ADMIRALS

IN THE AGE OF NELSON

ADMIRALS
IN THE AGE OF NELSON

Lee Bienkowski

. . .

Naval Institute Press
Annapolis, Maryland

Naval Institute Press
291 Wood Road
Annapolis, MD 21402

Library of Congress Cataloging-in-Publication Data
Bienkowski, Lee, 1960–
    p. cm.
Includes bibliographical references and index.
ISBN 1-55750-002-9 (alk. paper)
    1. Admirals—Great Britain—Biography. 2. Great Britain. Royal Navy—Officers—
Biography. 3. France—History—Revolution, 1789-1799—Naval Operations, British.
4. Napoleonic Wars, 1800-1815—Naval operations, British. I. Title.
    V64.G7 B54 2002
    359'.0092'241—dc21

                                                              2002009165

Printed in the United States of America on acid-free paper ∞
10 09 08 07 06 05 04 03   9 8 7 6 5 4 3 2
First printing

All illustrations, unless noted, are reproduced from William Jerdan's *National
Portrait Gallery of Illustrious and Eminent Personages of the Nineteenth
Century* (London: Fisher, Son, & Jackson, 1830).

Contents

Preface   vii

1   RICHARD HOWE   1

2   ALEXANDER HOOD   28

3   SAMUEL HOOD   52

4   JOHN JERVIS   78

5   ADAM DUNCAN   104

6   GEORGE KEITH ELPHINSTONE   131

7   JAMES GAMBIER   152

8   JOHN DUCKWORTH   170

9   JOHN BORLASE WARREN   190

10   JAMES SAUMAREZ   214

11   EDWARD PELLEW   238

Glossary   261

Notes   267

Bibliography   277

Index   283

Preface

The period of the French Wars (1793–1815) was the golden age of fighting sail for Great Britain. During that period the Royal Navy was undefeated in fleet actions and frequently enjoyed success over apparently overwhelming odds. Several factors contributed to the nearly uninterrupted litany of victories enjoyed by the British Navy in the late eighteenth and early nineteenth centuries. One was the deterioration of the other major European naval powers, such as France, Holland, and Spain.

Another factor that contributed to the Royal Navy's impressive collection of victories was experience on the part of the officers and men. Great Britain had been involved in no fewer than four major wars with naval components between the beginning of the eighteenth century and the start of the French Wars. Some officers still active in 1793 had served in three of those wars and had seen most of what the sea and the enemy could throw at them.

There can be little doubt that leadership in the Royal Navy reached a peak in the late eighteenth and early nineteenth centuries—not only by the old admirals who had served in three earlier wars, but younger men as well. The best-known example is Lord Nelson, whose exploits dominate most accounts of naval activities during the French Wars. Indeed, the period is often termed "the Age of Nelson." However, to apply the term to the entire period 1793–1815 is both inaccurate and unfair to the services of other officers. Nelson's main contributions to the war effort came between 1797 and 1805. Before 1797 both fleet and amphibious victories had been won, and afterward, there were numerous successful actions in which the most famous of admirals took no part.

As one of the greatest admirals who ever lived, Nelson deserves to be lauded. A large number of excellent books have done so. However, in concentrating on Nelson, many general books on the era of the French Wars leave the impression that there were no other significant flag officers in the British service during that time. In fact, there was a wealth of admirals of varying talents who won victories during the war and a short time afterward. They too deserve to have their stories told, and that is one of the goals of this work.

Eleven admirals were selected for this book. Out of the number of significant commanders of the era, it was difficult to make an impartial selection, so a few criteria were set up to limit the number of qualifiers. The first qualification was that the officer in question had to have held the rank of rear admiral or higher at some point during the period 1793–1815. This disqualified Captain Hoste, the commander of the frigate squadron that won the Battle of Lissa in 1811, who died before he reached flag rank. It also disqualified Lord Cochrane, who was not promoted to flag rank until well after the conclusion of the war.

The next selection criterion was that the officer must have been commander in chief of a station during the war. Both Calder and Strachan, victors of squadron actions before and after Trafalgar, were disqualified because neither ever served as a station commander.

The final criterion was that the officer in question had to be in command from start to finish of a full fleet or squadron action or a major amphibious expedition. Although both Hotham and Cornwallis qualified in other respects, their only fleet actions as commanding officers took the form of partial engagements. Collingwood succeeded to command of the British fleet before the last shots were fired at Trafalgar, but it was Nelson who had made most of the decisions in the critical early phase of the action.

After applying the criteria listed above to the British admirals of the French Wars, eleven emerged as candidates for portraiture in prose. They were not necessarily selected on the basis of ability. Some deserve to be included in a list of history's most distinguished sea commanders, but others were mediocre men whose victories were largely due to the excellent state of training in the Royal Navy and weakness and lack of morale on the part of their foes. It requires both types of commander to develop a balanced view of flag officers during the era in question.

As the length of each biography is limited, the treatment of certain topics of interest is necessarily cursory. Nonetheless, in describing the lives of officers whose active careers together covered nearly a century, there are many opportunities to observe the changes that took place in the Royal Navy during one of its most active periods. The final goal of this work is not only to provide verbal portraits of historical characters in terms of both career and personality, but also to give a sweeping view of naval history, covering most of the important political battles and tactical innovations. Each of the admirals profiled in this book had his own distinctive character, but all were ix

products of the time in which they lived. Therefore, this book is not only a collection of short biographies but an assessment of how personalities affected the Royal Navy and vice versa.

• • •

The author would like to thank the following people for helping to make this book possible: Rick Coyle, Robbie Zukauskas, and Brian Hathaway for reading some of the chapters and making useful suggestions for improvement; Kate Johnson for providing tips on preparing for publication; and Bart Reynolds for some valuable sources. The author would also like to acknowledge the following organizations for their assistance: the Public Record Office at Kew and the National Maritime Museum in Greenwich.

ADMIRALS

IN THE AGE OF NELSON

Chapter 1

RICHARD HOWE

1726–1799

THE FIRST OF JUNE 1794 dawned promisingly for the British. A steady breeze blew from the south by west, the sea was nearly flat, and the sky clear. After four frustrating days of fog and contrary winds, it appeared that nature was finally smiling on the Royal Navy. The French fleet of twenty-six ships of the line lay approximately six miles to leeward.

By this time, Admiral Lord Howe was close to exhaustion. He had scarcely quitted the deck since the enemy had been sighted four days earlier. Yet when it appeared that the enemy was finally within his grasp, he showed no hesitation. As soon as it was light enough for his signals to be read, Howe organized his battle line. Then, shortly after 7:00 A.M., he signaled that he would pass through the French line and engage them to leeward. Although at the admiral's insistence the latter signal had been on the books for a few years, this was the first test of the tactical innovation in a full-scale battle.

Once he had made his proposed method of attack known, Howe hove to so that his men had time to eat breakfast. But not long after 8:00 he was again bearing down upon the foe. Soon both fleets were nearly even and not far out of the range of their heaviest guns. Then again the British commander in chief paused to reorder his fleet so that the largest of the French fleet would be opposed by his own most powerful vessels. Shortly before 9:30 the opening shots of the battle were fired by the French van. Within half an hour the engagement became general, and Howe hoisted the signal for close action. With that he shut his signals book and awaited results.

• • •

Richard Howe—Earl Howe and Baron Howe of Langar, Knight of the Garter, Admiral of the Fleet, and First Lord of the Admiralty—was known in naval circles as "Black Dick" for two reasons. First, he had a swarthy complexion with dark hair and eyes, and second, his face generally bore a depressed expression. The only time he is reported to have smiled is when there was a prospect of action. "I think we shall have a fight today," one of his men is reported to have said on the morning of 1 June 1794; "Black Dick has been smiling."[1]

Howe was noted for courage in battle, attention to detail, and in his younger days, indefatigability in action. He was a favorite with the men before the mast because he sincerely cared about their well-being. In one case he even went so far as to divide his own share of prize money among some British prisoners who had been captured by the French but had been retaken.[2] No wonder Howe was trusted more than most other officers of his time.

Serving in four wars, he was involved in many of the great historical events, such as Anson's voyage, the Battle of Quiberon Bay, the relief of Gibraltar, and the Glorious First of June. Some authors have derided him for lack of imagination and for not following up his victories to the maximum possible extent. Because he failed to pursue the fleeing French fleet at the conclusion of the Battle of the First of June, Nelson termed an incomplete victory a "Lord Howe victory."[3] However, Nelson changed his tune after the Battle of the Nile, when he wrote a letter to Howe describing him as "our great master in naval tactics and bravery."[4] It is well that he paid tribute to his senior, because Howe was indeed one of the most influential officers of the eighteenth century.

Born in London on 8 March 1726, Richard Howe was the second son of Emanuel Scrope Howe, second Viscount Howe of the Irish peerage. His mother was Mary Sophia Charlotte, daughter of the Baroness of Kielmansegge, who had come to Britain as one of the mistresses of King George I. The baroness's daughter was widely believed to have been fathered by the king. The fact that Richard Howe's profile bore a resemblance to that of the first of the Hanoverian kings added credence to this theory.[5]

In 1732 the second viscount was appointed governor of Barbados, but it is not known if Richard joined him or remained at school in Britain. Lord Howe remained at his post until his death in March 1735. He was succeeded as viscount by his eldest son, George. All three of the Howe brothers (George, Richard, and William) were dedicated to the service of their country. George fell at the Battle of Ticonderoga in July 1758, while in command of the Fifty-fifth Regiment of Foot. He had been an innovator in wilderness tactics and was greatly mourned. William too entered the army and rose to the rank of general.

After early schooling at Westminster School and Eton, Richard was sent to sea in July 1740. Although this is the first period when he is known to have been afloat, his name had been borne in the books of other vessels earlier. It was a common practice in the eighteenth century for captains to include the names of their sons or the sons of friends in their books even if they were not physically on board. This was because an officer who presented himself to take the examination for a lieutenant's commission had to prove that he had been six years at sea. The only proof required was entries from ship's muster books, so many youths, Howe among them, gained sea time in absentia to satisfy the regulation.

When Richard Howe came aboard the *Severn* (50)[6] as a midshipman, the vessel was part of a fleet destined to sail under the command of Commodore Anson. Britain was at war with Spain, and it was decided that a profitable method of chastising the enemy was to attack its trade in the Pacific. Beginning early in 1740, a squadron was assembled at Portsmouth to essay this task, but it was not until 18 September that it took to the sea.

Almost from the start, the expedition was plagued with bad weather, which created delays throughout the voyage. When the squadron reached Cape Horn, it was struck by tremendous storms and soon became scattered. The *Severn* and the *Pearl* (42) remained together, but they lost sight of the rest of the squadron on 10 April 1741. These two ships spent more than a month trying to regain contact with Anson and the others, but failed. Finally, with both vessels leaking and their crews sick, they put about for Rio de Janeiro, where they arrived on 6 June. After making repairs there, the *Severn* sailed for Barbados and later returned to Britain. She was paid off on 24 June 1742.

Meanwhile, Anson successfully rounded the Horn and captured the fabulously wealthy Manilla Galleon near the Philippines. But the expedition took a tremendous toll on ships and human life. Out of the eight ships that set out, only the flagship, *Centurion* (60), completed the circumnavigation.

Howe did not remain long without a ship. On 17 August he came aboard the *Burford* (70) under the command of Franklin Lushington. This vessel was destined to take part in a series of assaults on the coast of Curaçao, so before long, the midshipman again found himself sailing for the Caribbean. It should be noted that throughout the eighteenth century the West Indies were notorious for disease. Yellow fever and malaria caused far more casualties than did enemy action. But Howe seems to have been virtually immune to the hazards of the climate. Although he served in the West Indies and other tropical regions for approximately six years, he is not recorded to have suffered from illness.

On 18 February 1743, the British began their attack with a naval bombardment. Late in the day, a shot cut the *Burford*'s cable and set her adrift, making her a tempting target for the Spaniards. Captain Lushington had one of his legs struck off by a piece of chainshot. He died of his wound five days later. With her captain slain and her hull severely damaged, the *Burford* was docked for repairs.

Wishing to continue his active career, Howe soon transferred to the *Suffolk* (70), commanded by Charles Knowles, and sailed for Puerto Cabello. For two weeks in April the British made assaults upon the town, but without success. Finally they drew off and returned to Jamaica. Later in the year the *Suffolk* cruised off Martinique. Finding himself short a lieutenant, and having gained a good impression of Howe's ability, Knowles gave him a temporary promotion. He served as acting lieutenant of the *Suffolk* from July into October before returning to the lesser rank of midshipman.

Although relegated to the midshipmen's berth again, Howe was not to remain there long. On 24 May 1744, at the age of eighteen, he took and passed his examination for lieutenant at Antigua. This is where his having been borne upon the books as a child paid off, because he had in fact served at sea for only half the required six years. However, the ship's books told another story, and the examining board turned a blind eye to an obviously common practice.

For some officers, early promotion appears to have been a mistake, but not in Howe's case. He met the challenge of each increase in responsibility without flinching. The day after his lieutenant's exam, Howe was placed in command of the fireship *Comet,* in which he sailed for a year. Upon his return to Britain in August 1745, his ship was paid off, and Howe was appointed to the *Royal George* (100). He remained a lieutenant for only a few months before he was made commander of the sloop-of-war *Baltimore* (14) on 5 November.

The latter part of 1745, and the beginning of 1746, was a critical period in British history. The followers of Bonnie Prince Charlie were rampaging throughout Scotland and even progressing well into England. Soon after he assumed command of the *Baltimore,* Howe was sent off the coast of Scotland to prevent the French from sending troops to support the rebellion. But it was not until the insurrection was completely defeated at Culloden that Howe had his first experience of a sea fight.

In the spring of 1746, several French vessels were sent to cruise off the coast of Scotland to pick up the prince and those of his followers who had managed to escape after Culloden. Among these vessels were two large privateers of thirty-two and thirty-four guns. The *Baltimore* encountered these vessels on 1 May when she was in company with two other small men-of-war. Although they were severely outgunned, the three British ships flew down upon the privateers with cannons blazing. But the French ships were too large and heavy-gunned for them to face for long. The *Baltimore* and her companions were driven off. Howe was wounded in the head by a musket ball. Meanwhile, the privateers made their escape and succeeded in taking aboard a number of Bonnie Prince Charlie's supporters before turning back to France.

When Howe reached shore again, he received news that probably made his wound smart less for a while. While he had been cruising off the coast of Scotland, he had been made a post captain into the *Tryton* (24) on 10 April, only a month after his twentieth birthday. This was a critical move for him, or indeed for any officer of the eighteenth-century Royal Navy. A commander or even a lieutenant could be called "captain" if he held command of a ship. But only a post captain (captain of a ship with twenty or more guns) could rise by seniority to become an admiral.

Howe assumed his new command on 19 July and spent the best part of the next year on convoy duty. Then, on 13 May 1747, he exchanged into the *Rippon* (60), whose captain had become ill and needed a change of climate. In this vessel he returned to the West Indies, and on 29 October 1748 he became captain of the *Cornwall* (80), the flagship of his old friend Charles Knowles, now a rear admiral. They sailed together until the flagship was paid off in July 1749, and Howe went ashore.

In March 1751 he was appointed to command of the *Glory* (44) and set sail on a long voyage. His first destination was the Guinea coast, where he concluded an agreement between feuding British and Dutch settlers. Then he crossed to the West Indies before returning to Spithead in April 1752. Soon after his return to England, Howe was transferred aboard the *Dolphin* (24), in which he was sent to the Mediterranean. It was more than a year before he saw England again. He spent the autumn of 1753 in negotiations with the Barbary pirates, and the spring of 1754 scouting out the state of the French navy, as it seemed likely that the two ancient foes would be at odds again. While Howe was employed in the Mediterranean, trouble was brewing between British and French settlers in North America. In 1754, colonial forces clashed at the confluence of the Monongahela and Allegheny Rivers, sparking an already tense situation into undeclared war. In 1755 the British government decided to increase the size of their naval force off the coast of North America to counter the sailing of a large French fleet to those waters. On 27 April a fleet sailed under the command of Adm. Edward "Old Dreadnought" Boscawen.

Having returned to Britain in July 1754, Howe was appointed to command of the *Dunkirk* (70) the following January and ordered to accompany Boscawen. Reaching the Newfoundland Banks, the British began to cast about for the French force that had preceded them. They failed to find the main squadron, but they did encounter a small group of four ships of the line on 6 June. Although they gave chase, Boscawen's ships soon lost their quarry in the region's famous fog. But two days later, the weather cleared enough for the French to be exposed and the chase to begin again. The *Dunkirk* ran herself alongside the sixty-four-gun *Alcide* and demanded her surrender. When the Frenchman refused, Howe ordered his men to fire a broadside. Finding himself outgunned and in danger from other vessels coming to the assistance of the *Dunkirk,* the captain of the *Alcide* swiftly hauled down his flag.

The *Dunkirk* did not remain off the North American coast for long. She became separated from the fleet in the autumn of 1755 and returned to English coastal waters. By the summer of 1756, Howe found himself in command of a squadron cruising off the Channel Islands. At home more than he had been accustomed to, Howe stood for Parliament at the request of the Duke of Devonshire, a leader of the Whigs. He was elected Member of the House of Commons for Dartmouth in May 1757, a position he continued to hold for the next fifteen years.

On 2 July the captain and the entire crew of the *Dunkirk* were transferred aboard the *Magnanime,* a seventy-four-gun two-decker that had been taken from the French in 1748. Once again Howe found himself under the command of Vice Admiral Knowles, who held a squadron under Admiral Hawke. On this occasion, the mission was to attack Ile d'Aix, near Rochefort on the northern coast of France. On 23 September, a force consisting of five ships of the line and two bomb vessels fell upon the fortress defending the island. They swiftly overpowered the battery, and when the British landed they destroyed the fortifications. It was then decided that Ile d'Aix would make a superior base for an attack on the mainland. The British attempted an attack late in September, but the weather was against them. Conceding that the plan had little chance of success against the weather and a strong enemy, Knowles put about for England and returned on 6 October. Although the attack was not a success, the captain of the *Magnanime* distinguished himself in one of the actions. He brought his ship in as close as he could to the bastions and then "began so furious a fire that the *Monsieurs* said that something more than a man must be on board that ship."[7]

The year 1758 was an eventful one for Richard Howe. On 10 March he wedded Mary Hartopp, a lady six years his junior, whose intrepidity matched his own. They were to have three daughters. In May, Howe was commissioned as a commodore (a temporary rank in the eighteenth century) for an attack on St. Malo and hoisted his broad pennant aboard the *Essex* (70) at Spithead. Soon after he joined his new command, he issued a book of signal codes to his captains, the first of many in his career, and the first ever issued by a British squadron commander.[8] Throughout his life, Howe had a singular interest in improving communications between naval vessels.

Howe's squadron weighed anchor on 1 June and succeeded in landing the troops safely. However, when the soldiers reached St. Malo, they discovered that an assault would cost them too dearly. They returned to the ships and set sail again. Attempts were made upon Le Havre and Cherbourg but were foiled by bad weather and enemy gunfire. After a month of adventures, the squadron returned to Spithead.

Later in the summer the British decided to make another attempt on Cherbourg. Although the defenses of the town had been strengthened since the previous visit by Howe's squadron, the troops were landed successfully and spent a week cutting a swath of destruction. By the time they reembarked, they left behind wrecked piers, blown-up magazines, and sunken vessels. But the Admiralty decided there was more to be done. The next destination for Howe and his squadron was the Bay of St. Lunaire. The soldiers were again disembarked but soon encountered resistance, and when they learned of the presence of a large body of French troops close by, they decided to return to the fleet. Most of the army successfully regained the safety of the ships, but about seven hundred remained ashore when the French attacked. Some of the British still managed to escape, but others, including several naval officers who had been overseeing the evacuation, were taken prisoner.

When the commodore returned to England he learned that he had become Lord Howe by the death of his brother on 5 July. Although all three of the brothers were to bear this title in turn, Richard bore it the longest.

In the summer of 1759, Howe returned aboard his former command, the *Magnanime*. This time he brought with him a midshipman of the royal blood—Prince Edward Augustus, the second son of King George II.

For most of the summer and autumn, the British under Admiral Hawke kept a close watch upon the French fleet at Brest. It was not until they were driven off by a storm on 9 November that Conflans, the French commander in chief, dared poke his nose out of the shelter of his home port. On

14 November the weather moderated enough for the British to put to sea again. Two days later, the admiral learned that Conflans was out. Having guessed from the news his scouting vessels brought him and from his past experience with the French that the enemy was making for the area of Belle Ile, Hawke immediately ordered his fleet to change course. Although the British set sail promptly, they were held back by head winds. It was not until 20 November that they sighted the coast of France. On the morning of the same day, they also located Conflans and his fleet off Quiberon Bay.

The French, with twenty-one ships of the line, decided that if they had the choice, they would not fight.[9] They were numerically inferior to the British, who had twenty-three ships, and they also were close to a dangerous, rocky portion of their own coast, with a strong northwesterly gale starting to blow.[10] In Conflans's opinion, it would be madness for the British to pursue him closely under such conditions—they would not attempt it. He was wrong.

In spite of the danger, Hawke was determined not to let the French fleet escape. He ordered his ships to crowd on all sail, and his captains took his orders to heart, setting sails that were normally reserved for fair weather. By 2:00 in the afternoon, the leading British vessels were within range of the rearmost French, and half an hour later Hawke hoisted the signal to engage.

Howe's *Magnanime* was among the first to fire on the French. He laid his ship close alongside the *Thésée* and poured broadside after broadside into her. But the engagement was broken off when the *Magnanime* lost some of her smaller spars and was fouled by one of her sisters. Her place in action was taken by the *Torbay,* which remained hotly engaged with the *Thésée* until the French ship foundered.

Meanwhile, the *Magnanime* swiftly cleared herself of obstruction and once more joined the chase. The next opponent Howe chose for himself was the *Formidable.* He treated her to a couple of broadsides, but soon pressed on as other vessels came up to engage his opponent. (The *Formidable* was later battered to a hulk.) While the battle raged astern, the *Magnanime* charged on, nipping at the heels of the rearmost enemy vessels, which were seeking the safety of the bay. Following close behind the French, imitating their every move, Howe passed safely through the rocky channel and flung his command upon the *Héros.* This seventy-four-gun ship had already suffered battle damage, but the *Magnanime* was about to give her a great deal more. Howe positioned his command astern of his foe and subjected her to a merciless raking fire. Under this terrible barrage the *Héros* "lost every officer on board down to a midshipman, and had near 400 killed and wounded."[11] She surrendered, but the weather was too rough to get a prize crew into her.

This action ended the battle for the *Magnanime*. With darkness falling and the weather growing worse, she anchored and signaled her prize to do likewise. However, by morning the *Héros* had run aground and was soon battered to pieces. Several of her compatriots also ran aground or forced their way up shallow channels not generally used by such large ships.

Howe and most of the rest of the squadron remained cruising outside Quiberon Bay for much of the winter, watching for any attempts to refloat the vessels that had run aground or retreated to the shallows. The weather made cruising uncomfortable, especially as it was difficult to supply the fleet from England. But their vigilance had its reward. Few of the French ships of the line that survived the battle ever returned to active service. Over the following two years, Howe remained under Hawke's command in the Channel. On 22 March 1760 he was made colonel of marines in recognition for his role in the victory at Quiberon Bay. The following summer he captured Dumet Island, which he thought would make a good anchorage for the fleet in bad weather. In 1762 Howe was appointed to command of a squadron cruising in the Basque Road. He kept a close watch on the enemy, but they had received such a blow at Quiberon Bay that they did not wish to risk another battle in the Channel. They remained at anchor in their harbors while the commodore and his squadron prowled outside.

Howe's last service as a captain was as commander of the *Princess Amelia* (80), the flagship of his former midshipman, the Duke of York, who had been promoted to rear admiral with exceptional speed because of his royal blood. He commanded the two-decker during the latter half of 1762, and the following year he came ashore to become a member of the Board of the Admiralty. In August 1765 Howe was appointed treasurer of the navy. Unlike most such appointees of the day, he proved incorruptible. Although he did not use public funds to enrich himself, Howe acquired the wherewithal to purchase an estate. Shortly after the conclusion of the Seven Years' War he bought Porter's Lodge, a country seat near St. Albans, where he settled down during his rare periods of inactivity. In the autumn of 1770, it appeared possible that Britain might go to war with Spain over the possession of the Falkland Islands. In preparation for this conflict, a number of senior captains were promoted to rear admiral, Howe among them. Because of his new rank, he resigned as treasurer of the navy and colonel of marines. In preparation for war against Spain, Howe was appointed to command of the Mediterranean Fleet. He had already begun to make preparations for assembling the fleet when the two contesting governments reached an agreement, averting a war. The admiral returned to the more peaceful pursuits of family and Parliament.

Although the British people had been spared a war with Spain, there was trouble brewing in the North American colonies. Protests against taxes had escalated to a state of near rebellion by 1774, especially in New England, where strict sanctions had been imposed on the city of Boston. As a Whig, Howe found the idea of war between the Englishmen in England and the Englishmen across the Atlantic distasteful. He wished for a diplomatic solution to the troubles before matters took a more serious turn. He offered his services as a mediator, but his offer was ignored. The tension in the colonies continued to mount until the first shots were fired at Lexington and Concord in April 1775, and the American Revolution began.

At first the new war had little effect on Richard Howe's life. In December 1775 he was promoted to vice admiral. His brother, Sir William, was already on the other side of the Atlantic, commanding all British forces in the colonies. In March 1776 he was forced to leave Boston to the rebels and retire to Halifax to reorganize and await reinforcements.

While Sir William was still in Boston, his brother was appointed to command of the North American station, which was badly in need of additional ships. At the start of the war, the British had a mere twenty-four vessels to patrol the coast from Halifax to St. Augustine.[12] Vice Admiral Howe with his flag in the *Eagle* (64) would bring a substantial addition. The fleet required several months to assemble. It was not until 1 July 1776 that the admiral arrived at Halifax to find that General Howe had gone on to New York. His lordship followed and arrived off Sandy Hook on 12 July. He joined forces with his brother on Staten Island.

Both of the Howe brothers wanted the revolution to be settled peacefully. They would have preferred to negotiate with the colonists rather than fight them, but they were handicapped by the powers that had been granted them for treating with the rebels. They were allowed to offer only a demand for abject surrender. By the time the admiral arrived, it was already too late for an easy peace, especially as the Declaration of Independence had been proclaimed days prior to the admiral's arrival outside New York Harbor. Nonetheless, Howe was willing to make the attempt at a peaceful settlement. Shortly after his arrival in North America, he sent a naval officer under a flag of truce with a letter for General Washington. But the general's secretary refused to accept it, because it was addressed to "Mr." Washington, which the secretary considered a slight to his employer's rank.[13]

In spite of this unpromising beginning, the admiral continued to attempt a negotiated settlement and sympathize with the Americans for as long as he remained on the western side of the Atlantic. When loyalists wrote to him demanding letters of marque so that they could send out privateers against the rebels, he replied, "Will you never have done oppressing these poor people? Will you never give them the opportunity of seeing their error?"[14]

In spite of their sympathy for the rebels, the Howe brothers were determined to act against the rebellion to the best of their abilities. First, the admiral sent a pair of frigates up the Hudson River to test American defenses in that quarter. When he found that they could do little against his fleet, he knew that he must only make a push and New York would be his. On 22 August the push began. Fifteen thousand British troops were transported from Staten Island to Long Island. These were soon joined by five thousand Hessians. The Americans had a force of approximately nine thousand men, many of whom were half-trained militia, to face the enemy.

The rebels attempted to hold Long Island by fortifying Brooklyn Heights to the north of the British position. On 27 August the two armies clashed to the south and east of these fortifications, and the Americans were swiftly compelled to seek shelter behind their ramparts. They were trapped because Washington did not have enough boats assembled for an evacuation, and if the British had pressed home their advantage, they could have captured nearly half of Washington's army. But General Howe hesitated. He put off the attack, giving the rebels time to slip away under cover of darkness on 29 August. For some reason unknown, Admiral Howe did not choose to block the American retreat with his fleet.

Once the British were in firm control of Long Island, Lord Howe again tried to end the war by diplomacy. His efforts met with no better success than earlier (and subsequent) attempts, and in the meantime, not wishing to poison his chances of a negotiated settlement, the admiral allowed an informal truce to exist between the two sides.

While Lord Howe awaited the result of his mission of peace, the rebels persisted in hatching plots against him. Under the guidance of David Bushnell, they built the world's first functioning submarine—the *Turtle*. This device, which looked like an enormous flattened keg with a pointed lead bottom and a primitive conning tower on top, was large enough to contain a crew of one. This single individual propelled his vessel by means of a hand-cranked propeller, steered it with a tiller, controlled his depth by means of a foot pump, and viewed the outside world through small glass portholes set in the "conning tower." The goal of this contraption was to attach a mine, in the form of a barrel containing 150 pounds of gunpowder, to the hull of a ship. To the rebels, the best target appeared to be the flagship *Eagle*.

On the night of 7 September, the *Turtle* was launched against her target. After an exhausting journey, Sergeant Ezra Lee reached the side of the *Eagle*. He had remained undiscovered, although the "conning tower" had been above the surface throughout his voyage. Only when he reached his goal did he submerge completely. To fix the mine to the hull of the flagship, he had been provided with a drill, but either the bit was not strong enough to pierce the *Eagle*'s copper bottom or Lee lacked enough purchase to force his drill in. Whatever the cause, he could not fix the mine to his target. So after a couple of attempts, he gave up and successfully returned to his own side, leaving his mine behind as a nasty surprise for a British boat's crew that stopped to investigate. Another attempt against the *Eagle* was made at a later date, but on that occasion the *Turtle* never made it close to the target. The submarine was eventually destroyed, when the ship on which she was stored was sunk by a British attack.

By the middle of September the Howe brothers abandoned hope of a diplomatic solution. Once again they were on a war footing, and the unofficial truce was over. Soon they began landing troops on Manhattan. In spite of some rather feeble resistance by the rebels, the British soon entered New York City, which appeared relieved by their presence. Once the city had been secured, Lord Howe settled in. He maintained a patrol outside the harbor throughout the winter, while his brother's troops were surprised at Trenton in December and defeated at Princeton in January. The general was not present on either of these occasions, preferring the comforts of New York society and the company of his mistress to the rigors of a winter campaign. It was not until spring that the British forces again set forth to repair the damages wrought by winter.

General Howe traveled from New York to New Jersey in early June 1777, and there began to lay plans for an invasion of Pennsylvania. His brother remained in New York for a while longer, assembling his fleet to support the army. In late July, Lord Howe departed with his fleet for the Chesapeake. Due to persistent headwinds, the fleet needed more than three weeks to reach its goal. There it disgorged the troops sent to attack Pennsylvania from the south and then remained to guard the line of retreat. As it soon became clear that no line of retreat was needed, Howe eventually sailed up the Delaware River and reached Chester, a few miles downriver of Philadelphia, on 6 October. Meanwhile, the general had been moving against

Philadelphia, which he reached on 26 September. In spite of rebel attempts to dislodge him, he remained in Philadelphia until the middle of the following year.

Once the admiral arrived, the battle for control of the Delaware River began in earnest. First the Americans tried to drive the British off with gunboats and fireships. Then they bombarded the fleet from Fort Mifflin, which proved a stubborn nut to crack. It was not until a small armed vessel was guided through a channel flanking the fort that the rebels were compelled to abandon their works, on 20 November. With this final obstruction cleared, the Delaware was safe for the passage of British ships, and it appeared that the rebellion was well on its way to being crushed. But then came the news of Burgoyne's defeat at Saratoga, and it became clear to the admiral that this war was far from over. Disappointed in his hope to bring the revolution to conclusion with as little bloodshed as possible, Lord Howe asked to be relieved of his command late in November. His brother too asked to be relieved of his command and was replaced by General Clinton in May 1778.

With unusual speed for the time period, the admiral received his permission to resign two months after posting his request. However, he was not yet free of his responsibility. Until another senior officer could be sent to take his place, he would remain commander in chief of the station. The appointment of a successor and the assembly of a fleet for him to command would take several months.

In the meantime, France joined the war on the side of the United States in February 1778. In April a fleet was sent under the command of Admiral d'Estaing with the original intention of bottling the British fleet in the Delaware River. But before the French could reach their destination, Howe departed Philadelphia, which was abandoned to the rebels, and returned to New York on 30 June. It was scarcely a moment too soon. D'Estaing and his fleet arrived at the mouth of the Delaware a week later. Finding that he was too late to close the trap on his enemy, the French admiral set his course for New York. He arrived off Sandy Hook on 11 July.

Howe was severely outnumbered. His force consisted of six ships of the line, whereas the French had twelve, and virtually all of them were larger than anything the British admiral had available. But his lordship was determined to set up a stout defense and hope for the best. He took the majority of the force available to him and anchored it in a tight line along Sandy Hook, a strip of land and shoals that the French would have to pass to enter New York Harbor. The vessels were anchored with springs in their cables so that they could employ their guns across a wide arc. They were positioned so close to shallow water that no man-of-war could pass between them and the land, and the line had a slightly concave configuration so that any enemy that came within range would be subjected to the fire of several vessels at once.

When d'Estaing reached Sandy Hook and saw the reception that had been prepared for him, he balked at accepting the invitation to battle. Not only did the defenses appear formidable, but also the bar he was required to cross was too shallow for his deep-drafted flagship, except under rare conditions. He cruised about for ten days, waiting for a spring tide, but even then he did not think he could get his flagship across. He put about and sailed away from New York. By 26 July, Howe came to the conclusion that d'Estaing had refused his invitation and unceremoniously departed for a more promising venue.

Upon leaving the vicinity of New York, the French fleet sailed north to Newport, Rhode Island, which was held by approximately 3,500 British troops. D'Estaing made arrangements with Washington to attack the town from land and sea. However, the coordination between the French admiral and the American General Sullivan was not harmonious, and in spite of every advantage, they failed to take the town. Meanwhile Howe received four new ships (a 74, a 64, and two 50s) from various locations and decided that he had sufficient strength to challenge the French as long as he could meet them on his own terms. On 6 August he sailed for Rhode Island and anchored off Point Judith on the ninth.

As soon as he heard that the British fleet was off the coast, d'Estaing sailed out to meet it. In spite of his reinforcements, Howe's force was considerably weaker than that of his opponent. He decided not to give battle until circumstances turned in his favor. For most of 10 August the French, who had the wind gauge, tried to close with the British, who continued to slide off to leeward while maintaining a tightly packed formation. While the fleets maneuvered, the British admiral shifted his flag to the frigate *Apollo* (32) and tacked in toward the enemy so that he could more closely follow their movements. Observing that the French appeared to be approaching his rear, he strengthened that end of his line by placing his lone 74 in the aftermost position. For a time it appeared that the French would engage the British rear, but then the wind began to freshen, and as the day drew to a close, d'Estaing decided to hold back, expecting to bring his foes to action the following day.

But during the night the weather grew worse, developing into a gale that continued for the next three days. Howe was unable to return to his flagship throughout this time and so remained a guest of the *Apollo.* By the time the storm blew itself out, both fleets had been scattered far and wide. As the *Eagle* was nowhere to be seen, Howe shifted his flag first to the *Phoenix* (44) and then to the *Centurion* (50). He finally rejoined his flagship and returned to Sandy Hook on 17 August; on 22 August his squadron was sufficiently recovered to sail again in search of the enemy.

While Howe had been stranded aboard the *Apollo,* d'Estaing was experiencing difficulties of his own. The weather had pounded his flagship, the *Languedoc* (90), so severely that she had lost all of her lower masts and her bowsprit. Her tiller too had been broken, so she was virtually helpless when she was sighted by the British *Renown* (50). The British man-of-war attacked but was beaten off when several other French vessels came to the rescue of the flagship. Nevertheless, it had been a close-run thing. D'Estaing had been so certain at one point that he would be taken that he had ordered all the confidential papers thrown overboard.[15]

Finding that the facilities at Newport were not sufficient to repair the damage suffered by his fleet, d'Estaing decided to leave for Boston. Howe pursued him northward, hoping to cut him off before he reached Boston Harbor. Arriving at Boston behind the French, he discovered that the defenses were too strong to be forced. Reluctantly he put about and returned to New York.

Upon Howe's return to New York Harbor on 11 September, he found Rear Adm. Sir Hyde Parker with six ships of the line, the vanguard of a larger fleet under the command of Vice Adm. John Byron. This was the replacement he was waiting for, and now he felt free to depart for England. He left a fortnight after his return from Boston, ready to put up a fight in Parliament in defense of his own and his brother's actions. Howe arrived at Portsmouth on 25 October and hauled down his flag five days later. Once he came ashore, he resumed his parliamentary duties but made no attempt at gaining another command as long as Lord Sandwich remained First Lord of the Admiralty.

While Howe remained on the sidelines, controversy raged in the navy between the supporters of Admiral Keppel and Vice Admiral Palliser. Although Howe was a longtime friend of Keppel, he stayed aloof from the quarrel. He was expecting Parliament to institute an inquiry into his activities as commander in chief of the North American station, and feared that his support would damage Keppel's cause. Nothing came of the inquiry, but the Howes continued at odds with the Tory administration. They refused an offer to be junior members of a new commission to be sent to treat with the American revolutionaries in 1779. Howe continued to be active in the House of Commons but declined any offers of command until the government was changed.

While Howe remained inactive, the war went badly for Britain. Spain and Holland entered the conflict on the side of the rebels, and a combined French and Spanish fleet gained control of the Channel. On the other side of the Atlantic, the British fleet was driven off by the French under de Grasse at the Battle of the Capes, and General Cornwallis was compelled to surrender at Yorktown in October 1781. With each failure, the Tory ministry became increasingly unpopular. At last the king was compelled to appoint a Whig ministry at the end of March 1782.

Within days of Sandwich's departure from the Admiralty, Howe was appointed commander in chief of the Channel fleet. He hoisted his flag as a full admiral of the blue aboard the *Victory* (100) on 20 April. On the same day the Irish viscount became a peer of Great Britain, propelling him from the House of Commons to the House of Lords.

During the spring and summer of 1782, Howe and his fleet spent much of their time at sea seeking a Dutch fleet that never showed itself. Finding that many of the ships' captains and crews had grown lax with the years under less active commanders, he held frequent exercises to improve the coordination of the fleet. He also experimented with new signals and ideas about tactics.

At the beginning of August the fleet returned to Portsmouth, where it began preparations to sail for Gibraltar. Spain had entered the War of American Independence with the intention of regaining possession of Gibraltar, which it had lost in 1704. No sooner had Spain declared war on Britain than it laid siege to the Rock, hoping to starve out the garrison. In spite of many privations, the garrison held on, but by the autumn of 1782, the situation was beginning to grow desperate. Howe was placed in command of a force of 183 assorted sail, including 34 ships of the line.

Howe's fleet sailed on 11 September, hoping to reach Gibraltar before the Spaniards made their impending assault. They were too late to prevent the assault, but the Spaniards were driven back by the British defenses without help from the fleet. They retired to Algeciras, a few miles away, and were joined there by a French squadron. Meanwhile, due to inclement weather and the size of the convoy, Howe's progress was slow. He did not come in sight of the Rock until 11 October, and even then he was unable to anchor. The wind swept most of the vessels under his protection past the mole and into the Mediterranean. A week was needed to gather them all together again and bring them to safety under the guns of the fortress. The enemy made a halfhearted attempt to prevent the British from reaching Gibraltar, but no shots were fired. When the transports finally reached their destination, the combined fleet was nowhere to be seen.

Now unencumbered by the transports, Howe sailed in search of the enemy on 19 October. He passed through the straits and waited for the French and Spanish forces to come up to him, which they did on the following day off Cape Spartel. Having the wind gauge, the allies bore down upon the compact British line. But in spite of superior numbers and having Howe cornered against the coast of Africa, the Spanish commander in chief, Cordova, would not press the attack. He cannonaded the British at long range, and they returned his fire. At the end of four hours, the British sustained 276 killed and wounded, and the allies 380. Then night fell, and the two fleets parted ways. The French and Spanish made for Cadiz while Howe continued for home. He reached St. Helens on 14 November.

In later years Howe considered the relief of Gibraltar to be the feat of which he was most proud. However, at least one of his contemporaries did not feel that he had done all he could have. Captain Hervey of the *Raisonnable* published a letter concerning the desultory battle of 20 October, stating, "If we had been led with the same spirit with which we should have followed, it would have been a glorious day for England."[16] Howe took exception to this statement and challenged Hervey to a duel. However, when the two officers met on the ground, the captain made a full retraction. In December the House of Commons moved and passed a vote of thanks to Admiral Howe for "the important service he had rendered to his country by his relief of the fortress of Gibraltar, and by his gallant and able maneuvers of the fleet under his command against a superior force of the enemy."[17]

The relief of Gibraltar was the admiral's last service at sea during the American War. Within a fortnight of his return from the Mediterranean, a preliminary peace treaty was signed. On 28 January 1783, he was appointed First Lord of the Admiralty when Keppel resigned temporarily. Howe held the post for only a little more than two months before Keppel returned to office, but at the end of December, Howe once more became First Lord.

During Howe's first short term as First Lord, he was called upon to settle a situation that was becoming increasingly common in the navy. The sailors were disgruntled by low wages and having to serve so long in an unpopular war. With the war on the verge of ending, they were eager to return home and were inclined to be unruly. One ship, the *Janus* (44), which had just returned to Portsmouth from the West Indies, was ordered to refit for sea. The rumor spread that she was to return to the Caribbean. Having already survived the region's notorious fevers, and fearing that they would not be so lucky a second time, the ship's company rebelled. They locked up their officers and threatened to fire on any ship that dared interfere with them. The spirit of rebellion caught on with other discontented crews, and soon the town was full of rioting sailors.

Hearing of the disturbance, Howe posted down from London and announced to the crew of the *Janus* that he would be coming aboard alone. The seamen received him respectfully and listened to what he had to say. He told them that the rumor they had heard was false and that their ship was to be paid off.[18] Hearing that they were not be sent to sea again, the crew of the *Janus* honored the admiral with three cheers, and ended their mutiny.

The unpopular task of reducing the navy fell to Howe during his second administration. In the course of his five years in office, he was vilified in Parliament and the press. One pamphlet described him as "a man universally acknowledged to be unfeeling in his nature, ungracious in his manner, and who, upon all occasions, discovers a wonderful attachment to the dictates of his own perverse, impenetrable disposition."[19]

Although these accusations were painful to him, the admiral continued to act according to what his conscience told him was best for the service. He reformed dockyard administration and introduced technical improvements. But in the end, feeling that Prime Minister William Pitt was not giving him the support he needed, he resigned his office and was replaced by Pitt's brother, the Earl of Chatham, in July 1788. In consolation for the difficulties he experienced at the Admiralty, Howe was created Earl Howe and Baron Howe of Langar and permitted to pass the barony on to his eldest daughter.

The admiral was allowed two years of relative peace at his estate until a threat of war with Spain developed. The cause of the dispute was Nootka Sound, a spit of land on the west coast of North America. The British had established a trading post in this disputed area, and when Spain heard of this it sent two small men-of-war to destroy the post and capture the traders. Incensed by Spain's cavalier treatment of his subjects, King George urged Parliament to place the nation upon a war footing. Immediately a fleet was prepared to face that of Spain, and in May 1790, Lord Howe hoisted his flag aboard the *Queen Charlotte* (100), flagship of the Channel fleet. Once his fleet was assembled, the admiral led them out and performed exercises, which intimidated the king of Spain. In July, Spain agreed to repair the damages done to the trading post and pay compensation. The whole affair withered away without the firing of a shot, but wishing to take advantage of the opportunity to exercise a fleet that had grown rusty after seven years of peace, Howe kept his command at sea into September. Spain officially ceded Nootka Sound to Britain in October, and two months later Howe struck his flag again.

While the situation in France and neighboring countries deteriorated, the admiral lived in peace. He was appointed Vice Admiral of England in May 1792, but did not again receive orders to command a fleet until 1 February 1793. By this time it was becoming clear that there would be war between Britain and the French republic. Shots had already been fired the previous month, but neither side was fully prepared for the conflict, and for both, the reinforcement of foreign stations took first priority. It was not until well into the spring that Howe had a fleet worthy of the name.

In May 1793, his lordship hoisted his flag again aboard the *Queen Charlotte,* with the temporary rank of Admiral of the Fleet. The fleet sailed for the first time in the new war on 14 July to seek its French counterpart. But due to various mishaps, it spent little more than a week at sea before returning to Torbay. The British sailed again soon afterward and actually sighted the French off Belle Isle, but due to contrary winds, they were unable to get within range. Then the weather became stormy, forcing the fleet to put back to Torbay after about a fortnight at sea. On 23 August the fleet sailed yet again to escort a convoy past the hazards of the Channel, which included the French fleet, cruisers and privateers. They encountered no threats and returned once again to their anchorage.

All these apparently pointless short cruises with long periods at anchor in between began to grow irksome to the admiral's officers. Some of them derisively nicknamed him "Lord Torbay." The general public, too, appeared disappointed that Howe was not more active in pursuing the enemy. Miss Berry, a lady of decided opinions, wrote: "Rumors there have been for some days, and still are, of overtures having been made from Brest to Lord Howe—but his lordship is not rapid, he moves like a king at chess at the end of the game, one square inch from Torbay, and the next back again."[20]

Indeed the admiral thought he had excellent reasons for keeping his fleet mainly at anchor in home waters. There were two schools of thought in that period concerning the blockade of an enemy. One believed that the best way to keep watch over the French fleet was to maintain a substantial presence outside Brest at all times. But the school to which Howe subscribed stated that the maintenance of a fleet outside the enemy's port for long periods of time was too costly in terms of wear and tear. In his long career, the admiral had seen the effects of a close blockade in terms of ships sunk or driven home in need of extensive repairs. To his mind the fleet was better anchored at readiness in Torbay, whence it would emerge in good condition as soon as the French were reported.

When Howe put to sea on 27 October, he stayed longer out of port, cruising the Bay of Biscay for the next two months. On 18 November one of his scouting frigates sighted a force of six French ships of the line and four smaller vessels. The commander of this force, Commodore Vanstabel, at first thought the fleet belonged to his countrymen, and he sailed toward it. But soon he was disabused of his supposition, when the British started to chase after him. Vanstabel turned and fled with the British snapping at his heels. One of Howe's frigates managed to come within range of two French frigates but was soon driven off by a pair of enemy two-deckers. Before the rest of the British fleet could come up, the enemy had reached safety.

While the admiral was still hoping the French would come out, a rumor sprang up in England that he had fought the enemy and captured five of their vessels. For the first part of December, the British public waited eagerly for confirmation of the report and to see the prizes brought in, but as time wore on without any news, they became impatient. Miss Berry wrote: "That there may have been such persons as King Arthur, and the Wandering Jew, and Lord Howe and his fleet, I will not take on me to deny; yet as History is silent on what became of them, I will not easily credit their re-existence."[21]

When the fleet returned at last with no prizes, the public became even more disenchanted with "Lord Torbay." "Completely has Lord Howe disappointed us all at last. . . . I hope we shall not soon again hear of him in command," wrote Mrs. Montagu, another strong-minded lady.[22]

During the winter of 1793–94, conditions in France grew desperate. The autumn harvests had been paltry; it was clear that if a large stock of food was not imported, the Republic might die of starvation. In the spring of 1794, a large convoy, reported to be as many as 350 sail (although 117 appears a more realistic number) of storeships was assembled from a number of American ports.[23] These, under the escort of Commodore Vanstabel, sailed from the Virginia coast on 2 April. Their arrival was eagerly anticipated in both Britain and France.

In Brest the main fleet was prepared to sail under the command of Rear Adm. Louis Thomas Villaret-Joyeuse, to protect the convoy for the final phase of its voyage. To make certain that the storeships reached their destination safely, Jean Bon Saint-André, a representative of the convention, was sent to accompany Villaret-Joyeuse aboard his flagship. If the British took the convoy, the admiral would pay with his head.

Meanwhile, the British too were assembling a convoy of impressive proportions. The vessels that comprised it were bound for the East and West Indies and for Newfoundland. Howe and his fleet would escort it as far as the western end of the Channel and then cruise in search of the French convoy on its way from America. The entire cavalcade, consisting of 148 ships and including forty-nine men-of-war, sailed on 2 May. The convoy parted company two days later, taking eight two-deckers and six or seven frigates to protect the merchantmen further on their way. Howe took the rest of his fleet, which amounted to twenty-six ships of the line, seven frigates, and six assorted other vessels to Ushant to await the French.[24] He cruised the bay through 18 May without seeing any sign of the enemy.

On 17 May a dense fog settled over the area of Brest, which allowed the French, who had sailed the day before, to slide past the British without being observed. This fleet consisted of twenty-five ships of the line, fifteen or sixteen frigates, and corvettes.[25]

On 19 May Howe learned of an expected conjunction of two smaller French forces to the west, threatening the convoy that had parted from him earlier in the month. The day after he received the news he left Ushant, heading westward in hopes of driving the enemy away from the convoys. Early in the morning of the following day, Howe learned that Villaret-Joyeuse was out and in close proximity to his fleet. Immediately upon hearing this news, he dashed off to the southwest in search of the main French fleet.

Although Howe missed Villaret-Joyeuse in the first pass, he made a few captures from which he learned information to help him narrow the scope of his search. Finally, on 28 May the British came in sight of the main French fleet. Immediately Howe made the signal to prepare for battle.

The enemy lay to windward (south by west) of the British, so Howe sent four of his ships of the line, under the command of Rear Adm. Thomas Pasley, to investigate.[26] This small scouting force had not gone far when the enemy was seen to be bearing down upon them, seeking to cut them off from the main fleet. As soon as this move was observed, his lordship issued the command for Pasley's squadron to shorten sail so that the rest of the fleet could come up to them.

Seeing that he would not be able to cut off the four advanced vessels from their compatriots, Villaret-Joyeuse signaled his ships to lay to on the larboard tack. Then he formed his fleet into a line of battle variously described as "rather ragged" or "indifferent," but as he held the wind gauge he could not be approached save in a dangerously piecemeal manner. Only Pasley was in a position to attack. When the *Révolutionnaire* began to fall astern of her compatriots, the rear admiral decided to take advantage and brought his flagship, the *Bellerophon,* within range of the massive French three-decker. She soon took some damage aloft, but before long the *Marlborough, Russell,* and *Thunderer* came to her assistance. Finding that the two-deckers were more than she could handle alone, the *Révolutionnaire* wore around and began to retreat before the wind. Several British vessels continued to harass the three-decker, nearly dismasting her, and the captain of the *Audacious* reported that the Frenchman had struck her flag. But because most of the pursuing British ships were disabled aloft, none could take possession of the supposed prize. The *Révolutionnaire* made her escape but was of no further use to Villaret-Joyeuse. In exchange, the *Audacious* was rendered incapable of providing any further assistance to Lord Howe.

At the close of the foregoing action, the two fleets parted ways, but they remained on parallel courses throughout the night at a distance of approximately six miles. On the morning of 29 May, Howe signaled his fleet to tack in succession, hoping to close the distance between himself and the French. When that maneuver had been completed, he directed his vessels to pass through the enemy's line in order to gain the wind gauge. This movement threatened the rear of the French fleet, which wore around to meet it and exchanged a distant cannonade with their foes. Meanwhile, Howe continued his effort to gain the wind gauge by passing through the enemy's line.

Due to the superior seamanship of the sailing master, James Bowen, Howe's flagship managed to pass through the enemy line and take the wind gauge. In admiration of his officer's feat, the admiral exclaimed, "Mr. Bowen, you may call me My Lord! You yourself deserve to be a prince."[27] A few other British vessels also managed to pass through the line, and it appeared for a short time that a general engagement would result. But the French admiral was able to extricate himself by disabling the leading British ship before others could enter the action and turning away, surrendering the wind gauge to Howe. Each side reformed to protect its cripples and repair its damages.

On the morning of 30 May the two fleets were still within sight of each other, with the French lying to leeward. Once again Howe attempted to renew the action, but the arrival of a dense fog stopped all hope of battle for the day. On the day following, the British had little better success in bringing the French to action. Villaret-Joyeuse's force withdrew slowly before the foes, maintaining a nearly impregnable line of battle that would be murderous to any enemy who assailed it. Howe remained in contact while he looked for an opening, but finding none until late in the day, he put off the engagement until he could be certain of a long period of daylight in which he could order the battle according to his tastes.

Finally, on 1 June, the conditions were right for battle. The weather was clear, and the wind blew from the south by west, giving Howe the wind gauge. Due to a few changes over the past days—*Révolutionnaire, Indomptable, Montagnard,* and *Mont-Blanc* replaced by *Trajan* (74), *Téméraire* (74), *Trente-et-un Mai* (74), *Patriote* (74), and *Sans Pareil* (80)—the fleets were nearly equal. The French had twenty-six, and the British twenty-five, ships of the line. At about 7:00 in the morning, Howe made the signal to pass through the enemy's line.

The British bore down and attempted individually to pass through the French line, but that proved a hazardous undertaking for many of the English vessels. There were few gaps in the enemy line large enough for a ship of the line to sail through without running the risk of collision. A small number of Howe's ships managed to pass through and engage the enemy to leeward, but most remained to windward and attacked at varied distances.

The rules of combat during the Age of Chivalry dictated that opposing leaders should seek to duel single-handed against each other on the field of battle. So it was with flagships in the Age of Sail, not only because flagships were generally the heaviest vessels in their respective fleets, and it was best to counter weight with weight, but also because the lesser commanders of both sides looked to the flags for guidance. It was one thing to make a signal and expect it to be obeyed, and quite another to lead by example. From the Battle of the First of June to Trafalgar and beyond, the British commander in chief set the standard, and woe betide any captain who failed to measure up.

At Howe's command the *Queen Charlotte* made for the space astern of the *Montagne.* The gap was so narrow that the flagship barely squeaked through. But once she was on the other side, the British flagship ran herself close alongside Villaret-Joyeuse's vessel and proceeded to pour broadside after broadside into her. Meanwhile, the *Queen Charlotte* was receiving fire from both sides, the *Jacobin* having run alongside her unengaged starboard side. One of her shots carried away the flagship's foretopmast, but she did not remain alongside the three-decker for long. Her captain soon found the contest too hot for him and steered her out of the battle.

After sustaining about ten minutes of concentrated fire from the *Queen Charlotte,* the *Montagne* made more sail to get away. The British flagship could not follow, due to the injury done to her masts, and was left with a less worthy opponent, the *Juste.* In a short time the two-decker was dismasted, but in fighting her, the *Queen Charlotte* lost her maintopmast, which rendered her nearly unmanageable. She was almost overwhelmed by the three-decker *Républicain,* but was spared when the enemy lost her main- and mizzenmasts. With her foe crippled, the flagship was able to cruise slowly forward and come to the assistance of the *Queen,* which had been severely mauled by several of the enemy. Joined by several other British vessels, the *Queen Charlotte* drove off the second rate's attackers. With that action, the battle ended as far as she was concerned.

Although Howe was denied the epic ship-to-ship duel that creates legends, a few single-ship actions of note developed within the Battle of the First of June. The most famous is the contest between the *Brunswick* and the *Vengeur.*

The *Brunswick* was one of the few British vessels that successfully passed through the French line. At her station directly astern of the *Queen Charlotte,* she first tried to cross the wake of the *Jacobin,* but she was thwarted by the *Achille* and then the *Vengeur.* Determined to break the line in spite of the danger of collision, she set her sights on the narrow gap between the *Achille* and the *Vengeur.* She did not make it. As the *Brunswick* passed, her anchors hooked in the *Vengeur's* chains, fastening the two vessels together. The French and British ships were locked so closely that the *Brunswick's* guncrews could not open the gunport lids. Instead they blew them off with their first shots. This first round was followed up by a number of savage broadsides, which rocked the *Vengeur* from stem to stern. The French vessel was not able to counter her foe's broadsides with many of her own guns, but she discharged a fusillade of musketry and light cannon fire on the decks of the *Brunswick,* mortally wounding the captain and killing and wounding a number of officers and men.

After about three hours of bloody fighting, the two vessels were finally separated, allowing the *Brunswick* to discharge a few more guns into her opponent's stern, disabling her rudder. The *Brunswick* fell away, but her place was soon taken by the *Ramillies,* which completed the devastation of the *Vengeur.* A few hours after she parted from the *Brunswick's* embrace, she sank, with a large loss of life.

By shortly after 1:00 P.M. most of the battle was over. The *America, Impétueux, Juste, Achille,* and *Northumberland* were secured as prizes, while the rest of the French fled to leeward. Little attempt was made to pursue them, partly because many of the British ships were badly damaged and also because Howe and his men were exhausted. In the course of five days in contact with the enemy, they had lost 290 killed and 858 wounded, while the French losses amounted to close to seven thousand killed, wounded, or taken. Although the British failed in their main objective by allowing the convoy to escape, the battle was accounted a great victory by the standards of the time.

The victorious admiral returned to Spithead with his prizes on 13 June, but the news of his feat had preceded him by more than a week. He was greeted with a tremendous outpouring of public approval. The king himself determined to come down to Portsmouth to congratulate Howe in person and present him with a diamond-hilted sword and a gold chain. He also promised to induct his lordship into the Order of the Garter at the first vacancy.

Other rewards flowed in for the subordinate officers. Peerages and baronetcies were distributed like candy to the various vice admirals and rear admirals, gold medals were granted to certain captains and flag officers, and a hoard of lieutenants were promoted to the rank of commander. It was unfortunate that the celebration was marred by divisions between those who were granted medals and those who were not but felt that they too deserved them. Howe was blamed for playing favorites when in fact he had been compelled against his wishes by Lord Chatham to weed out the captains who had been less distinguished, and had not been allowed to amend the list later.

The admiral was not allowed to rest long upon his laurels. By 22 August he and his fleet were back at sea on a cruise that extended to October. Then they weighed anchor once more for most of the month of November, but they did not encounter the French again that year.

All this cruising was beginning to take its toll on Howe's constitution. At the time of the Battle of the First of June he was sixty-eight years of age, the oldest sea officer to win a battle in the eighteenth century. In the spring of 1795, he sailed again with the fleet aboard the *Queen Charlotte,* but he returned in ill health and never put to sea again.

Although the admiral did not go out with the fleet, he remained the official commander in chief of the station all through 1795 and 1796. In March 1796, at the death of the octogenarian Admiral Forbes, he became Admiral of the Fleet, the most senior officer in the entire Royal Navy. But his ill health prevented him from taking on any duties more active than to sit on the occasional court-martial. Although eager to retire, he was persuaded by the king and the First Lord to remain officially in command for longer than he would have liked. Nevertheless, he spent most of that time in Bath, being treated for gout, and left the day-to-day running of the fleet to Lord Bridport.

It was unfortunate that Bridport should have been designated second-in-command of the Channel fleet under Howe. There had been bad blood between the two of them since the period of the Keppel court-martial, and further antipathy had been nurtured in the bed of politics. By the time they served together in the Channel fleet, they were scarcely on speaking terms. This lack of communication between them was to have serious repercussions in 1797.

For a long time the seamen of the Royal Navy had been dissatisfied with the service. In spite of inflation, their pay had not been raised since the middle of the seventeenth century. They were often not given the full rations they were entitled to by law, and they were frequently mistreated by bad officers. To rectify these faults, in early 1797 many of the seamen of the Channel fleet wrote petitions to Lord Howe, long known for humane treatment of his ships' companies, asking him to intercede on their behalf. The admiral was ill and not feeling inclined to pursue the matter far. Besides, it appeared to him that these petitions had been written by only a few people who had disguised their handwriting. He forwarded them to Lord Spencer, who had replaced Chatham at the Admiralty in 1795, and promptly forgot about them. He passed no word to Admiral Bridport at Spithead.

Hearing no response to their petitions, the seamen of the Channel fleet grew frustrated and decided that they could solve their difficulties only by taking action. Lord Howe officially resigned as commander in chief on 13 April, and two days later, his entire former command mutinied. The mutineers treated their superiors with respect, but they refused to weigh anchor when commanded to do so by Lord Bridport. Various officers were sent ashore, some more willingly than others, but generally the action was characterized by a lack of violence.

Parliament swiftly met and voted to increase the sailors' pay, but because of a lack of trust between the two sides, the seamen continued to hold out until the middle of May. As a gesture of good will, Lord Spencer decided to send Howe to negotiate the final settlement with the mutineers. When asked who he would like to accompany him on this delicate mission, he replied, "Lady Howe."[28] On 9 May 1797, the elderly admiral and his lady boarded the mail coach that ran from London to Portsmouth. They arrived early on the following day, and immediately his Lord Howe set to work. Leaving his wife at the home of a kinswoman, he had himself rowed out to the fleet. For three days he traveled from ship to ship, speaking with each vessel's company, hearing their grievances and persuading them that if they returned to their duties, they would not be punished. On the thirteenth he met with delegates from each of the ships aboard the *Royal William* (84) and spent most of the day negotiating with the mutineers. They had presented him with a long list of officers they wished removed from their vessels. Although the admiral had not been granted the right to remove officers, he quickly saw that to remove a few of those on the list would be the surest way the end the mutiny quickly. He went down the entire list, removing some officers and persuading the crews to allow the rest to remain.

By the morning of 14 May a settlement had been reached. A total of 114 officers were removed from the ships stationed at Spithead and Plymouth, and the seamen agreed to return to work. In celebration of this new accord, Lord Howe was paraded through the fleet. Upon landing at the Sally Port, the admiral invited the chief of the mutineers to drink a glass of wine with him. The next morning the delegates and a band of music repaired ashore to serenade the old admiral and his wife until they agreed to come out and join them for a final triumphal procession. Once again, his lordship was rowed all through the fleet. When they finally returned to the house where the Howes were staying that evening, Lady Howe invited all the delegates to stay for supper. Then, with his final service to the nation complete, the admiral returned to his retirement.

Within a fortnight of his return to London from Portsmouth, Howe was inducted into the Order of the Garter. It was a fitting end to a distinguished career. From that point on, the old admiral lived quietly, bearing patiently painful attacks of gout. Electrical cures were all the rage in the late eighteenth century, and in the summer of 1799, Howe was persuaded to see what the treatment could do for him. According to Barrow, the application of electricity drove the gout to his head and killed him, on 5 August 1799. His devoted wife survived him by little more than a year.

The admiral was buried in the family vault at Langar, and was succeeded as Viscount Howe by his brother William. His eldest daughter inherited his English barony, which passed down to her son.

Chapter 2

ALEXANDER HOOD

1727–1814

ONE SOURCE OF CONFUSION in the literature on the mid- to late-eighteenth-century Royal Navy is the four Hood cousins, whose era of active service ranged from 1741 to 1812. These officers were two sets of brothers—both named Samuel and Alexander, and three of the four lived long enough to achieve flag rank. In reading some sources, it is occasionally difficult to determine which Hood is meant if only the last name is used, but to set the record straight, the four Hoods were: Samuel Hood, Lord Hood (1724–1816); Alexander Hood, Lord Bridport (1727–1814); Alexander Hood (1758–98); and Sir Samuel Hood, KB (1762–1814). The pair most commonly confused are Lords Bridport and Hood. Even the Admiralty was guilty of forgetting which was which, as will be demonstrated below.

The biographical details on Lord Bridport and Lord Hood will be provided in this chapter and in chapter 3. Sir Samuel Hood was one of Nelson's famous "Band of Brothers" and appears in several chapters in this book. Alexander Hood the younger accompanied Captain Cook on his second voyage. A description of his death in battle with the French ship of the line *Hercule* is included in this chapter.

• • •

Sometimes the most trivial occurrences can have far-reaching consequences. For example, who could have guessed that a carriage accident would bring four distinguished officers into the king's service? But that is precisely what happened with the Hoods.

Samuel and Alexander were the only sons of the Reverend Samuel and Mary Hood of Butleigh, Somerset. Both boys were educated at home, but to what intended end is not recorded. Whatever plans the good vicar had for his sons were set at naught on the day in 1740 that Capt. Thomas Smith had a carriage accident. Because the damage to his carriage was not something that could be repaired quickly, the captain remained a guest of the vicar and his family for a few days. During that time he met the two young Hood brothers, and before he left, he agreed to take the younger to sea with him.

So, on 19 January 1741, Alexander Hood was entered aboard the *Romney* (54) as a captain's servant. It was a common practice in the eighteenth century for young gentlemen to be brought aboard men-of-war as captain's servants although they were destined to be officers. This was because each ship was allowed a limited quota of midshipmen, but a captain was allowed a larger number of servants than he needed. So the best way to advance a young relation or the son of a friend was to take him aboard as a servant. Then he could mess with the young gentlemen and learn the ways of the sea until a vacancy occurred in the midshipmen's berth. It did not matter when it came time to take the exam for lieutenant as long as one could show that one had been six years at sea, and had been a midshipman for at least two of those years.

Later in the year Captain Smith was replaced by Captain Grenville, and in early 1742, the *Romney* set sail for the Mediterranean. When the little two-decker arrived on station, the commander in chief was Rear Adm. Richard Lestock, a contentious man who was once described thusly: "Unconciliating in his manners, austere in command, restless when in a subordinate station, he had fewer friends than fell to the lot of most men, and that number, which was gradually diminishing, his behavior never appeared of a nature to recruit."[1] In May he was superseded by Vice Adm. Thomas Mathews, which fired up his already smoldering resentment. Not only were Mathews and Lestock personal enemies, but the more junior officer felt that to appoint a commander in chief over him was an affront from the Admiralty. The admirals' mutual dislike was to have far-reaching repercussions a couple of years later.

Meanwhile, well away from the politics of high command, young Mr. Hood was learning his duty aboard the *Romney*. The main fleet blockaded a combined French and Spanish force anchored in Toulon while the reserve, under Lestock, remained at Villa Franca. Performing this rather tedious but essential duty, Alexander passed a year. Then, in April 1743, he departed the *Romney* and soon found himself, now a proper midshipman, again under the command of Captain Smith, aboard the yacht *Princess Mary*.

Little is known of Mr. Hood's life over the next two years. But during that time, a furor erupted among the more senior officers of the fleet. In February 1744 the British Mediterranean fleet under Mathews, with Lestock as second-in-command, engaged with the French off Toulon. The result was a disorganized, scrambling action in which the British took no prizes before the enemy effected his escape. In the aftermath Mathews blamed Lestock for failing to support him. Both flag officers were eventually tried by court-martial, with the result that Mathews was dismissed from the service and Lestock acquitted of wrongdoing.

Because he wanted to get at the enemy as quickly as possible and so came at them in a disorderly manner, Mathews was cashiered. Lestock, on the other hand, was acquitted of all charges against him, on the grounds that he had been obeying the signal for line of battle that had been kept flying until near the end of the action. These judgments gave many officers the impression that maintaining a strict line of battle was the only way to stay out of trouble with their superiors. For the next generation, with few exceptions, naval battles were fought with that premise in mind.

In December 1744 Mr. Hood followed Captain Smith aboard the *Royal Sovereign* (100), in which they remained only four months before removing to the *Exeter* (60). In the latter vessel Hood remained for slightly more than a year and then followed his patron aboard the *Hawk* (10) in May 1746. This was the last ship in which he served as a midshipman. On 2 December 1746 he was promoted to lieutenant and commissioned to the *Bridgewater* (24). Like most small ships of rate, the *Bridgewater* was mainly employed in escorting convoys and cruising independently. With the coming of peace toward the end of 1748, the sixth rate was paid off, and Hood was placed on half pay. What followed was the longest period of inactivity in Hood's life. Like many other naval officers during peacetime, he could not find employment until another war erupted. Fortunately for naval officers of the eighteenth century, they generally did not have long to wait for the next war.

With the beginning of the Seven Years' War in 1755, the future began to seem considerably brighter for Mr. Hood. In January of that year he was commissioned lieutenant of the *Prince George* (90) under the command of Capt. Charles Saunders, one of the most distinguished captains then in the service. Alexander did not serve under Saunders for long, because the captain left his ship to become comptroller of the navy in December, but he appears to have made a favorable impression during the time they were together in the same ship. In his position at the Admiralty, Saunders was able to influence promotions, and before long (11 January 1756) Hood was promoted to commander of the *Firebrand* (20). Normally a ship of twenty guns would have been a command for a post captain, but the *Firebrand* had recently been converted into a fireship, which made her a post for a commander.

Hood's first command did not begin auspiciously. He made a number of mistakes that betrayed his youth and inexperience. First, when he been in command for less than a month, he chased a suspicious brigantine too close to shore and barely avoided running aground near Dartmouth. Then, only a few days later, he decided to press a few sailors out of some merchantmen. But when he tried to land, he discovered that a number of the men he had pressed had come from ships under quarantine, which placed the *Firebrand* under quarantine as well.[2]

As the Admiralty might well be expected to be displeased at losing the use of one of its men-of-war for the period of quarantine due to a piece of carelessness on the part of its commander, Hood took the liberty of writing an explanation of how the whole mess was not his fault. He explained: "If I have been guilty of an error, it has proceeded from my not having any particular instruction relative to this Order in Council, and the Laws of Quarantine, for had I been well informed concerning them, I would have carefully avoided my present situation."[3]

It was typical of Alexander Hood to write self-justifying letters to the Admiralty every time anything questionable took place aboard one of his commands; and questionable occurrences were not uncommon, especially during his early years as a captain. On 11 March, after a mere two months in command, Hood was removed from the *Firebrand*. He remained aboard the *Lovely Sukey* tender for about a month before he was placed in command of the *Merlin* (10).

Alexander commanded the *Merlin* for less than three months before he was made post as flag captain to the newly created Rear Admiral Saunders on 10 June. This promotion was strong proof of Saunders' approval, because the junior admiral had been given the choice of his own flag captain. Among all the officers he could have selected for that honor, he picked Hood. Together with Saunders and Vice Admiral Hawke, he boarded the *Antelope* (54), which was bound for Gibraltar to deliver the new commanders of the Mediterranean fleet to their station. In their place, she was to take up Vice Adm. John Byng and Rear Adm. Temple West and return them to England. The former officer was returning to England to attempt to explain his actions at a battle fought on 20 May 1756. To his surprise, he found himself on trial for his life.

Byng, with a fleet of twelve ships of the line, had fought a French force of approximately equal size off Minorca. The situation at the opening of the battle was typical of contests between the two navies. The British had the wind gauge, and both sides were in a tight line of battle. Because of the decision against Mathews, Byng was reluctant to charge down haphazardly upon the enemy. He chose a more sloping angle of attack that maintained his line of battle but exposed him to enemy gunfire for a long period of time. Soon many of his vessels were too damaged to continue; the French made off, and Minorca fell to the enemy.

At the news of the loss of Minorca, the British public began to look about for a likely scapegoat. Byng was the most obvious choice, and when he reached Spithead aboard the *Antelope* on 26 July 1756, he was arrested. The judges at Byng's court-martial were compelled to try him under the Twelfth Article of War, which specified the death penalty.[4] The judges found Byng guilty but recommended him for clemency, which was denied. He was executed aboard the *Monarch* (74) on 14 March 1757.

Meanwhile, Rear Admiral Saunders raised his flag aboard the *Prince George,* bringing Hood with him as flag captain. For the latter half of 1756, the rear admiral served as second-in-command under Hawke. Then, after the departure of his senior, he was commander in chief for a year. While he remained in the Mediterranean, Saunders shifted his flag from ship to ship, taking Hood with him on each occasion. In the course of a year and half, the young captain commanded the *Prince George,* the *Culloden* (74), and the *St. George* (96). Finally, at the end of 1758, Saunders was released from the Mediterranean command, and returned to Britain aboard the *Royal George* (100). Hood, as ever, accompanied him.

Shortly after the *Royal George* returned to England in December 1758, her captain was appointed to the *Minerva* (32). This was his first independent command since his days with small ships, but it appeared that he had learned much about leadership while he had sailed with Saunders. Although he still had a tendency to write for Admiralty approval of the slightest act, he was considered a very promising young captain by his superiors. Hood took command of the *Minerva* about a fortnight before she was launched, and spent the next two months preparing her for sea. In March 1759 he weighed anchor and made for the French base at Brest. For the remainder of the year, he cruised the Channel, taking prizes and scouting for Admiral Hawke.

When the British and French fleets met in the stormy Battle of Quiberon Bay on 20 November 1759, as described in chapter 1, the *Minerva* was on hand. But with a mere frigate, Hood's command did not take an important part in the contest between the two- and three-deckers.

Although the main French fleet had been crushed, the blockade of Brest continued. For the year following the Battle of Quiberon Bay, Hood cruised his old grounds without encountering an enemy of note. Then, in January 1761, the *Minerva* was presented with two opponents within a short time of each other. While cruising in the Bay of Biscay, she first encountered the privateer *Ecureuil* (14), and then the troopship *Warwick* (60). In conquering the latter vessel, Captain Hood finally began to make a name for himself independent of his patrons.

The *Warwick* had been captured from the British by three French vessels in March 1756. She was a weak two-decker and dull sailor, so the French decided she would serve better as a troop transport. They stripped her of many of her heavy guns and filled her with soldiers intended to relieve a garrison at Pondicherry in India. Although she no longer carried her full armament, she still had thirty-four cannon, most of which could fire heavier shot than the *Minerva*'s 12-pounders.

Captain Hood was not discouraged by the disparity in the size of the two ships. He gave chase and, by the middle of the morning, ran his vessel alongside the *Warwick* and opened fire. After an hour's exchange of shot, the troopship's mainmast and foretopmast fell, causing her to fall astern of the frigate. But Hood hove to and waited for the enemy to come up to him. In the following cannonade, the *Minerva* lost her foremast and bowsprit. Then, both ships being unmanageable in heavy seas, they collided, but afterwards parted before either side could attempt to board. In the confusion the Frenchman again tried to escape, but Hood swiftly cleared away the wreckage and set sails on his remaining masts. He caught the crippled *Warwick* and pounded her until she struck her flag late in the afternoon. The casualties suffered by each side were nearly even—fourteen French and British killed, and thirty-two French and thirty-four British wounded.

For attacking a larger foe so fearlessly, Hood enjoyed public acclaim for the first time in his career. Because of the prominence this feat had given him, he was selected to command part of a squadron that escorted Princess Sophie Charlotte of Mecklenburg-Strelitz to the homeland of her future husband, King George III, in August 1761.

Upon the return of the escort squadron, Hood was placed in command of the *Africa* (64) and sent to join the Mediterranean fleet. He served in those waters for approximately a year and a half, but by that time most of the action was taking place across the Atlantic. The captain enjoyed a relatively peaceful cruise, after which he returned to England, and his ship was paid off in April 1763. As the Seven Years' War had concluded in February, it was to be some time before Hood gained the opportunity to distinguish himself again.

Not long after the captain's return from the Mediterranean, he was wed to Mary West, of whom it is written that she brought a large fortune.[5] Judging by most accounts of her husband's fondness for money, that is likely to be the principal reason that he married her. His lady wife also had a less substantial, but still useful, dowry—some distant family connections to the powerful Lyttleton and Grenville families.

In September 1763 Alexander was sent a commission to command the *Thunderer* (74), but he realized that the vessel was intended for his brother Samuel and declined the post. However, he did not remain without a command for long. In December he was appointed to the *Katherine* yacht, a vessel he commanded for the next fourteen years. Although a yacht might seem a less challenging command than the third rate his brother received, it had its compensations. Not only were the duties comparatively easy, but the captain of a yacht received the same pay as the captain of a second rate. Certainly, Hood was able to pursue other interests while he commanded the *Katherine*. When Admiral Saunders resigned his position as treasurer of Greenwich Hospital in September 1766, Hood succeeded him, while keeping his command of the yacht. For the next decade the captain lived a peaceful existence. War started in North America, but Hood does not appear to have been eager to join in. He remained ashore until it appeared that the French were likely to join the war on the side of the rebels. In December 1777 he was appointed to command the *Robust* (74).

In the first half of 1778, the Royal Navy drastically increased its operations. Simultaneously, one fleet was prepared to sail for North America, and the other was readied to cruise the Channel. Each competed for limited resources, delaying the date of departure for both. It was not until the beginning of June that either fleet was ready to sail. But on 9 June, Byron finally sailed for America to relieve Howe as commander in chief of that station. A few days later the Channel fleet, the *Robust* included, sailed for its first cruise off Brest.

The first cruise of the Channel fleet in the War of American Independence was relatively uneventful. The fleet returned to port after a fortnight. But on 8 July the French fleet, commanded by Lt. Gen. Louis Guillouet, the Comte d'Orvilliers, put to sea with thirty-two ships of the line.[6]

The day following the emergence of the Brest fleet, Keppel too weighed anchor, hoping to catch the enemy and force them into a decisive battle. As some new vessels had been made ready since the beginning of June, the size of his fleet was ultimately increased to thirty ships of the line.[7] Although the French had a slight advantage in the total number of ships of the line, the British fleet had more guns.

Keppel was one of the most distinguished officers then in the king's service. As described in chapter 1, the duel between his *Torbay* and the French *Thésée* at the Battle of Quiberon Bay was one of the great single-ship actions of the Seven Years' War. But the admiral bore several burdens. He was suffering from a back injury that often deprived him of the use of his legs. Also, he was on bad terms with Lord Sandwich, the First Lord of the Admiralty. As a Whig sympathizer with the American rebels, he had refused to take any command until the French declared war, and even then, he insisted that he remain on the eastern side of the Atlantic. Sandwich would have preferred to appoint another commander in chief of the Channel fleet, but Keppel was immensely popular with the public, and there were no other admirals with sufficient rank and ability to take his place. So the First Lord made up for it by making a follower of his own, Vice Adm. Sir Hugh Palliser, the third-in-command.

D'Orvilliers also had a handicap, which consisted of conflicting orders from a government that wanted to see the British fleet beaten but without appreciable cost. To the ministers, the admiral replied, "I will avoid a disproportionate action as well as I can; but if the enemy really seeks to force it, it will be very hard to shun."[8]

For the first fortnight after they sailed, the two fleets cruised the Channel without sighting each other. Then, finally, on the afternoon of 23 July 1778, they made contact about one hundred miles west of Ushant. The British had the wind gauge as they started toward their foes. But the sun went down before they got into range, so Keppel commanded his fleet to heave to, expecting to see battle in the morning. However, during the night the wind shifted and strengthened, allowing the French to overreach the British and obtain the wind gauge, which they used subsequently to avoid action. Two French ships of the line became separated from their fleet, and the British tried to take advantage of their vulnerability. But in spite of all efforts, Keppel's men-of-war were unable to catch them. Nonetheless, d'Orvilliers was deprived of their services for the remainder of the campaign.

By dawn 27 July, the two fleets were approximately five miles apart, with the French still to windward. In trying to come up into range, the British fleet had become spread out. Vice Admiral Palliser's squadron, to which the *Robust* belonged, trailed Keppel's flagship, the *Victory,* by three miles.[9] As the morning wore on, with the British trying to force an action and the French continuing to slide away, Palliser in the *Formidable* (90) dropped farther and farther astern of the main fleet. His squadron remained by him, opening a large gap in the line of battle until Keppel signaled the rear division to give chase and catch up with the rest of the fleet.

At around 10:00 in the morning, first the French wore and then the British tacked, drawing the two lines slightly closer together. Soon afterward a rain squall obscured the fleets from each other. D'Orvilliers decided to take advantage of the squall to change tack again and open up more distance between the fleets. But with the squall came a change in the wind direction, which favored the British, allowing them to draw within range of the enemy.

At 11:20 Admiral Keppel made the signal for battle. Because the two fleets were sailing on opposite tacks, the vans of both forces took little part in the action. They were carried away from the enemy soon after they were within range. The brunt of the fighting fell on the center and rear. For nearly three hours the two fleets pounded each other, the British firing into the hulls and the French into the rigging.

Palliser's squadron remained within range of the enemy longer than did the rest of the fleet. As a result, the vessels' masts, sails, and rigging absorbed tremendous punishment that disabled five of them so badly they could not maintain contact with the rest of the British fleet. Observing the vulnerability of the five disabled vessels, d'Orvilliers put about again and tried to cut between Keppel and the cripples. But the British managed to form their van and center into a line of battle to windward of the French, placing themselves between the cripples and the enemy. Foiled in his original intention, d'Orvilliers drew up out of range, maintained a tight line of battle, and awaited results.

The latter stage of the battle was the most controversial. Keppel's van and center were ready to renew the action. But the rear, under Palliser, had fallen a good way astern. The vice admiral's flagship had been badly damaged during the initial pass and could not come up to join her compatriots as swiftly as the commander in chief desired. What was more, the captains of the squadron considered it their duty to remain by Palliser's flagship rather than join the main fleet on their own. It was not until 7:00 P.M. that Keppel signaled each ship individually to join the line of battle. This finally effected the admiral's desire for a full line of battle, but darkness fell before the action could be renewed. The French then took advantage of the night to slip away.

Although the Battle of Ushant was indecisive, the casualties were significant, especially in the ships of the center and rear squadrons. The *Robust* lost 5 killed and 17 wounded out of a company of approximately 600 men.[10] Total British losses were 133 killed and 373 wounded. The French lost 161 killed and 513 wounded.[11]

When the main body of the British fleet returned to Plymouth on 31 July, the initial reaction to the news of the battle was relief. The French fleet had been met at sea and had retreated, thereby removing a perceived threat of invasion. But after a few months had passed, reaction began to set in. While the Channel fleet spent the end of the summer and beginning of autumn cruising in hopes of another meeting with the French, some people began to search for a scapegoat. In mid-October, the following paragraph was published in the *Morning Intelligencer:* "The principal cause of Mr. Keppel's not reattacking the French, at half-past three in the afternoon . . . was Sir Hugh Palliser's not joining him, agreeable to signal to form the line. . . . Mr. Keppel, observing a non-compliance, made other signals for the respective ships of Sir Hugh's division to bear down to him, which, in complying with, Sir Hugh called them back into his wake."[12]

The article went on to state that the vice admiral had failed to make a satisfactory excuse for his not allowing the ships of his squadron to join the main fleet. By implication, the *Morning Intelligencer* placed the blame for the inconclusive nature of the battle squarely on the shoulders of Sir Hugh Palliser.

Offended by the article's insinuations, the vice admiral wrote a letter to Admiral Keppel, which included the following paragraph: "I think myself much entitled to have my conduct . . . justified by you . . . from those foul aspersions. I have been expecting your offer to do it. I have waited for your coming to town to ask it. Being now informed of your arrival, I lose no time in desiring you will contradict those scandalous reports that have been propagated as before mentioned, by publishing in your own name the enclosed paper, which I have the honour to enclose herewith."[13]

The enclosed paper was a highly laudatory description of Palliser's actions, which stated that "his conduct on that day [27 July 1778] was in every respect proper, and becoming a good officer."[14] Although the commander in chief had not found fault with his junior's actions during the battle, he considered his demands impertinent and rejected his requests. Keppel's refusal to sign the paper prompted Palliser to go to the *Morning Post,* a Tory newspaper, and submit his own version of the battle for publication. This article cast aspersions on Keppel's abilities as an admiral and created such a furor among naval officers and political officials that the vice admiral finally demanded that the Admiralty try Keppel on the charge of misconduct and neglect of duty. Because of the result of Byng's court-martial more than twenty years earlier, there was the possibility that the admiral was on trial for his life.

The court-martial of Admiral Keppel began aboard the *Britannia* on 7 January 1779. Because of the defendant's ill health, the proceedings were later moved to the Governor's House at Portsmouth. Every available captain who had been present at the Battle of Ushant was called upon to testify, Hood among them.

Before the captains had their chance to stand before the judges, the sailing masters of all the ships were called upon to swear to the accuracy of their logs. Robert Arnold, the master of the *Robust,* refused to take an oath to that effect and testified that Captain Hood had made alterations to the log after the news of the court-martial had been released. This testimony made it appear that Hood had purposely altered his log to support Palliser's claims. Soon word of his alleged action spread throughout the nation, which was following the court-martial closely, and Hood acquired an unenviable reputation. The public reaction ran so strongly against him for a time that the word *hooded* meant to manufacture false evidence.[15]

When the captain's turn came to give evidence, he was questioned about the alterations to his log, to which he replied that the log had been written up carelessly at first and that when it appeared that it would be produced as evidence in court, he thought it wise to improve its appearance and accuracy. Although the court accepted this explanation, Hood continued to pursue the issue, even when the judges tried to ask for information on other matters. Finally the exasperated president told the captain to speak no more about the altered log books: "We shall never get through a court martial if we are to follow this practice."[16]

In the rest of his testimony, Hood proved evasive. When asked if Admiral Keppel flew or appeared to fly from the enemy, he replied that there was one point when the commander in chief appeared to fly, but he added that he thought it was only the judges' supposition. At the end of his period of giving evidence, Hood was asked if he had ever seen Admiral Keppel behave in a manner unbecoming of a flag officer. To this the captain replied, "I have long had the honor of knowing the honorable admiral and will respect him notwithstanding my evidence."[17]

Some modern authors take a lenient view on Hood's alteration of his log. However, many of the captain's own contemporaries took a dim view of his alterations and his lukewarm support of Admiral Keppel. Captain Jervis of the *Foudroyant,* who also stood as a witness at the court-martial, condemned Hood's testimony.

Because of the uproar produced by his testimony, Hood resigned as captain of the *Robust* and was reappointed to the *Katherine* yacht before the court-martial ended in early February. Keppel's acquittal became an excuse for an antigovernment mob to riot through the streets of London, breaking windows and looting the houses of unpopular officials. Captain Hood's house was attacked, but it did not sustain the sort of damage inflicted on the houses of Lord Sandwich and Sir Hugh Palliser.

On 26 September 1780 Alexander Hood was promoted to the rank of rear admiral of the blue, but was not employed for two years. Then, toward the middle of 1782, the British began outfitting a fleet to relieve the garrison at Gibraltar. As described in the previous chapter, this fleet was under the command of Admiral Howe. One of the subordinate admirals appointed to the expedition was Rear Adm. Richard Kempenfelt, who hoisted his flag in the *Royal George*. But when the flagship sank at Spithead, taking the admiral to the bottom with her, Hood was appointed to take his place. In early September the new admiral hoisted his flag aboard the *Queen* (90) and set sail with the rest of the fleet a few days later. The details of the relief of Gibraltar are included in chapter 1. The *Queen* took part in the partial action between the British and allied fleets on 20 October 1782, but sustained few casualties.

Soon after the return of the fleet to Portsmouth in November, a preliminary peace was signed, and Hood went ashore. Although his first service as a flag officer had not been notable, he was established as a worthy junior admiral. While he waited for another war, the admiral determined to pursue a more peaceful form of public service. He was elected Member of Parliament for Bridgewater in 1784, and soon afterward represented Buckingham.

In 1786, the admiral's first wife died, and on 26 June 1788, he wedded Mary Bray, the daughter of a private gentleman. Although the lady was some twenty years younger than her spouse, she was not a fresh young maiden. Her age at the time of their marriage was forty-two.

When the Tories regained control of the government in July 1788, Hood was nominated to receive the Order of the Bath. By the king's hand he became Sir Alexander Hood. During the threat of war with Spain over Nootka Sound, Hood, now a vice admiral, received his commission as third-in-command of the Channel fleet. He hoisted his flag aboard the *London* (98) in May 1790 and spent the next few months cruising and performing drills in preparation for war. At the successful conclusion of these preparations, he was appointed Rear Admiral of England and given leave to return to his life ashore.

Then, at the beginning of 1793, war threatened again, this time with republican France. In February Vice Admiral Hood received another commission as third-in-command of the Channel fleet. He hoisted his flag aboard the *Royal George* (100). When the newly reconstituted Channel fleet set sail on 14 July 1793, the *Royal George* was among the fifteen ships of the line that cruised along the coast of France. As described in chapter 1, it was not until the end of the year that the Channel fleet was able to keep the sea for more than a few weeks at a time. Howe's fleet returned to Spithead after the final cruise of 1793 in mid-December and did not sail again until the following spring. In April 1794, Hood rose to the rank of full admiral of the blue, but in the meantime, there was little activity on either side of the Channel. That, however, was soon to change.

The Channel fleet weighed anchor in early May to escort a large convoy past the most dangerous portion of the coast and in hopes of capturing a French convoy from America. They never encountered the convoy, but on 28 May, as described in chapter 1, they sighted the French fleet, which had escaped from Brest some days earlier. A few ships of both sides managed to get into action, but without any more result than the crippling of one vessel on each side.

On the following day the action become more general. Commanding the British van, Hood approached within gunshot of the French line and exchanged a number of broadsides. The fire of the flagship and supporting vessels severely damaged the leading enemy vessel, *Montagnard* (74), but at the cost of damage to their own rigging. When Admiral Howe made the signal to tack in succession with the intention of passing through the French line, some of Hood's squadron were unable to comply.

The *Royal George* succeeded in tacking, and with the support of the *Invincible* (74), fell upon the rearmost French ships, the *Tyrannicide* (74) and the *Indomptable* (80). In the fierce battle that followed, the *Royal George* suffered the loss of two officers and eleven seamen killed and a large number of wounded.[18] Her hull suffered a number of shot holes, which rendered her leaky, and she had her mizzen yard shot away.[19] Her opponents were badly crippled, but the French admiral, Villaret-Joyeuse, brought the rest of his fleet to their support and prevented their capture.

For a short time it appeared that the *Royal George* was in danger of absorbing the concentrated fire of the bulk of the French fleet, but Howe commanded his own force to run down to her protection. The vans of both fleets engaged briefly at long range, and then the fleets reformed to lick their wounds and await another day.

Fog prevented the two fleets from meeting on 30 May, and Howe spent the following day preparing his forces to attack the enemy on the following morning. Finally, on 1 June, the full French and British forces engaged in action. On this occasion Hood commanded the rear of the fleet, his *Royal George* fourth from the end of the British line of battle. When Lord Howe gave the signal to pass through the enemy's line and engage him to leeward, Hood's flagship bore down on the *Sans Pareil* (80) and the *Républicain* (110), the latter being the flagship of the admiral commanding the French rear. She gave them a few broadsides as she came up into range, then passed between the two and concentrated her fire on the *Républicain*. She was eventually assisted by the *Glory* (98), and between them, they severely damaged the French three-decker's main- and mizzenmasts. But the *Républicain* crippled both of her foes enough that she was able to make her escape. The departure of the *Républicain* ended the battle for the *Royal George*.

In the Battle of the First of June, Hood's flagship lost one officer and four seamen and marines killed, and four officers and forty-five seamen and marines wounded.[20] Her foremast was toppled, both remaining topmasts fractured, and the ropes that connected the wheel to the tiller were shot away.

As third-in-command of a fleet that had won a great victory, Vice Admiral Hood came in for a number of rewards. Not only did he receive a gold medal and chain, but on 12 August, he was created Baron Bridport of Cricket St. Thomas in Somerset. Because he was a member of the Irish peerage, he was not required to give up his seat in the House of Commons.

Due to Lord Howe's deteriorating health, more and more of the responsibility for running the fleet fell to Lord Bridport. Although the commander in chief continued to cruise during the late summer and autumn of 1794, most of the day-to-day business fell to the officer who had risen to second-in-command following the retirement of Lord Graves. When the fleet returned to Spithead at the end of November, Admiral Howe posted almost immediately for Bath, seeking treatment for his ills. He left Bridport to deal with a situation that erupted a few days later.

The *Culloden* (74) was in poor condition, and many of her company thought that if they went to sea in her again, she would founder. The seamen believed that their requests to be given a new ship would be ignored by the Admiralty, so, without warning, they mutinied in the late evening of 3 December. While the captain was ashore, the mutineers suddenly burst up onto the deck, unshipped the ladders and barricaded themselves below. Capt. Thomas Troubridge informed Admiral Bridport of what had occurred; then, early in the morning, he proceeded aboard the *Culloden*. The mutineers released loyal men they had been holding prisoner and demanded that their ship be dry-docked and repaired or they be transferred aboard a new vessel. The captain had no authority to make arrangements of this nature, and none of his attempts at persuasion could lure the seamen back to their duty.

As the day wore on and affairs aboard the *Culloden* remained at an impasse, Lord Bridport himself decided to come aboard to see what he could do. But the mutineers remained adamant even in the face of such a display of condescension.

For a week the mutineers remained in control of the *Culloden.* Then, on the eleventh, Capt. Thomas Pakenham of the *Invincible* (74) came aboard. The mutineers allowed the visiting captain to come below and talk with them. What Pakenham said is not recorded, but he managed to persuade them to return to their duty. The mutineers understood that the captain had offered them a pardon, so they were shocked when ten of the ringleaders were seized once they emerged onto the deck. These men were tried for their actions, and five of them were eventually hanged. The result of this mutiny was a further erosion of trust between the officers and the men who served before the mast, and was to have resounding repercussions two and a half years later.

In February 1795 Lord Howe sailed out with the Channel fleet for the last time, but although the commander in chief was present, Bridport again held the reins. After that spring's cruise, there were no further pretenses of who was in charge. Howe retired to Bath, maintaining command in name only, leaving the second-in-command to order the fleet as he saw fit. On 12 June, Bridport sailed from Portsmouth to escort an expedition bound for Quiberon Bay. His fleet consisted of fourteen ships of the line.[21]

The French, commanded again by Vice Admiral Villaret-Joyeuse, sailed the same day as the Channel fleet. Their force consisted of twelve ships of the line.[22] The first British force the French encountered was a small one under the command of Vice Admiral Cornwallis. With too few ships to engage the French on anything approaching equal terms, and hampered by slow sailing on the part of some of his squadron, Cornwallis conducted a masterful retreat. He held the French at arm's length and then drove them off by having one of his frigates make false signals to an imaginary fleet in the offing, and by turning about as if he were on the verge of receiving reinforcements. When Cornwallis and his squadron reached the safety of Plymouth on 18 June, Villaret-Joyeuse put about for Brest. Just as he was at the point of reaching his destination, a strong gale blew up out of the north, which forced the fleet to anchor off Belle Ile.

Meanwhile, Bridport escorted the expedition as far as Belle Ile, which he reached on the nineteenth. Soon after he had parted from his charges, the British admiral learned that the French fleet had been sighted in the vicinity, so Bridport placed himself between the threat and the expedition. However, in spite of being within the same general area, the two main forces did not catch sight of each other until the early morning hours of 22 June.

Villaret-Joyeuse had one goal—to get his fleet away from the British force that outgunned him so substantially. He set all sail to the light southeasterly wind and fled. Observing that the French did not intend to fight him, Bridport signaled his fleetest sailers—the *Sans Pareil, Orion, Colossus, Irresistible, Valiant,* and *Russell* to give chase. But soon he signaled for the rest of the fleet to join in.

Now Villaret-Joyeuse was hampered by having to protect his slowest ships. For the whole of a long midsummer's day, the British fleet drew ominously closer and closer. By 7:00 P.M. Bridport was able to signal his leading vessels to harass the enemy's rear. A few shots were exchanged at long range, and by sunset it appeared that general action could not be far away. But then, at around 10:30 P.M., the wind died, leaving both fleets adrift until a light breeze blew up from the southwest at 3:00 A.M. on the twenty-third.

When the sun rose, it revealed the French fleet lying in a disordered clump approximately three miles distant from the British van. The leading vessels of Bridport's fleet were the *Queen Charlotte* and the *Irresistible.* Not far behind them were the *Orion, Sans Pareil, Colossus,* and *Russell.* These vessels surged down upon the French fleet, ready to offer battle as soon as they were within a respectable range.

Villaret-Joyeuse's slowest ship was the *Alexandre.* At the admiral's command, she was taken in tow by a frigate, but the order came too late. By shortly before 6:00 A.M., she and one or two of her compatriots began firing their stern chasers on the advancing enemy. The frigate cast off, and soon the *Alexandre* was engaged by the *Irresistible* and the *Orion.*

Meanwhile the *Queen Charlotte* surged forward to engage the *Formidable,* with the *Sans Pareil* in support. Between them, the two British vessels pummeled her hull, slashed her rigging, and started a fire on her poop deck. Before long the *Formidable* was compelled to strike to the *Queen Charlotte.* The former flagship, although crippled by damaged rigging, managed to drop back and finish off the already battered *Alexandre.*

By the time the first French prize had been taken, the action had become more general. The *Colossus, Russell, London,* and *Queen* had caught the *Peuple, Mucius, Redoutable, Wattigny,* and *Nestor.* Off to one side, the *Sans*

Pareil and the *Tigre* fought a duel until the *Queen* and *London* came up to support their compatriot. Hopelessly outgunned, the *Tigre* surrendered.

With every sail drawing, the flagship *Royal George* finally entered the action shortly after 8:00 A.M. Bridport called off the *Colossus* and the *Sans Pareil,* and then she herself engaged the vast French flagship, the *Peuple.* The battle of the flagships did not last long. At 8:37 A.M., the *Royal George* turned away, and the admiral directed the rest of his fleet to follow him. Although British reinforcements were on the verge of joining the battle, and several French ships were within range, Bridport sailed away, leaving a disbelieving but grateful Villaret-Joyeuse to gather up his remaining vessels and retreat into the shelter of Ile de Groix. The British admiral later explained that he considered the land too close for the action to be continued.

The British fleet got off lightly in terms of damage and casualties. A total of 31 men were killed and 113 wounded in the eight ships that managed to get into action.[23] The day following the conclusion of the Battle of Ile Groix, Admiral Bridport wrote the following self-congratulatory letter to the Admiralty:

> It is with sincere satisfaction I acquaint you . . . that his Majesty's squadron, under my command, attacked the enemy's fleet . . . on the 23rd instant, close in with Port L'Orient. The ships which struck are the *Alexander, Le Formidable,* and *Le Tigre,* which were with difficulty retained. If the enemy had not been protected and sheltered by the land, I have every reason to believe that a much greater number, if not all the line-of-battle ships would have been taken or destroyed.
>
> When the ships struck, the British squadron was near to some batteries, and in the face of a strong naval port.[24]

Although some modern authors condemn Bridport for not gaining a more complete victory, by the standards of the time he had done well enough. He and two of his subordinate admirals received the thanks of Parliament, and the public received the news with great rejoicing.

The public might have received the news of the victory with joy, but the glories of a royal visit, a golden chain, and a bejeweled sword did not fall to Lord Bridport's lot. For one thing, he was kept at sea until 20 September in support of the Quiberon Bay expedition. By the time he returned to Spithead, the novelty of his victory had worn off. Also, by that time, other reports of the battle had filtered back to Britain. No other officers' accounts make mention of the close proximity of land or enemy batteries, so by the time Bridport came ashore, his victory may have seemed less glorious than at first.

Following his return to England at the end of September, Bridport remained in Portsmouth for the rest of the year. His cruisers off Brest informed him that the French were staying close to home, so he saw no reason to hazard his fleet to the dangers of the Channel if there was little prospect of meeting the enemy.

The *Royal George* spent most of 1796 at anchor in Spithead while squadrons under lesser admirals kept watch over the French and Bridport directed operations from Portsmouth or from London. On 15 March, he was appointed Vice Admiral of England. On 31 May, Bridport was made a peer of Great Britain, which removed him from the House of Commons to the House of Lords. Otherwise, the year was uneventful for the admiral until its waning days.

Through much of the year the French fleet had been preparing for an invasion. The British could clearly discern the progress made on the ships and the increase in the number of troops in the area, but they could not be certain of the fleet's destination. Some thought the invasion was intended for Ireland, others Gibraltar and still others suspected that it was bound for Portugal. To be ready for any eventuality, the squadrons of the Channel fleet cruised all the likely routes.

The French originally intended their invasion force to sail in October, but some of the expected reinforcements were delayed by the presence of the British squadrons, and others never reached Brest at all. Finally, not wishing to allow the season to grow any more advanced, the French set sail on 16 December. The fleet, which was destined for Ireland, consisted of seventeen ships of the line, twenty smaller men-of-war, and seven transports loaded with approximately eighteen thousand soldiers under the command of General Lazare Hoche. Vice Adm. Morard de Galles commanded the naval force, flying his flag in the frigate *Fraternité* (40).

Although the invasion force was of impressive size, it soon encountered difficulties. In trying to slip past the watching British squadron during the night, some of the ships became separated from the main body, and the *Séduisant* (74) ran aground.

On 17 December a portion of the French fleet under the command of Rear Admiral Bouvet emerged into the open waters of the Channel. As Bouvet could see nothing of the rest of the fleet, he decided to proceed to Ireland, where he hoped to rendezvous with his compatriots. En route to the southwest coast of Ireland, the French admiral gathered up most of the scattered force, but de Galles's flagship was not among them. As senior officer in the area, Bouvet retained command. He made the signal to anchor in Bantry Bay on 21 December.

Meanwhile, Admiral Bridport did not learn that the French were out until the day they reached Bantry Bay. He immediately gave orders for the fleet to make ready to sail, and on the twenty-fifth, they weighed anchor. But in trying to emerge from Spithead, the *Prince* (98) collided with the *Sans Pareil,* severely damaging the smaller of the two men-of-war. Another collision occurred, between the *Formidable* and the *Ville de Paris* (110), while the *Atlas* (90), in trying to avoid running afoul of a sister ship, ran aground. In the face of this debacle, Bridport had no choice but to postpone his emergence from the harbor until he had repaired the worst of the damage. He did not again attempt to put to sea until 3 January 1797.

Back in Bantry Bay, some of the French succeeded in anchoring, but a stiff wind swept many others back out to sea. On 24 December they made an attempt to land troops, but a gale soon put a stop to the proceedings, and shortly afterward the weather became so foul that all their vessels were eventually forced out of the bay. By the time the weather cleared, on 29 December, the French had been scattered far and wide, and provisions were running short. Bouvet decided to turn back to Brest, which he reached on New Year's Day. Most of the rest of the fleet eventually arrived safely in home waters, although the *Droits de l'Homme* (74) was lost off the coast of Ireland under circumstances that will be related in chapter 11.

Bridport reached the British cruising grounds off Brest in time to chase a couple of late arrivals, but he failed to capture any of the force. He continued cruising in hopes of taking some prize he could bear home in triumph, but finally he gave up and returned to Spithead on 4 February.

On 13 April, the fiction that Lord Howe commanded the Channel fleet finally ended. For the first time in his career, Bridport was officially commander in chief of his own station. This was a goal that the admiral had hoped to achieve for a long time, but it could not have come at a worse moment.

During the early months of 1797, the admiral had observed a degree of restlessness among his seamen. The sailors had been constructing a list of grievances for several years, and their pay was at the top of the list. The army had recently received a pay raise, but navy wages had remained the same. After their abortive cruise in search of the French fleet, several seamen of the Channel fleet had sent petitions to the man who was still officially their commander in chief. The old admiral had glanced at the letters, dismissed them as the work of one or two disgruntled individuals, and forwarded them to the Admiralty without informing his successor.

As stated above, Howe and Bridport were an odd pair to have been harnessed together for so long. The senior admiral had long held his junior in contempt because of his behavior at the Keppel court-martial. This situation was made worse because Bridport did not accord Howe the kind of deference the older man felt he deserved. The acrimony between the two senior officers of the Channel fleet resulted in a disastrous lack of communication. Bridport was left to his own devices to try to discover the source of the restlessness he had observed among his seamen. On the day that he officially became commander in chief of the fleet, he wrote the following letter to the First Lord of the Admiralty:

> I am sorry to inform your Lordship that a circumstance reached me yesterday which gave me much concern. It has been stated to me that representations have been made by the crews of the Channel fleet to Lord Howe and the Admiralty for an increase in pay. If this should be the case it would be very desirable for me to know what steps have been taken in consequence thereof. I am particularly anxious to receive such instructions as your Lordship and the Board may think expedient with as little delay as possible as I yesterday heard that some disagreeable combinations were forming among the ships at Spithead on this subject.[25]

Regardless of the admiral's warning, the Admiralty ordered him to sail on 15 April. But as Bridport suspected, when the command was issued for the seamen to weigh anchor, they refused. Some of the admiral's subordinates took offense at this mutinous act, and attempted to force the men to their duty at the point of the marines' bayonets. But Bridport was determined not to allow bloodshed. He permitted the mutineers to proceed with their meetings. Then he sent an officer to the Admiralty to report on developments.

At first Lord Spencer refused to take the mutiny seriously, but after consideration, he decided to go down to Portsmouth himself to settle the matter. The First Lord and the officials who accompanied him arrived in town on the eighteenth and met with Bridport to discuss their options.

By the time Spencer arrived at Portsmouth, the seamen had drawn up a document listing their demands. The primary demands, in summary, were: (1) wages should be increased, (2) provisions should be measured in pounds of sixteen ounces, not fourteen, as had been the custom since time immemorial, (3) the sick should receive better treatment, and (4) seamen should be granted more shore leave. The First Lord was not interested in the new petition, but he opened negotiations by informing Bridport that he would increase the seamen's wages. The admiral, acting as Spencer's agent, passed the offer to the men who demanded a higher raise than the one initially offered and wanted other grievances addressed.

After debating the matter with many of the senior officers of the fleet, the First Lord finally countered by granting the full pay request but still refused to address any other issues. The seamen appeared willing to accept the offer, but they were suspicious. They all knew the tale that the *Culloden's* mutineers had been offered a pardon, and then some of the ringleaders had been hanged. They wanted to make certain that the same thing did not happen to them. They informed Spencer that they would not return to their duty until the king granted them a pardon.

The First Lord agreed with this demand and sought out the king at Windsor Castle. He soon obtained the pardon, which he sent to Bridport with instructions that it be read aboard every ship in the fleet. When the admiral read his copy of the pardon aboard his flagship, he was greeted with cheers of approval. It appeared that the mutiny was over.

On 23 April Lord Bridport commanded his fleet to put to sea. A few ships' companies still felt they had special grievances that needed to be addressed, but the rest weighed anchor and followed the admiral as far as St. Helens. There they encountered winds too strong to allow them to proceed further, so they anchored to wait for the gale to die down.

In order to prevent further mutinous incidents, Lord Spencer sent instructions to all the commanding officers of the fleets from the Channel to the East Indies to treat their men better and to use force against the first signs of mutiny.

While the gales raged outside St. Helens, the seamen waited to hear that the bill for their requested pay raise had been passed by Parliament. The houses of government had every intention of fulfilling the First Lord's promise, but they felt the need to discuss it at length first. As a fortnight passed and nothing happened, the seamen grew impatient. A rumor circulated that the bill had been "hove out."[26] By 3 May the men of the Channel fleet were growing decidedly restless. The crew of the *Queen Charlotte* sent a message to Bridport stating that they would not sail until they knew that the bill had been passed.

On 7 May the wind finally died enough for the fleet to emerge, but the admiral did not issue the order to get under way. He was certain it would not be obeyed. Bridport penned the following note to the Admiralty: "I have endeavored to prevent this mischief by every argument in my power, but without effect; and I cannot command this fleet, as all authority is taken from me. My mind is too deeply wounded by all these proceedings, and I am so unwell that I can scarcely hold my pen to write these sentiments of distress."[27]

Meanwhile, matters had taken a more sinister turn aboard the *London,* flagship of Vice Adm. Sir John Colpoys. Confined below to prevent them from joining the growing mutiny, some of the ship's company got drunk and demanded to be allowed to come out on deck. When the seamen forced their way through the hatchways, a handful of officers and marines fired on them, mortally wounding one of the mutineers. The seamen immediately seized the lieutenant who had fired the fatal shot and prepared to hang him. Colpoys pleaded for the young officer's life, stating that he had only been obeying the commands of the Admiralty. To prove it, he produced the order sent out after the end of the first mutiny. This saved the officer's life but further convinced the seamen that the Admiralty was determined to betray them. The renewed mutiny took on a more serious complexion. Not trusting the officers now that they knew they had been commanded to put down the first sign of mutiny by any means, many crews sent their officers ashore. Admiral Bridport was one of the few officers allowed to remain in his ship.

Galvanized into action by the new mutiny, Parliament met and swiftly passed the bill. The king signed a new pardon covering the latest acts, and on 9 May, Lord Howe was sent to Portsmouth to meet with the mutineers.

Although Bridport must have been disgusted at having his chief rival called down to supersede him again, he did everything in his power to make sure Howe's mission was successful. The former commander in chief commended his successor for his helpfulness in Bridport's "endeavors to promote the benefit of his Majesty's service upon this most intensely interesting occasion."[28] Both admirals working together in spite of their differences brought the "intensely interesting occasion" to a successful conclusion.

Thanks to Howe's removal of many officers from their ships, Bridport's fleet was shorthanded. It finally sailed on 17 May, but it did not remain out for long. Several ships were damaged by accidents, and so the fleet put into Plymouth to make repairs. By the beginning of June, the fleet returned to sea, but not all was well within many of the hulls that made up Bridport's command. Having grown accustomed to joining forces to compel their officers to redress grievances, the seamen were often unruly. Many ships' companies demanded a return to Portsmouth because of a shortage of provisions or a lack of sufficient men to adequately crew the vessel.

Toward the end of 1797, the flame of mutiny finally burned down to smoldering embers in home waters, and the situation returned to near normal in the Channel fleet. Bridport continued to cruise sporadically off the French coast but spent much of his time ashore. In early 1798 he detached a number of squadrons to watch Brest or Ireland, but the French were not yet ready to make their move.

On 21 April the *Mars* (74), commanded by the admiral's namesake and cousin, encountered the *Hercule* (74) off Brest. The British vessel gave chase and brought the Frenchman to bay. In the early stages of the battle, the anchors of the two ships of the line became hooked together, and the two vessels engaged with the muzzles of their guns almost touching. For an hour the pair pounded each other mercilessly, until the *Hercule* surrendered. The French captain had been mortally wounded, but in accordance with tradition, sent his sword as a token of surrender. But Captain Hood too lay dying. He touched the sword of his conquered foe and soon afterward expired.

During the spring and summer of 1798, the French made renewed attempts at Ireland, where many of the local people were already in a state of rebellion. In August, they landed a force of approximately 1,150 troops on the west coast without encountering resistance of any kind from the Royal Navy. The first success encouraged the French to try again with a much larger force, and on 16 September a squadron of nine vessels under the escort of the seventy-four-gun *Hoche* sailed from Brest. But unlike the previous expedition, this one encountered difficulties. Some of the French were taken, and others were driven back to Brest. None succeeded in landing troops in Ireland.

The winter months of 1798–99 saw little action on either side of the Channel. But on 17 April, Lord Bridport came out in the *Royal George* to join the force blockading the French at Brest. A few days later a large fleet of twenty-five ships of the line, five frigates, and a number of smaller vessels left the French base. Guided by false information, the British admiral assumed that this force was bound for Ireland. He immediately sent word out to all the commanders in the area that he would need assistance, and losing touch with the enemy, he made for Cork where he cruised in daily expectation of regaining contact with the French. But, unfortunately for Bridport, the French were bound for the Mediterranean. It was not until more than a month later that the admiral began to suspect that he had made a mistake, and by then it was too late. Although he eventually sent sixteen ships of the line to reinforce Admiral St. Vincent in the Mediterranean, the French fleet had long since disappeared. They were obviously intent on mischief, but due to disagreements in enemy government circles, little came of the excursion.

In March 1800 Lord Bridport sailed in the *Royal George* off the coast of France. But his health had suffered from age and nearly sixty years of service, and he soon returned ashore. On 24 April he hauled down his flag for the last time.

Having given up command, the old admiral enjoyed a peaceful retirement. For his long years of service he was made a viscount on 10 June 1801. No further events disturbed the quiet of old age, and on 2 May 1814, he died.

As Lord Bridport had no children by either of his wives, his British title became extinct at his death. However, the Irish title was passed on to his great-nephew, another Samuel Hood. This Hood made a different kind of naval connection from the rest of his family. In 1810 he married Charlotte Nelson, a niece of Lord Nelson and the heiress to the Sicilian dukedom of Bronte bestowed upon the Hero of the Nile. Duke of Bronte continues among the titles of the Hood-Bridport family to the present.

Chapter 3

SAMUEL HOOD

1724–1816

M ANY CONTEMPORARIES who knew both of the Hood
brothers—Samuel and Alexander—commented on how little alike
they were. In appearance they had some similarities. Each had a long, rather
hooked nose, like the beak of a bird of prey. Each had a thin face, with a small
mouth and a haughty expression. The main differences lay in their personalities.

According to the *Dictionary of National Biography,* they "differed . . . in
their general habits, for Lord Bridport [Alexander Hood] was rather penuri-
ous and rich, and Lord Hood quite the reverse and very poor."[1] The differ-
ence between them could not have been more pronounced than in how they
selected their wives. The younger brother, Lord Bridport, waited until he
was in his thirties and established in his profession before he married, and
then to an heiress, whereas his elder brother married young, to a lady with
little money but a few good connections. In reading about Alexander, one
gets the impression that he married for money, while Samuel showed such
great fondness for his wife on many occasions that he could almost be
termed uxorious.

In their professional and political lives the two brothers differed as well.
Where Alexander, though personally brave, tended to be cautious in
action, Samuel was more impetuous. But it was Samuel rather than Alexander who nearly retired from the service to take up a shore appointment.
Presumably he wanted to be near his family as much as possible. When he
spent time at sea, he was generally a long way from home. His brother never
even crossed the Atlantic, in spite of an active career spanning more than
fifty years.

Although both brothers were Tories and served as members of Parliament, only Alexander became embroiled in the heated debates that coin-
cided with the court-martial of Admiral Keppel. Samuel remained aloof,
which led to the reactivation of his nearly stalled career.

Although Samuel might have remained on the sidelines during political disputes, he could wield an acid-tipped pen against his fellow officers. Unlike his brother, who appears to have kept his less flattering opinions of his superiors to himself, Hood was more than ready to write criticisms of his seniors to anyone he thought would read them. At one point he went so far as to call his commander in chief a common thief.[2]

The modern assessment of both men as admirals varies from author to author. But while some consider Lord Hood to have had a streak of brilliance, none have ever attributed the same level of talent to Bridport.

• • •

Samuel Hood was born the elder son of Rev. Samuel and Mary Hood of Butleigh in Somerset on 12 December 1724. Like his younger brother, he was educated at home until the day that Capt. Thomas Smith had a carriage accident, in 1740. An arrangement was swiftly made for the younger brother who, at thirteen, was more of an age for first entry into sea service. But on 6 May 1741 accommodation was found for the elder brother as a captain's servant aboard the *Romney* (54).

Both Hood brothers served aboard the *Romney* for all of 1742 while she cruised the Mediterranean in the squadron of Rear Admiral Lestock. Thomas Grenville replaced Smith as captain during that time, but the two brothers remained in the ship. It was not until April 1743 that they were split up. From then on their careers followed different paths, and only once again did they briefly serve in the same ship. While Alexander's early career was closely tied to his original patron, Samuel found new captains to follow. When Captain Grenville was transferred aboard the *Garland* fireship, the elder Hood brother went with him. Some months later Samuel made his first acquaintance with an officer whose path would cross his own with important consequences in future years. In November 1743 Midshipman Hood was sent aboard the *Sheerness* (24) under the command of George Brydges Rodney, then a post captain of only one year's standing. Aboard the sixth rate, Hood cruised the Channel, and followed his captain into the forty-four-gun *Ludlow Castle* the next year. The midshipman's first significant taste of battle occurred in 1745 when the *Ludlow Castle* captured a large French privateer out of the port of St. Malo.

In January 1746 Samuel briefly rejoined his brother and Captain Smith aboard the *Exeter* (60), but in May he was made acting lieutenant of the *Winchelsea* (20). By the middle of June his commission was confirmed, and at the age of twenty-one Samuel was entered into the Navy List after only four years at sea.

Although Lieutenant Hood had experienced a relatively uneventful early career, that was about to change. On 19 November, while cruising in the Channel in company with the *Portland* (50), the *Winchelsea* sighted the *Subtile* (26). Both ships gave chase, and soon the smaller British vessel left her consort behind and ran herself alongside the Frenchman. The two vessels traded heavy blows in an action contemporary sources describe as "severe." As the iron, lead, and splinters flew, Hood was wounded in the hand, the only wound he is known to have suffered throughout his long career. After an action in which blood flowed heavily and both combatants suffered to a nearly equal extent, the *Portland* at last came up. Observing that an attempt to escape would be futile and to fight further would only waste more lives, the *Subtile* lowered her flag.

In March 1748 Hood was appointed to the *Greenwich* (50), under the command of Capt. John Montagu. He remained in that ship for only a few months before he was transferred to the *Lion* (60), flagship of Rear Admiral Watson, which soon afterward led a squadron to the coast of North America. However, by the time they reached their cruising station, the war was nearly over. After a short stay on the western side of the Atlantic, the squadron turned around and returned to England. The *Lion* was paid off in November, and Hood found himself on the beach for the first extended period in his career. Samuel's stretch ashore gave him time for romance. On 25 August 1749, he married Susanna Linzee, daughter of the mayor of Portsmouth. The evidence indicates their union was a love match. The son of a country parson with only a lieutenant's half pay to offer was no great catch, and while Miss Linzee was related to the powerful Pitts, she had little fortune to give her husband. Sometimes for an officer to marry so early in his career was fatal to his chances of advancement, but that did not appear to weigh with Lieutenant Hood.

The couple was deeply attached to each other. They were little more than a year apart in age and were able to spend more time in each other's company than was typical for a naval couple. It is likely that Hood's affection for his wife was one of the reasons that he gravitated toward shore appointments for much of his career. When he had to leave her to go to sea, he missed her terribly. "The parting was very severe," he wrote when he was compelled to sail some years after their wedding. "I did not think it would have affected me so much, but I find I love my sweet wench better than I thought."[3] In nearly sixty years of married life, she presented her husband with three sons, but the elder two died young.

The Hoods enjoyed a long honeymoon before Samuel was appointed to a ship, and even then he did not have far to go. In January 1753 he was commissioned aboard the *Invincible* (74), the guardship at Portsmouth.

Appointment to a guardship was the wish of every married officer in peacetime. It meant active service under full pay without most of the discomforts of service at sea. A man could see his family regularly, and the duties were light, consisting mainly of patrolling the harbor and providing seamen to work on other ships. War, with the increased chance of advancement and profit for active officers, made guardship duty unpopular for the ambitious, but in peacetime the berths were much sought after.

In the spring Lieutenant Hood was transferred aboard the *Terrible* (74), another guardship. He continued to enjoy the post for the rest of the year. Then, in May 1754, with war threatening in North America, Samuel was promoted commander of the *Jamaica* (14), which at the time of his appointment was on the other side of the Atlantic. In search of his new command, Hood sailed for Charleston, but when he arrived, he learned that the *Jamaica* had sailed for Philadelphia. It was not until September that the commander was finally united with his command.

In the autumn the *Jamaica* returned to Charleston, where it was her duty to protect British trade in the southern reaches of the colonies. The *Jamaica* sailed out of Charleston until the spring of 1755, and then traveled to Philadelphia to spend the summer before returning again to Charleston.

As was related in chapter 1, shooting at sea began on 6 June 1755, but the little *Jamaica* did not become involved in action until the following year. The *Jamaica* served in a small squadron, which nearly cut off a couple of small French forces near Louisbourg. These both got away, and the exchange of shots between the squadrons was minimal.

During his service off the North American coast, Hood attracted the attention of Commo. Charles Holmes. Recognizing ability in the commander, the commodore posted him to the *Lively* (20) on 21 July. (It is an interesting coincidence that the two Hood brothers, although serving on opposite sides of the Atlantic, were made post within little more than a month of each other.) Samuel served aboard the *Lively* for a short six months before he was made captain of the *Grafton* (70), the commodore's flagship. Late in 1756 Holmes returned to Britain, where his flagship was paid off. The *Grafton* was soon recommissioned, but Hood remained on the beach.

For the first half of 1757, Samuel took a pair of temporary commands. It would sometimes happen that a captain would be out of his command for an extended period of time, to attend Parliament, to recover from wounds, or to take part in a lengthy court-martial. The original captain intended to return to his command, but lest the ship lie idle during his absence, a temporary captain would be appointed.

At the end of December 1756, a court-martial assembled to try Admiral Byng for actions that led to the defeat of the British fleet by the French off Minorca. The details of this court-martial are covered in greater detail in chapter 2. By the beginning of January 1757, it became clear that the trial would go on for quite some time and that Captain Keppel of the *Torbay* (74), one of the judges, would need a temporary replacement. Hood held the position until the court-martial ended on 27 January.

Samuel did not remain on the beach for long after Keppel returned to the *Torbay*. On 1 April he was appointed to the *Tartar* (28), again as a temporary commander, in place of Captain Lockhart, who had been wounded in action. In less than a month Hood was removed from the *Tartar* and placed in temporary command of the *Antelope* (54). Disliking temporary command, and impatient to distinguish himself, Hood wrote to the Admiralty requesting a ship he could call his own. On 3 July he received a reply with the promise of a permanent command, and less than a fortnight later, the First Lord made good on his promise. Samuel was appointed to the *Bideford* (20).

When Hood came aboard his new command, he had some initial difficulties with a few members of his ship's company. He found himself without a purser when the gentleman who held the warrant for the *Bideford* was left behind when the ship sailed. The captain was certain that the purser had missed the ship intentionally. To make matters worse, the purser's steward was a "drunken worthless fellow" who could not be trusted to assume the purser's duties.[4] Then, only days later, Hood was compelled to suspend his sailing master for disrespect to the lieutenant. But after the captain had been in command for a few months, he had no further difficulties with that ship's company.

The *Bideford* was attached to the command of Adm. Sir Edward Hawke in the Channel. As part of a large fleet, she set out on 8 September bound for the Ile d'Aix, off the coast of France. The abortive attempt to capture the island is described in the chapter on Howe, who was only one of several future great commanders who were present at this campaign. The *Bideford* came into Plymouth on 4 October, and the main fleet returned home not long after. But soon they set sail again, hoping to intercept a French squadron from the New World. Before Hawke met the French, a gale scattered his fleet and prevented anything more than a disappointing partial action. The fleet returned to its home port on 15 December.

At the beginning of February 1758, Hood was commissioned aboard the *Vestal* (32), a large frigate for her time, but he did not take command until a month later, because the *Bideford* was on a cruise when the order arrived.

Once again he was attached to the command of Admiral Hawke, who was determined to attack Ile d'Aix another time.

On 11 March, Hawke set sail with a squadron of seven ships of the line and three frigates, among them the *Vestal*. They arrived at their destination on 3 April and lost little time in attacking a convoy of merchantmen and transports bound for North America. After a brief chase, the British drove most of the enemy vessels ashore and then turned away, lest they take the ground themselves. This done, Hawke's fleet directed its attention on the island itself. They landed a force of 150 marines and destroyed the batteries that overlooked the harbor. On 6 April the squadron set sail for home, having completed their mission with relatively little trouble.

After blockading Brest for most of the summer, Captain Hood enjoyed a winter ashore. Then, early in 1759, he was assigned to the command of his old friend Holmes, now a rear admiral, who was to take a squadron to North America. The squadron sailed on 12 February, but on the twenty-first of the month, the *Vestal* sighted the *Bellone* (32), and Hood was given an opportunity to distinguish himself.

Cruising ahead of the rest of the squadron, the *Vestal* sighted a strange sail ahead, and determined that it must be an enemy. Holmes gave the order for Hood to give chase and sent the *Trent* (28) in support. Although the smaller frigate had a reputation as a fine sailor, she was soon left far behind.[5] The *Vestal,* however, ran herself alongside the French ship and proceeded to engage her at close range. For four hours the two frigates were locked in a violent embrace until the *Bellone* was dismasted and had forty members of her company slain. She had defended herself stubbornly, but she could fight no longer. As dusk settled she hauled down her flag. By this time the *Vestal* had only her lower masts standing and was little better off than her prize.

After the battle the *Vestal* was in no state to continue to North America. She returned to Spithead with her prize, which was bought into the Royal Navy under the name of *Repulse*. Prevented from following her original squadron to North America, the *Vestal* was reassigned to the Channel under the command of Hood's former captain, now Rear Admiral Rodney. During the spring the frigate cruised off the coast of Normandy. In the summer, the admiral gathered a squadron to destroy the landing craft and supplies that had been assembled at Le Havre in preparation to invade England.

On 3 July 1759 Rodney's ships appeared off Le Havre and wasted no time in getting his bomb ketches into position to throw shells at virtually anything of military use. To approach closer to the action than the draft of his flagship would allow, the admiral transferred his flag aboard the *Vestal*. The frigate played a strong supporting role, which won her captain the admiral's praise. However, there was no opportunity to take a more active part in the bombardment. The efforts of the bomb ketches were sufficient to destroy most of the invasion fleet within two days of the squadron's arrival. But once the main action had been concluded and the bomb ketches sent home, more opportunities arose for Hood and his fellow frigate captains. They were allowed a few cruises, during which they snapped up a number of prizes.

Although the Channel was proving a lucrative station for Hood and the *Vestal,* the captain requested transfer to the Mediterranean fleet in April 1760, for his health. He might really have needed a change in climate, but many officers used their health as an excuse to leave postings they did not like. It is possible that the blockade or Rodney's personality did not agree with Captain Hood's constitution. Whatever the cause, Hood was permitted to leave the Channel in May and spend the remainder of the Seven Years' War cruising and escorting convoys in the Levant. He returned to England in April 1763, and the *Vestal* was paid off.

As usual, the coming of peace brought unemployment to many officers in the king's service, but Mrs. Hood's relations made certain her husband was not among them. Within five months of the paying off of the *Vestal,* the captain was commissioned into the *Thunderer* (74), the Portsmouth guardship.

However, the rebellious spirit that was born in Britain's North American colonies in the wake of the Seven Years' War intruded upon Captain Hood's domestic bliss. In response to resistance in New England against taxes imposed to help pay the mother country's war debt, a regiment of soldiers was sent in the summer of 1765, to help restore order. Samuel commanded the convoy that brought the soldiers across the Atlantic and then remained as second-in-command of naval forces in the region.

The first two years of Hood's stay in North America were relatively peaceful, although relations between the colonists and the British government continued to deteriorate. By the time Samuel succeeded as commander in chief of the station in April 1767, Boston had emerged as a seat of rebellion.

Hood hoisted his broad pennant aboard the *Romney* (50). Although his official headquarters were at Halifax, he was compelled to spend much of his time in Boston, trying to cow into submission those who objected to King George's taxes. Unlike some of his contemporaries who were sympathetic to the colonists, the commodore believed that all signs of rebellion should be sternly repressed.[6] While he remained commander in chief of the

North American station, Hood did his utmost to quash the rebellion. But when he departed for home late in 1770, he left his successor a far more volatile situation than had fallen to his lot upon his arrival.

When Samuel returned to Britain in January 1771, he was appointed to command of the *Royal William* (84), the current guardship at Portsmouth. Once again he was able to enjoy the company of his family and begin to forget the stresses of high rank in a rebellious foreign station. It is likely that Hood's stressful tenure as commander in chief of the North American station influenced him to think about terminating his seagoing career. He began to look about him for a promising position ashore.

For seven years Samuel commanded a guardship at Portsmouth. In November 1773 he and his ship's company were transferred from the *Royal William* to the *Marlborough* (74). Hood continued to perform the not terribly onerous duties of guardship captain while the rioting he had witnessed in Boston flared into an armed rebellion. Although he had advocated stern repression of the colonial protesters, he showed no desire to sail across the Atlantic and bear a hand. He remained comfortably ensconced aboard the *Marlborough* at Portsmouth until the guardship was severely damaged by an explosion on 5 July 1776. Then he transferred himself with his surviving officers and crew aboard the *Courageux* (74).

In January 1778 it appeared that Hood's shipboard career had come to an end. He was appointed commissioner at Portsmouth and governor of the Naval Academy. These positions generally went to officers who had no further desire to go to sea and were on the point of retiring from active service. In May of that year, King George III paid one of his periodic visits to Portsmouth. The king always took a special interest in his fleet, and visited Portsmouth every few years during the first decades of his reign. On these occasions he bestowed honors upon some of the more prominent men stationed there. On a visit in 1773, he distributed five knighthoods to various active officers and two baronetcies to the controller of the navy and the present commissioner of Portsmouth in compensation for the probability that they would be unable to win such a reward by actions at sea. On his return to the base in 1778, he bestowed a baronetcy upon Captain Hood. It appeared that Sir Samuel had swallowed the anchor.

However, there were other matters afoot that prevented the newly made baronet from remaining for the rest of his life in his shore appointment. The bitterness aroused by the court-martial of Admiral Keppel (see chapter 2) and the disaffection of many senior officers for the Sandwich administration led a majority of Britain's most able commanders to refuse to serve, even as the number of their nation's enemies was expanding. Unlike his younger brother, Sir Samuel had steered clear of the Keppel-Palliser maelstrom and was thus one of the few officers of rank who had no strong political affiliations with either side.

In September 1780 the Admiralty was looking for officers near the top of the Captain's List for promotion to flag rank. Hood fit the bill and was apparently willing to serve at sea if called upon to do so. Accordingly, he was promoted to the rank of rear admiral of the blue and soon appointed to command of a squadron that was to sail for the West Indies to reinforce Hood's old acquaintance Admiral Rodney.

The old admiral should have been pleased that the position of his second-in-command would go to an officer whom he knew well and of whom he appeared to approve. When he received the news, he wrote to the new rear admiral, "It gives me the highest satisfaction that the Admiralty have appointed you to serve with me, as I know no-one whatsoever that I should have wished in preference to my old friend, Sir Samuel Hood."[7] However, behind his back he complained, "They might as well have sent me an old apple woman."[8]

Having hoisted his flag in the *Barfleur* (90), the rear admiral sailed for St. Lucia with a squadron of eight ships of the line in December 1780. Just after Hood had left Britain, his country had declared war on the Dutch Republic. The principal reason for this declaration was that the Dutch had been supplying the rebellious colonials with arms and ammunition since the beginning of the war. The tiny Dutch West Indies possession of St. Eustatius, positioned as it was at the northern end of the Leeward Islands, was an ideal location for carrying on a trade in contraband. Merchants of many nationalities would exchange muskets, gunpowder, and cloth for American tobacco and indigo, thereby keeping up resistance against the British on the mainland and enriching themselves in the process.

Rodney eagerly heard the news of war against the Dutch. He had eyed St. Eustatius for quite some time and was delighted to have the opportunity to act against the island. Not only was St. Eustatius an aid to the rebels, but the island was immensely rich, and the admiral lusted for prize money. The commander in chief of the British fleet in the West Indies was not a wealthy man, but he had expensive tastes and loved to gamble for high stakes. Before the war he had been compelled to flee to France to escape his creditors in England, but while residing in Paris he had racked up still more debts and had been stranded there until his creditors had been paid for him. Soon after his return, he was given employment and had already won a running battle against an outnumbered Spanish fleet by the time Hood joined him. But in spite of his victories, Rodney was still a poor man by his own lights. He needed one grand prize to ensure that he need never worry about debt again. It seemed that St. Eustatius would fill that bill perfectly.

The commander in chief wasted no time after he received the orders to attack St. Eustatius. He sent Hood and his squadron to patrol between Monteserrat and Nevis and keep away any vessels attempting to make for his target. It was likely that the Dutch on the island had not yet heard that war had been declared, and Rodney wanted to catch them by surprise. Then, on 30 January, the commander in chief sailed.

The fleet arrived off the island in the morning of 3 February. Taken completely by surprise, the Dutch had no choice but to surrender. The British took over the main town of Oranjestad, but the crafty Rodney left the Dutch flag flying, the better to lure more unsuspecting prizes into his net.

The value of the plunder obtained from St. Eustatius and the ships anchored in the harbor amounted to more than £3,000,000.[9] The share of this staggering sum that was likely to fall to Rodney would be more than enough to ensure that he could live as high as he pleased for the rest of his days. In order to make sure of every penny that was due him, the admiral elected to remain at St. Eustatius. He stated in his correspondence that he was merely remaining to protect the defenseless island from the enemy, but Hood, who was sent to cruise in the vicinity of Martinique soon after the island's capture, suspected him of other motives. He had wanted to take the whole fleet and fall upon the Dutch colonies of Surinam and Curaçao, but Rodney had denied him the opportunity by remaining close to the honey pots of St. Eustatius.

The second-in-command thought he should have some representation to the board that was taking charge of gathering and disposing of the booty. But when the plunder was collected and tallied, Hood's representatives were shouldered out of the process. As he cruised off Fort Royal, waiting to intercept a French fleet that never seemed to arrive, the rear admiral became increasingly agitated, especially as every communication he received from St. Eustatius told him that vast sums of money were being divided up in his absence. Although Hood professed a profound disregard for money, he could not bear that unfair advantage might be taken of him.

In his lonely station, the rear admiral brooded on the wrongs done to him. He suspected that the rumor of a French fleet en route to the West Indies was an excuse to get him out of the way while Rodney enriched himself at his expense. But on 28 April, he was shown that his suspicions were unfounded. On that date a fleet of twenty ships of the line and a large convoy under the escort of Admiral de Grasse came into view. With the eighteen ships of the line under his command, Hood attempted to prevent the French from reaching Fort Royal.[10] But betrayed by unreliable winds and a strong current, the British were swept so far to leeward that they were unable to come within range of de Grasse. Rodney blamed his second-in-command for allowing the French to get past him, but it appears that there was little Hood could have done to prevent it.

Having increased his force to twenty-four ships of the line, the French admiral emerged from Fort Royal with the apparent intention of giving battle to the outnumbered British. But Hood gave him no opportunity to close. He remained within maximum range, hoping to lure the French into disorder and give him the opportunity to fall upon isolated ships or squadrons, but that was not to be. De Grasse's fleet inflicted a number of casualties by long-range gunfire, but they did not lose their cohesion. So Hood called an end to the action and, with his ships all coppered and comparatively free of weed, soon left the uncoppered French astern. From there the rear admiral proceeded to Antigua, where he and Rodney were reunited on 11 May.

The reassembled fleet of twenty ships of the line put into Barbados on the fifteenth, where Rodney and Hood remained while the third-in-command cruised in search of the enemy. He discovered them off Tobago and immediately proceeded to Barbados to report. Rodney reached Tobago on 4 June, only to learn that the French had taken it two days earlier. De Grasse and his fleet were still in the vicinity and were sighted by the British, but neither commander in chief wished to risk a battle, so the two fleets never closed to within range. They returned to their respective bases to make ready for a campaign season in more northerly waters, away from the hurricanes that frequent the Caribbean in late summer and early autumn.

Rodney had been in ill health for the past several months and began to speak of resigning his command, but he seemed unable to come to a decision. An exasperated Hood wrote:

> It is quite impossible from the unsteadiness of the commander-in-chief to know what he means three days together: one hour he says his complaints are of such a nature that he cannot possibly remain in this country, and is determined to leave the command with me: the next he says he has no thought of going home. The truth is I believe he is guided by his feelings on the moment he is speaking, and that his mind is not at present at all at ease, thinking that if he quits the command he will get to England at a time that many mouths

perhaps may be opened against him on the topic of Tobago, and his not fighting the French fleet off that island after the public declarations he made to everyone of his determined resolution to do it: and again, if he stays much longer, his laurels may be subject to wither.[11]

While Rodney feared that he would be chastised in England for not fighting the French when he had the chance, Hood suspected that he had another for not wishing to leave the Caribbean just yet:

> The money brought from St. Eustatius was put on shore upon the island so soon as we arrived: and the very day before we sailed . . . it was all reembarked and put on board two of the most crazy ships in the fleet . . . that almost a single shot in either under water would have sent them down. But the commanders-in-chief could not bear the thought of leaving the money then and notwithstanding they talk aloud of their disregard of money, they will find it very difficult to convince the world that they have not proved themselves wickedly rapacious.[12]

At last, toward the end of July, Rodney decided to go home to Britain for a few months to have his ills treated and to escape the brutal West Indian climate. He gave up command of the fleet to Hood, who sailed on 1 August to try to intercept de Grasse before he could reach the mainland. Rodney himself sailed the following day, escorting a large convoy. Doubtless much of the plunder he had appropriated for his own use went with him.

It was as well for the senior admiral that he had secured some portion of the proceeds of the looting of St. Eustatius, because most of the rest of the plunder never reached England. A convoy under the command of Commodore Hotham sailed from St. Eustatius on 20 March 1781. At the entrance to the Channel, they were met by a French squadron, which attacked the convoy and captured most of it. Virtually all the valuables plundered from St. Eustatius, collected together and divided amid such contention, fell into enemy hands.

Having convoyed a herd of merchantmen to Jamaica, Hood continued northward up the coast of North America. The original plan had been for Sir Samuel to rendezvous with Rear Adm. Thomas Graves off the mouth of Chesapeake Bay, where de Grasse's fleet was expected to arrive to assist the American and French armies facing Cornwallis. Hood had sent two small men-of-war ahead to inform Graves of the arrangement, but one was lost and the other captured before word could reach the commander in chief at New York. When Sir Samuel reached the Chesapeake on 25 August, he found no sign of Graves or the French. Fearing that his dispatches had gone astray, he led his fleet on to New York, which he reached three days later.

Although it was a matter of urgency, Graves was not prepared to sail at a moment's notice. He required three days to prepare his fleet to join Hood, his junior in rank by the matter of a year. Although he was itching with impatience, Sir Samuel could not hurry his senior officer. They left New York with a force of nineteen ships of the line on the last day of August.

On the morning of 5 September, Graves's fleet sighted the French already comfortably settled in close to shore. As the British approached, de Grasse ordered his ships to get under way and form line of battle. The French, with twenty-four ships of the line, slightly outnumbered the British, so Graves was determined to use caution. Instead of sweeping in and attacking de Grasse while he was still trying to organize his forces, the British commander in chief waited at the mouth of the bay for the enemy to come to him. By that time the French fleet had formed a compact line of battle on the larboard tack. Initially the British had been on the starboard tack, with Hood commanding the van, but in order to match the enemy, Graves ordered his fleet to wear together, transforming the van into the rear. Then he used the northeast wind to bear down on the French. It was already well into the afternoon before the first shots were fired.

As commanded, the van ships of the British fleet ranged themselves against the French van at a good fighting distance and began banging away. But abaft of the first six ships in the British line, matters began to go awry. The *Europe* (64) approached the enemy at a steeper angle than did her sisters ahead. As the signal for line ahead was flying from the flagship, the captains following her did not dare break out of the line to engage the enemy more closely. Thus, the rear two-thirds of Graves's fleet angled farther and farther away from the French until most of Hood's division was nearly out of range for the duration of the action.

Finally, after an hour of ineffective cannonade, Graves ordered the signal for line of battle hauled down to allow his rear to engage. Hood immediately bore down for the enemy, but as the French slid away out of range, he was frustrated in his attempt to bring them to grips. The sun set a short time later, and the battle ended there. The British suffered 90 killed and 246 wounded, and several of their vessels were badly crippled, while the French remained in possession of the anchorage, denying the Royal Navy any chance of supporting Cornwallis.

Following the Battle of the Virginia Capes, the British commanders took council about what to do next. They knew it was critical to regain control of the bay, or the besieged army would be compelled to surrender, but Graves could not see a way to drive off de Grasse without risking the destruction of his own fleet. According to Hood's statements at a later date, he urged his senior to engage the French again, but Graves was in favor of a return to New York, where he hoped to find reinforcements. On 23 September the British fleet returned to their main base in the colonies, where they were joined a day later by Rear Admiral Digby and five ships of the line.

Now with a force of twenty-three ships of the line (the badly crippled *Terrible* had been burned before the retreat from the Chesapeake), Graves again set forth, but it was not until 18 October that he was able to get to sea. Cornwallis surrendered the next day.

Unaware of the change in circumstances, Graves reached the mouth of the Chesapeake on 24 October, and there he learned two disturbing facts: first, that the enemy had received reinforcements, which brought the number of their fleet to thirty-six ships of the line; and second, that Cornwallis had already surrendered. The British fleet put about and returned to New York. Little more than a week later, Hood detached eighteen ships of the line and sailed again for Barbados, which he reached on 5 December.

At around the same time that the British left New York, de Grasse also began his voyage to the south. Returning to the West Indies, the French decided to continue what appeared to be an uninterrupted plan of conquest. The next obvious target was Barbados, but two attempts to make for that island were foiled by bad weather. St. Kitts, just south of St. Eustatius, which had been taken by the British on 26 November 1781, seemed a more reasonable target. The island was to leeward of Martinique, closer to French bases than to sources of British support, and less well defended than Barbados. On 14 January 1782 Rear Admiral Hood learned that de Grasse was off St. Kitts, and weighed anchor immediately. He sighted the French fleet on the twenty-fourth.

Hood had hoped to make the last portion of his passage by night so as to come upon the French at daybreak and surprise them. But in the dark the *Alfred* (74) collided with the frigate *Nymphe* (36), forcing the fleet to heave to while the vessels made repairs. So dawn found the British still well out to sea, and the French sighted them long before they were in position to attack. When the French first sighted their enemy, they had been anchored in the harbor, but hoping to drive the British off with a show of aggression, de Grasse ordered his fleet to sea. He had a force of twenty-four ships of the line and two smaller two-deckers to oppose Hood's fleet of twenty-two.[13] From his previous experience with the British, he expected to engage at long range, cripple a few enemy ships, and drive them off, leaving him master of the field. However, the British commander in chief on this occasion had other plans.

At dawn on the twenty-fifth, Hood made the signal to form line of battle on the starboard tack. Once his line was formed, he hove to, to allow the enemy to approach a little closer, their line at an angle to his own. Then he gave the order to proceed while the French struggled to close. By the time de Grasse was within range, the only portion of the British fleet he could fire on was the rear. Meanwhile, while the enemy was engaged with his rear, Hood had turned his van toward the anchorage the French had abandoned the previous day. Crowding on all sail, the foremost ships in the British fleet sped on until their keels nearly touched the substrate. Then they began to anchor in a close line ahead, each succeeding vessel farther from land than her next forward. For a time the British rear overlapped the firing range of the anchored van, but as more ships swung into the line, the van began to open fire. Thus the few remaining ships that had not yet anchored were supported until they too joined the line.

The final formation stretched from the shore to a sharp dropoff at about one hundred fathoms and then bent to follow the edge of the dropoff, presenting a formidable obstacle to de Grasse. Not only could he not cut through any portion of the tightly ordered line, but also he could not envelop the rear, because to do so would have invited fire from two sides. At 5:30 P.M. the baffled French commander in chief pulled away to consider the situation.

Sir Samuel's captains were impressed with the masterful way in which their maneuver was planned and carried out. The following morning, the French attempted to dislodge the British from their position. At first they sought to cut between the foremost vessel and the shore, but soon found the wind and the depth of water prevented them. So de Grasse's fleet turned away from shore and proceeded to follow the anchored line, firing and receiving fire as they went. They passed and inflicted considerable damage, but did nothing to dislodge Hood and his fleet. A halfhearted attempt by the French center and rear in the afternoon was repulsed with little difficulty, and de Grasse retreated out of range. Although he cruised in the area for some time afterward, he did not again try to assail the British position.

Although Hood's brilliant maneuver had secured the anchorage for the British, he could do little to keep the island of St. Kitts in English hands. The garrison was already besieged, and Sir Samuel had no troops to reinforce them. On 13 February the British garrison was compelled to surrender, and the French ashore threatened to turn their guns on Hood's fleet. With the prospect of being caught between the shots from the shore and those of a larger fleet, Hood appeared to be in a difficult position. Calling his captains to a conference aboard his flagship, he made his plans. That night each ship in the British fleet cut her cable, leaving a light tied to a buoy to deceive the enemy into thinking they were still in place. In silence they slipped away and rounded the northern end of St. Kitts. When the sun rose the next morning, the French found the anchorage empty.

On 25 February, Hood was again reunited with Admiral Rodney, off Antigua. The commander in chief had returned from Britain only the week before and brought with him twelve ships of the line. Now the British had a force powerful enough to challenge de Grasse's fleet at sea.

In March, Rodney sailed, hoping to prevent the French from returning to Martinique, but de Grasse passed to the north and reached Fort Royal without encountering the British. Once he reached his base, the French admiral began making preparations for his most ambitious campaign yet—the conquest of Jamaica. In order to achieve his aim, he first needed to convoy his supply ships to Cape François on the island of Hispaniola, where he would join a Spanish squadron. Then, with overwhelming force, they would fall upon Jamaica, and there would be nothing the British could do to stop them. The most dangerous part of the campaign would be the voyage to Cape François. But de Grasse thought that by taking his fleet on the inside track of the Lesser Antilles, he could avoid the enemy, because most of the islands on his route were French or Spanish possessions. If the British tried to force him into a fight under less than ideal conditions, he could put into a friendly port and wait for the enemy to be driven off by the weather.

De Grasse set sail with thirty-five ships of the line on 8 April. Rodney, anchored at St. Lucia, heard the news the same day and immediately put to sea with his own thirty-six ships of the line. Within hours the leading British frigates were within sight of the enemy, and by sundown the lookouts in the main body of the fleet could see the French from their respective mastheads.

The following morning the two fleets were off Dominica; the French, near the shore. Because of the unreliability of the winds close to land, the rear division of the fleet was nearly becalmed and clustered together, while the van was spread out in the passage between Dominica and Guadeloupe. Seeing an opportunity to cut out two of the enemy that had become separated from the rest by the unreliable winds, Hood crowded on all sail, and with eight of his ships, he bore down on the isolated Frenchmen. At first it

appeared that these two vessels would be snapped up while their countrymen stood by helplessly, but just as they were preparing to engage in a desperate defense, the wind filled their sagging sails, and they were able to
speed toward their compatriots.

Hood continued in pursuit for a short time longer, but seeing that he was
drawing dangerously far from his own fleet and too close to the enemy, he
hove to. Suddenly the tables were turned, and he was in danger of being cut
off by a superior force as de Grasse turned the fifteen ships that had successfully weathered Dominica toward Sir Samuel's isolated squadron. Having
the wind gauge, the French bore down and commenced their attack on the
rear of the squadron. Each ship in succession passed along Hood's line of
battle at about half cannon shot and then tacked and sailed back to the rear
to commence the same maneuver over again. Thus each of the fifteen ships
initially with de Grasse had her turn to fire at the enemy, but at no time was
the French admiral's full force brought to bear.

While de Grasse's ships were politely queuing up to make certain that
everyone had his fair chance at firing on the British, the elements of both
fleets that remained under the lee of Dominica struggled to get into battle.
By ones and twos, various vessels were finally able to work their way into the
action. The British line became longer, while the number of French turning
circles also increased. Finally, as the rearmost British vessels were preparing
to enter the battle and even the numbers, de Grasse broke off and sailed
away into the early afternoon.

Thus the French admiral lost his opportunity to win as decisive a victory
in the Caribbean as he had won in the Chesapeake. He later gave as his reason for not fully engaging the British that he did not wish to have his ships
severely damaged when he still had a long voyage to Jamaica ahead of him.
He hoped to cripple the enemy enough to discourage them from following,
without risking his own spars in the process. But in the end, the damage to
the enemy was so minimal that it was repaired at sea, so his cautious
approach gained him nothing.

The night following the Battle of Dominica, the British hove to, to make
repairs. Then they continued in pursuit of the enemy, but they began to fall
behind. By the morning of the eleventh, Hood, now in the rear, could see
only stragglers from the masthead of his flagship. It began to appear that de
Grasse would be able to escape after all.

Then, during the night, the French flagship, *Ville de Paris* (110), collided
with the *Zélé* (74), causing the loss of the smaller vessel's bowsprit and foremast. The *Zélé* was taken in tow by a frigate, which left the fleet, intending

to seek shelter at Guadeloupe to the north, but much of de Grasse's lead had been lost. At daybreak on the twelfth, the British fleet was no more than eight miles distant from the *Ville de Paris*. The *Zélé* was in sight and apparently vulnerable to attack. Rodney signaled Hood to detach four of his vessels to chase the crippled third rate. In order to defend the *Zélé*, de Grasse gathered his fleet and turned back toward the enemy, hoping that the threat of attack would force Rodney to recall his four detached vessels.

At the first stage of the action that eventually developed into the Battle of the Saintes, the wind blew softly from the southeast. The British were on the starboard tack; the French, on the larboard tack. De Grasse again had the wind gauge and intended to take advantage to engage the enemy at a distance of his own choosing. He formed his line of battle close hauled, bearing southward toward the British. Rodney's own line also remained close hauled, headed northward until they encountered the French and began to work up their line from the van to the rear. At first it appeared that this battle would end as inconclusively as the one off Dominica. The French continued to hold their foe at arm's length, hoping to pass out of range before the British gunnery could inflict much damage. But there was a danger in the tactics de Grasse had been compelled by circumstances to adopt.

To avoid too close an approach to Dominica and its fluctuating winds, the French admiral attempted to tack his fleet and resume its northward course. But the near approach of the British made that maneuver impossible, so de Grasse could only pray that the wind would hold long enough for him to fight his way clear. That was not to be.

Just as the French flagship was passing the center of the British line the wind shifted from the east to south-southeast. Finding the wind blowing directly into their faces, the French turned westward to avoid being thrown aback. This carried them closer to the enemy and opened a few sizable holes in their line.

There has been a great deal of controversy about who first realized the implications of what had just happened to the French. At first smoke so obscured the scene that it was not immediately apparent that there were holes in the line. According to one account, Sir Charles Douglas, Rodney's chief of staff, is said to have been the first to realize how vulnerable the French were.[14] Dramatically, Sir Charles approached the admiral, swept off his hat, and said, "Sir George, I give you joy of the victory."

Rodney was not inclined to listen to the officer's histrionics and replied with an irritable, "Pooh!"

Then Douglas explained what he meant—that the gaps in the French line allowed the British to break through. At first Rodney was reluctant to break his own line, but after a few minutes of hesitation, he decided to allow Sir Charles to turn the helm of the *Formidable* toward the enemy and through the gap in the line. As she passed between two enemy vessels, she fired with both her broadsides and did great execution.

True to the creed of maintaining the line of battle regardless of circumstances, the five ships astern of the *Formidable* followed the flagship through the line. But the *Bedford* (74), the sixth in line, unable to see her next ahead through the smoke, reacted to the change in wind direction by turning toward the enemy. She passed through the line independently, taking the rest of the fleet with her. The actions of the *Formidable* and the *Bedford* split six ships, including the *Ville de Paris,* from the French line and divided both fleets into three squadrons. The British now had the wind gauge and were in better order than their foes. As soon as all his fleet had passed clear of the enemy, Rodney signaled his ships to tack back toward the French. With the enemy in disorder and to leeward, the situation seemed perfect for a general chase. Hood certainly thought so, as he wrote later: "I am very confident we should have had twenty sail of the enemy's ships before dark. Instead of that, he pursued only under his topsails . . . the greatest part of the afternoon, though the flying enemy had all the sail set their very shattered state would allow."[15]

Because the British did not press their pursuit of the French, most of de Grasse's fleet escaped. But the French admiral himself became a British prisoner. The three ships that had been severely mauled when Rodney's fleet passed through the enemy line were swiftly snapped up. Then the pursuit focused on the *Ville de Paris,* one of the finest warships afloat. One after another the *Torbay, Canada* (74), *Monarch* (74), *Marlborough,* and *Russell* (74) came up to exchange broadsides with the huge three-decker. But the *Ville de Paris* lumbered on, shaking off the third rates as a bear does dogs. Finally, the *Barfleur* caught up with her. Hood held his fire until he was close alongside. Then he let fly with broadsides so devastating that de Grasse hauled down his flag inside of ten minutes. The commander in chief of the French fleet arrived aboard Sir Samuel's flagship as a prisoner.

With the capture of the *Ville de Paris,* the Battle of the Saintes, named for a small cluster of islands lying between Dominica and Guadeloupe, came to an end. The scattered French fleet fled in disorder, but the British did not trouble them further. Although his second-in-command was eager to continue the chase, Rodney signaled his fleet to heave to. He was afraid to further scatter his own fleet and leave them vulnerable to a counterattack, especially as it was beginning to grow dark.

In spite of Hood's complaints, the Battle of the Saintes was a great victory by the standards of the time. Not since the Battle of Quiberon Bay in 1759 had a contest between two evenly matched fleets resulted in such a clear victory. Rodney's losses were 243 killed and 816 wounded. French losses are unknown, but the *Ville de Paris* alone is known to have suffered more than 300 casualties. In spite of Hood's remonstrance, the commander in chief felt he had reason to be pleased with himself.

Following the battle, the British fleet continued to cruise off Guadeloupe. They spent their time making repairs and looking into various inlets to see if any French stragglers might be hiding there. Then, on 17 April, Hood, who had been anxious to continue toward Jamaica, was sent to the Mona Passage between Puerto Rico and Santo Domingo with ten ships of the line. Two days later he was fortunate enough to sight a small French squadron, to which he immediately gave chase. After a short action, he captured two small two-deckers, a frigate, and a sloop. In his report to the commander in chief, he took the opportunity to make another pointed remark concerning that officer's lack of pursuit: "It is a very mortifying circumstance to relate to you, Sir, that the French fleet which you put to flight on the 12th went through the Mona Channel on the 18th, only the day before I was in it."[16]

While Hood had been visiting the Mona Passage, Rodney had continued on directly toward Jamaica. He encountered no sign of the enemy, and his second-in-command rejoined him off Cape Tiberon on the twenty-fifth. Together they continued on to Jamaica.

The British prepared a vast fleet to meet whatever the French and Spanish chose to send against them. However, even though most of de Grasse's convoy and soldiers reached the rendezvous safely, the allies balked at making the assault upon Jamaica. In the end, nothing came of their plans.

Meanwhile, back in England, the bad news of Cornwallis's surrender had brought about a change of ministry. Sandwich was ousted from the Admiralty in favor of Admiral Keppel. Due to the political bitterness that was the legacy of the Sandwich administration, certain appointees of the old administration were replaced by supporters of the Keppel faction. One of the first to be removed from his post was Rodney, from whom nothing positive had been heard for quite some time. The undistinguished but loyal Admiral Hugh Pigot was commissioned to be the new commander in chief of the West Indies. He gathered up a convoy and an escort and set sail for his post. A mere day or two after Pigot sailed, word of the Battle of the Saintes reached England, and the new government feared it would be subject to negative publicity if it became known that they were replacing an admiral who had won such a splendid victory. A swift frigate was sent immediately with orders recalling Pigot, but it was too late. The frigate never located the convoy, and the new commander in chief arrived at Jamaica on 10 July.

Although Rodney was leaving, Hood was ordered to remain as second-in-command. The old admiral departed on 22 July, and never again served at sea. With the hurricane season coming on, Pigot and Hood left Jamaica for New York soon after Rodney's departure. Although the war was not officially over, there was little fighting taking place in North America. Neither side wished to waste further lives and resources while the diplomats negotiated a treaty.

Rodney had been granted a peerage soon after the news of the Battle of the Saintes reached England, but Hood had to wait a little longer for his reward. On 12 September 1782, he was created Baron Hood of Catherington, Hampshire, in the Irish peerage.

The main British fleet returned to the West Indies in October, and soon the rear admiral was sent to patrol off Cape François with thirteen ships of the line. His purpose there was to make certain that the allies had no further designs upon Jamaica. But by that time the project was truly dead. Lord Hood enjoyed an uneventful cruise, and the following year both he and Admiral Pigot returned to England.

In 1784 Hood, who felt once again that his years at sea were over, decided to stand for a seat in the House of Commons. As a Tory he opposed the most notorious Whig of them all, Charles James Fox, for the seat for Westminster. Eighteenth-century political campaigning was an expensive business. While, obviously, there were no television spots to buy, the voters had to be treated to free food and drink, and the more influential often had to be bought outright. The admiral, never a wealthy man, had friends to help him financially with his campaign.

The election of 1784 was a famous one and strongly contested. The king sent some of his own household to the Westminster polls on election day to cast their votes for Hood, while the beautiful Duchess of Devonshire promised kisses in exchange for a vote for Fox. In the end Hood was elected, but Fox was also returned. The admiral's parliamentary career was not a tremendously distinguished one. He appears to have continued his practice of staying out of political embroilment. He was a professional, and never much of a politician.

On 1 May 1786 Hood returned to his primary career. He hoisted his flag aboard the *Barfleur* as commander in chief of the fleet at Spithead, a position he held for the next two years. In 1788 Samuel, now a vice admiral, left

Parliament and became one of the lords of the Admiralty. He later returned to Parliament in 1790, while keeping his role at the Admiralty. Then, in response to the threat of war against Russia the following year, Hood was given command of a squadron of thirty-six ships of the line in home waters. He hoisted his flag aboard the last and greatest of his flagships—the *Victory* (100).

Although the possibility of war with Russia came to nothing, the situation in France prompted the British to maintain a larger-than-usual peacetime force in the Channel. In July and August 1792, Hood paraded his fleet along the coast to the French as an indication of what they might be facing if they dared to go to war against England. That was the last major fleet exercise before the wars began.

Upon the declaration of war against France in February 1793, Hood was appointed commander in chief of the Mediterranean fleet. To get as large a fleet as possible into the area quickly, a few smaller squadrons preceded the main one. The vice admiral himself sailed with the most powerful fleet on 22 May.

Before the commander in chief's arrival, the British had been blockading the main French Mediterranean base at Toulon. However, not only did the French fleet show little signs of being ready to put to sea, there were also indications that the city might be willing to declare for the king if they had some force to back them. Shortly after his arrival at Gibraltar, Hood gathered most of his forces and sailed for Toulon with twenty-one ships of the line.[17]

Shortly after the fleet arrived in mid-August, two envoys from Marseilles came aboard the flagship to discuss the surrender of Toulon to the British. They pledged their honor that the citizens of Toulon were heartily sick of the revolution and would soon send delegates on their own account. The delegates never materialized, but Hood decided that the proposition merited further investigation. He sent a couple of junior officers ashore to meet with the royalists of Toulon and attempt to obtain a document surrendering the port. They eventually brought off Captain Baron d'Imbert, the royalist special commissioner, who met with the admiral and promised the assistance of the royalists in securing Toulon for the British.

However, there was no unity of feeling in the town. Republican forces manned the forts on the west side of the harbor, determined to resist any efforts to dislodge them. In response Hood landed approximately 1,500 troops and 200 seamen and marines under the command of Captain Elphinstone on 27 August. These men took possession of the forts on the east side of the harbor, threatening the French ships at anchor there. All further resistance was suspended for the time, and the British fleet sailed into the harbor, followed by a Spanish force of seventeen ships, of the line under the command of Adm. Don Juan de Langara, which had arrived that day.

Having secured Toulon, the commander in chief appointed Rear Admiral Goodall governor of the town. Meanwhile, the republican army was advancing from Marseilles. At the end of August, the two sides skirmished and the French were driven back. But soon the enemy received enough reinforcements to be able to surround Toulon from the land.

On 18 September, the republicans had approached close enough to establish a masked battery at the head of the northwest arm of the inner road, from which they could fire on some of the smaller vessels that lay there. The next day another battery began to fire, rendering the inner road untenable for all but the stoutest ships. For the next few weeks, British and Spanish ships of the line dueled with the batteries, but neither side gained a clear advantage. For most of the autumn, battles were waged back and forth through the hills around Toulon. The allies gave a good account of themselves, but they were too few to hold so vast an acreage for long without reinforcements. In the meantime, the number of their enemies grew continually.

There was conflict within the lines as well as without. The British and Spanish officers and troops had difficulty understanding each other, which led to frequent disputes. Even at the top there was little harmony. At the beginning of November, Admiral Langara informed Lord Hood that the king of Spain had promoted him to the rank of lieutenant-general, and that as such he now outranked the British commander in chief. His lordship chose to ignore the letter, but Don Juan felt he was not to be slighted. He paraded his fleet, which then outnumbered the British force in the vicinity, in a threatening manner, but his allies were unimpressed. They felt certain that the Spanish would never dare to fight them if they called their bluff. Soon the affair blew over and Hood remained overall commander in chief.

Nonetheless, the allies held on against increasing odds. It was not until the middle of December that nearly four times their number broke through their outer defenses and forced the allies to consider abandoning the operation. Lord Hood called a council of war, which decided to begin evacuating Toulon as soon as arrangements could be made to carry off as many of the royalist inhabitants as possible. On 18 December nearly fifteen thousand French civilians were loaded aboard any ship that would float. Although they could take little with them, those who escaped by sea were the lucky ones. Once the republicans entered the town, the guillotine became busy. By the end of the orgy of executions, more than six thousand Toulonese had lost their lives.[18]

While Lord Hood was shepherding his fleet and flock of refugees away from Toulon, the dashing captain Sir William Sidney Smith led a mixed British and Spanish expedition to set fire to the ships which could not be carried off. There was a tremendous show of fires and explosions, but the destruction was not as effective as had been hoped.

From Toulon the British fleet sailed on to Hyères Bay, approximately ten miles to the east. Hood remained there for the balance of the year. Then, in January 1794, he learned that the republicans in Corsica were running short of supplies. Now that he was unencumbered by his Spanish allies, the admiral decided that the time was ripe to separate the island from its French overlords. On the twenty-fourth, he set out with his fleet, bound for San Fiorenzo. Unfortunately, on the following day a storm blew up, which scattered the fleet and damaged the rigging of some of them, including the *Victory*.

Needing to reorganize and make repairs, the fleet put into the island of Elba. Even though his flagship was not yet fit to sail, the commander in chief did not wish to risk losing his opportunity. He sent a squadron of three ships of the line and two frigates under the command of Commo. Robert Linzee straight on to San Fiorenzo to make sure that no convoys slipped through to succor the republicans. With the squadron came a number of transports carrying the soldiers that had held Toulon in the face of the French.

On 7 February this force arrived at Mortella Bay, and the soldiers were landed the same evening. The following day a third rate and a frigate attacked the Mortella Tower from the sea while land-based artillery bombarded the fortress. The tower was strong enough to hold out against two and a half hours of steady cannonading from the sea, which so impressed the English that they later produced copies of the tower on their own coast. The ships were forced to draw off. But the number of men (only thirty-three) defending the fortress was not sufficient to maintain control under the steady bombardment from ashore, which included the use of hot shot.[19] When one of these set fire to the lining of the parapet, the garrison was compelled to surrender. With a firm foothold ashore, the British then drove toward San Fiorenzo, only briefly held back by republican resistance. On 19 February they took the town.

By the time San Fiorenzo fell, Lord Hood had arrived with the main fleet to take overall command of the campaign. Having secured his first base on the island, the admiral next opted to concentrate on Bastia, a more difficult proposition. The army commander, Major-General Dundas, wanted to wait until reinforcements were received from Gibraltar, but the impatient

Hood was eager to move ahead. In spite of the general's refusal to support him until he had more men, the admiral sailed on 23 February and cruised off Bastia until early March, hoping for an opportunity to attack. As none came, he returned to San Fiorenzo.

Still no reinforcements had arrived, and Dundas remained adamant about making no more attacks until they did. Hood waited for nearly a month for an augmentation to his force. But when none arrived, he decided he could do without. He sailed again on 2 April. Two days later he disembarked a force of soldiers and marines under Lieutenant Colonel Villettes and some seamen under Capt. Horatio Nelson. While this force descended upon the town from the north, the fleet anchored in the harbor just out of gunshot and sent in a flotilla of smaller vessels to attack the town's seaward side. The land force constructed a number of batteries and prepared to train them on the town.

Before he gave the command for the batteries to fire, Hood offered the governor of the town the opportunity to surrender, but the offer was refused. A short time later the thunder of cannon sounded from all sides, but with little immediate effect, except for the burning of one of Hood's smaller vessels. Soon the sides had settled down for a siege that was to last for thirty-seven days. Finally, on 21 May, the town surrendered, and soon afterward the island was formally given up to the British.

However, that was not quite the end of all action in Corsica. The town of Calvi remained in the hands of the republicans. Hood, who felt anxious about French activities at Toulon, especially after hearing that a squadron had put to sea, left Nelson in command of naval forces in the area and sailed with the majority of the fleet to the mainland.

Meanwhile off Toulon, Hood, now a full admiral, encountered a fleet of thirteen French ships of the line and gave chase. But the French were too quick for him. They escaped into Gourjean Bay, and foul weather kept the British from following in their wake. Hood then left Vice Admiral Hotham in command, and turned back toward Corsica.

At Calvi, Nelson went ahead with landing seamen and troops and setting up another siege. Soon afterward, on 27 June, Hood arrived to assume command, although there was little he could do to improve the situation. Calvi held out for fifty-one days before surrendering on 10 August.

The capture of Calvi was Lord Hood's last action at sea in the service of his king. In the late summer of 1794, he disputed with First Lord of the Admiralty, Lord Chatham, over the number of ships he felt should be allotted to his command. Finding that the First Lord would not give way to his demands, he sailed for England on 11 October, leaving Hotham—temporarily, he thought—in charge of the station. When Chatham was replaced by Lord Spencer the following year, Hood tried to return to his station but found the new administration little more agreeable to him than was the old. He formally resigned in the spring of 1795.

Although Hood's sea service was over, he still had many years of shore duty ahead of him. In March 1796 he was appointed governor of Greenwich Hospital, the main form of pension available to aged and wounded seamen. He held that post until the end of his life.

On 1 June 1796, in recognition for his long years of service, the admiral was created Viscount Hood of Catherington in the peerage of Great Britain. This was the last great honor bestowed upon him. In 1815 he was nominated to receive the Grand Cross of the Order of the Bath, but was turned down because he was too infirm to undergo the ceremony of investiture.

The admiral's final years were long and peaceful. After his wife died, on 25 May 1806, he wrote, "A better woman, a better mother or better wife never existed."[20] He did not follow her for nearly another ten years. Finally, on 27 January 1816, he passed away quietly at the age of ninety-one. The Hood title was passed down to the admiral's only surviving son, Henry. His descendants still hold it to this day.

The Hood family was one of the most distinguished naval families in British history. Not only were there the four Hoods mentioned at the opening of chapter 2, but also several other members of the family served at sea in later years. The most famous was Rear Admiral the Honorable Horace Hood, who was killed aboard his flagship, the *Invincible,* at Jutland.

Chapter 4

JOHN JERVIS

1735–1823

THE MEDITERRANEAN fleet was in great danger. All of the major fleets in home waters had mutinied, and now it appeared that the fleet blockading the Spanish in Cadiz might be next to succumb to the contagion. But any seamen who were thinking seriously about importing mutiny to this fleet had to reckon with the commander in chief, Admiral the Earl of St. Vincent.

Ever a stern disciplinarian, his lordship introduced new ceremonies and regulations designed to instill greater awe and respect for the officers by the men under their command. At his command the marines were to parade on the poop deck every morning at 8:30, descend to the quarterdeck at 9:00, and present arms as the entire company stood at general quarters with hats off and the band played "God Save the King."[1] Those officers or men who did not attend the ceremonies or show proper respect were stricken with the direst penalties. With ceremonies and a few well-publicized hangings of mutineers, the admiral hoped to keep order.

As the officers stood to attention with their hats off as required, a certain Lieutenant Cumby of the *Thalia* (36) felt inspired to write a lampoon of the new ceremonies, which he passed through the fleet. Unfortunately for the lieutenant, some careless gentleman happened to leave a copy of his masterpiece lying about the quarterdeck one day, when it came into the hands of the commander in chief. Having read the piece, the earl decided to wreak a trifle of comic revenge upon Cumby.

It came to pass that the lieutenant received an invitation to dine with the admiral. He came willingly, unaware of the potential doom that awaited him. He enjoyed a hearty dinner, but when the meal was done, he was handed a copy of his lampoon and asked to read the work aloud before the assembled guests. With a trembling voice he did so, and all the while the admiral's visage became increasingly stern.

But when the young officer neared the end of his recitation, the Earl of St. Vincent allowed himself to laugh. Then he informed the lieutenant that he would be granted an extended period of leave as a reward for his wit. Cumby later took over command of his ship at Trafalgar when his captain was mortally wounded and was promoted to post captain soon after.

Of all the great officers who served in the Royal Navy, few had greater influence or a more marked personality than John Jervis (aka "Old Jervie"), the Earl of St. Vincent. In many respects, he was a Roman of the old republic translated into mid- to late-eighteenth-century Britain. He was supremely competent, fearless, and utterly incorruptible. He was also inflexible in the enforcement of discipline, intolerant of those who could not meet his standards, and prejudiced against anyone whose background was not close to his own. He was singularly constant in love and hate. He was capable of courting the same woman for twenty years, but once an officer had transgressed against one of the often arbitrary rules he set, that unfortunate was cast into damnation and never considered for the admiral's favor again. A study in contrasts, he could be merciless toward mutineers, but he cared enough for the welfare of the seamen in his ships that he went out of his way to make their lot more tolerable. But, in spite of Jervis's efforts, he was always more respected and feared than loved.

During his long lifetime, Jervis left behind a wealth of correspondence and dispatches. His strong wording makes no doubt of his meanings, most of which were uncomplimentary to his contemporaries. Few were exempt from his censure. Even Nelson, whom he fostered at the expense of more senior officers, did not completely escape condemnation. Years after the Battle of Trafalgar, his former commander in chief was heard to say that "Lord Nelson's sole merit was animal courage, his private character most disgraceful in every sense of the word."[2]

The admiral was even less charitable toward lesser talents. Many pithy sayings have come down in his correspondence. For example: "Commissioner Inglefield is an honest man and sufficiently intelligent, but pompous, flowery, indolent and wrapped up in official forms, stay-tape and buckram."[3] He was most critical of his fellow naval officers, few of whom lived up to his standards: "The promotion to the Flag has happily removed a number of officers from the command of ships of the line who at no period of their lives were capable of commanding them."[4]

Jervis resembled a republican Roman not only in personality, but also in profile. The medal that was struck following his victory at the Battle of St. Vincent shows his strong, slightly hooked nose, balding head, and forceful jaw. He resembles a Roman general whose image has been preserved in marble. The impression, however, is destroyed in most portraits. In full lengths he is shown to have been a stocky man of average height, with legs short for the length of his body and a pronounced stoop.

Although Old Jervie seemed excessively stern and unyielding to the casual observer, his sense of humor implies a more complex personality than that of an undiluted martinet. There are numerous stories concerning the practical jokes he enjoyed playing on his subordinates. The one described at the beginning of this chapter was relatively mild compared to putting a number of ship's chaplains together in a small boat during a gale in hopes that their sincere prayers would calm the winds. Many of his jokes were cruel; nevertheless, he occasionally showed that he could laugh at himself, a trait that gives him an unexpected hint of humanity.

. . .

John was born on 9 January 1735, the second son of Swynfen and Elizabeth Jervis. Although he stated in later life that his father "had a very large family with little means" four children did not constitute a very large family by eighteenth-century standards.[5] The "little means" might be more accurate, because Swynfen does not appear to have been a great success in his career as a barrister.

When John was born the family lived in Meaford, Staffordshire, and the boy received his first schooling in Burton-on-Trent. But in 1747 Swynfen was appointed treasurer of Greenwich Hospital, a position he was to hold with little distinction for the next nine years. He moved his family to Greenwich, where John completed his education and first developed an interest in going to sea.

When the younger Jervis boy expressed enthusiasm for a naval career, his father tried to discourage him. He intended that his son should be a barrister. But John was not to be denied. He ran away from school and hid aboard a ship docked at Woolwich for three days. Cold, wet, and hungry, he eventually came home, chastened but undaunted. The family finally decided that if he was that determined to go to sea, he should be accommodated. On 4 January 1749 he was entered aboard the *Gloucester* (50), under Captain Lord Colville.

Although Swynfen had been persuaded to give way to his son's ambition for his future, he was not generous. Young Jervis reported aboard his first ship in clothes too large for him with sleeves that covered his hands and coat skirts touching the ground. He must have presented a ridiculous, yet pathetic, figure. In addition to this embarrassment, his father provided him with £20 and informed him that was all he could expect from that point forward. He never received a penny from Swynfen again.

Soon after Jervis joined the *Gloucester,* she sailed for Jamaica. The War of Jenkins Ear had just recently ended, so except for minor piracy and smuggling, there was little excitement in the West Indies. The climate was brutal and rife with disease, and conditions on shipboard were harsh. Doubtless, Swynfen confidently expected for his son to apply to come home to stay after such an experience, but showing a determination that was to characterize him for life, John remained adamantly attached to the navy.

After two years in the Caribbean, Jervis returned to Britain and was soon taken aboard the *Severn* (50), with Capt. Henry Dennis, as a midshipman. He served in the *Severn* from June 1752 to June 1754, and then followed his captain aboard the *Sphinx* (24) for a cruise in foreign waters. Following his return to England in the autumn of 1754, he served for a month each in the *Seaford* (22) and the *Mary* yacht. These two brief periods of sea service gave him the full six years of service required for a young man to take his lieutenant's examination. He passed, apparently without difficulty, on 22 January 1755.

The following month, Lieutenant Jervis was commissioned to the *Royal George* (100), but moved aboard the *Nottingham* (60) a month later. It was aboard the *Nottingham* that John met the officer who was to become his patron and have a more profound influence over him than any other. The vessel's commander was Capt. Charles Saunders, already a distinguished officer and on the verge of becoming a great name in mid-eighteenth-century naval history. Saunders had been one of the officers who accompanied Lord Anson on his voyage around the world and was now a favorite with the First Lord of the Admiralty. With such a patron, Jervis could be certain of opportunities for advancement. The *Nottingham* was among the ships that followed Admiral Boscawen's flag across the Atlantic prior to the beginning of the Seven Years' War. For the summer they cruised off Louisburg, and in the autumn, returned to Britain.

In March 1756 Jervis boarded the *Devonshire* (74), but only three months later he was commissioned aboard the *Prince* (90), bound for the Mediterranean. When the lieutenant arrived in the Mediterranean, he rejoined his patron, now a rear admiral, second-in-command of the fleet under Admiral Hawke. In October, Saunders hoisted his flag aboard the *Prince,* and when he moved aboard the *Culloden* (74) a month later, he took Jervis with him. As a lieutenant aboard Saunders's flagship, John served for a few months under the command of flag captain Alexander Hood.

Hawke's departure from the Mediterranean in December left Saunders commander in chief of the station. Now Lieutenant Jervis was in an enviable position. He was a favorite with the commander in chief of the station. It did not seem long before he would have the chance at his own command.

Jervis's first command was a temporary one. In January 1757 he was appointed to the *Experiment* (24), whose captain was ill, and sent to cruise off Cape Gata. In the middle of March, he encountered a large Moorish privateer xebec of twenty-six guns and went in on the attack. But the xebec was too large and heavily armed for the *Experiment,* and drove her off with enough damage to prohibit further pursuit. A few days following his encounter with the privateer, Jervis returned aboard the *Culloden* at Gibraltar. In April the fleet weighed anchor to try to intercept a French squadron that had been reported sailing from Toulon. The British managed to sight the French, but they were unable to close within anything more than extreme range. The enemy escaped, and the next month Vice Adm. Henry Osborn arrived to assume command of the station.

At the beginning of June, Saunders transferred his flag aboard the *St. George* (96), and once again, he took Jervis with him. They remained in the Mediterranean through the rest of the year and into the next.

In February 1758, the British fleet captured an enemy vessel that was to figure later as one of Jervis's most famous commands. Off the lieutenant's old cruising ground of Cape Gata, Osborn's fleet sighted a small French force and immediately gave chase. Although the French scattered, the British pursued them separately. Three small British ships of the line trailed the largest of the Frenchmen, a tremendous two-decker of eighty guns. First the *Monmouth* (64) caught up with the *Foudroyant* (80) and fought her for two and a half bloody hours. Then the *Swiftsure* (70) came up and added her broadside to that of her sister, forcing the huge two-decker to surrender. By the end of the battle, the Frenchman had nearly two hundred casualties, compared to just over one hundred British killed and wounded. She was carried triumphantly into Gibraltar, where she was fitted out for the voyage to England.

By May the *Foudroyant* was ready to sail for Britain, and Jervis was chosen to command her for the journey. At around the same time that his lieutenant left the Mediterranean, Saunders returned to the north and joined the Channel fleet for a time. But the Admiralty had plans for Vice Admiral Saunders other than mere cruising in the Channel. The government had determined that the time had come to make a sincere attempt to capture Quebec. Saunders was appointed to command the naval portion of the expedition, while command of the army resided in the person of Maj. Gen. James Wolfe.

On 15 January 1759 Jervis rejoined his patron aboard the flagship *Neptune* (90). A month later they sailed for North America. The fleet designated for the attack on Quebec consisted of twenty-two ships of the line, thirteen frigates, fourteen smaller men-of-war, and a number of transports. The force assembled off Louisbourg through the spring and started up the St. Lawrence River in the beginning of June. By the time they sailed, Jervis had already been promoted to the rank of commander, but he did not yet know his good fortune, and he had to wait a short time longer before obtaining his first permanent command. He remained in the flagship while the fleet made its slow way up the river.

On 26 June the British fleet anchored a few miles below Quebec. Two days later the French tried to dislodge them with fireships, but the British had prepared their defenses, and the attack come to nothing. The British established themselves at their first landing point and then prepared to work closer to their goal. On 4 July, Jervis was appointed acting commander of the *Porcupine* (16), the ship designated to lead the British forces past Quebec to their point of attack. Five days later he took General Wolfe aboard and set sail. During their short time together, the officers struck up a friendship that was close enough for Wolfe to ask Jervis to deliver his effects to his mother in case he should be killed (although it was an aide-de-camp who actually delivered the slain general's possessions into the hands of Mrs. Wolfe).[6]

Following the capture of Quebec, Jervis returned to England as commander of the *Scorpion* (14). In January 1760 he was appointed to command of the *Albany* (14), assigned to escort a convoy to New York.

When he returned to Britain in May, Jervis was attached to the squadron commanded by Rear Admiral Rodney and cruising off Le Havre. Then, on 13 October, he was made post into the *Gosport* (44) and sent to serve in the North Sea.

The years following the devastating defeat of the French fleet by Admiral Hawke at Quiberon Bay (see chapter 1) were quiet for British officers in home waters. But by 1762 the enemy was beginning to recover. In the spring of that year, the *Gosport* set sail with a valuable convoy of East and West Indiamen. To help with the protection of these vessels were the *Superb* (74) and the *Danae* (32). Before the convoy reached the point where it would break up into three separate units bound for different destinations, it encountered a French fleet under the command of Commodore de Ternay. The squadron had escaped the Brest blockade and was on its way to attack Newfoundland, but the valuable convoy made a tempting target.

Although outgunned, the three escort vessels closed ranks and placed themselves between the French and the merchantmen. Observing that if he wanted to take any part of the convoy, he would have to fight hard for it, the French commodore decided to concentrate on his assigned mission. He sailed on, leaving the Indiamen unmolested. He did, however, capture Newfoundland.

In September the *Gosport* joined the force under Commodore Lord Colville, which soon retook Newfoundland from the French. De Ternay and his fleet managed to escape, but the last aggressive act on the part of the enemy ended in failure. The war concluded early in 1763, and the *Gosport* was paid off soon afterward.

Although the navy was considerably reduced during the peace, Jervis had a good prospect of employment. His old patron, Vice Admiral Saunders, stood high in government circles. In September 1766 he became First Lord of the Admiralty, but unfortunately for Jervis, he did not remain in office long. Admiral Hawke succeeded him as First Lord in December. However, Hawke too appears to have gained a good impression of Captain Jervis. In February 1769 he commissioned him aboard the *Alarm* (32), one of the first British ships to have her bottom sheathed in copper.

In May the *Alarm* sailed to the Mediterranean for an extended cruise. While the frigate lay at anchor off Genoa in the autumn, two escaped slaves from a Turkish galley managed to reach the sanctuary of one of the *Alarm*'s boats. One of the slaves had managed to seize the cloth of the British flag that flew from the boat's stern. But dockside guards forcibly removed both men, one of them still firmly grasping a portion of the flag, and returned them to the galley. Zealous for the honor of his country and a strong opponent of slavery, Captain Jervis protested vigorously enough that the slaves were freed.[7]

The *Alarm* was ordered home early in 1771, and she arrived off Portsmouth in May. But in the summer she was ordered to return to the Mediterranean to attend to the king's youngest brother, the Duke of Gloucester. The duke was in ill health and had been ordered by his doctors to spend the winter in the mild climate of Italy. The royal guest spent most of his time aboard the frigate until May 1772, when he departed, and the *Alarm* was ordered home to be paid off.

Free of responsibility, Jervis decided that the next few years would be well spent in travel of a different kind than he had been accustomed to. The autumn following his return to Britain, he set out to visit France. First he traveled to Paris and then to Lyons to learn the language, and once he felt he had mastered it sufficiently, he toured much of the country. He returned to England in November 1773, after more than a year abroad.

The following summer Jervis embarked as a passenger in a merchantman bound for Cronstadt. In company with Capt. Samuel Barrington, he visited many of the major ports of the Baltic and North Seas, making observations of naval matters throughout his travels. He and Barrington enjoyed their excursion so much that the next spring they took a yachting cruise off the west coast of France. That was to be the last period of leisure that Jervis was to enjoy for several years.

In June 1775 he was appointed captain of the *Kent* (74), but within three months he was transferred aboard the *Foudroyant*. For the first two years of his command, the vessel served as guardship at Plymouth, but when the French entered the American War, she was called up for more active service. On 9 July 1778 the *Foudroyant* put to sea as one of the fleet of thirty ships of the line under the command of Admiral Keppel.

The first fortnight of the cruise of the Channel fleet and the preliminaries of the Battle of Ushant are described in chapter 2. In the line of battle, the *Foudroyant* was directly astern of Keppel's flagship, the *Victory,* and thus her captain had a much closer view of the battle than did Bridport, who was in the rear division.

In the action that took place on 27 July 1778, the *Foudroyant* lost five killed and eighteen wounded. Jervis did not ascribe the inconclusiveness of the action to any fault on the part of the British flag officers. As he wrote to the Secretary of the Admiralty a few days later, he doubted such a battle could be decisive because "two fleets of equal force never can produce decisive events, unless they are equally determined to fight it out; or the commander-in-chief of one of them bitches it so as to misconduct his line."[8]

In the dispute that developed between Admiral Keppel and Vice Admiral Palliser following the Battle of Ushant, Jervis was a strong partisan for the former. He wrote to Admiral Keppel: "I have read, with a mixture of contempt and indignation, the publication in the *Morning Post,* signed 'H. Palliser.' It is replete with vanity, art and falsehood, and, though I agree with the rest of your friends, that it would be unbecoming your exalted character and station to write in a newspaper, I am clearly of an opinion the public should be undeceived somehow."[9]

When called to the witness stand at the court-martial, Jervis spoke with evident admiration of the accused. Among those who testified, his language was strongest in praise of the commander in chief: "I cannot boast of a long acquaintance with Admiral Keppel; I never had the honor of serving under him before; but I am happy in this opportunity to declare to this court, and to the whole world, that the whole time the English fleet was in sight of the French fleet, he displayed the greatest naval skill and ability, and the boldest enterprise . . . which . . . will be the subject of my admiration and of my imitation as long as I live."[10]

This is strong praise indeed from an officer so critical of his fellows as Captain Jervis. When Keppel was acquitted, he received a kind letter from the admiral thanking him for his assistance.

Following Keppel's resignation, his place as commander in chief of the Channel fleet was taken by Sir Charles Hardy. As one of the few officers with sufficient seniority willing to serve under Lord Sandwich, he was brought out of semiretirement and installed aboard the *Victory*.

Meanwhile, Spain had joined the war against Britain and succeeded in bringing most of her fleet northward to join with the French in the Channel. With a force of sixty-six ships of the line, the allied fleet cruised off the English coast for much of the month of August. The Channel fleet too was at sea, with a total force of thirty-five ships of the line. Toward the end of the month, the two fleets finally sighted each other. Considering the disparity of forces, Hardy had little choice but to keep his distance. Fortunately the enemy did not appear to be any more eager to meet him than he was to meet them. The two fleets parted without exchanging a shot.

Although the British had chosen not to engage nearly twice their number, the more aggressive captains burned with shame at being compelled to allow the enemy to sail on unmolested. Jervis wrote to his sister after he returned to Spithead at the beginning of September: "I am in the most humbled state of mind I ever experienced, from the retreat we have made before the combined fleets all yesterday and this morning."[11] It was fortunate for the British that the French and Spanish admirals had conflicting orders and could agree on nothing. The opportunity to take control of the Channel was wasted, and never repeated. The allied fleet put into Brest in the middle of September having accomplished nothing.

Toward the end of the year a force was collected under the command of Adm. George Rodney to bring relief to the garrison of Gibraltar, then besieged by Spanish forces. The *Foudroyant* was included in the fleet of twenty-two ships of the line, fourteen frigates and smaller men-of-war, and abundant storeships, victualers, ordinance vessels, troopships, and merchantmen.[12]

On 16 January 1780 Rodney's fleet sighted a Spanish squadron of eleven ships of the line off Cape St. Vincent. Although it was growing dark, the

British commander in chief made the signal to give chase, loosing his hounds of war against the outnumbered Spaniards. A detailed account of the Moonlight Battle, as this action came to be called, is included in the next chapter. In the end, only four Spanish ships escaped. There is no record that the *Foudroyant* played a major role in this action, but it certainly was not due to lack of zeal on the part of her captain.

Toward the end of January, the fleet arrived at Gibraltar, unopposed by the enemy who remained snug at Cadiz. The garrison was resupplied for another year, and the fleet weighed anchor again on 13 February. A few days later Rodney split off to assume command of the West Indies while the remainder of the fleet returned to Spithead.

Hardy having resigned due to ill health, Adm. Francis Geary assumed command of the Channel fleet. He led his force in an uneventful cruise during the summer after the first relief of Gibraltar. Then both sides appeared content to spend the winter in harbor.

The following spring, the government decided that it was again time to resupply Gibraltar. In the middle of March 1781, a fleet of twenty-eight ships of the line, the *Foudroyant* among them, sailed from St. Helens. The voyage was less eventful than the year before, and again the enemy offered little resistance as the British sailed in. Only after the fleet had already reached its destination did the Spanish make a serious attempt to punish them. They sent in a number of oar-propelled gunboats that harassed the transports and men-of-war, but did little to prevent resupply. Within a week the Gibraltar garrison had enough provisions and ammunition to last another two years. Then the fleet departed, returning to Spithead on 22 May.

The spring of 1782 saw a yet another new commander in chief of the Channel fleet. Now that Sandwich had left the Admiralty, Howe had returned to service. One of his subordinate flag officers was Jervis's traveling companion, Samuel Barrington, now a vice admiral. It was while cruising under the vice admiral's command that the captain of the *Foudroyant* won his greatest distinction prior to the start of the French Wars.

On 20 April, Barrington's squadron sighted a French convoy that had just emerged from Brest. The convoy was guarded by two ships of the line—the *Pégase* (74) and the *Protecteur* (74). As the latter vessel had a large sum of money aboard, she parted from the rest at the sight of the enemy and made all sail toward the horizon. The *Pégase* remained behind to give the convoy a chance to escape.

No sooner had the vice admiral made the signal to give chase than the *Foudroyant* was off. She was so much faster than her sisters that she soon left them far astern. Leaving the merchantmen for the rest of the fleet to collect, she made straight for the *Pégase*. The Frenchman turned willingly to present her broadside to the larger two-decker and began a battle that lasted for three hours before the *Pégase* hauled down her flag. Although the French vessel suffered more than eighty casualties, the *Foudroyant* had none killed and only eighteen wounded. Among the wounded was her captain, who suffered a painful splinter wound to his forehead. For this feat, Jervis was made a knight of the Bath, a very rare distinction for a naval officer who had not yet reached flag rank. In honor of his opponent, the crest of his coat-of-arms bore a flying horse.

At the end of the summer of 1782, the *Foudroyant* joined the grand fleet under Lord Howe, which sailed for the final relief of Gibraltar. Although the Spanish and French made an attempt to fight the British on their way back, the action was only partial, and neither side suffered extensive casualties.

On 15 January 1783, after an unusually long period of more than seven years in command of the same ship, Jervis left the *Foudroyant*. Having been appointed commodore of a squadron bound for the West Indies, he hoisted his broad pennant aboard the *Salisbury* (50), but the war ended before his squadron was ready to sail. He hauled down his pennant and came ashore.

Soon after the end of the war, Jervis married his first cousin Martha Parker. This was no case of sudden romance. The captain, persistent as always, had been courting the same fair maiden for more than twenty years. But Martha came from the wealthier, more highly placed side of the family. Her father was Sir Thomas Parker, First Baron of the Exchequer, a far more successful man than the fellow his sister had married. Although John Jervis aspired to the daughter's hand in the early 1760s, he was hinted away as being too far beneath Martha to be considered. But although he had been turned away, he continued to meet his cousin when he could, and she remained unwed. She appears to have been partial to the captain. As an heiress, she could have been married long before she tied the knot at the age of forty-two. But she held fast until the capture of the *Pégase* made her swain a more desirable connection in the eyes of her parents. Jervis's married life does not appear to have been easy. His wife was demanding and jealous, and often not in good health. Nonetheless they were generally very fond of one another.

Jervis was wed and elected to Parliament in 1783. He stood for Launceston as a Whig and was installed on the Opposition Bench. He was never tremendously active during his parliamentary career except when naval matters were brought before the House.

During 1787 a short crisis of diplomacy between Britain and France over affairs in Holland induced the government to make a round of promotions in preparation for the expected war. On 24 September, Sir John Jervis was raised to the rank of rear admiral of the blue. He hoisted his flag aboard the *Carnatic* (74), but as the dispute was resolved without war in October, he returned ashore. Again, when the dispute with Spain over Nootka Sound increased naval readiness, the admiral hoisted his flag aboard the *Prince* (90). Although once again national differences were settled peacefully, the fleet did have the opportunity to perform maneuvers in the Channel.

Following the conclusion of the Nootka Sound armament, Sir John saw no more sea service until the beginning of the French Wars in 1793. He was promoted to the rank of vice admiral in February, virtually on the day that war was declared against republican France. When the vote to go to war was brought before Parliament, he was one of the few who voted against it. But when his country required his services as commander in chief of the Leeward Islands, he showed no reluctance. He hoisted his flag aboard the *Boyne* (98) and sailed for the Caribbean on 26 November. When he arrived at Barbados at the end of January 1794, he immediately gathered a fleet of five ships of the line, eight frigates, four sloops-of-war, a bomb ketch, and two store ships and set sail for Martinique.

Arriving off the island on 5 February, the British fleet disgorged some six thousand troops against a mere six hundred armed Frenchmen. Although the enemy put up a good fight, costing the British more than two hundred casualties, most of the island was overrun in less than a fortnight. Only Fort Royal and Fort Bourbon were still in French hands. While a pair of naval vessels bombarded Fort Royal from the sea, a combined force of soldiers and sailors was landed to storm and carry the works. By the twenty-second, the last French resistance had been crushed, and the island was under British control.

Leaving a small squadron and garrison to protect his new conquest, Jervis departed for St. Lucia on 31 March, and arrived the following day. Within three days, that island had changed hands, leaving the admiral free to concentrate on Guadeloupe. On 10 April he anchored in Gosier Bay, and even though some of his transports had not yet arrived, he launched an attack on the enemy's batteries the following day. Once the majority of the troops arrived on the twelfth, pressure was brought to bear upon the French. Attacked on all sides, General Collot was compelled to surrender on the twentieth. Then Jervis sailed off, leaving Major General Dundas in command.

Sir John was at St. Kitts when word reached him on 5 June that the French had retaken Guadeloupe. Wasting no time, he sailed on the day the news came to him and arrived two days later. This time the British enjoyed less success than on the previous occasion. They made landings at different points and fought several inconclusive skirmishes with the enemy, but neither side could gain a firm advantage, until the French received reinforcements in late September. From that time on, the republicans took the initiative, forcing the British to give ground until they held only Fort Mathilde. There they were besieged for two months, starting at the beginning of October. Vice Admiral Jervis did not remain for the end. He sailed for England in November, leaving Vice Adm. Benjamin Caldwell to oversee the removal of the last British troops from the island on 10 December.

Arriving at Spithead in February 1795, Jervis struck his flag and went home. He was promoted to full admiral in July and soon was considered for another command, although he did not assume it until November. At that time he was appointed to the position where he won his greatest fame—that of commander in chief of the Mediterranean fleet. The admiral himself stated that the "Mediterranean should always have an officer of splendour."[13] Many great flag officers held command of that fleet throughout its history, but few with more splendor than Jervis.

Sir John sailed aboard the *Lively* (32) to join his fleet, and on 3 December he hoisted his flag aboard the *Victory* (100) off the coast of Corsica. Soon after he assumed command of the fleet, the admiral sailed to blockade Toulon. His fleet consisted of eighteen ships of the line as well as many smaller men-of-war. These were more than enough to keep the fifteen French ships of the line bottled up in port. But Jervis had arrived at a time when the political situation in the Mediterranean was taking a turn for the worse for the British. The French army was making strides in Italy, and the Spanish were becoming increasingly dubious allies. To counter both threats, he sent a squadron to blockade Genoa, and another to keep the Spanish squadron at Cartagena under surveillance. In spite of all the British could do, the French continued to dominate the Continent, and the Spanish signed a treaty of alliance with the enemy in August 1796.

Shortly before the treaty between Spain and France had been ratified, a squadron of seven ships of the line under the command of Rear Adm. Robert Man left Cadiz for Corsica. But in September, Admiral Jervis received orders to abandon Corsica, which was becoming too costly to maintain under the British flag. When Man reached the island, his ships were too poorly supplied to remain, and the commander in chief ordered him to Gibraltar for reprovisioning. On his way he encountered a Spanish fleet of nineteen sail of the line, which gave chase to the smaller British force. They succeeded in capturing a brig and a transport, but the rest escaped and reached Gibraltar.

However, once Man provisioned his ships, instead of returning to Corsica, he and his officers decided to return to England. It seems likely that their nearly disastrous encounter with the enemy had scared them badly, but their desertion meant that Jervis was left with only fourteen ships of the line against a Spanish force that eventually rose to a total of twenty-six. It was fortunate for the commander in chief that Adm. Don Juan de Langara made for Toulon instead of Corsica. But Sir John was left with little choice. His fleet was insufficient to face a combined French and Spanish fleet. Rather than risk being trapped between the two, he was compelled to abandon the Mediterranean altogether. Gathering his forces as he went, he reached Gibraltar on 1 December.

Soon after Jervis's fleet reached Gibraltar, five French ships of the line commanded by Rear Admiral Villeneuve sailed past the Rock. Thinking they were bound for the West Indies, the British commander in chief sent warnings to Jamaica and Barbados. Instead they made for Brest. Meanwhile, the Spanish fleet, which had accompanied Villeneuve, put into Cartagena.

Toward the end of December, Jervis sailed from Gibraltar for the coast of Portugal, Britain's last ally in western Europe. From Lisbon he thought that he could keep a better watch upon the Atlantic approaches than from Gibraltar. One of the admiral's first actions from his new base at Lisbon was to sail with eleven ships of the line to protect a valuable convoy bound for Brazil. He escorted the convoy through the latitudes commonly frequented by enemy vessels and turned back to rendezvous with reinforcements off Cape St. Vincent. When Sir John met his reinforcements on 6 February, they brought his fleet strength up to fifteen ships of the line.[14]

It was fortunate for Jervis that his reinforcements arrived when they did. A fleet of twenty-seven ships of the line under the command of Adm. Don Jose de Cordova had already sailed from Cartagena on 1 February and was headed his way.[15] Cordova's orders were to make for Brest, where he was to unite his force with the French and seize control of the Channel. On his way he was to put into Cadiz for provisions.

The Spanish fleet passed Gibraltar on 5 February, and in passing, the admiral sent three of his two-deckers to escort some gunboats and transports into Algeciras. One of these rejoined the fleet swiftly, but the other two did not sail until the tenth, and were sighted the next day by a British frigate, which carried the news to the commander in chief off Cape St. Vincent.

With their head start, the Spanish fleet should have been able to make

Cadiz before the British came close enough to intercept them. But a persistent east wind kept Cordova from gaining safety. He sighted his adversaries toward the end of the day on 13 February but, mistaking them for part of a convoy, showed no concern. At around that time, the wind had finally shifted to allow a closer approach to Cadiz, and the Spaniards were making the most of it. Having no suspicion that the enemy was close at hand, and eager to make the most of the fair wind while it lasted, the Spanish fleet sailed haphazardly. But Jervis had heard from a Portuguese vessel that the foe was no more than five leagues distant, so he knew to be prepared. His fleet was formed up in two divisions on the starboard tack with the wind in the west—well ordered, disciplined, and eager for battle.

At daybreak on 14 February, the leading British two-decker, the *Culloden,* made the signal for five sail of the line to the southwest. Having received confirming reports from his scouts, the admiral made the signal for the fleet to assume close order and to prepare for battle. At this early stage of the action, neither fleet was fully aware of the force of the other. The Spanish had received false intelligence that Jervis had only nine ships of the line with him, and the British could not see the full extent of the enemy fleet because of intervening patches of fog. As the two fleets drew ever nearer, more and more Spanish ships were reported by the scouts.

According to one account of the Battle of St. Vincent, Captain Hallowell, a passenger aboard the *Victory,* listened while the scouting reports were repeated to the commander in chief. As the odds increased against him, Jervis finally retorted: "Enough, sir no more of that; if there are fifty sail I will go through them."

At these words Hallowell, a man "of gigantic frame and vast personal strength," gave the admiral a great thump on the back.[16] He cried out, "That's right, Sir John, that's right! And by God! we'll give them a damned good licking!"[17]

In their effort to make port while the wind allowed, the Spanish ships had divided into two clumps, with six ships of the line in one and the rest in the other. As soon as the number of the enemy could be made out, the smaller Spanish group made all sail to rejoin the rest of the fleet, but Jervis too was closing, making for the gap between. The wind was in the west, with the British fleet on the starboard tack bearing south. The main Spanish fleet was sailing southeast while the smaller squadron bore northwest to meet them. All three forces were aimed at a point somewhere in the middle.

At 11:00 A.M. the British commander in chief made the signal for his fleet to form line of battle. His well-drilled force assembled into a tight-knit line, with the *Victory* near the middle. Meanwhile, the Spanish fleet made no effort to form a line of their own. They were far more interested in closing the fatal gap than in organizing themselves for the fight.

By the time the British reached the gap in the Spanish fleet, the nearer of the two divisions was the larger one, which lay to windward. At approximately 11:30, the foremost of Jervis's fleet opened fire on Cordova's van and began to pass down the leeward side of the fleet, exchanging broadsides with those Spaniards who could fire without the danger of hitting a friend. Meanwhile, three Spanish ships of the line managed to cross in front of the British van and join forces with the smaller force to leeward, which reduced the main fleet to sixteen. For the next half hour, the British fleet and the larger Spanish force sailed past each other on opposite tacks and exchanged broadsides. Then, once the leading British ship, the *Culloden,* passed the rear of the Spanish clump, Jervis made the signal for the fleet to tack in succession.

Captain Troubridge of the *Culloden* had anticipated the command and was ready as soon as he could make out the signal flags through the smoke. His action won the approval of his commander in chief, who considered him the best officer in the British service. The next three ships astern of the *Culloden* tacked in their turn and bore back northwestward to close with the enemy. But the fourth astern was too disabled to tack and had to wear instead, and, as she was threatened by a large enemy, her next forward backed her sails to assist her. As the Spanish did not press the attack, the two vessels pressed on toward the gap, this time to engage the enemy more closely than they had been able to in the first pass. The *Victory* and the ships immediately ahead and astern tacked in turn to follow in the wake of the van. The Spanish vice admiral made an attempt to break the British line ahead of the flagship, but skillfully handled, the *Victory* denied him and gave him a good raking for his pains.

Meanwhile, with most of the British rear now past his van, Cordova thought to take the opportunity to lead his main fleet to swoop down before the wind and rejoin his smaller force to leeward. The intention was to cross the gap astern of Jervis's line. In the third ship from the rear, Commo. Horatio Nelson observed the Spanish action and decided to act immediately, without orders. He commanded his flag captain to wear the *Captain* (74) so as to cut across before the Spanish van. Having completed the maneuver, he made for the massive *Santissima Trinidad* (130), the largest ship in the world, and opened fire on her and those around her. The *Culloden* soon joined the *Captain,* and other vessels of the British van approached near enough to force Cordova to abandon his attempt to close the gap. The Spanish admiral again directed his fleet to the north.

At the extreme rear of the British line was the *Excellent* (74), under the command of Capt. Cuthbert Collingwood. In obedience to a series of signals from the *Victory,* he came about out of turn and made straight for the Spanish van. First he engaged a three-decker and then closed with the crippled *San Ysidro* (74), which he forced to surrender. Meanwhile, two other vessels in the British fleet mobbed the *Excellent*'s first opponent, the *Salvador del Mundo* (112). Ranging themselves on her weather bow and lee quarter, they brought down her main- and foretopmasts, and when the *Victory* joined in, the Spanish three-decker surrendered.

After the flow of the action had forced him away from the *Santissima Trinidad,* Nelson passed on to trade broadsides with the *San Nicolas* (80) and brought down her foremast, but the *Captain* too was seriously damaged. The two vessels remained close alongside, exchanging blows until the *Excellent* approached the *San Nicolas*'s starboard side and fired a powerful broadside into her. Recoiling from the new assault, the *San Nicolas* collided with the *San Josef* (112), a vessel that had already suffered damage from earlier engagements with the British fleet. While the two Spanish ships reeled from their contact, the nearly unmanageable *Captain* ran alongside the *San Nicolas* and hooked her larboard cathead into the Spaniard's starboard quarter gallery. Then came the command to board.

Nelson's flag captain led a party of soldiers onto the deck while the commodore broke through a quarter-gallery window into the Spanish captain's cabin. While Nelson pressed forward, his flag captain pressed aft, and meeting on the poop deck, they lowered the Spanish flag. While the captured officers were surrendering their swords, Nelson and his men came under fire from the *San Josef.* Immediately the commodore led his boarding party aboard the larger vessel, which promptly surrendered.

Although Nelson personally accepted the surrender of two enemy ships of the line and garnered most of the credit, other British vessels played a major role in the Spaniards' decision to capitulate. Not only was the *San Nicolas* threatened by the *Excellent,* but the *Prince George* (98) was engaged with the *San Josef* at the time that Nelson and his men boarded her.

Following the capture of the *San Nicolas* and *San Josef,* the *Excellent* pressed on to join the mob of British vessels around the *Santissima Trinidad.* Many of the officers present at the battle declared that the huge Spanish ship struck her colors, although other sources deny it. But then her compatriots crowded around her and forced the British away.

Shortly before 4:00 P.M., Admiral Jervis observed that fresh ships from the smaller squadron that had become separated at the outset were now closing in to join the battle. Lest these vessels snatch his victory from him, he made the signal for his fleet to form line ahead in close order. This action covered the prizes and the crippled British ships, and discouraged the Spaniards from making a counterattack. Cordova appeared willing to accept his losses and make for Cadiz without further ado. Although the two fleets remained in sight of each other for most of the next day, neither side made any effort to renew the engagement. The British were encumbered by their prizes and by the crippled *Colossus, Culloden,* and *Captain,* and their foes were pleased to be allowed to make their escape without further molestation. When the Spanish fleet was last seen on the afternoon of the fifteenth, it was making its way for Cadiz with the *Santissima Trinidad* in tow.

In spite of the numerical odds against him, Sir John Jervis had won a great victory. At the cost of 73 killed and 227 wounded, he had taken four enemy ships of the line, including two first rates, and caused 603 casualties in the captured ships alone. At the Battle of St. Vincent, Admiral Jervis proved the truth of one of his own maxims—that a decisive victory could be won only if one commander misconducted his line. The British fleet, highly trained and well disciplined, kept a compact line and worked together in mutual support against a foe that was inexperienced, disorganized, and surprised. The Spanish fleet, although impressive in appearance, had defended itself to little better effect than a flock of sheep. They fought bravely, but their lack of sailing skills often made them their own worst enemies.

On the evening of the fifteenth, Jervis led the majority of his fleet to Lagos Bay, but he left behind a squadron of frigates to see if they could pick up the crippled *Santissima Trinidad.* One of the frigates did encounter the first rate at the end of the month and tried to capture her but did not have sufficient firepower to make an impression on the huge vessel and was compelled to part company when more Spaniards came into sight.

Meanwhile, at Lagos, the British commander in chief wrote a public account of the battle. Some of the admiral's contemporaries complained that the letter was too short and gave no credit to officers by name, but it is likely that Jervis remembered all too well the jealousies that arose from the distribution of honors after the Battle of the First of June. In his opinion, all the officers in his fleet had served as best they could, and none deserved to be singled out at the expense of the others. However, Nelson did receive the Order of the Bath.

Although he had won a victory likely to make the enemy think twice about coming out again, Jervis was not one to rest on his laurels. Having repaired his damages at Lagos, he sailed for Lisbon on 23 February, and for Cadiz on 31 March. He spent the spring prowling around outside the port, hoping the Spaniards would come out and give him another chance. When they refused to be lured out that way, he sent in a bomb ketch and supporting ships to bombard the town on 3 July. This action resulted in a small-boat engagement, but no men-of-war were involved. Another similar attack two days later had the effect of forcing the Spanish fleet to warp out of range.

While he continued his blockade of Cadiz, Jervis learned that he had been created Baron Jervis of Meaford and Earl of St. Vincent on 23 June. Of his subordinate admirals at the battle, Vice Adm. Charles Thompson and Rear Adm. William Parker were made baronets, and Vice Adm. William Waldegrave was appointed governor of Newfoundland. Unlike with the First of June, all captains were granted gold medals, although Collingwood of the *Excellent* refused the St. Vincent medal until he also received his medal for the earlier battle.

On 15 July the newly created Admiral the Earl of St. Vincent sent Rear Admiral Nelson with a force of three ships of the line, a fifty-gun ship, three frigates, and a cutter to capture a rich galleon reported to have arrived at Tenerife from Manila. This expedition proved a costly failure that cost Captain Bowen of the *Terpsichore* (32) his life and Nelson his right arm. It could have been much worse, because the landing party was cut off and their ammunition was wet. But thanks to a bluff by Captain Troubridge, who threatened to burn the town if the Spanish attacked, the British were allowed to depart in peace.

While the Mediterranean fleet had been blockading Cadiz, the Channel and North Sea fleets had mutinied, as described in preceding and succeeding chapters. Some of the spirit of Spithead and the Nore infected a few of the vessels under St. Vincent's command, and an undercurrent of mutinous rumbling increased. The commander in chief of this station was more empowered than his colleagues in home waters to enforce his own justice. At the first hint of rebellion, he ordered the offenders court-martialed, and those who were found guilty were hanged at the yardarm by their own shipmates. In a speech following one such hanging, he told his officers that "there is much greater merit [in stopping a dangerous conspiracy] than in taking a ship of war by force from the enemy."[18]

All through the summer, more ships from the Channel fleet were sent to

join their brethren in the Mediterranean. Although the Spithead mutiny
had ended amicably, there were still many seamen whose heads had been
turned by their success, and some of them were inclined to be disrespectful
of authority. St. Vincent's methods soon taught them to mend their ways,
but the admiral was becoming demoralized by the seemingly endless series
of courts-martial and hangings. Finally he complained, "Why do they send
me mutinous ships? Do they think I will be hangman to the fleet?"[19]
Although it was the common seamen who were hanged, St. Vincent placed
the blame for the mutinies elsewhere: "The decay of the vigour and discipline of the navy has originated with the officers, not with the men, and I
am sorry to observe that the license of speech, and constant attempts to lower
the authority of superiors, is almost become universal."[20]

Throughout the rest of 1797, the Mediterranean fleet remained off
Cadiz. Little effort was made to return to its namesake sea, although a few
of the smaller men-of-war were sent on brief cruises just to the east of
Gibraltar. But with the coming of spring in 1798, the British admiralty
began to take a more active interest in the Mediterranean. When Nelson
returned to the fleet after some months spent in England recuperating
from the loss of his arm, he brought with him orders for a squadron to be
detached to visit Toulon and see what the French were doing there. The
selection of Nelson to command the squadron angered rear admirals Sir
William Parker and Sir John Orde, who were senior to Sir Horatio and
thought they should have been chosen. Parker's ruffled feathers were eventually smoothed, but Orde's resentment continued to rankle, and a feud
developed between Orde and St. Vincent that continued even after the rear
admiral was sent home.

In spite of the protests of more senior flag officers, Nelson was sent off in
May with a force of three ships of the line, two frigates, and a sloop. Upon
learning that a French fleet was at sea in the Mediterranean, St. Vincent sent
the rear admiral a reinforcing squadron of ten ships of the line and a fifty-
gun ship later in the month. He could afford to spare them by then, because
Rear Adm. Sir Roger Curtis had arrived from England with a squadron
from the Channel fleet. The reinforcements joined Nelson on 7 June, and
the chase was on after Gen. Napoleon Bonaparte and his fleet. (The details
of the pursuit and the battle that followed will be presented in chapter 10.)

While St. Vincent was waiting anxiously for news from Nelson, he continued his blockade of Cadiz. The Spanish made little effort to emerge, and
by October the commander in chief felt certain enough that they would
remain where they were that he detached another squadron, under the

command of Commo. John Duckworth, against Minorca.

Early in 1799 another squadron from England, commanded by Vice Adm. Lord Keith, reached Cadiz to assume the blockade. This released St. Vincent from that duty, allowing him to proceed to Gibraltar. But in May a large French fleet from Brest entered the Mediterranean, threatening the scattered British forces in those waters. As soon as he learned of the French presence in his vicinity, the commander in chief summoned Keith from Cadiz to join him. With sixteen ships of the line, they proceeded to Minorca to join forces with the four ships of the line under Duckworth. Then, hearing that the French fleet was in Toulon and most of the Spanish fleet had made Cartagena, he placed his own force between the two, hoping to prevent a union. However, neither enemy fleet elected to emerge and face the British at that time.

After almost four years of nearly constant cruising in all weathers and under many sources of stress, the commander in chief's health began to fail. By 2 June he was too ill to continue in command, so he left Keith as commander in chief and headed for home in his flagship. That he took one of the largest ships in the British fleet with him instead of transferring to a frigate for the journey home indicates how ill he was. It was feared that he might not survive if he had to be moved from his flagship. However, he reached England safely and went ashore to recuperate.

When St. Vincent returned home, the resentful Sir John Orde was waiting for him. The rear admiral allowed his former commander in chief three months to recover his health. Then he drove out to the old man's country home and issued a challenge to a duel. The authorities were apprised of the challenge, and on 5 October, Orde was arrested. St. Vincent too would have been arrested before he set out for the appointed dueling ground, but his opponent opposed the suggestion, saying that the arrest would alarm Lady St. Vincent. Instead, the senior admiral was picked up on the dueling ground, and both men were compelled to give bail to keep the peace. To finish the matter, the king himself intervened. He wrote a letter to Lord Spencer commanding the two admirals to end their quarrel.[21]

When Lord Bridport retired as commander in chief of the Channel fleet, in April 1800, St. Vincent was asked if he was in condition to succeed him. Although his health was still far from good, he accepted the appointment, declaring, "The King and Government require it, and the discipline of the Navy demands it. It is of no consequence whether I die afloat or ashore."[22] Shortly afterward he hoisted his flag again aboard the *Ville de Paris* in Spithead harbor.

When the admiral had been offered command of the Channel fleet, he had been informed that Bridport's friend and second-in-command, Sir Alan Gardner, had no desire to command in chief. This information proved false. Gardner felt himself ill used when he learned that he would not succeed to command of the station. He made no secret of his feelings, and St. Vincent was pained by the malicious gossip spread by his second-in-command: "I cannot account for his rudeness to me in any other way than his having been worked up by a party which considers my elevation as an obstacle to the further aggrandizement of them—I mean the Hoods who have shown hostility to me ever since the court martial on Admiral Keppel."[23]

Even after more than twenty years, the Keppel-Palliser affair still had a bearing on the relations between senior officers. Eventually Gardner was removed from the fleet and, as consolation for not being made commander in chief, was granted a peerage. Then the Earl of St. Vincent prepared to remold the Channel fleet according to his personal tastes.

In the years under the command of Howe and Bridport, the officers of the Channel fleet had grown accustomed to an easy-going manner of conducting the blockade. Although a small squadron of lighter vessels kept watch outside Brest on a regular basis, the large ships of the fleet were kept mainly in port to preserve them from the rigors of sea service. This manner of blockade was popular with the officers and their families. Many senior officers lived ashore, and others went on lengthy excursions at some distance from Portsmouth. These gentlemen pitied their colleagues in the Mediterranean fleet under St. Vincent, and one captain is said to have given the following toast at Lord Bridport's table, "May the discipline of the Mediterranean never be introduced into the Channel fleet."[24]

Although he knew that the changes would be unpopular, the new commander in chief instituted a series of sweeping reforms. He issued orders to the effect that no officer should sleep on shore and that those on ordinary day leave were to go no more than three miles from the landing place. Meanwhile, he kept a substantial inshore squadron on constant duty outside Brest, so that even the privilege of going ashore was denied to all and sundry. This style of blockade proved beneficial to the professionalism of the officers and seamen and, although uncomfortable at times, was in no way detrimental to their health. However, it did result in a great deal of wear and tear on the ships in the squadrons. Also, it was not completely effective in keeping the French bottled up. Squadrons could occasionally slip through in foggy or stormy conditions.

In spite of his age and dubious health, the admiral experienced the same discomforts as his officers by keeping station with them. There he ruled through an inflexible code of regulations that could not be broken for any reason, as the following anecdote from an officer's journal shows:

> Joined the said fleet on the night of June 26 off Ushant. On this occasion, an incident occurred very demonstrative of the character of this commander-in-chief, Lord St. Vincent. The ship had joined the fleet at midnight, and Captain Fancourt, with the intention of going on board the admiral's ship, *Ville de Paris,* early in the morning, kept close to the admiral. He had made the night signal and it was answered. Soon afterwards, a gun was fired by the admiral, and a night signal made, which was supposed to be to the fleet in general. Shortly after this a second gun was fired, with a shot, which went very near our ship. This excited some surprise, when bye and bye a third shot was fired close to the bows. Captain Fancourt was now convinced that the admiral made a demonstration to him, and instantly ordered his boat to be hoisted out of the ship still under sail. For Lord St. Vincent never altered his course nor waited for boats to come alongside, which was a most tedious and harassing conduct to people in the boats, as they, poor fellows, were obliged to pull and sail, with all their might, to reach the admiral. So with much difficulty and danger, Captain Fancourt got on board the *Ville de Paris* about 2 or 3 o'clock in the morning. The admiral was up and walking the deck, when the captain entered. He was immediately saluted with rough language, upbraiding him for not having come on board immediately on joining the fleet, and reporting himself and his ship to the commander-in-chief of the Grand Channel fleet. The captain very properly replied that he had kept close to the flagship on purpose to go on board early in the morning, and did not think it proper or necessary to disturb his lordship in the middle of the night. His lordship replied, in a surly tone, a commander-in-chief is never disturbed, and all officers must do their duty, without admission of any impediments. Ordering him to attend particularly to his duty in future at all times, he bowed to and dismissed him. The earl was a polite man.[25]

However unpopular St. Vincent's rule was with his officers, it was doubly so with their families. One lady went so far as to wish him a quick demise with the following toast: "May his next glass of wine choke the wretch."[26]

In February 1801 Pitt's Tory government, which had been in power since before the beginning of the war, fell. In its place, a government under Addington was formed, and Admiral St. Vincent was appointed First Lord of the Admiralty.

While the Addington government began the process of making peace with France, the new First Lord set about reforming naval administration with the same ruthless energy he showed in reforming the lifestyles of the captains of the Channel fleet. Immediately upon assuming office, he set about ferreting out sources of corruption and abuse in dockyards, pay offices, and victualing. He personally visited all royal dockyards and made inquiries into the most minute details of their administration. In so doing he uncovered such abuses as horses carried on paybooks under fictitious names, men still listed as receiving pay after they had been dead for three years, and repair bills to ships that cost ten times the cost of building a new vessel from the keel up.

To cure these ills, he determined to make a complete overhaul of dock-yard administration. However, when they learned of his plans, the ship-wrights threatened to go on strike, and with the war still raging unabated to near the end of 1801, the admiral was temporarily compelled to back off. But as soon as the preliminaries of peace were signed in October, he essayed a program so sweeping that nothing like it had been seen in more than a century. Had St. Vincent remained in office longer, his investigations would have led to a streamlining of ship construction and repair, but when he left the Admiralty, the dockyards reverted to their old practices.

St. Vincent insisted that a royal commission of inquiry be appointed to look into corruption. Although many other members of the cabinet objected to the admiral's plans, he was so persistent that they were forced to concede. The commission was authorized in December 1802 and continued for the next two years, until St. Vincent left office. During that time so much dis-honesty was exposed in high officeholders of earlier administrations that it caused the impeachment of the next First Lord.

A renewal of war between Britain and France was formally declared on 18 May 1803. The greatest concern in the early stage of renewed warfare was an invasion fleet that was being built at Brest. All through the summer and early autumn, various expeditions of small craft were launched against this force, nipping into the harbor, bombarding and burning the assembled craft, and then bustling out again. In spite of all the activity, however, neither side was able to make much of an impression upon the other.

In May 1804 Pitt became prime minister again, and St. Vincent knew that his days at the Admiralty were over. He had had too many hard words with the new prime minister over the reorganization of the navy for him to stay in office. He retired to his home, thinking to live out the rest of his life in peace. But his nation still needed his services.

When Adm. William Cornwallis retired as commander in chief of the Channel fleet in February 1806, St. Vincent was appointed to succeed him. The month following his appointment, he hoisted his flag in the *Hibernia*

(110). Most other admirals of his age would have elected to remain in comfort ashore, while their subordinates stood the strain of close blockade, but not St. Vincent. He sailed with his fleet to Ushant and spent the summer cruising off the coast of France.

While the admiral was cruising in the Channel, a question arose concerning Mr. Clerk of Elden, who had written a book on naval tactics in the early 1780s. Some of the proposals he made in his book seemed to resemble the tactics used by the great admirals of the next three decades, and his friends thought he might be due for a reward. As part of the investigation into the matter, the current First Lord consulted the most respected admiral then living—the Earl of St. Vincent. In his reply, the old admiral made several characteristically pithy observations concerning the tactics used by his contemporaries in battles described in this book:

> Lord Rodney passed through the enemy's line by accident, not design, although historians have given him credit for the latter.

> On the 29th May a maneuver, by which Lord Howe proposed to cut off the rear of the enemy, by passing through his line, failed in its effect, owing to the mistake or disobedience of signals; the only advantage gained was the weather gage, which he preserved to the first of June.

> Lord Duncan's action was fought pell-mell (without plan or system); he was a gallant officer (but had no idea of tactics, and being soon puzzled with them); and attacked, without attention to form or order, trusting that the brave example he set would achieve his object, which it did completely.

> Upon the whole, [Clerk's] tactics are certainly ingenious, and worthy of the study of all young and inexperienced officers. But the great talent is to take prompt advantage of disorder in the fleet of the enemy, by shifts of wind, accidents, and their deficiency in practical seamanship, to the superior knowledge of which much of our success is to be attributed, and I trust it will never be sacrificed to frippery and gimcrack.[27]

The French navy in the summer of 1806 was still licking its wounds from Trafalgar, and Napoleon's main interest lay upon the Continent. The enemy showed no interest in coming out and challenging St. Vincent and his fleet. One of the European nations that Napoleon had his eye on was Portugal, Britain's most loyal ally on the Continent. To give support to the Portuguese royal family, the admiral was sent with a fleet to Lisbon, but for the time being, Napoleon's threats were empty. He was otherwise occupied with the Prussians and Russians. St. Vincent remained at Lisbon for a few months and then returned to his station off Brest. His fleet wintered in Cawsand Bay, and in deference to his failing health, the admiral resided in a house ashore. When the ministry changed again in March 1807, he requested to be relieved. On 24 April he hauled down his flag for the last time and came ashore.

The remaining years in the life of this great naval officer were peaceful. He attended the House of Lords at infrequent intervals, mainly to speak on naval matters. His last appearance was in 1810.

Lady St. Vincent had never been in good health, and during the last years of her life became an invalid. She died in February 1816 and was buried at Caverswall in Staffordshire. Hers was perhaps the only funeral her husband attended in his later years. He refused to attend those of Nelson and Collingwood because he feared that standing in the icy drafts at St. Paul's would be the death of him.

When George IV was coronated in July 1821, he raised St. Vincent to the rank of Admiral of the Fleet. Although the king's brother the Duke of Clarence had already been granted the rank, and only one was allowed at a time by custom, a special exception was made in St. Vincent's case. The king sent him a gold-mounted baton as a mark of honor.

The admiral of the fleet was to enjoy his new rank for less than two years. On 14 March 1823, following a few days of excessive weariness and unrest, he died. Like his wife, he was buried in Staffordshire, but a monument was raised to him in St. Paul's.

Because the admiral died without issue, the earldom became extinct. But the viscounty of St. Vincent passed to a nephew. The old man was disappointed in his heir. He had been close to his sister Mary since early childhood. When he was granted a peerage, having no children of his own, he was allowed to leave his title to anyone in his family he chose. He thought well of Mary's eldest son, a young naval officer, and proclaimed him his heir. But just as the young man seemed to be doing well and was appointed to command of his own ship, he was drowned in a boating accident. With the line of succession unalterably set in stone, Mary's next son became heir, a man who had disobliged his family by wedding a woman unacceptable to them. The only revenge the old admiral could take was to refuse to speak to the nephew who would succeed him as Lord St. Vincent.

Chapter 5

ADAM DUNCAN

1731–1804

O N 14 MAY 1797 a mutiny broke out aboard the *Adamant* (50), one of the many small two-deckers that made up the main force of the North Sea fleet. This particular vessel had been among the foremost of the troublemakers in a fleet whose men were itching to show their solidarity with their mutinous brethren at Spithead. The commander in chief of the station, Admiral Duncan, was maintaining constant vigil to prevent his fleet from dissolving. On each occasion that a ship threatened to revolt, he would go aboard, hoist his flag, and make a speech pointing out the foolishness of mutiny. Because of his formidable physique and the respect his seamen had for him, the admiral had been able to keep order, but the situation was growing increasingly unstable. He had already come aboard the *Adamant* several times, and now he could see that if drastic measures were not taken, the vessel would become a prize of the mutineers, encouraging other vessels to follow her example.

As soon as Duncan clambered aboard the *Adamant,* he mustered the ship's company. Glaring down at them from the quarterdeck rail, he told them, "My lads, I am not in the smallest degree apprehensive of any violent measures you may have in contemplation; and though I assure you I would much rather acquire your love than incur your fear, I will with my own hand put to death the first man who shall display the slightest signs of rebellious conduct." He then demanded to know if there was any individual who presumed to dispute his authority or that of the officers.[1] Surprisingly, one seaman stepped forward and said, "I do."

Before the sailor could say another word, the huge admiral swept down upon him and hoisted him up by the collar. Holding the man at arm's length in one hand, Duncan took him to the bulwarks and dangled him out over the side. The admiral gestured toward his squirming captive and bade the rest of the ship's company, "Lads, look at this fellow, he who dares to deprive me of the command of the fleet."

The reaction of the men is not recorded, but they must have laughed to see their self-appointed leader dangling ignominiously over the side. After that, the *Adamant* became one of the more reliable vessels in the fleet.

A would-be mutineer would have needed confidence in himself to have challenged Admiral Duncan. The Scottish-born commander in chief was the tallest man on the flag list, standing six feet, four inches tall; and in spite of his sixty-five years of age, he still displayed the vigor of a younger man. Virtually every author who writes of him mentions that he was singularly handsome, with snow-white hair, a high forehead, and regular features.

Except for his outward appearance, Duncan is a shadowy figure who enjoyed his privacy. He left few writings beyond his correspondence with the Admiralty, but except for Admiral St. Vincent, most contemporaries spoke well of him. One young officer who served under both admirals wrote: "Earl St. Vincent . . . was haughty and imperious, rigidly and unnecessarily strict. . . . Many others fulfilled their commands in a more agreeable and equally efficient manner. For instance Lord Nelson, Lord Duncan, etc., etc., without his severity."[2] A civilian who met the admiral late in his career described him as "really an interesting man, with a peculiar naïveté, which in an old sea officer, and one who has distinguished himself so much, is remarkably striking."[3]

By most accounts Duncan lived frugally but was generous with his resources. When his sister was having difficulties finding the money to send her children to school, her brother gave it to her. He was also fiercely loyal to both patron and protégé. He nearly wrecked his career by his unwavering support of Admiral Keppel and was willing to challenge even the First Lord of the Admiralty for the sake of one of his protégés. Although generally tactful in dealing with those around him, in times of stress he became sarcastic. His correspondence with Lord Spencer is peppered with demands for better conditions for his seamen, whiny complaints about his flagship, and threats to resign his command.

Although Duncan's appearance dominates most accounts, there was an unexpected subtlety to his personality. A trait that was unique to him was the way he cut some of the Gordian knots more than fifty years of service threw his way. Few other officers might be able to dangle a mutineer over the side of a ship—but most others were unlikely to think of setting fire to a pair of ships holding up negotiations at disease-ridden Havana or think to use the excuse of a fictitious mutiny to maintain his seat at a court-martial. Episodes such as these hint at a far more complex individual than the physically impressive but dull-witted officer some authors make him out to have been.

. . .

When a third son was born to Alexander Duncan, provost of Dundee, he had no way of knowing that this was the son who would eventually inherit the family lands. As was typical of the landed gentry of eighteenth-century Britain, the eldest son inherited all lands intact. Younger sons had to make their own way in the world, and the Duncans of Lundie were no exception. As the eldest son, John, would inherit the modest family lands and the quasi-noble title of Laird of Lundie, the younger two, Alexander and Adam, were placed in professions appropriate to their social standing. As it was common for the second son of a landed family to go into the army, Alexander became an officer of the Fifty-fifth Regiment of Foot. Because John died young, Alexander inherited the family lands when his father died, in 1771.

Adam, born 1 July 1731, met the fate of a great many third sons of landed gentlemen. He was sent to join the navy. The navy was a fine choice for a younger son in the eighteenth century. A man did not require money to buy a commission as in the army, and if he was lucky, he might win enough prize money to make up for the lack of inheritance. All one needed to start on a naval career was the good will of a captain of one of His Majesty's vessels. Adam, whose cousin Robert Haldane commanded the fourteen-gun *Tryal* sloop-of-war, had no trouble in obtaining the influence to provide him with a berth in April 1746.

The boy's first days in the king's service must have been exciting. The risings in favor of Bonnie Prince Charlie were ending, and the *Tryal* was in the vicinity of Inverness at the time of the Battle of Culloden. Like young Commander Howe's *Baltimore,* her mission was to prevent the escape of the defeated Jacobites. To close off one avenue of escape, she was sent to cruise off the Hebrides in the aftermath of the battle. In spite of the efforts of the *Tryal* and other vessels, Bonnie Prince Charlie and several of his supporters escaped to France. The sloop continued cruising until September 1747 and reached Plymouth in November.

On 22 November 1747 Captain Haldane transferred himself and his followers aboard the twenty-four-gun frigate *Shoreham.* The first cruise of the *Shoreham* under her new commander appears to have been a busy one. Inside of two months, she captured three prizes and attempted a cutting-out action against a privateer.

All went well for Captain Haldane and the *Shoreham* until the ship ran aground on 22 June 1748. She was towed off after her guns and supplies had been taken off, but the captain was brought before a court of inquiry, in consequence of which he resigned his command on 13 September 1748.

Presumably, Duncan left the ship with his cousin, but he never sailed under his command again. In the last months of 1748, he made an acquaintance that was to guide him through his career for the next fifteen years.

By early 1749 the Honorable Augustus Keppel, second son of the Earl of Albemarle, was already an officer of distinction. As a midshipman he had sailed around the world with Commodore Anson. Still a favorite of the influential Anson and having some politically powerful relations, Keppel had risen swiftly through the ranks. He had been made a post captain in December 1744, a few months shy of his twentieth birthday. At the time of his first meeting with Duncan, he commanded the sixty-gun two-decker *Centurion.* In early January 1749 Duncan was mustered aboard the *Centurion* as a midshipman. Shortly thereafter Keppel was appointed commander in chief of the Mediterranean station and entrusted with a diplomatic mission to the Barbary States.

The Barbary pirates had been especially bold while the navies of Europe had been preoccupied with the war that ended in October 1748. But as soon as the British government had the leisure to think of something other than the war, they turned their eyes on the latest outrages perpetrated by the Algerians. These included capturing British ships in defiance of an existing treaty between the two nations and plundering them of large sums of money. Keppel's squadron was entrusted with the task of obtaining reparation for these acts of piracy.

The *Centurion* arrived in the Bay of Algiers at the end of June, and soon Keppel went ashore to meet with the dey. The embassy had an unpromising start, but after two years of negotiations and periodic cruising by the squadron throughout the western Mediterranean, a treaty was signed. The *Centurion* sailed back to England, arriving in July 1751, and was there paid off.

Duncan spent the next three years ashore, but when his friend Keppel was reappointed to the *Centurion* late in 1754, the captain did not forget his protégé. Duncan returned to sea as a midshipman, but when the third lieutenant of the *Norwich* (50), another vessel in the squadron, became ill, he was made acting lieutenant in his place. His commission was confirmed on 10 January 1755, and he returned to the *Centurion.*

The first mission of Keppel's squadron when it reached the American coast was to escort a body of transports containing General Braddock and his men up the Potomac River. After the troops were disembarked, the navy blockaded the coast to prevent supplies and reinforcements from reaching the French. Once Admiral Boscawen arrived to assume command of the North American station in July 1755, Keppel was sent home as too junior to bear the rank of commodore. Duncan remained with the *Centurion* on the North American station until the squadron returned to England in November.

Keppel assumed command of the *Torbay,* a seventy-four-gun third rate in January 1756, and Duncan, now a second lieutenant, rejoined him in July. By that time the events of the previous two years in North America had touched off a formal declaration of war.

In September the *Torbay* was sent with a small squadron to cruise off Cape Finisterre. These vessels took a number of prizes, including the thirty-six-gun frigate *Chariot Royale.*

Soon after he returned to Portsmouth, Keppel was called upon to sit as one of the judges in the court-martial of Admiral Byng, as described in chapter 2. This court sat from the end of December 1756 to the end of January 1757, during which time Keppel became so involved in the trial that Capt. Samuel Hood was brought aboard temporarily to take his place.

The *Torbay* spent the rest of 1757 and the first half of 1758 cruising in and out of Portsmouth. She captured several prizes, but met nothing that came close to giving her an even fight. Then, in September 1758, Keppel was once again made a commodore with the right to select a flag captain. He chose Thomas Owen, an officer who had served under his command for many years. Duncan took another step upward in his own career, becoming first lieutenant of the flagship.

The task before Keppel and his squadron, consisting of five two-deckers, three frigates, a sloop, and two bomb vessels, was to capture Gorée, a fortified island off the coast of Africa, which served as a center of the slave trade. The expedition was assembled and supplied at Cork. Bad weather plagued the British from the start. Indeed, a first attempt to sail was thwarted by the *Torbay* striking a rock during a gale, forcing the squadron to return to Cork for a fortnight. The expedition finally sailed again on 11 November 1758.

Storms continued to hound the squadron as it made its way southward. On 19 November, the *Torbay* was struck by lightning, which killed one of her crew. On the twenty-ninth of the same month, the vessels were caught on a lee shore and nearly run aground. One of their number, the fifty-gun *Lichfield,* was wrecked, with a loss of 130 of her crew. Those who survived to reach shore were stripped of all their belongings by the Moors and sent to Morocco, where they were kept in slavery until ransomed by the British government.[4]

Meanwhile, the rest of the squadron reached Gorée on 28 December, and commenced the attack the following morning. The troops were loaded into flat-bottomed boats and held at the ready behind the transports. In the meantime, the ships of the squadron bombarded the batteries and fortresses that defended the island. The strength of the bombardment alone drove the French from their guns and caused the governor of the island to sue for peace.

During the action Lieutenant Duncan was wounded by a musket ball in the leg. It is remarkable that an officer whose naval career spanned more than fifty years and included service in four wars, and who presented such a large target, should have been wounded only once.

In January 1759 the *Torbay* left Gorée and, with a short stop at Senegal, made for Portsmouth. Because Keppel's commission as commodore had been for the Gorée expedition only, Owen left the ship shortly after her return. From May until September the *Torbay* cruised off Ushant under the command of Admiral Hawke. Then a position as commander of a hired vessel came open, and Duncan left the *Torbay* to take his first independent command on 21 September 1759.

Once the new commander had come aboard the hired lugger *Royal Exchange,* she commenced escorting small convoys. This was a difficult first command. According to the *Dictionary of National Biography,* the vessel had "a miscellaneous ship's company, consisting to a large extent of boys and foreigners, many of whom . . . could not speak English, and all impressed with the idea that as they had been engaged by the merchants from whom the ship was hired they were not subject to naval discipline."[5] The difficulty with the ship's people led to a short term of hire. In April 1760 Duncan was again without a ship.

Although it was likely that the promotion to commander had been welcome at the time, it proved a disservice. Had Duncan remained in the *Torbay* two months longer, he would have taken an active role in the Battle of Quiberon Bay on 20 November 1759. As first lieutenant of a ship that had taken a major part in the fight, he would have won more distinction than as the commander of an obscure hired lugger. Instead, he had to wait some time longer before he was able to win a name for himself.

Duncan's luck took a turn for the better in early 1761, when Keppel received a commission as commodore of a squadron assembled to capture the island of Belle Ile, off the coast of France. Once again he was allowed to select a flag captain, and this time Duncan received the appointment. His post captain's commission was dated 25 February 1761. Shortly thereafter he moved aboard the *Valiant,* a new seventy-four-gun ship of the line that Keppel had been given in place of the worn-out *Torbay.*

The Belle Ile expedition set sail on 29 March 1761. The force consisted of one three-decker, ten two-deckers, eleven frigates, fireships, and bomb vessels. Having to make the entire journey against the wind, the squadron required nine days to reach its destination. However, once Keppel reached Belle Ile, he lost no time in beginning the attack. On the day following his arrival (8 April), he loaded troops into flat-bottomed boats and attempted a landing but was repulsed, with the loss of about five hundred men. It was not until 22 April that the British made a successful landing. Over the ensuing days the French were forced to seek cover in the citadel, which was subjected to bombardment by the bomb vessels from the water and a number of batteries that had been set up ashore. On 7 June the citadel finally surrendered.

The *Valiant* spent most of the remainder of 1761 at anchor off Belle Ile while Keppel commanded the advance squadron, whose duty was to keep an eye on the French fleet at Brest. Finally, on 27 December, the commodore's flagship set sail. She spent the new year off Ushant, at which time her captain began to notice some ominous signs. All the while the *Valiant* had remained anchored at Belle Ile, she had seemed a sound vessel, but once she was subjected to the rough weather of the Channel in winter, she began to leak. On the last day of 1761, she was making three and a half feet of water an hour, and by 2 January, the rate had increased to five feet an hour.[6]

As the weather and the leak continued to worsen, the *Valiant* turned for home in company with a squadron. She was nearing England when she encountered her severest trial, as related in the captain's log: "Strong gales and thick weather . . . at 6 the shot locker in the after hold broke down; the shot fell out and stove a butt of wine; at 10 very hard gales; the mainsail and mizzen staysail split and blew to pieces; hauled up the foresail and lay to under ball mizzen . . . in wearing the spritsail blew away; at 1/2 past four having taken in much water between decks and making 6 feet an hour, fired a gun and bore away."[7]

Close to sinking, the *Valiant* reached the shelter of Torbay on 14 January, and once her company had recovered from their ordeal, they attempted to repair the leak. A makeshift repair proved unsuccessful, and on 19 January the ship sailed to Spithead to be put in the docks.

Although Keppel's commission for Belle Ile was terminated in February, he immediately received a new commission as second-in-command of the naval forces in an expedition against Havana. Because of this, Duncan was able to remain in the *Valiant* as the commodore's flag captain. On 5 March a fully repaired *Valiant* sailed with a force of five ships of the line and two frigates protecting a vast number of transports, victualers, ordnance, and hospital ships. The fleet was commanded by Adm. Sir George Pocock. The army served under Lord Albemarle, the commodore's elder brother.

The fleet reached Barbados on 20 April, and hearing that Martinique had been taken by the British, set sail for that island three days later. At Martinique, Pocock collected the rest of his forces, which swelled the total to 20 ships of the line, 11 frigates, 11 smaller men-of-war, and 156 storeships and transports.[8] At Keppel's urging, this vast fleet elected to take passage through the Old Straits of Bahama rather than the more commonly used route along the southern coast of Cuba. Although the former passage was more dangerous, it was quicker and would result, if successful, in surprise.

All went well until 2 June, when the British fleet encountered a small Spanish patrol. Most of the Spanish ships were taken, but a schooner escaped and brought a warning to the governor of Havana. Hot upon the heels of the warning, the British arrived on 6 June and, the following day, began landing troops. By the end of June, the defenders had been driven to take shelter in the great fortress of El Morro and behind the city walls.

Seeing El Morro as the key to the city's defenses, the British concentrated on that. Many ships' guns were hauled ashore and placed in batteries trained on the fortress. An attempt was made to attack El Morro from the sea on 1 July, but it proved a mistake, and cost the captain of one of the ships his life. From that point onward, the British concentrated their efforts on assaulting the fort from the landward side, using sailors to man the guns. The battery manned by guncrews from the *Valiant* had a reputation as one of the best. Although an effort was made to change the crews periodically, many more men died as a result of disease and bad water than from action with the enemy.

For more than a fortnight, the British subjected El Morro to a tremendous bombardment, which eventually dismounted all the Spanish guns and weakened the walls. Still, there could be no final assault until the walls had been mined, and on 30 July the mines were sprung. Immediately British troops charged into the gaps created by the springing of the mines, and soon forced their way into the fortress. After about twenty intense minutes of hand-to-hand fighting, the Spanish were forced to surrender.

The day of El Morro's capture was a busy one for the captain of the *Valiant*. At 4:00 in the morning, two Spanish floating batteries emerged and opened fire on the British troops massing in readiness for the springing of the mines. Boats from several ships were manned and sent under Duncan's command to chase away the floating batteries. Soon after the captain's return aboard the *Valiant,* he was sent out again with more boats full of men "in case he should see, upon the springing of [the] mine, that his people could be of service, to seize the opportunity."[9]

After Havana surrendered on 12 August, there remained only the task of collecting and dividing the plunder. The negotiations dragged on for more than a month as each interest debated what belonged to whom. Meanwhile, the death toll among the seamen of the fleet and the soldiers ashore was appalling. The *Valiant* alone lost twenty-one men in July and another nine in August.[10] One of the sticking points in the negotiations was a pair of ships of the line that had not yet been completed and were still upon the stocks. Apparently hoping to speed the day of departure and reduce the losses in his ship's company, Duncan took his boat's crew ashore one night in September. They set fire to the ships in the stocks, thereby removing one of the barriers to concluding the negotiations.

By the time the *Valiant* sailed with six other ships of the line in company, on 10 October, 560 British had been killed or died of wounds and 4,708 had perished from sickness.[11] The loss in life had been tremendous, but the fortunes gained by the senior officers of the fleet were stupendous. Admiral Pocock and the Earl of Albemarle each gained £122,697, and Keppel received £24,539. As one of the forty-two captains involved in the taking of Havana, Duncan received £1,600.[12]

The *Valiant* spent all of 1763 in the Caribbean, shuttling between Port Royal, Jamaica, and Havana. Keppel was made a rear admiral on 1 January 1764, to the jubilation of the men under his command, who held him in affection.

In March 1764 the *Valiant* left Port Royal with the intention of returning to England, but she was found to be leaking so badly, she had to put back. After an extensive series of repairs, the ship sailed again on 9 May and dropped her anchor at Spithead on 26 May. On 12 July the *Valiant* was paid off, and Duncan went ashore, ending his fifteen-year professional relationship with Admiral Keppel. He never served directly under his old patron again.

In the first years after the *Valiant* was paid off, some time ashore was welcome. Duncan's health had been affected by his service in the West Indies, and for the three years following the end of the war he lived as a semi-invalid.[13] Once he began to recover his former vigor, he grew restless and started to write letters to the Admiralty requesting employment. This was a bad time for any naval captain looking for a ship. In the years following the Seven Years' War, the British government sought to pay off its wartime debt by reducing the fleet. There were few commands available for even the most distinguished and well-connected captains. Worse for Duncan was his association with Keppel, who had become an outspoken member of the opposition.

Meanwhile, the captain lived with his mother after the death of her husband and, in 1774, traveled to Italy to visit Lady Mary Duncan, the widow of his uncle. By November 1776 he was writing to the Admiralty again requesting employment, but continued to be ignored. Then, on 6 June 1777, he took a step that proved to be the turning point in his life. He married Miss Henrietta Dundas, a lady with some powerful Scottish Tory connections.

There were several good, if unromantic, reasons for Duncan to make an alliance of this kind a trifle late in life. His elder brother was married but had no children; if the captain left no descendants, the Duncan lands would go to a distant relation. He needed to marry a woman young enough to bear children and, even better to have the sort of connections that would advance his career. In return, he could promise her the eventual enjoyment of the family estates and enough money to live on for the time being.

Although no letters survive between the captain and his wife (it was a common custom in the eighteenth century for a wife to burn her husband's letters after his death), there are indications that the relationship was an affectionate one. For all that Duncan was nearly twenty years her senior, he was still a handsome man. He appears to have been the choice of her heart, and in his turn, he spoke glowingly of her on the rare occasions that he spoke of her in public. They produced nine children.

The newly married couple settled in Nellfield, near Edinburgh, where they lived out the short time until the captain became employed again. Duncan's first naval appointment in thirteen years was not a flattering one, but it gave hope of better things to come. On 25 July 1777 he became the commanding officer of a press gang based on the upper part of the Thames. Many officers—Duncan included—thought poorly of impressment as a method of recruitment, but when there was a war on, there was little alternative. And for a captain who had been unemployed for thirteen years, any sort of appointment that would bring him to the attention of the Admiralty was better than nothing.

Eventually the period as captain of a press gang seemed to pay off, because on 16 May 1778, he was commissioned into the seventy-four-gun *Suffolk*. It turned out to be a dubious reward. When he joined the ship a month later, he made a number of unpleasant discoveries. Upon arriving aboard, the new captain discovered that the *Suffolk* had no purser and that the man filling the rank of carpenter was unfit for duty and had to be replaced. When the new carpenter finally arrived, he lacked the all-important warrant to prove that he had been appointed to the ship and knew his duty. By 18 July the captain was growing increasingly frustrated:

> Never since I commanded his Majesty's ship *Suffolk* has there been either purser or any other person to act in that capacity on board, which has put us into many difficulties particularly so now, as we have got a number of men on board who have no conveniency to make them comfortable, and therefore to request as we have been some time ready to take on board sea stores that you will please to give such directions about a person to do that duty as you shall think fit, for until one is appointed the service must stop.
>
> (I am just informed that the master of the *Suffolk* is warranted for the *Dunkirk* and the surgeon for the *Princess Amelia.* This I cannot help complaining of as a hardship when the ship is fitting for immediate service to have the officers taken away without any previous notice and particularly so when I find they were put into this ship as a step for their own conveniency.)[14]

While Duncan was struggling with the task of keeping his warrant officers, his old patron, Admiral Keppel, was in difficulties of his own. As noted in previous chapters, the Battle of Ushant had resulted in a serious breach between Keppel and his third-in-command, Vice Admiral Palliser, and ultimately in the order for a court-martial against the senior officer. The trial was arranged to begin in January 1779.

Meanwhile, the *Suffolk* sailed with a convoy on 5 September 1778 and joined the Channel fleet a week later. At the end of October, the fleet returned to Spithead. That was Duncan's sole service afloat in the *Suffolk.* On 4 December he was appointed to the *Monarch,* another seventy-four-gun third rate. When he moved aboard his new command, he brought most of the crew from the *Suffolk* with him. However, there were still a few difficulties in acquiring the right number of officers. This time the trouble was the first lieutenant. Originally, a Mr. Potts had been appointed first lieutenant of the *Monarch,* but on 22 January 1779 Duncan wrote a sarcastic letter to the Admiralty to the effect that as Potts had not appeared by that time, he must assume the man had died.[15]

When the court was assembled to try Admiral Keppel, Duncan was appointed one of the judges. In the eighteenth century, courts-martial were formed from the second-in-command of the station, who served as president, and the twelve (or fewer) next most senior post captains or flag officers. At Keppel's court-martial, many of the court had served under the accused and were inclined to favor him.

The trial began on 7 January 1779. By most accounts Duncan appears to have behaved with impartiality throughout the trial, unlike one or two of his colleagues who tended to badger witnesses hostile to the defendant. But when the court finally announced its verdict "that the charge was malicious and ill-founded," on 11 February, he was obviously jubilant.[16]

Even after the acquittal, there was no love lost between Keppel and Lord Sandwich. On 12 March, the admiral resigned his command at the request of the First Lord and came on shore, never to serve afloat again.

Meanwhile, after the verdict of the Keppel court-martial was announced, Palliser's position deteriorated rapidly. Soon he was obliged to request a court-martial upon himself to clear his name. To make certain that the verdict would be to his liking, he requested that Lord Sandwich pack the court in his favor. One of the first people he wished removed was Keppel's former flag captain. "It would be very much to be wished Captain Duncan could be out of the way," he wrote to his lordship on 8 April.[17]

The First Lord of the Admiralty lost no time in obliging him. On 9 April, Admiral Arbuthnot, who was expected to sail at any moment, received the following orders: "Whereas we think fit that His Majesty's ship the *Monarch,* whose Captain is directed to obey your orders shall . . . accompany you 100 leagues to the westward of the Lizard for the greater security of the transports, victualers and trade put under your convoy. . . ."[18]

Duncan, who knew that his assignment to the convoy was merely to make certain he would not be available for the court-martial, sent the following message to Arbuthnot two days later: "Late last night, I received your orders to place myself under your command and to proceed with the utmost dispatch to St. Helens with His Majesty's Ship *Monarch* under my command. In consequence of which I made preparation to sail with all possible dispatch, and tho' the ship was in no condition to put to sea, gave directions this forenoon for her to be unmoored, to drop down, which the people refused until they were paid."[19]

It was becoming increasingly common during this period for sailors to refuse to sail until they were paid, but the claim of mutiny aboard the *Monarch* is suspicious. There is no mention of any mutinous activity aboard the ship in the ship's log or any other document save this one letter to Arbuthnot. In light of the timing and Duncan's later record in suppressing mutiny, it seems probable that the refusal by the ship's company was a story concocted by the captain to keep from being sent out of the way.

By 12 April it was too late to find some other way to keep the *Monarch*'s captain off the court-martial. Accepting the inevitable, the Admiralty commanded that the *Monarch* should remain at Spithead until further notice.

Palliser's court-martial was slightly shorter than Keppel's, but it was close to a month before it ended. The vice admiral was acquitted of any wrongdoing, but the verdict included a slight reprimand for not giving his superior better information concerning the condition of his ship.

Following the courts-martial, the *Monarch* became an active member of the Channel fleet, which passed to the command of Sir Charles Hardy. This was a dangerous time for the Royal Navy. Spain soon joined the war and united its fleet with that of France. On 1 September 1779, Hardy found himself with thirty-eight ships of the line under his command facing an enemy fleet of sixty-six. To the disgust of some of his officers, he slunk away up the Channel and returned to Spithead. Like Jervis, Duncan was among those frustrated by the refusal to fight the enemy and could "only stand looking over the stern gallery of the *Monarch*," longing to engage the foe.[20] Luckily for Britain, the French and Spanish combined fleet made little use of their control of the Channel and soon returned to Brest.

Toward the latter part of 1779, Admiral Rodney was placed in command of a fleet whose ultimate destination would be the Leeward Islands. But before the fleet proceeded to the West Indies, it would first stop at Gibraltar to bring supplies and reinforcements to the besieged garrison. The *Monarch* was among the twenty-two ships of the line chosen for this expedition, which sailed on 29 December.

At first the voyage was uneventful, but in the afternoon of 16 January 1780, a Spanish force of eleven ships of the line and two frigates was sighted. Rodney lost little time in sending his own vessels after the Spaniards, beginning what has been called the Moonlight Battle. The following is an account of the action, taken from the captain's log of the *Monarch:*

> At 1 the admiral made the signal for the line of battle abreast; made sail and cleared ship for action. At 2 the signal for a general chase. . . . Thirteen sail in sight. The admiral made the signal for battle. . . . At 1/2 past 3 the headmost ships began to engage. At 4 one of the enemy's ships blew up in the action; the ships ahead engaged with the enemy and we in chase. . . . At 9 the enemy began to fire their stern chasers at us; 1/2 past 9 got up alongside 3 of the enemy's ships and came to a close engagement with them, which continued till 1/2 past 11 when one of the enemy struck to us and we brought to under the mizzen, the rest of our sails being shot and cut to pieces, likewise a great part of our running rigging.[21]

In the action the *Monarch* lost three men killed and twenty-four wounded. Her prize was later identified as the *San Augustin* of seventy guns, but because the sea was too heavy for a boat to be launched, a prize crew could not be sent, and the Spanish ship eventually escaped. Of the rest of the Spanish fleet, only four managed to get away.

Following the defeat of the Spanish fleet, Rodney and company sailed on to relieve Gibraltar. Afterward, Rodney continued to the West Indies with four ships in company while the rest returned to Britain. For the spring and summer of 1780, the *Monarch* cruised the Channel and captured a few small prizes. Then, in September, orders arrived for the ship to sail for the West Indies. Having suffered from the insalubrious Caribbean climate, Duncan begged to be excused on medical grounds.[22] In accordance with his request, the captain was relieved of his command on 1 October.

Duncan spent the next year and a half ashore. The Tory North government fell in March 1782, and his old friend Keppel became the new the First Lord of the Admiralty. The ink had scarcely dried on his appointment when the new First Lord commissioned Duncan to command of the ninety-gun three-decker *Blenheim,* then in dry dock at Chatham.

After several months of preparation, the second rate sailed on 31 August to join Lord Howe's fleet, gathering for another relief of Gibraltar. In the battle off Cape Spartel on 21 October, the *Blenheim* led the larboard division of Howe's squadron. She was engaged with the enemy as much as any British ship and lost two men killed and three wounded. Following the successful relief of Gibraltar, the *Blenheim* returned to England, and upon hearing that his ship was to be ordered to the West Indies, Duncan again resigned command, in December.

This time the captain was not long ashore. On 15 January 1783, he succeeded Captain Jervis in command of the *Foudroyant.* However, his commission to that ship was of short duration, and the vessel was paid off on 30 January. While Duncan commanded the *Foudroyant,* news reached Britain of the signing of the treaty that ended the war. Word spread throughout Portsmouth that most of the fleet was to be paid off, and the seamen, who were eager to go home, immediately began dismantling their vessels without orders. Several ships' companies, including that of the *Blenheim,* rioted on the docks. Hearing that the people of his former command were playing the devil, Duncan assembled the crew of the *Foudroyant* and led them against the mob. He "convinced the mob that he had spirit and firmness to enforce obedience if they were determined to resist. His frankness and generosity spared that alternative; he joked them into good humor, and then separated in peace."[23]

As long as the Whigs remained in power, Duncan had no need to fear that he would be passed over for command. On 15 April 1783 Keppel appointed him to the *Edgar* (74), the guardship at Portsmouth. An officer who served aboard the *Edgar* a couple of years after Duncan's tenure recalled a story concerning the former captain and one of his warrant officers: "This Johnny Bone [the boatswain] was a devil of a fellow at Cap-a-bar, and would stick at nothing. It is related that the late Lord Duncan, when he commanded the *Edgar,* once said to him, "Whatever you do, Mr. Bone, I hope and trust you will not take the anchors from the bows.""[24]

In July 1785 Keppel retired as First Lord of the Admiralty, and on 22 September he paid a visit aboard the *Edgar,* where he was treated royally. Shortly afterward he took ship for Naples. This is probably the last meeting of master and pupil, because Keppel died in October 1786. Meanwhile, the *Edgar* was paid off on 9 August 1785, and Duncan left his last command as a captain.

Although Britain was officially at peace between 1783 and 1793, there were several occasions during which war threatened but was averted. In preparation for one possible war, a number of new admirals, Duncan among them, were created on 24 September 1787.

But peace continued, and few commands were available for admirals, especially for adherents of the party that was once again out of office. Rear Admiral Duncan spent most of his time in Scotland, especially in Edinburgh visiting with his wife's relations. It was fortunate on one occasion that he was such a frequent visitor, because the grasping Dundas clan was not popular with the mobs who sympathized with the French Revolution. On 4 June 1792 rioters assaulted the house of the widow of Robert Dundas, with whom the admiral happened to be staying. In defense of his mother-in-law's house, Duncan sallied forth to fight single-handedly against the mob. During the melee the little finger of his left hand was broken by a blow from a stick. Some soldiers eventually drove the mob away, but the admiral's finger never healed properly. For the rest of his life he wore a double ring that connected the little finger to its sounder neighbor.

As war with France loomed on the horizon, another round of promotions was made on 1 February 1793, which made Duncan a vice admiral, but he remained unemployed. In December 1794 two things occurred that were to profoundly influence the admiral's hitherto quiet existence. First, Lord Spencer, who though a Tory had many Whig connections, became First Lord of the Admiralty. Then France invaded Holland and compelled the Dutch to become their allies, making it necessary to form a fleet to patrol the North Sea.

Early in 1795 Vice Admiral Duncan was appointed to command the newly formed North Sea fleet. He hoisted his flag aboard the seventy-four-gun *Venerable* on 31 March at Yarmouth and undertook as frustrating a task as ever confronted any flag officer. Because the Dutch were considered less of a threat than the French, the North Sea fleet was kept small. It consisted of only four two-deckers, although this number was later increased. The ships too were generally of the smaller types considered too weak to stand against the French, and even those could be spirited away for convoy duty on short notice. The administration too was unusually complex. Although the ships of the fleet were based out of Yarmouth, as that port was closest to the Texel, they had to come down into the Nore to be paid or repaired.

Then, to add to the confusion, a Russian fleet of twelve sail of the line and six frigates was sent to the North Sea and placed under the admiral's command. This Russian force, which first arrived in August 1795, was generally more trouble than it was worth. Neither side could understand the other's signals; the Russian vessels were always under repair when they were most needed; and there were disputes over the command structure. Early in the commission the British second-in-command was Rear Adm. Thomas Pringle, who was junior to the Russian admiral. This led to disputes over whose orders were to be obeyed when Duncan himself was absent, which caused him to lament, "I am the first British admiral that ever was ordered on service with foreigners only."[25]

For the first year of its existence, the North Sea fleet spent most of its time at Yarmouth, with only a few frigates keeping watch on the Dutch at the Texel. Duncan, who became a full admiral of the blue on 1 June 1795, visited the Texel in person only in August and November of that year. The Dutch came out for a short time in August but returned to port before the main British fleet could put in an appearance.

After a winter in which the Dutch were frozen in and the British concentrated at Yarmouth, Duncan came out to the Texel in March 1796, where he relieved Pringle. Because of the difficulties over seniority with the Russian admiral, the departing second-in-command was replaced by Vice Admiral MacBride. The newcomer was a good choice because of his prior experience in the North Sea. He had his own ideas about the best way to blockade the Dutch with the varied number and quality of vessels available to him. He wrote to Duncan: "I have begun to wean them, as I term it, by keeping closer in—the cutters as near the Texel as they can safely get, the frigates next them, then two line of battle ships to cover them, and the rest of us without and still further off so as not to be seen from their lookout.

This keeps them in suspense as to the amount of our force."[26] This method of watching the Texel was to have an unforeseen benefit the following year.

In August 1796 the admiral finally inherited the family estate. However, this made little change in his life. The estate brought him approximately £500 per year, which was less than he was already earning as commander in chief of a fleet. Also, he soon had other matters to concern him.

In September, Pitt and Spencer between them concocted a scheme to land troops at the Texel. They had gained the impression that there was a strong royalist contingent in Holland that would rise up against the French if a British force was landed. The plan was to capture the fortress of the Helder, overlooking the Texel, bombard the Dutch fleet, and use local support to make Holland untenable for the French. When Duncan was consulted about the plan, he raised a number of objections, as reported by letter to the First Lord: "Admiral Duncan considers that the Dutch fleet may escape from their present anchorage out of reach of the guns of the Helder. . . . He further thinks that at this season in those seas so little dependence can be had on the weather that it might be many days before the troops could reembark, and that they would consequently be cut off, from the probable force which could be sent against them in a short time."[27]

In spite of the admiral's objections, the scheme went forward. Troops were embarked at Yarmouth in mid-October and sailed with the fleet across to the Texel. However, once they reached their destination, they encountered inclement weather, making it too dangerous to attempt a landing. Spencer gave up the scheme in early November, but Duncan continued to beat about the coast, looking for an opportunity to land the troops until the end of the month. He returned to Yarmouth on 27 November. During the excitement of the Texel project, Vice Admiral MacBride suffered a stroke. He was replaced by Vice Adm. Richard Onslow.

When 1797 began, Duncan had no way of knowing that it was to be the most critical year of his life. In early March a Dutch squadron was reported to have sailed from the Texel, but by the time Duncan got there with the fleet, they had already returned to the safety of their home port. The commander in chief and his fleet remained off the Texel for the better part of two months, returning to Yarmouth late in April.

While the North Sea fleet had been sitting outside the Texel, tension had been building in the Channel fleet, resulting in the Spithead mutiny. Soon after the North Sea fleet returned to Yarmouth, signs that the conflagration from Spithead had caught there too began to show. On 30 April the ship's company of the *Venerable* gathered together and gave a cheer that indicated their solidarity with their brethren of the Channel fleet. As Duncan reported to the Admiralty, he took steps to maintain order aboard his flagship:

> I immediately assembled the officers and ordered the marines under arms. Being thus prepared I went on the forecastle and demanded to know the cause of such improper conduct, to which they made no reply; but five of them appeared more forward than the rest I ordered aft onto the poop, and directed the others to disperse, which they did. Soon after I ordered all hands to be sent aft on the quarterdeck and the five men to be brought from the poop. I then interrogated them on their conduct. They had nothing to say for themselves but that as their friends at Spithead had done so they thought no harm. . . . I pointed out the enormity of the crime of mutiny and pardoned the offenders. Good order was again established, and I have the satisfaction to say they have behaved very properly ever since.[28]

According to other sources, the incident was more serious than the admiral's letter implied. When the cheering was first heard aboard the *Venerable,* he charged up on deck in a fit of rage, and had to be restrained by the chaplain from running one of the mutineers through with his sword. However, he swiftly regained his composure and was soon in a state to meet the crisis in the manner he described above. For the manner of his handling of the aborted mutiny aboard the *Venerable,* he received the following compliment from Lady Spencer: "The success attending such well-judged and vigorous conduct makes me lament that we have not more Adam Duncans. However, since we can't cut him up into several pieces (tho' there is certainly enough of him to make many reasonable-sized men), we must be contented with having one of that name who will keep the North Sea fleet in good order."[29]

As far as Duncan was concerned, that was the end of the matter. He predicted that there would be no more mutinous demonstrations in the North Sea fleet. Indeed, for a time, all was quiet at Yarmouth. As word of the continuing events at Spithead reached the North Sea fleet, the admiral countered the news with a few lectures to his ship's company, and seemed pleased with the results. He reported to Spencer: "A report has gone about that the ships would not go to sea. I today put the question to this ship's company, as I thought it better it should be known before we put them to the trial; their answer to a man was they 'would go to any part of the world with me,' and seemed most penitent for their past faults."[30]

While the admiral kept his fleet in order with a round of personal appearances and speeches, a mutiny erupted at the Nore on 13 May. If the ships at the Nore had not mutinied just as the Spithead affair was drawing to a close, it is likely that the North Sea fleet would have settled back into a more peaceful state. Instead, matters went from bad to worse until Duncan was compelled to use physical force against the mutineers as described at the beginning of this chapter.

After the incident aboard the *Adamant,* the mutinous rumblings were stilled for a while in the North Sea fleet. On 17 May, Duncan reported to the First Lord, "It is now with much pleasure I can almost assure you we shall keep all right in this fleet."[31] Accepting this assessment, and having heard rumors that the Dutch were preparing to come out, the Admiralty ordered the North Sea fleet to the Texel on 25 May. The ships obeyed the command to sail, except two who refused to weigh because they had not been paid, but there were danger signs aboard many of those who had followed their admiral.

Duncan still hoped to hold his fleet together by keeping it at sea and away from evil influences ashore, but on 28 May five ships mutinied and returned to Yarmouth. These vessels were followed by most of the rest of the fleet the next day. Some remained at Yarmouth through the duration of the mutinies, but seven others proceeded to the Nore, where they arrived in time to shore up the waning enthusiasm of the mutineers there.

With all of his fleet gone except the two-deckers *Venerable* and *Adamant* and a pair of smaller vessels, the admiral decided to blockade the Dutch with what he had. He announced to his crew that the *Venerable* was to block the Texel and that "the soundings were such that his flag would continue to fly above shoal water after the ship and company had disappeared."[32]

On 1 June the sorry remnant of the North Sea fleet arrived off the Texel. The two ships of the line took up stations in the narrowest part of the channel, with the smaller vessels still closer in. If the *Venerable* and *Adamant* had been sunk in action when the Dutch came out, as the admiral predicted, they would have made it difficult for the enemy to sail out any farther. It was at this point that the method Vice Admiral MacBride had chosen for keeping the Dutch guessing the force of the North Sea fleet came to have unforeseen utility. Now Duncan had the opportunity to fool the enemy into thinking that he was stronger than he was. As he reported to the First Lord: "Shall therefore continue off the Texel and make up as well as I can for the want of my fleet by making a number of signals as if the fleet was in the offing. I shall from time to time change my flag for deception, a humiliating situation to my former one."[33]

For three days the *Venerable* and the *Adamant* stood constant vigil. Although the Dutch showed few signs of wishing to come out, the wind would have allowed them to attack if they chose. On 4 June the wind shifted to the west, and the blockading force was able to withdraw from the bottleneck into which it had been crammed. The next day they were joined by two ships of the line from the Channel fleet. With these vessels to assist him, the admiral was partly relieved of the cares that had been riding him since the desertion of his own fleet and was able to think of matters in England. He wrote to the First Lord: "I shall be glad to hear my scoundrels are come to their senses again, and that the gentlemen delegates will be pleased to let them come to sea again; am sure it will give me much satisfaction to hear some of them are hanged, as they deserve."[34]

Although the letter above does not hint at it, having been written while the memory of the desertion by his fleet in spite of all the promises of his men was still fresh, Duncan was exceptionally ready to forgive. Later in the year, after the guiltiest men had been tried and punished, he requested that the king pardon the remainder. He took them back into the fleet, and the troubles seem to have been forgotten.

On 10 June more reinforcements from the Channel fleet arrived, bringing the fleet up to ten ships of the line. While the Nore mutiny ground to an end on 14 June, the Texel was secure. This was fortunate, because toward the middle of July the Dutch began to make serious preparations to embark troops and invade Britain. They were at one point actually weighing anchor when the wind failed them. Eventually the wind was against the enemy for so long that they gave up the attempt and sent the soldiers ashore to recuperate after their long and useless stay aboard ship.

Also in July, the idea of granting Duncan some form of reward for his service during the mutiny was put forward. The king seemed willing, and Spencer made a suggestion in a manner that reminds one of a waiter with a wine list: "[i]f I might venture to offer an opinion to you, I should recommend your choice of an Irish peerage. In case you should agree with me, I must trouble you to let me know by what title you would wish to be distinguished. If you should feel any objection to this, perhaps you might like the Order of the Bath, to which, if you are desirous of an honor which may remain in your family, I have reason to suppose that his Majesty would be pleased to add a baronetage."[35] With one thing and another, this proposal never came to fruition, but Czar Paul of Russia granted the admiral the Order of St. Alexander Nevsky.

Through the summer the North Sea fleet continued off the Texel. The borrowed ships of the Channel fleet returned to their proper stations, while vessels that had abandoned their commander in chief earlier began to straggle back in. Many of the admiral's letters from this time report that the crews were still unruly and less respectful to their officers than they had been before their experience in the mutiny. Between the unruliness of his crews, the length of the cruise, and the condition of his flagship, Duncan began to grow tired of the business, as he wrote to Lord Spencer: "Now, my Lord, as to myself, should this treaty with France not end in a peace, which to give you my opinion really think will not be the case, hope you will have no objection to my retiring. . . . The *Venerable* cannot hold out a winter's cruise, I am sure for [when] it rains even in my cabin am not dry, as is the case with everybody in the ship."[36]

In spite of the admiral's complaints, nothing changed, and he continued in command. As summer gave way to autumn, the weather deteriorated, and still the North Sea fleet kept off the Texel in case the Dutch should decide to come out. Finally, on 26 September, the word came that the fleet should return to Yarmouth.

Although there was now no chance of using their fleet to support an invasion, the Dutch Admiralty decided to send it out anyway, before the season became too advanced. Apparently they hoped that an action of some kind would improve the flagging morale of their sailors. Soon after the departure of the British fleet, Vice Adm. Jan de Winter received orders to put to sea. He was commanded to seek out the enemy and bring them to action, preferably close to the coast of Holland, where the shallow draft of his own vessels might give him an advantage. Although he disapproved of his orders, thinking it likely he would meet with defeat if he stood against the British, de Winter set sail from the Texel on 7 October.

Meanwhile, the greater part of the North Sea fleet returned to Yarmouth on 2 October. Duncan originally intended to stay in port less than twenty-four hours, but when it became clear that the fleet would have to remain longer, the admiral sent the *Russell* (74), *Adamant* (50), and *Beaulieu* (40) back to the Texel to join a squadron of smaller vessels that had been left behind. The reinforcements arrived in time to observe the Dutch weigh anchor and issue forth from their harbor. Immediately the *Speculator*, a lugger, was dispatched to Yarmouth with the news. The rest of the force shadowed the enemy, keeping well out of range but watching to report their movements to the admiral when he arrived with the rest of the fleet.

On 9 October the *Speculator* reached Yarmouth with the news that the Dutch were out. Eleven ships of the line put to sea in such haste that some left part of their crews behind. A few more followed later. By the time

Duncan rejoined the *Russell* and the *Adamant* off the coast of Holland, early in the morning of 11 October, his total force was sixteen two-deckers, two frigates, and a number of smaller vessels.[37] Observing that the British were attempting to cut them off from their home port, de Winter, who lay to the southeast, immediately set his course for the Texel to the northeast. Determined not to let his foe get away this time, Duncan hoisted the signal to prepare for battle and attempted to get his scattered fleet into an effective line.

As the wind was from the northwest, the British had the wind gauge, giving them the option to close at will. But Duncan preferred to meet the enemy, whose force was only slightly less than his own, with an organized fleet.[38] He spent the first hour after hoisting the signal for battle trying to form his line. All the while the Dutch were sliding closer and closer to their home port and into shallow water, where it would be dangerous for the deeper-drafted British to follow. Finally, at 10:12 A.M., he made the signal to give chase, compelling his fleet to come into action as swiftly as possible without much regard for the line of battle.

After an hour of charging down upon the enemy, Duncan made the signal for the fleet to bring to. He tried to make a few quick adjustments to his line, hoping to bring his most powerful ships to bear on the larger vessels in the enemy's fleet. But soon he realized that there was no time for any fine-tuning of his force. If he was to meet the Dutch before they reached the shallows, he would have to attack them as he was. At 11:25 the *Venerable* signaled for each ship to steer for and engage her opponent. In response, the vessels of the North Sea fleet turned their sterns into the wind and closed rapidly with the opposing force. Then, shortly after 11:30, Duncan made a series of orders that turned the Battle of Camperdown into a tactically significant engagement. He first commanded the lee division under Onslow to engage the enemy's rear and then ordered the weather division under his own flag to engage the enemy's center. The result of this was to mass the entire force of his fleet on two-thirds of the enemy and leave the Dutch van to their own devices. The final important signal of the battle was made at 11:47. This was: "Having the weather gauge, pass through the line and engage them to leeward." The purpose of this command was to place British vessels between the Dutch and their own coast, forcing them to stand and fight.

With Duncan in the *Venerable* leading one division, and Onslow in the *Monarch* leading the other, the British bore down on the Dutch in two disordered clumps. The *Venerable* attempted to pass through the line astern of de Winter's flagship *Vrijheid,* but her way was blocked by the *Staten-Gener-aal.* She was able to pass astern of that vessel, firing a devastating raking broadside into her. Then she continued forward to engage the *Vrijheid,* which had already come under fire from the *Ardent* to windward. The rest of the ships in the weather division attacked the Dutch center, but few made it through the line. Meanwhile, the lee division under Onslow had better luck in passing through the line. They massed on the Dutch rear and swiftly overpowered it.

The fighting was a great deal hotter for the weather division, and the victory was not at first assured. The *Venerable* was fighting the *Vrijheid* on her larboard side and the *Staten-Generaal* to starboard. During this part of the action, the admiral's flag was shot down from the mainmast. This was a serious loss, especially because the Dutch *Hercules* caught fire at around this time, and in the confusion was thought by some of the British to be the *Venerable.* It was imperative for the admiral's flag to be hoisted again, but with the halyards shot away, there was only one way to raise it. A seaman named Jack Crawford volunteered to climb aloft and nail the flag to the mast, regardless of a wound he received by the enemy's fire.

It was approximately 12:30 when the *Venerable* broke the Dutch line. By 3:00, better than half the enemy fleet had surrendered, and the remainder was making for the Texel with all speed.[39] The *Vrijheid* was dismasted by her final opponent, the *Director.* When the *Director's* first lieutenant rowed over to the Dutch flagship, he found de Winter attempting to make hasty repairs to a boat in which he hoped to escape. Realizing that he now had no hope of avoiding capture, the Dutch admiral took an emotional leave of his ship's company, many of whom were dangerously wounded. He then allowed himself to be rowed to the side of the *Venerable.*

When de Winter reached the quarterdeck, he was met by Duncan, who assured him that he had nothing to be ashamed of in his loss. The Dutch admiral offered his sword in token of surrender, but his British counterpart waved it away. "I would much rather take a brave man's hand than his sword," he said.[40]

There has been a considerable amount of debate over the Battle of Camperdown. The results made for one of the most smashing successes in British naval history to that time and showed the way for others to follow. The debate lies in Duncan's abilities as an admiral. Some authors claim that he was little more than a lucky dolt and that his concentration of his whole force on a part of the enemy was an accident. Indeed, he himself stated that his tactics were forced upon him by circumstances: "I was obliged to lay all regularity and tactics aside, we was so near the land, or we should have done nothing."[41]

But there are circumstances in which one makes one's own luck. If Duncan had held back waiting to form his line of battle, the Dutch would probably have escaped safely back to the Texel and there would have been no battle. Instead he chose on the spur of the moment to set the example and place his own flagship between the enemy and their own coast, relying on the fighting spirit of his captains to follow him. If the result was an unintentional tactical innovation, Duncan, at least, should be given credit for thinking effectively in a swiftly changing situation and being willing to change his plans at a moment's notice.

The news of the victory was greeted with public jubilation. Church bells rang and a grand illumination was decreed for the city of London. By the time Duncan arrived at the Nore, shepherding his leaking prizes and his own fleet in scarcely better condition, he found that he had been created Viscount Duncan of Camperdown. The king himself attempted to travel down to the Nore to visit the fleet as he had done for Howe, but he was held back by bad weather.

Although the admiral himself appears to have been content with his title, there were others who thought he had not been treated fairly. Lady Mary Duncan, the aunt he had visited in Italy many years earlier, penned the following to Henry Dundas: "Report says my nephew is only made a viscount. Myself is nothing. But the whole nation thinks the least you can do is give him an English earldom."[42]

Indeed the admiral appears to have been a prime favorite with the public for the latter part of 1797. When he visited London in November, he went out to eat with his brother-in-law. Toward the end of the meal, one of the other diners asked if that was not Admiral Duncan sitting there. Finding that it was indeed the case, the stranger toasted the admiral's health, announcing that he was present. The result of this news was pandemonium. To avoid being mobbed, Duncan and his brother-in-law tried to escape into a hackney cab. But the people outside took the horses out of harness and themselves drew the cab around Covent Garden.

Not everyone joined the general enthusiasm for the admiral. William Windham, a Tory MP wrote:

> You will have heard of our rejoicings here and the impression made by Lord Duncan's victory. It was a good work and as well done, I believe, as was possible; but we should not have heard so much of it had it not been Duncan. For

Lord St. Vincent's victory, the greatest beyond all example in naval annals, not a candle burnt. For the same reason, hardly anything said of Admiral Onslow, though, had Duncan been Onslow and vice versa, the whole honor of the victory would have been ascribed to him.[43]

Following all the excitement and the court-martial of one of his captains who appeared reluctant to attack during the Battle of Camperdown, the admiral returned to Scotland for more fetes and adulation. Judging by letters written at the time, fame had begun to pall on Duncan, and he was only too glad to resume a peaceful existence at home for a time.

In August 1798 the admiral hoisted his flag aboard the *Kent* (74), a brand-new two-decker. For the remainder of the summer he cruised outside the Texel and then returned to Yarmouth in time to celebrate the first anniversary of Camperdown. Little happened in the North Sea fleet for the rest of the year, except that in December, Vice Admiral Onslow retired and was replaced by Vice Admiral Dickson.

In the summer of 1799, Pitt and Spencer again began to think about another attempt to invade Holland. This time they thought they had a better chance of success. It appeared that the Dutch were growing weary of their French allies, and after Camperdown they had less of a fleet to send against an invading force. In addition to British troops under General Abercromby, a number of Russian soldiers had been promised. Vice Adm. Andrew Mitchell was assigned to the North Sea in command of the escort. The expedition set out from Yarmouth on 12 August 1799. By agreement Duncan had command of all sea forces, but Mitchell had the freedom to act independently inshore. The commander-in-chief would remain in deeper water until needed.

On 27 August the first attack was made against the batteries of the Helder, overlooking the Texel. To his regret, the admiral took no part in this action, as he wrote to the First Lord: "I cannot say I ever experienced a more anxious day than yesterday, for I find it requires better nerves to look at fighting than to be in it."[44] Three days later, the Dutch fleet in the Texel surrendered.

Throughout the expedition Duncan's health had not been good. Toward the end of August, it took a turn for the worse, and on 1 September he returned to Yarmouth. For most of the first half of September, the admiral was severely ill, and was even reported to be near death. He recovered, but he never again went to sea in command of a fleet.

Meanwhile, back at the Helder, little progress was made after the early days of the invasion. Soon the British and Russian forces were pinned down near the coast. Fighting continued until the middle of October, and the land forces were evacuated in November.

Although Duncan had recovered from the worst of his indisposition by the middle of September, it was some time longer before he regained his normal level of activity. In spite of the fact that he was in better health, the old admiral decided to retire. Not only was his constitution no longer fit to face the rigors of the North Sea, but also, as the Dutch fleet had been virtually eliminated, there seemed no further use for an officer of his rank in those waters. In late April 1800 he hauled down his flag and went ashore for the last time. The North Sea fleet, now much reduced, fell to the command of Vice Admiral Dickson.

Although Duncan was eager at first to return to Scotland to live in peace and quiet, he had a restless retirement. He took Vice Admiral Mitchell to court over the prize money from the Dutch ships captured during the Helder expedition. This sort of dispute was in no way unusual. Throughout the eighteenth and early nineteenth centuries, court cases over the distribution of prize money were a favorite recreation of senior officers.

But even a bit of haggling over prize money did not satisfy the admiral's need to remain active. By the time Pitt's administration fell in February 1801, he felt he was ready to take another command. In a letter to Lord St. Vincent congratulating him on becoming First Lord, he strongly hinted that he was available, but nothing came of it. In August 1803 Admiral Cornwallis considered retiring from command of the Channel fleet, and Duncan was named as the prime candidate to succeed him. However, Cornwallis changed his mind, leaving Duncan on shore.

When his wife's uncle, Lord Melville, became First Lord in May 1804, the old admiral hoped that he would be employed again. In July, at the age of seventy-three, he traveled down to London to offer his services, but was turned down as being too old and infirm. Disappointed, the old man turned for home. He never reached it.

Having retired to bed in apparent good health at an inn near Coldstream on 3 August 1803, he was awakened shortly before midnight by stomach pains. He took a draft of medicine, but this had no effect. Within less than two hours, he was dead.

The admiral was succeeded by his third son, Robert (his eldest son, William, died in infancy, and his second son, Alexander, died in 1803). In 1831 William IV, who as a young man had been friendly with Duncan and his family, was coronated king of England. Apparently he was one of those who had thought that Duncan should have been made an earl after

Camperdown. Not only did he create the admiral's son Earl of Camperdown, but also he made the unique decree that all the admiral's children should rank as the children of an earl. The admiral's great-grandson served as a lord of the Admiralty in the 1870s.

That grand old ship the *Venerable* did not long survive her most famous commander. On 24 November 1804 she ran aground on some rocks near Berry Head. Nearly all her officers and men were saved. As a final irony, the last British ship to bear the name of *Venerable,* an aircraft carrier built in 1943, was sold to the Dutch in 1948. She was swiftly renamed the *Karel Doorman.*

RICHARD HOWE, 1726–1799

Engraving by W. T. Fry from a painting by Gainsbro Dupoint

ALEXANDER HOOD, 1727–1814

Engraving by S. Freeman from a painting by L. F. Abbott

SAMUEL HOOD, 1724–1816

Engraving by James Northcote Henry Kingsbury

U.S. Naval Academy Museum

JOHN JERVIS, 1735–1823

Engraving by J. Cochran from a painting by J. Keenan

ADAM DUNCAN, 1731–1804

Engraving by J. Andrews from a painting by J. Hoppner

GEORGE KEITH ELPHINSTONE, 1746–1823

Engraving by W. Holl from a painting by J. Hoppner

JAMES GAMBIER, 1756–1833

Engraving by W. Holl from a painting by Sir William Beechey

EDWARD PELLEW, 1757–1833

Engraving by W. Holl from a painting by William Owen

Chapter 6

GEORGE KEITH
ELPHINSTONE

1746–1823

C APTAIN ELPHINSTONE of the *Robust* (74) was one of the more senior captains in the fleet assembled under the command of Admiral Lord Hood. For a naval officer, he had more experience in land warfare than most. During the American War of Independence, he had taken part in the siege and capture of Charleston. For that reason the commander in chief of the British Mediterranean fleet selected him to lead the naval contingent in the first attack on the republican forces at Toulon.

On 27 August 1793 the fleet landed a force of about 1,500 soldiers accompanied by 200 seamen and marines.[1] These men were landed near Fort La Malgue, a battery that commanded the harbor and prevented British ships from resting comfortably at the main French Mediterranean base. Taking command of both military and naval forces, Elphinstone led them up the slope, and the republicans fled before them. Before long the British were in full possession of the fort, and the captain was appointed governor.

But that was far from the end of Elphinstone's activities ashore. A few days later he learned that a large republican force lay only five miles from his position. Gathering up a collection of British and Spanish troops with six pieces of artillery, the captain led his men (about six hundred all together) toward a heavily defended bridge. For a short time the republicans resisted, but finding that they could do nothing to stop the onslaught, they deserted their posts for the rear. The artillery and ammunition they left behind were put to good use by their enemies. As James states, the "success of Captain Elphinstone in this affair gained him many compliments on his knowledge of military tactics, so little expected in an officer of the navy."[2]

The Honorable George Keith Elphinstone, later Viscount Keith, was a dour, sardonic Scotsman. From his correspondence and accounts of his life, it appears that the comprehension of a simple joke would have stretched his imagination to its limits. His personal life was virtuous, if unromantic, which made him intolerant of the marital failings of others. Elphinstone himself appears to have been ruled by the head rather than the heart in his dealings with women. He married twice, both times to women with generous expectations. However, he must have possessed a certain degree of charm to convince the scholarly and independent Hester Thrale to accept him as a husband.

Elphinstone's best qualities as a commander appear to be steadiness and perseverance. At no time in his career did he demonstrate the flashes of brilliance that characterized some of his contemporaries, but neither did he become embroiled in controversy or commit any irreparable errors. His reputation was for luck rather than native talent, but luck was considered a valuable commodity in the eighteenth- and early-nineteenth-century navy. Because of these qualities and his noble connections, he rarely had difficulty finding employment.

In appearance Elphinstone was no more distinctive than in his career. He was of medium height and build, with regular features and a ruddy complexion. The erect carriage of his head, the heaviness of his eyelids and eyebrows, and the set of his mouth give him a haughty expression in virtually every portrait. This appearance is a reasonable reflection of his personality. In his long career he made no strong friendships and never wrote enthusiastically about the deeds of a fellow officer. In comparing him with other admirals already profiled in this book, he was in truth as aloof as Howe appeared to be, and he possessed all of St. Vincent's coldness, unleavened by a sense of humor or sincere regard for the welfare of his subordinates.

. . .

Charles Elphinstone, the tenth lord Elphinstone, was not a wealthy peer, and he possessed the questionable blessing of a large family. When his fifth son, George Keith, was born on 7 January 1746, it was plain that all but his eldest son would have to make their own ways in the world. For an impecunious nobleman with a plenitude of children, the least expensive method for establishing his sons was to send them aboard His Majesty's ships. Of George's four elder brothers, two preceded him into the navy. Lord Elphinstone's second son, Charles, was a midshipman aboard the *Prince George* (90) in the Mediterranean when she accidentally caught fire and burned in 1758. Mr. Charles Elphinstone was among the 485 crew members who lost their lives in the conflagration.[3]

The third son, William, joined the navy in his turn, but soon found the service of the East India Company more profitable. He amassed a large fortune in the East and was later in a position to aid his younger brother when the navy was unable to find a ship for him.

Like his brothers, George was educated in Glasgow with the intention of sending him to sea as soon as he was old enough to stand the rigors of a midshipman's life. Mr. Elphinstone was fortunate in his first ship. In the autumn of 1761, he was entered aboard the *Gosport* (44), under the command of Capt. John Jervis, the eventual Earl of St. Vincent, then a novice post captain. As described in chapter 4, the *Gosport* spent the majority of her time in convoy duty.

In 1762 the *Gosport* joined the squadron under Commodore Lord Colville, who was blockading the French commodore de Ternay at Newfoundland while troops fought ashore. The British soon recaptured the disputed territory, but the French fleet managed to escape when the blockading squadron was driven off by a storm. Thus a sea battle was avoided. After a year and a half in the wartime navy in which he had yet to hear a shot fired in anger, George left the *Gosport* when she was paid off in the spring of 1763.

During the mid-1760s Midshipman Elphinstone served in turn aboard the *Juno* (32), the *Lively* (20), and the *Emerald* (32). These vessels were commanded by undistinguished captains, and the duty was routine. In search of more steady and profitable employment, Elphinstone entered aboard the East India Company ship *Triton* in 1767. This vessel was commanded by his elder brother William, making it easy for the twenty-one-year-old George to find a berth as third mate. For the next two years, the Elphinstone brothers sailed between Britain and the Orient.

Then, in December 1769, a short time after his return to England, George was appointed to the *Stag* (32), a naval vessel bound for the East Indies. It is likely that his familiarity with the passage and the lands the ship was to visit were useful to him in gaining the appointment that rejuvenated his naval career. From that point on, there was never again any question of which service George Elphinstone would follow.

While stationed in India, Mr. Elphinstone was promoted to the rank of lieutenant, on 28 June 1770. In the following October, he left the *Stag* and returned to England.

Lieutenant Elphinstone did not remain on the beach long after his return. In May 1771 he was commissioned aboard the *Trident* (64), flagship of Rear Adm. Sir Peter Dennis, commander of the Mediterranean fleet. As many other officers had learned before him, appointments to flagships generally led to promotions. On 18 September 1772 Elphinstone made the transition to the rank of commander. He came aboard the *Scorpion* (14) sloop-of-war and soon was on his way to England with dispatches. Toward the end of the year, he was sent back to the Mediterranean and thence for a cruise in the vicinity of Minorca and the Italian coast.

After one and a half years of uninterrupted Mediterranean service, the *Scorpion* was sent home and paid off in 1774. On 12 March 1775 Elphinstone was made post into the *Romney* (50) and soon sent as an escort protecting merchant convoys bound for Newfoundland.

Captain Elphinstone served in the *Romney* for a year, during which time he journeyed to the New World and back. Then, in March 1776, with the war in North America well under way, he was commissioned to the *Perseus* (20), a new frigate to be made ready for service in the western Atlantic. The new vessel required some months to fit out, and then a while longer to gather her convoy. Finally, in late July, the *Perseus* set sail for New York and successfully brought her charges into port.

For the next two years, Captain Elphinstone spent his time cruising in and out of New York. While at sea he escorted coastal convoys and sought out enemy privateers. Closer in to shore he supported the troops fighting the rebels.

In December 1779, Vice Adm. Marriot Arbuthnot received orders to embark 8,500 soldiers commanded by generals Clinton and Cornwallis. The original intention had been to relieve the king's forces that had been under siege at Savannah since the beginning of October. But before the fleet departed on 26 December, the news came that the siege had been lifted. Nonetheless, General Clinton was determined to make his presence felt in the southern colonies. If others had secured Savannah for the king, Charleston, the fourth-largest city in the rebelling colonies, lay ripe for the taking. Clinton decided to conquer Charleston and then turn north as the opportunity allowed.

The force that accompanied Arbuthnot's five ships of the line and the transports southward included nine frigates, among them the *Perseus*.[4] The journey was plagued by weather so foul that one of the transports was blown all the way to Cornwall. But finally, at the end of January, the fleet reached the sheltered waters off Tybee Island near Savannah. Clinton allowed his men about a fortnight to rest. Then he reembarked the troops and sailed northward. He arrived approximately thirty miles south of Charleston on 10 February and started landing troops the next day.

At the time the British landed, Charleston was poorly defended. The fortifications that had driven off an earlier attack in 1776 had been allowed to deteriorate, and the men immediately available to the rebel General Lincoln were few. As soon as he heard that the enemy had landed to the south, the American commander set about rebuilding his fortifications and gathering as many troops as he could lay his hands on. Ultimately he managed to collect a total of slightly over five thousand assorted Continentals and militia.

Meanwhile, the British were moving with great deliberation. They marched up the coast until they reached the banks of the Ashley River immediately across from the city. But it was not until the fleet entered the harbor that the army attempted to move farther.

Arbuthnot's fleet arrived off the harbor entrance on 4 March. The only obstacles to their entering were a few small rebel vessels, a bar too shallow for the ships of the line to cross, and Fort Moultrie on the north end of the entrance. More than a fortnight was needed to unload sufficient cannon, provisions, and water for the larger vessels to float high enough to clear the bar. In the middle of the month, the fleet started to cross into the harbor. Then the officers met to consider how they would face their next obstacle, Fort Moultrie. This fort had fought off a squadron under the command of Sir Peter Parker in 1776, so Arbuthnot was inclined to approach it cautiously. He decided not to make Sir Peter Parker's mistake of attacking the fort from the sea. He chose to avoid it, but it was not until 9 April that he was ready to attempt the run past. Although the fort fired and several vessels were hit, three ships of the line and an equal number of frigates successfully passed into the inner harbor. The few American ships present were withdrawn behind a barrier of sunken vessels and a boom in the Cooper River to the north of the city. Charleston was now completely cut off by land and sea.

The day following the passage of British ships into the inner harbor, Clinton and Arbuthnot called upon Lincoln to surrender, but the American general refused. Both sides settled in for a siege. By 13 April a combined army and navy force had constructed batteries that rained shells and red-hot shot down on the city's defenders. One of the naval officers commanding the shore detachments was Captain Elphinstone.

By the time the siege was a fortnight old, the situation inside the city was growing desperate. It was clear that they could expect no help from outside, so if the British were to be driven off and the largest concentration of American regulars in the south saved, it must be done from within. On 24 April, Lincoln attempted a sortie, but with little success. The British drove his men back into the city, suffering few losses.

On 6 May, Fort Moultrie fell into British hands, and by the eighth Lincoln was ready to surrender. His only condition, that his troops be allowed full military honors, was rejected by the enemy high command. So the siege continued with more shot and shell, pounding the city into ruins. Finally, on 12 May, Lincoln surrendered unconditionally. With the city of Charleston, the British captured 4,500 rebel troops and a quantity of supplies and weapons. The price of victory was 76 killed and 189 wounded against approximately 250 American casualties.[5]

Shortly after the surrender of Charleston, the *Perseus* was sent back to Britain with dispatches. The frigate was paid off a month after her arrival in June, but her captain was immediately commissioned to the *Warwick* (50), in which he spent the balance of the year cruising Britain's coastal waters.

While Captain Elphinstone was stationed near home, he was elected to Parliament for Dumbartonshire. Unlike many officers of his era, he took no side in the intense political debates that continued as long as the Earl of Sandwich remained First Lord of the Admiralty. Indeed, he was one of the few who attempted to reach a compromise between the two sides.

While cruising in the Channel at the beginning of January 1781, the *Warwick* encountered the Dutch two-decker *Rotterdam* (50), which had recently fought another British fifty-gun ship but had managed to escape. This time the Dutchman was not so lucky. Although a sizable fraction of the *Warwick*'s crew was away in prizes, Captain Elphinstone engaged the *Rotterdam* and took her without the loss of any of his own men.

Toward the end of March, the *Warwick* sailed from Cork as one of the escorts of a convoy bound for North America. Once again Elphinstone found himself on the western side of the Atlantic for an extended stay. He continued on convoy duty between New York and Charleston and therefore took no part in the action off the Virginia Capes (see chapter 3) in September. He returned to New York in time to meet the fleet coming back for reinforcements after the battle, and joined it as it traveled south again. The *Warwick* was used as a scout ahead of the fleet, and it was her captain who discovered that Cornwallis had already surrendered.

Late in the year a new midshipman came aboard the *Warwick*. The lad was in most ways typical of junior officers of the era—except that his father happened to be king of Great Britain. His name was Prince William Henry, later to become Duke of Clarence and ultimately King William IV. The prince was to encounter a number of future great admirals during the active portion of his naval career. Not only did he serve with Elphinstone and Lord Hood, and dine at Duncan's table, but also he became friends with Nelson in the West Indies after the war.

Although most of the action on the North American continent was completed by the beginning of 1782, the war with France continued. Through the year the *Warwick* convoyed and cruised between Halifax and New York. On 12 September, while in company with the *Lion* (64), *Vestal* (28), and *Bonetta* (14) off the Delaware River, she encountered two French vessels, the *Aigle* (38) and the smaller *Gloire*. These two ships had earlier in the day captured the British brig *Raccoon* (14), but they had no desire to face such a formidable squadron. They fled up the Delaware, electing to enter a shallow channel where they hoped the British would not be able to pursue them. But they had reckoned without the persistent Captain Elphinstone. He followed close on their heels for two days. He did not come close enough to compel the French to face him broadside to broadside, but eventually he managed to force the *Aigle* to run aground. The *Warwick* followed no farther, fearing to meet the same fate as the French ship, but the *Vestal* and *Bonetta* ranged themselves alongside the helpless *Aigle* and pounded her into submission. Before he struck his flag, the French commander cut away his masts and tried to scuttle the ship. But the British were able to keep her afloat and soon had her repaired. She was to serve in the Royal Navy until 1798.[6]

Some time after the pursuit of the *Aigle,* Captain Elphinstone turned the care of his royal midshipman over to Lord Hood. The commander of the *Warwick* was beginning to feel unwell after such a long period of nearly constant service in foreign waters. He requested to be allowed to return home, and in November he arrived, and the *Warwick* was paid off. Briefly Elphinstone commanded the *Carysfort* (28) at Portsmouth, but with the war drawing to a close, that vessel too was soon paid off.

After he left his last frigate command, Elphinstone lived ashore and attended Parliament. As he began to feel more energetic, he found the opportunity to court Jane Mercer, the elder daughter and coheiress of Col. William Mercer, whom he married on 10 April 1787. Although at the age of forty-one he was a trifle tardy in starting a family, it was not long before the union was blessed with a daughter, Margaret, who was born 12 June 1788. Unfortunately, Jane died in December 1789, leaving her husband with a child a year and half old.

The captain had considered marriage no bar to his continued career. Less than half a year after his wedding, he was writing to the Admiralty to inform them that he was "ready to receive their lordships' commands."[7] Like many another naval officer in peacetime, he sent periodic missives to the Admiralty to remind them of his merits, but no commands were forthcoming. The years 1790 through 1792 were among the quietest of Elphinstone's career. He left Parliament and held no commands. But with the beginning of war in 1793, he resumed his active life. Virtually simultaneously with the news that Britain was at war came the captain's commission to the *Robust* (74) and orders to prepare her to sail to the Mediterranean.

Squadrons departed for Gibraltar throughout the spring of 1793, but the *Robust* remained at Portsmouth until Admiral Hood himself was ready to sail in May. As described in chapter 3, when the British fleet arrived off Toulon in August, they were invited by royalist delegates to take possession of the town. His lordship accepted the invitation, and on 27 August sent Captain Elphinstone ashore with soldiers, seamen, and marines to seize Fort La Malgue, thereby permitting safe passage of the British fleet into the Great Road.

As governor of Fort La Malgue, Elphinstone spent much of his time ashore. While more and more republican troops swarmed around Toulon, skirmishes between the two sides became increasingly frequent and alarming. On 30 September the French took advantage of a foggy night to surprise a small Spanish force manning the heights of Pharon overlooking Toulon. They drove off or made prisoners of the Spaniards and started to settle in, preparing to drop various missiles on the town below. But the day after Pharon was taken, Brigadier General Lord Mulgrave led a mixed force against the enemy. Captain Elphinstone commanded the British naval contingent in this action, in which the allies completely overwhelmed the disorganized republicans. The allies lost only 8 killed and 72 wounded, whereas the French casualties amounted to as many as 1,500.[8]

Although the French were driven from the heights on this occasion, they continued to hem Toulon in greater numbers while the force of the allies was decreased by illness. By mid-November the republicans regained possession of Pharon, and in such numbers that the allies could not hope to drive them off. In the face of an increasingly untenable position, the allied commanders decided that their only option was evacuation. Captain Elphinstone remained ashore almost to the last. Fort La Malgue was abandoned on 18 December, only after nearly all those who could be evacuated had been loaded into the ships. Elphinstone still remained behind to oversee the final stages of the evacuation and left the shore in one of the last boats.

While Lord Hood undertook his operations to capture Corsica, as described in chapter 3, the captain of the *Robust* was sent back to England as commander of the escort protecting the French prizes taken at Toulon. Shortly after his homecoming, Elphinstone found that he had been promoted to rear admiral in April 1794. On 30 May he became a knight of the Bath in honor of his deeds as governor of Fort La Malgue.

The newly made rear admiral enjoyed a summer at home, and in the autumn he hoisted his flag aboard the *Barfleur* (98), one of the flagships of the Channel fleet under Lord Howe. However, he did not remain in home waters for long. Once the Netherlands became allies of the French, Britain decided to act against the Dutch colonies. One of the most strategic targets was the settlement at the Cape of Good Hope. The intention was to send a squadron sufficiently powerful to intimidate the governor of Cape Town into surrendering without a fight. But if force became necessary, the admiral commanding the squadron would be free to use it. On 4 April 1795 the squadron departed for the Cape of Good Hope. Sir George flew his flag aboard the *Monarch* (74). The rest of his command consisted of four ships of the line and two sloops-of-war.[9] Aboard the ships of the squadron was a detachment of the Seventy-Eighth Regiment.

After more than three months at sea, the squadron arrived at Simon's Bay in July. Thinking that the Dutch would prefer to give their allegiance to their hereditary prince rather than to a parcel of French-backed republicans, Elphinstone, who had become a vice admiral since weighing anchor, gave the governor of the colony the option of throwing off the revolutionary yoke. The governor refused and attempted to burn Simon's Town rather than let it fall into enemy hands. But he was forestalled by a foray of soldiers and marines on 14 July. The Dutch were compelled to withdraw to within six miles of Cape Town while the British settled in at Simon's Town. To reinforce the soldiers and marines already ashore, the admiral also landed one thousand seamen. By 7 August the entire invading force was ready to advance on the enemy. Supported by the two 64s and the two sloops, the soldiers marched along the coast. The Dutch had set up a few small batteries in an attempt to hold the British off, but a series of short bombardments from the men-of-war soon compelled the enemy to abandon their positions.

At the end of the first day, the British had advanced more than half the distance to Cape Town, and the Dutch had nothing to show for their efforts except the loss of their camp of the night before. The next day, with reinforcements, the enemy advanced from Cape Town. The British stood fast in the face of all that could be brought against them and soon compelled the Dutch to retreat.

For the rest of August the two sides remained where they were—the Dutch in Cape Town, and the British occupying the original enemy camp. Elphinstone set about seizing all Dutch vessels within Simon's Bay, including five Indiamen, one of which he had fitted out as a man-of-war of twenty guns.

At the beginning of September, the Dutch again made serious efforts to drive the British away, and at first it appeared that they might succeed. On the third they assembled every man under arms who heeded the call, and advanced. They might have succeeded in pushing their enemies back to Simon's Town, except that just as the Dutch prepared to attack, British reinforcements arrived from England, and they compelled the foe to retreat to the safety of their fortifications.

With his augmented force, Sir George felt he had enough strength to assail Cape Town directly. He allowed nearly a fortnight for his troops and supplies to be brought ashore. Then, on 14 September, he set off again, his seamen dragging ships' guns through the deep sand. Meanwhile, a few of the ships of his squadron sailed into Table Bay to create a diversion that would draw fire from the troops marching over land. Although the Dutch resisted as best they could, they were unable to stop such an overwhelming force. By evening, the governor was ready to capitulate. After a few days of negotiations, Cape Town became a British possession.

The British spent the remainder of the year making themselves at home in their new colony. The admiral's orders from Lord Spencer had stipulated that once Cape Town was taken, his next target was to be the Dutch colonies in the East Indies. But once he succeeded in achieving his first goal, Elphinstone's health broke down. He did not sail until the end of 1795. He reached Madras in January, only to find that Rear Admiral Rainier was well on the way toward capturing Ceylon. Although the senior flag officer remained in the region until the island capitulated on 15 February, he was too ill to take an active role.

Some time after the capture of Ceylon, Elphinstone learned that a Dutch squadron had eluded the North Sea fleet in February and was believed to be on the way to the Cape of Good Hope. Soon he put about for Cape Town. He arrived in May but found that there had been as yet no sign of the Dutch squadron. Confident that the enemy would eventually appear, the British admiral awaited them in Simon's Bay.

On 3 August, word reached the squadron off Cape Town that an enemy fleet had been sighted some fifty or sixty miles to the north. Unfortunately, this long-awaited news came at an inconvenient time. The weather was stormy, and the flagship was undergoing repairs. It was not until the sixth that Elphinstone was finally able to lead his squadron to sea. Hearing that several strangers had been sighted to the southwest, the admiral set his course in that direction. However, the weather again became violent, damaging some of the British ships so much that they were forced to return to

Simon's Bay for repairs. Finally, on the fifteenth, Elphinstone led a force of eight two-deckers, two frigates, and four sloops toward Saldanha Bay, where the Dutch still lay at anchor.[10]

The Dutch government had seriously underestimated the size of the force the British had in these far southern waters. They had sent Rear Admiral Lucas with only five small two-deckers, two frigates, and two sloops.[11] When the British arrived on 16 September, they sailed boldly into the bay, anchoring within gunshot of the enemy. In the face of this threat, Lucas had little choice but to surrender.

Still suffering from ill health, Elphinstone resigned his command, leaving Rear Adm. Thomas Pringle, who had joined him when he returned from the East Indies, as commander in chief of the station. He sailed for home in October and landed in England on 3 January 1797.

As a reward for the capture of Cape Town, Sir George Elphinstone became Baron Keith of Stonehaven in the Irish peerage. He rested for a time to recover his health. The only action he took on behalf of his country was to attend sessions of Parliament, now representing Stirlingshire. But as the spring of 1797 warmed, the admiral grew restless and wrote to the Admiralty to notify them that he was available. He soon received a reply assigning him to quell the mutiny raging at the Nore.

As described in chapter 5, the seamen of the fleet anchored in the mouth of the Thames had mutinied in the middle of May. Their original intention had been to support their brethren at Spithead, who had struck for higher wages in April. But when the matter at Spithead was settled soon after the beginning of the outbreak at the Nore, the seamen continued to defy their officers. They felt that they should be accorded the same treatment as the mutineers at Spithead, including a visit from the First Lord of the Admiralty and the removal of obnoxious officers. The port admiral was a weak-willed man unequal to the crisis. When Vice Admiral Keith began to express interest in resuming active duty, Lord Spencer had been seeking a stronger flag officer to assume the role of second-in-command. Although Keith was officially subordinate to Vice Adm. Charles Buckner, it was intended that he would take overall command of the forces being gathered to counter the mutineers. The commander of the station was instructed to cooperate with the new arrival and give him the benefit of his assistance.

When Keith arrived at Sheerness on 2 June 1797, he discovered that the mutineers had recently been reinforced by seven ships from the North Sea fleet, which had strengthened their resolve. Keith decided that the best way to defeat the mutiny was to maintain a strict blockade. Not only did he not allow supplies to be brought out to the seamen, but also he refused to let them ashore for any reason. Even sick men who were landed by their shipmates were sent back without delay. In addition he brought together a large body of trustworthy men to whom he gave the authority to patrol the waterfront and defend the town of Sheerness from any depredations by mutineers.

While the mutinous ships pooled their dwindling provisions as best they could, the admiral experienced his own shortages. The naval victualer in the vicinity had not been prepared to provide for Keith's defense force. His stock of beer was soon depleted, and the local brewers refused to supply the navy with any more of the vital fluid upon which the home fleets ran. The navy already owed them a large sum of money, and like the seamen of the Nore, they wanted to be sure the government was acting in good faith before they worked for it again. There were stores of rum and fortified wine available, but visions of drunken defenders doing worse damage than any party of mutineers prevented the admiral from issuing these stores to his men.

Although Keith had his difficulties ashore, the situation of the mutineers was far worse. Matters had progressed too far for the Nore mutineers to hope for the blanket pardon that had been granted their brethren at Spithead. If they surrendered, some would certainly hang. Those who were most in fear for their necks wanted to sail the fleet away and turn it over to the enemy or make for a foreign shore where they could lose themselves in anonymity. But the majority of the seamen felt secure that they would escape punishment if they surrendered, and they feared that if they tried to sail they would run aground because Keith had caused the channel markers to be removed. When the chief mutineer gave the order to weigh anchor on 10 June, not a single capstan was manned, and the ships remained at the Nore. After that, it was clear that the mutiny was doomed.

Several of the less dedicated vessels took advantage of the confusion after the attempt to weigh anchor to cut their cables and escape upstream. As soon as the ships that managed to get away reached safety, Keith had himself rowed out to them. He was not interested in congratulating the officers for their escape or their ships' companies for their loyalty. His chief concern was to gather as much evidence as he could find to be used in determining who the ringleaders were and in prosecuting them when they were brought to trial.

Meanwhile, the head mutineers desperately tried to rally the recanting seamen to the cause. But hoping to be treated leniently, most of the sailors were ready to return to duty. By 12 June all but two vessels had struck the red flag of rebellion. The harsh line dictated by the government, which demanded unconditional surrender, brought out a temporary resurgence, but most of the mutineers had had enough. As Lord Keith came aboard each ship over the next two days, the red flags were again hauled down in submission. A few desperate characters escaped, but most ringleaders were turned over to the admiral. By 15 June the mutiny was over.

As a reward for his efforts against the mutineers, Keith was appointed second-in-command of the Channel fleet under Lord Bridport on 23 June. At Portsmouth, Lord Keith hoisted his flag aboard the *Queen Charlotte* (100), former flagship of the Spithead mutiny. As mentioned in chapters 2 and 4, the period after the conclusion of the mutinies was marked by numerous acts of insubordination. The seamen had started to lose the habit of obeying their officers without question, and it proved difficult for them to regain the habit once the mutinies were over. Several ships in the Channel fleet reported difficulties during the summer and autumn of 1797. There are no incidents reported aboard the *Queen Charlotte* during that period, but later assessments of the ship indicated that she was still considered a hotbed of sedition.

As second-in-command to Lord Bridport, Keith cruised periodically off the coast of France, but he spent at least as much time at anchor at Spithead or St. Helens as he did off the enemy's port. Occasionally the French were able to slip through the weak blockade, but they rarely accomplished much. After a year of such service, the vice admiral began to look about him for a more active station. Early in 1799 Keith was commissioned second-in-command of the Mediterranean fleet, with an eye toward replacing the ailing Earl of St. Vincent. He hoisted his flag aboard the *Foudroyant* (80) and sailed southward before the coming of spring.

Upon his arrival Keith was first given the task of blockading the Spanish fleet at Cadiz with a force that varied between eleven and fifteen ships of the line.[12] He transferred his flag from the two-decker *Foudroyant* to the roomier three-decker *Barfleur*. Periodically, when his fleet ran short of water, he put in to Tetuan, leaving only a few frigates to watch the enemy. But even while the British were absent, the Spanish remained at anchor.

While Keith was keeping watch over Cadiz, a large French fleet, including twenty-five ships of the line, under the command of Vice Adm. Eustache Bruix, escaped from Brest on 25 April 1799. This fleet was bound for the Mediterranean, and the only force of size in its way was Keith's fifteen ships of the line.

The vice admiral was returning from a watering stop at Tetuan when the news reached him that five Spanish ships of the line had sailed from Ferrol and that Bruix had been sighted heading in his direction. Immediately he gave the command for his fleet to prepare for action. He also sent word to the commander in chief at Gibraltar.

Forming line of battle, Keith's fleet awaited the arrival of the French. On the morning of 4 May, they sighted the enemy to the west-northwest. At first it appeared that Bruix was willing to fight, and the two fleets sailed along on the same tack. But the French, having the wind gauge and a gale to push them along at a great clip, decided to decline action. By the end of the day, they had disappeared into the haze, with Keith still vainly trailing after them.

The next morning four French ships of the line were in sight, but these too soon escaped, and the British vice admiral decided that there was no point in chasing them any further. He returned to Cadiz to ascertain that the Spaniards were likely to remain in port; then he made for Gibraltar to meet up with the commander in chief. As described in chapter 4, Keith arrived on 10 May and sailed two days later for Minorca to join forces with Rear Admiral Duckworth. Bruix never approached Minorca, preferring to put into Toulon, but the absence of the British fleet outside Cadiz allowed the Spanish to put to sea and make for Cartagena. Although the British placed themselves in a position to intercept the enemy if they should try to make a juncture, they never met either fleet at sea.

Admiral St. Vincent left the fleet on 2 June, leaving Keith in overall command. One of the vice admiral's first acts after the departure of his senior was to shift his flag back to the *Queen Charlotte*. The British fleet chased over much of the central Mediterranean, following reported sightings of the French. But Bruix was long gone. He exited the sea on 24 June while Keith was still chasing his tail somewhere off the coast of Italy.

Not knowing that the enemy was on his way back northward, the new commander in chief made for Minorca, where he was reinforced by twelve ships of the Channel fleet. There he also received instructions from St. Vincent to sail westward. He arrived at Gibraltar on 29 July, only to learn that Bruix was long gone. But the vice admiral was tenacious. He continued in pursuit, hoping to catch the enemy at one of the ports between Gibraltar and Brest. He missed them off Cadiz by a little more than a week and, putting on a fine turn of speed, was only two days behind by the time he reached Cape Finisterre. But that was as close as he got. He arrived off Brest on 14 August to find the French and Spanish fleets safely anchored in the bay, having arrived only the day before.

Frustrated by failing to catch the enemy at sea, Keith sailed on to Torbay, where he remained until November. Then he received orders to return to the Mediterranean. Shortly after his return to Gibraltar in December, the admiral became involved in a matter that had been proceeding during his absence.

Although the French fleet off Alexandria had been destroyed during the Battle of the Nile in 1798, a strong French army still existed in Egypt under the command of General Bonaparte. A British squadron remained in the area to keep the enemy from being resupplied but had little direct impact on Bonaparte's conquests. Then, in March 1799, Commo. Sir William Sidney Smith assumed command of the squadron and stopped the French at Acre. Bonaparte then captured Alexandria but decided that he could further his ambitions better in France. He abandoned his army of approximately twenty thousand men under the command of Gen. Jean-Baptiste Kleber and sailed with a few followers on 23 August.

At first Kleber hoped that Bonaparte's return to France would produce either reinforcements or an evacuation fleet. But Bonaparte had other ideas. He made himself First Consul and completely forgot any obligation he had to the men he had left behind in Egypt. Kleber was disgusted when he learned he had been abandoned, but he determined to make the best of the situation and hoped that eventually help would come.

However, the British blockade cut off resupply, and the French soldiers were weary and ill. Hoping to save his army intact for more important campaigns on the Continent, Kleber opened negotiations with Commodore Smith in October 1799. By the beginning of January 1800, he and Smith had reached an agreement. Between them, they decided that Kleber and his men should be allowed to surrender with all the honors of war and then be returned to France in British ships. Because the French soldiers had been so poorly treated by Bonaparte, the English felt that they might help decrease the popularity of the First Consul and even topple him from power.

By the time Lord Keith returned to the Mediterranean, the capitulation agreement had been all but signed. But the commander in chief, newly arrived from home waters, was better informed on present British policy than an officer who had been acting independently in the Mediterranean for several years. The king had decided on a policy of unconditional surrender where the French troops in Egypt were concerned. Hearing of the negotiations at Alexandria, Keith wrote to Kleber, "I have received positive orders from His Majesty not to consent to any capitulation with the French troops which you command."[13] By the time Keith's correspondence reached Smith and Kleber, the French had already begun to evacuate their fortifications. But as soon as he learned that the government had disallowed his treaty, the commodore sent word to the general to reoccupy the fortresses.

Meanwhile, Lord Keith had more urgent matters to concern him. The island of Malta had been taken by the French in 1798 and had been blockaded by the British throughout the year that followed. Keith joined the blockade of Malta in February 1800, but in March he learned of a French invasion of Tuscany and turned his attentions there. On the sixteenth the admiral went ashore at Leghorn, instructing his flag captain to reconnoiter the island of Capraia in his absence. The following morning the *Queen Charlotte* was discovered to be on fire. According to accounts from the survivors, the fire was started by some hay that had been left lying about coming in contact with a piece of lit slow match used to fire a signal gun. The flames consumed the flagship so swiftly that few were able to escape with their lives. Out of 829 people who were aboard the *Queen Charlotte* when she caught fire, only 156 were saved. The flag captain remained behind to the last, trying to save the lives of his ship's company, and perished with the majority.

After the loss of his flagship, Keith hoisted his flag aboard the *Audacious* (74) and later moved aboard the *Minotaur* (74). Meanwhile, the British blockaded and bombarded Genoa, compelling the French to evacuate the city on 4 June. But the arrival of Bonaparte with reinforcements allowed the enemy to press forward again, and by the fourteenth, they had reoccupied Genoa.

While the admiral still had his flag in the *Audacious* in mid-May, the French attempted to attack the blockading force with a galley and a number of smaller oared craft. Although the British flagship was struck with a few shots, the damage was slight and the enemy returned to port. The following night, the British launched a cutting-out expedition against the galley. Although the members of the expedition met with several obstacles and some stiff resistance from the crew, the attackers managed to carry off the prize. Propelled by slaves who saw this as their opportunity to gain freedom, the galley was rowed out to the waiting fleet. As soon as the vessel was out of gunshot from the batteries ashore, the British officers gave permission for the slaves to be freed. The wretches liberated themselves with alacrity and fell to capering with delight about the decks while the galley sailed on toward the flagship. Doubtless they were familiar with Britain's reputation for unfriendliness toward the institution of slavery. Unfortunately for these poor souls, Keith lacked St. Vincent's firm hatred of bondage. He sent them back to the French, along with the prisoners captured with the galley, in hopes that the addition of all those extra mouths to feed would bring the siege to a speedier conclusion. But the French commander at Genoa had no desire to feed the slaves, especially after he heard they had aided the enemy. Instead, he had them marched into the town square and shot.

While the battle for Genoa was still taking place, the British government began to think that allowing General Kleber to return from Egypt with his army intact might not have been such a bad idea after all. In May, Lord Keith received new instructions concerning that campaign and forwarded them to Smith. Immediately the commodore reopened negotiations, hoping that the delay and the bad feeling occasioned by having to go back on his word would not preclude reaching an understanding. Unfortunately, there were factors at work besides the great powers of Britain and France.

On 14 June, Kleber was assassinated by a Muslim fanatic disguised as a beggar. With his death, the situation in Egypt changed. His successor, General Menou, had no desire to evacuate Egypt. He spurned the offer of capitulation with scorn.

Following the loss of Genoa, Keith led his squadron first to Leghorn and then to Minorca, where he shifted his flag aboard the *Foudroyant*. By the end of the summer, he arrived at Gibraltar, where he was joined by transports under the command of Rear Adm. Sir John Warren and troops under the command of Gen. Sir Ralph Abercromby. The original purpose for sending Abercromby with sixteen thousand men to Gibraltar was to assault Cadiz. But when the fleet arrived off the coast of Spain on 5 October, they learned that there was a plague raging ashore. Fearing disease more than Spanish guns, Keith and Abercromby abandoned the assault on Cadiz and decided to turn toward Egypt instead.

At the end of October the expedition sailed for Alexandria. The force under the admiral's command consisted of seven two-deckers, two frigates, two bombs, seven sloops, and thirty-nine transports.[14] Followed by stormy weather, the fleet put into Marmorice, where they disembarked the soldiers and remained until 22 February 1801. Lord Keith, who had become a full admiral on 1 January, finally led his fleet into Aboukir Bay on 2 March.

Once again Keith's movements were hampered by bad weather. He could not begin to land the troops until nearly a week after he put into Aboukir Bay. When the weather finally calmed enough for the invasion to begin, sixty flatboats capable of carrying fifty men apiece, more than ninety launches large enough for thirty men, and a vast number of smaller craft were employed to ferry more than seven thousand men ashore in a single day. In the face of the landing, the French put up a stiff resistance. They poured artillery fire down on the British from a ridge above the beach, the infantry sniped from behind sand dunes, and the cavalry charged with sabers. But all these efforts were to no avail. The British stormed the enemy defenses, drove off the defenders, and occupied the beach.

Both sides remained at rest for the first few days following the landing, but on 13 March the French returned in greater numbers. They were again driven off, and the invaders advanced to within three miles of Alexandria. By the eighteenth, they had possession of Aboukir Castle, and the prospects for the swift conquest of Egypt appeared good. On the twenty-first the French made a final effort to throw the British back into the sea. They attacked with great savagery, eventually causing more than 1,450 British casualties against approximately 1,500 of their own.[15] Among those wounded in the battle was General Abercromby, who received a musket ball in the hip. He was taken aboard the *Foudroyant* to receive treatment, but he died a few days later. He was succeeded by Maj. Gen. John Hutchinson.

Following the encirclement of Alexandria, the British sailed up the Nile to take Rosetta and eventually Cairo. Among those serving with the British under the command of Sir Sidney Smith were a number of French royalists. They had done significant service, but Lord Keith told them to be gone where they would. "I'll have no foreigners in the fleet," he wrote.[16] Smith too was soon relieved of his duties working with the army as they drove up the Nile.

While the army struggled on toward Rosetta, Keith and the large ships of the fleet patrolled the coast to discourage any French attempts to reinforce or rescue their army. A weak attempt was made by a squadron under the command of Admiral Ganteaume but was easily driven off. Meanwhile, the French at Cairo surrendered on 27 June, leaving only Alexandria to be subdued. The siege of the city, which had begun a few months before, tightened its grip until the besieged were compelled to surrender on 2 September. As part of the terms of their capitulation, the French soldiers were returned to France at British expense.

As a reward for achieving at great cost what Smith had almost accomplished nearly two years earlier by negotiations, Keith was granted the Turkish Order of the Crescent. On 15 December he became a peer of the United Kingdom.

With the signing of the preliminaries of the Peace of Amiens late in 1801, there was little activity in the Mediterranean following the capture of Alexandria. Keith returned home in July 1802, leaving Rear Adm. Sir

Richard Bickerton as commander in chief of the station. The admiral had little time to enjoy the pleasures of home. In March 1803 Keith was offered the command of the fleet based at Plymouth. He took up the post at first, but in May decided that the command of the North Sea fleet was more to his liking. He hoisted his flag in the *Monarch,* flagship of a fleet consisting of nine ships of the line and numerous smaller vessels. The Dutch gave the admiral little trouble, but the French at the southern end of his realm were extremely active.

Throughout the peace the French had been building up an invasion fleet. By the time the new war was a year old, the vessels at Boulogne alone numbered 150.[17] The British had watched the increase in the flotilla with interest, and by the autumn of 1804, they decided to act to decrease its numbers. On 2 October, Lord Keith's fleet attacked, as described in the admiral's own report:

> The operations commenced at a quarter past nine, P.M. and terminated at a quarter past four this morning, during which time several vessels, prepared for the purpose, were exploded amongst, or very near to the flotilla; but on account of the great distance at which they lay from each other, no very extensive injury seems to have been sustained, although it is evident that there has been very considerable confusion amongst them, and that two of the brigs and several of the smaller vessels appear to be missing since yesterday, at the close of the day.[18]

Although several British efforts against the invasion flotilla were largely ineffectual, the boats were never used for the purpose for which they had been constructed. Once his hopes were dashed again at Trafalgar in October 1805, the French emperor turned his thoughts away from the ocean, leaving the British in command of the sea. This was an accomplishment devoutly to be wished by the people of England, but it gave few opportunities for distinction for senior officers. After a relatively uneventful couple of years following the Battle of Trafalgar, Keith resigned command of the North Sea and came ashore in May 1807.

On 10 January 1808 Keith married again. This time he chose a lady who had more than mere wealth to recommend her, although to be sure, she was an heiress too. Hester was the daughter of Samuel Johnson's friends, the Thrales, and the author of the dictionary had a special fondness for this daughter of the family, whom he called "Queenie." By the time she was in her teens, she was described as "a very fine girl, about fourteen years of age, but cold and reserved, though full of knowledge and intelligence."[19]

She spent much of her adult life in seclusion studying Hebrew and mathematics.

At the time of the wedding the groom was sixty-two; the bride, forty-five. Remarkably, the pair produced a daughter in December 1809. Surprisingly, after having lived in seclusion for most of her life, the new Lady Keith become prominent in society. The admiral engaged in his wife's social activities until February 1812, when he was appointed commander in chief of the Channel fleet. This was still a post of honor, but the level of activity demanded had decreased since the days when Howe and St. Vincent held the command. Except for a few single-ship actions, little of note occurred in the Channel until Napoleon's abdication in April 1814. With the coming of peace, the admiral hauled down his flag again. During the ensuing celebrations, many of those who had served the British government throughout the war were rewarded. Among those honored was Lord Keith, who became a viscount.

When Napoleon escaped from Elba and precipitated the war's renewal, Keith was reappointed to the Channel fleet in March 1815. He immediately ordered elements of his fleet to cruise off the coast of France. His decisive action foiled Napoleon's attempt to escape to America following his defeat at Waterloo in June. On 13 July the French emperor boarded a frigate and sailed out, hoping to evade the blockade, but he was stopped by the *Bellerophon* (74). Two days later he surrendered himself to the captain of the same British vessel, who eventually ferried him to the coast of England.

Napoleon had hoped to remain in England for the rest of his days, but the government had determined to send him to St. Helena. Some of the former emperor's friends in England tried a legal subterfuge to keep him in England for a while longer, in hopes that governmental hearts would soften. They arranged to have Napoleon detained as a witness in a trial, but Lord Keith thwarted them by denying French agents access to their emperor. After all attempts to keep him in England failed, Napoleon was kept at sea while the final arrangements were made for his departure for St. Helena. The emperor was transferred to the *Northumberland* (74), where he was received aboard as a general and not as a head of state, in keeping with the policy dictated by the British government. Keith saw to it that his baggage was searched and that Napoleon was settled in the cabin he was to occupy for the duration of his voyage. Then he returned to his flagship, and on 10 August the *Northumberland* weighed anchor for St. Helena.

The sending off of Napoleon was the last act of the admiral's long career. He retired from active service as soon as he was formally relieved of command, and proceeded to live the rest of his life improving his estate of Tul-liallan on the banks of the Forth River. In 1821 he was presented with the Sardinian Order of St. Maurice and St. Lazarus in honor of his Mediter-ranean activities twenty years earlier.

Lord Keith died at his home on 10 March 1823. His elder daughter, wife of the French ambassador in London, succeeded to the title of Baroness Keith. But the barony became extinct upon her death in 1867. The dowager Lady Keith eventually turned her back on the society in which she had been so active while her husband had been alive. She remained in London and devoted herself to works of charity until her death in 1857. Her daughter married first the second son of the Earl of Jersey and then the younger brother of the Duke of Leeds.

Chapter 7

JAMES GAMBIER

1756–1833

THE FRENCH FLEET was in trouble. It was trapped in the Basque Roads with little defense save its own guns, and the main force of the British Channel fleet was patrolling the waters outside. The commander in chief of the Royal Navy forces in March 1809, Admiral Lord Gambier, seemed content to continue his patrolling, keeping the enemy bottled up. But both the Admiralty and his own second-in-command had other ideas. They felt that this opportunity should be used to destroy as much of the French fleet as possible, and they were willing to explore any available method.

Rear Adm. Eliab Harvey had grown tired of waiting for the commander in chief to do something, and he was eager for an opportunity to distinguish himself. He had fought at Trafalgar, but since then, moments when junior flag officers could secure everlasting glory were scarce. He assembled a list of officers and men who volunteered to attack the trapped Frenchmen with fireships and brought it aboard the flagship *Caledonia* (120). Admiral Gambier was awaiting his subordinate on the quarterdeck. He listened calmly as Harvey presented his list; then, when the rear admiral had finished, his lordship informed him that the Admiralty had already chosen Captain Lord Cochrane for the mission.

On learning that he was being passed over for an officer many years his junior, Harvey flew into a towering rage. In full hearing of every member of the flagship's company, he declared that "if he were passed by, and Lord Cochrane, or any other junior officer, appointed in preference, he should immediately strike his flag and resign his commission."[1] Gambier calmly replied to his excited subordinate. He explained that the Admiralty had made the selection, and both admirals would have to live with their decision. His lordship liked the situation as little as did his second-in-command, although for different reasons. He did not think the use of fireships would be either effective or moral. "It is a horrible mode of warfare, and the attempt very hazardous, if not desperate," he protested.[2]

Harvey was not to be mollified. He declared that "he never saw a man so unfit for command of the fleet as Lord Gambier, who instead of sending boats out to sound the channels, which he (Admiral Harvey) considered the best preparation for an attack on the enemy, he had been employing, or rather amusing himself with mustering the ships' companies and had not even taken the pains to ascertain whether the enemy had placed any mortars in front of their lines."[3]

Still in a passion, he swore that even if he received no sanction from the Admiralty or Gambier, he would take it upon himself to sail his flagship right into the bay and cut out a French three-decker. Then, addressing the flagship's complement of officers, he compared himself to the man he was confronting, "Well, this is not the first time I have been lightly treated . . . because I am no canting methodist, no hypocrite, no psalm-singer and do not cheat old women out of their estates by hypocrisy and canting!"[4]

Even this accusation made on his own quarterdeck failed to produce an immediate reaction from Gambier. He allowed the rear admiral to storm back to his own flagship and continue as second-in-command until the task at hand was done. Then, upon mature reflection, he had Harvey court-martialed.

. . .

Opinions on James Gambier the younger (the elder was his uncle, an admiral during the American War of Independence) differ widely, depending on the author consulted, but all agree that he was a deeply religious man, so much so that it was worthy of note even in an age when faith was a given.

In the Royal Navy, Gambier was noted for dispensing tracts and paying particular attention to the Sabbath services, which were often perfunctory on other vessels. For these character traits, he was known by the sailors as "Dismal Jimmie." One midshipman who served under him described the conditions of a ship under his command as follows: "Our captain in all his arrangements evinced a determination to enforce his religious principles on board the ship under his command. He had prayers in his cabin twice a day, morning and evening. I was obliged to attend every morning with the other young mids, he in person superintending."[5]

Gambier's religious convictions were so strong that he was one of very few captains who enforced the rule that the only women allowed aboard his ships were those who could prove they were the seamen's wives. He conducted a forceful campaign against swearing, by which a man found guilty of profanity was compelled to wear a wooden collar about his neck from which were suspended two 32-pound shot. The practice was discontinued only when the weight of the collar and the shot injured one of the men who had been forced to wear it.

Although Gambier could be a stern disciplinarian, he could also be a benefactor to some of the men under his command. A friend wrote: "I could relate many instances of his unwearied attention in forwarding the deserving and friendless sailor, not only in promotion, but to the hurt and wounded, pecuniary assistance, when he conceived the smart money or Greenwich pension inadequate. To the idle and the dissolute his punishments were with vigilance directed, but in no instance attended with cruel severity."[6]

Gambier's story appears to be one of a well-meaning man who, through family connections, was promoted more quickly than his experience and ability justified. By his own standards he was an honorable man who had little interest in money or glory. It was enough for him to have fulfilled his duties to the expectation of his superiors. To exceed his instructions was beyond his scope, and he preferred to err on the side of caution rather than to charge impetuously into a situation.

Virtually the only published portrait of the admiral is one painted by Sir William Beechey between 1805 and 1810. It shows a sparc individual with a thoughtful expression, a square face, and a receding hairline. There is perhaps a hint of sinful pride in the tilt of his head, but no evidence of either humor or choler.

• • •

The James Gambier who would eventually become Lord Gambier was born on 13 October 1756, in New Providence in the Bahamas. His father, John Gambier, was lieutenant governor of the colony. This younger son of John and his wife, the former Deborah Stiles of Bermuda, was named for his paternal uncle, already a post captain in the Royal Navy. It is likely that even as early as the christening, it had been determined that the babe's destiny would be to follow the sea.

To assist him in the service, James the younger would eventually have two very important connections. His aunt Margaret married Charles Middleton, eventually Lord Barham and briefly First Lord of the Admiralty. His sister, also named Margaret, married William Morton Pitt, a cousin of William Pitt, the prime minister. With such connections, only an utterly incompetent officer had any chance of failure.

At the age of eleven, young James was entered in the books of the *Yarmouth* (64), the guardship at Chatham under the command of his uncle.

James Gambier senior had taken part in the Battle of Quiberon Bay and the Belle Ile expedition. Thanks to political connections, he was employed when other officers went begging for commands. Unfortunately, he had made an enemy of Lord North, the eventual prime minister, who wrote of him to Lord Sandwich: "To say the plain truth I have seldom heard any seaman speak of Gambier as a good naval officer or as anyone who deserved to be trusted with any important command."[7]

Sandwich had nothing to say about Gambier's skill as a seaman, but he was willing to appoint him commissioner of Portsmouth at Middleton's recommendation. While Gambier senior was in that position, the First Lord paid him a visit and met a young woman in whom he took a carnal interest. He mentioned his attraction to the host, who promised to do what he could to arrange a second meeting. Although it is not reported if Sandwich met the fair maid a second time, Gambier was to remember the incident in a different light in later years. When he did not receive an appointment he had hopes of, he threatened to make public that Sandwich had tried to employ him as a panderer, this time stating that he had refused indignantly to have anything to do with the affair. This was a prime piece of hypocrisy. Gambier himself had been compelled to pay heavy damages for the seduction of the wife of a fellow officer.[8] He was eventually brought to see that he was making a fool of himself, and he withdrew his threats, with abject apologies.

Some officers' careers would have ended immediately if they had tried to blackmail the First Lord of the Admiralty, but the Gambier family connections kept him employed until his health failed following the end of the American War of Independence. Whatever James senior's abilities as a commander and his qualities as a human being, he was certainly his nephew's early patron and had the greatest influence on his professional and personal development.

Midshipman Gambier's early years in the service were far from difficult. While his ship remained moored at Chatham he was able to spend a considerable amount of time ashore while still racking up "sea time" against the day when he would be old enough to gain his commission. The lad's first real experience at sea came when his uncle was appointed commander in chief of the North American station, replacing Samuel Hood in 1770. He hoisted his broad pennant aboard the *Salisbury* (50) and sailed for New York late in the year.

Commodore Gambier arrived on the western side of the Atlantic to confront a volatile situation. Although affairs between Britain and its American colonies did not take any serious turns for the worse until after he had left the station, he must have resigned his command in the summer of 1773 with a sigh of relief.

By August, the Gambiers had returned to England, and the uncle was appointed commissioner at Portsmouth. Records of the nephew's service until 1777 are sparse, but it is likely that he served in the Portsmouth guard-ship until the beginning of the American Revolution. Then he took ship again across the Atlantic. At the age of twenty, he received his commission as a lieutenant, on 12 February 1777.

In January 1778 James Gambier senior, now a rear admiral, was appointed second-in-command of the North American station. He hoisted his flag aboard the *Ardent* (64), and sailed for the western side of the Atlantic in March. One of his first actions on reaching his new command was to make his twenty-one-year old nephew commander of the *Thunder* (8) bomb vessel.

The summer of 1778 was an exciting time on the North American station. As described in chapter 1, the French navy had entered the war, and d'Estaing led his fleet to the mouth of New York Harbor, only to be turned away by his reluctance to take his ships over the bar. The *Thunder* was one of the vessels that followed Lord Howe to Rhode Island in August, and when the storm blew up that scattered the fleets, the little ship became separated. She was still seeking her friends on 14 August when she blundered into the main French fleet. Designed for siege operations, the *Thunder* was too unwieldy to outrun the enemy and too weak to fight. Commander Gambier had no choice but to surrender his first command to the French.

In those days of gentlemanly warfare, it was not to be expected that the nephew of an admiral would remain a prisoner for long. James was allowed to give his parole, and lived in comfortable captivity until he was exchanged within a month of being taken prisoner. By the beginning of October, he was back amongst his friends, and on the ninth, he was made post into the *Raleigh* (32), a frigate recently captured from the Americans.

Within a few weeks, Rear Admiral Gambier became commander in chief of the station when Howe set sail back to England. He did not remain in charge long before he was superseded by Vice Adm. John Byron, but upon that commander's weighing anchor to spend the winter of 1778–79 in the West Indies, Admiral Gambier again became senior officer on the station. Tucked under his uncle's wing at New York, the young captain of the *Raleigh* played no major part in that period of the war. When the rear admiral left the North American station in March 1779, his nephew and his ship went with him. It was the last time James the younger was to serve under his uncle's command.

Soon after the *Raleigh* reached England, she was assigned to a squadron that had been swiftly formed to prevent the French from landing on the island of Jersey. The French were off Coutances when the British sighted them. Having a greater strength than his enemy, the English commodore decided to trap them between two squadrons. He led five vessels around the west of Jersey, while the eight remaining British men-of-war, the *Raleigh* among them, clapped on all sail to attack the French. The enemy, retreating from the squadron they could see, backed into the other five vessels and found themselves trapped. One maneuvered to safety, but the rest were driven ashore on the coast of France. Three were set on fire where they lay, and three more small men-of-war were carried off by the British.

Following her return from Jersey, the *Raleigh* lay for most of the summer at Plymouth while the Admiralty worked to replace her guns. The wheels of government turned slowly, so it was not until autumn that the frigate was again ready to depart for a foreign station. She carried as passengers the royal governors of New York and the Bahamas. The young captain entertained his distinguished guests to the best of his ability with Admiralty funds throughout the passage. The *Raleigh* arrived in New York in the evening of the year, and sailed for the south with Arbuthnot's fleet the day after Christmas (see chapter 6 for more details).

Unlike Captain Elphinstone, Gambier played no major role in the siege of Charleston. His frigate was one of the vessels that ran past Fort Moultrie on 9 April 1780. The campaign was satisfactory for the British commanders, but not one designed to allow a junior frigate captain to win a name for himself.

The *Raleigh* finally had her opportunity to fire back at her former masters in 1781 when she captured the *General Mifflin* (20), a privateer. However, Gambier's main duties were the unromantic services generally required of the commanders of smaller men-of-war. After the capitulation of Charleston in May 1780, he sailed with the fleet to New York and was later detached to the West Indies. While the frigate was in the Caribbean, her captain found time to court the daughter of Commodore Laforey, commander of naval forces at Antigua. But he apparently fell short of asking the lady for her hand, and her father sent him packing.

In early 1781 the *Raleigh* sailed to New York, but was soon sent to Britain with dispatches. On 23 April, after reaching Spithead, Gambier claimed illness and asked to be relieved of his command.[9] The captain appears to have recovered his health quickly, because by June, he was in command of the *Arrogant* (74). In January 1782 he took command of the *Endymion* (44), but before the month was out, he again requested to be relieved of command for health reasons. By the time he was fully recovered, the war was over and the navy was on a peacetime footing, with few positions available.

Up to this point in his career, the captain had seen little action, but he continued to climb the ladder of seniority during the years of peace that followed the end of the American War of Independence. When at last he returned to sea, although most of his command experience had been in smaller vessels, he was far too senior a captain to be given anything less than a ship of the line. Like many other naval officers, Gambier did his serious courting in peacetime. In July 1788 he married Louisa Matthew, the sister of the wife of his elder brother. Their marriage was a long one, lasting forty-five years, but the couple was not blessed with children. The remainder of Captain Gambier's time ashore was uneventful until the war with France, beginning in 1793, demanded his return to sea. He was commissioned to the *Defence* (74) in April and assigned to the Channel fleet.

The *Defence* was one of the ships in Lord Howe's fleet that met Villaret-Joyeuse in late May and on 1 June 1794. Gambier did not play a major role in the preliminary battles of 28 and 29 May, but his actions on 1 June were notable. His place in the line of battle was directly in front of the flagship of Rear Admiral Caldwell, slightly forward of the center of the fleet.

When the French van first opened fire at about 9:30 in the morning, they concentrated on the *Defence,* which in charging down toward the enemy line had gained ground upon her nearest compatriots. In spite of this concentration of fire, the two-decker came on and was the first of the British fleet to break the enemy line. Noticing her from the flagship, Lord Howe exclaimed, "Look at the *Defence,* see how nobly she goes into action!"[10]

She passed between the seventh and eighth ships in the French line, the *Mucius* (74) and the *Tourville* (74). Because the *Defence*'s next astern was unable to maneuver to the best advantage, both the *Mucius* and the *Tourville* were free to concentrate the majority of their fire on the *Defence.* Soon the British ship lost her main- and mizzenmasts, and her sailing master and boatswain were slain. But the *Defence* gave better than she received. The *Mucius* was the first to leave her by running forward, ostensibly to the assistance of another French ship. Then the *Tourville* sailed away, and the British vessel was too crippled to follow and compel her to continue the action. But the *Defence* did not remain without an opponent for long. Soon afterward the *Républicain* (110) came alongside and poured a powerful broadside into the smaller man-of-war, felling her only remaining mast.

Unable to maneuver, Gambier made the signal for assistance, but it was not until the *Républicain* abandoned the action that the dismasted *Defence* was taken in tow by the *Phaeton* (38). That ended the battle for Gambier. Although he took no prizes, he distinguished himself by facing superior odds without flinching. He won the praises of his fellow officers by remaining on deck while many of the men around him fell. The total casualties suffered by the *Defence* ship's company were seventeen killed and thirty-six wounded. Of the other British seventy-four-gun ships involved in the battle, only the *Marlborough* and the *Brunswick* suffered greater casualties. Observing the shattered state of the *Defence* following the battle, and being familiar with her captain's evangelical propensities, Captain Pakenham of the *Invincible* facetiously consoled Gambier with: "Jemmy, whom the Lord loveth He chasteneth!"[11]

The Battle of the First of June was Gambier's last active service as a captain. The *Defence* was too battered to see further duty without extensive repairs, so she remained at Spithead when the rest of the fleet sailed later in the summer. Toward the end of the year, Gambier was appointed to command of the *Prince George* (98), but he never took her to sea. Shortly after he received his commission, he was made a lord of the Admiralty, and his new command was taken from him. Gambier repaired to London, where he served within the Admiralty for the next six years.

Although Gambier was not on active duty, he continued to climb the ladder of seniority. He became a rear admiral on the first anniversary of the Battle of the First of June, and was promoted to vice admiral on 14 February 1799. From his desk in London, he passed his recommendations and commands to flag officers and captains around the world.

The admiral remained at the Admiralty until the change of ministry in February 1801. Although his connections were out of office, Gambier was not compelled to languish in unemployment. No sooner did he leave the Admiralty than he was appointed third-in-command of the Channel fleet and directed to hoist his flag aboard the *Neptune* (98).

Although the Channel fleet spent considerably more time at sea than it had in Howe's and Bridport's day, the position of third-in-command was not demanding. Gambier and the *Neptune* spent their time between Portsmouth and Brest, until the signing of the preliminary peace in October reduced the tightness of the blockade. The signing of the Peace of Amiens further reduced the fleet, and rather than leave Gambier unemployed, his masters appointed him governor and commander in chief of Newfoundland. He sailed for his new office in the spring of 1802.

The admiral remained in Newfoundland until the Whig ministry left office in May 1804 and the war with France was back in full swing. Then

Gambier was summoned back to England and to his post at the Admiralty. All through the invasion scares and the Trafalgar campaign, he remained at his desk, serving beside his kinsman, Lord Barham, now First Lord of the Admiralty. In the general promotion that followed the arrival of the news of Trafalgar in Britain, he became a full admiral in November 1805.

During his second term at the Admiralty, Gambier made two contributions of dubious worth that came to affect other officers for some time afterward. One was to discontinue the demand that all foreign vessels in the English Channel salute any British man-of-war they encountered, and the other was the creation of a new rank. According to *The Dictionary of National Biography*, "Gambier seems to have been as ignorant of naval history as careless of naval prestige, and must be considered as one of the chief of the perpetrators of the official blunder which, in the warrant of 9 Nov. 1805, appointing admirals of the red, spoke of the rank as restored to the navy, whereas, in point of fact, it had never previously existed."[12]

The ministry changed again in February 1806, leaving the admiral unemployed for the first time since the beginning of the war in 1793. It was little more than a year before he was recalled to the Admiralty, but this time he was no longer content to serve only in an office. In July 1807 he hoisted his flag aboard the *Prince of Wales* (98) at Yarmouth and prepared to sail for the Baltic.

A treaty had been signed between France and Russia on 7 July 1807. Among the secret clauses of the treaty was the resolution to deny British shipping the use of ports in Portugal, Denmark, and Sweden, some of the last countries in Europe open to British trade. Also, the fleets of these three countries were to be seized and used to further Napoleon's ambitions. Russia had agreed to use its influence on Sweden, while the French were to coerce the other two nations. However, the new ministry in London learned of these secret clauses. Because the greatest threat appeared to be the seizure of the Danish fleet by the French, it decided to act immediately by sending an expedition into the Baltic. Gambier was chosen for the command.

On 26 July the admiral sailed from Yarmouth, accompanied by seventeen ships of the line. Before the end of the expedition, his force would amount to twenty-five ships of the line.[13] In addition were forty smaller vessels, such as frigates, sloops, bombs, and gun-brigs.[14]

By 1 August the main fleet was off Göteborg. Gambier sent Commo. Richard Keats with four ships of the line, three frigates, and ten gun brigs to occupy the passage of the Great Belt. This prevented assistance being sent from other parts of Denmark while the main fleet concentrated on Copenhagen. Two days later Gambier led his fleet into the sound, meeting no opposition along the way. He anchored at Helsingör to await the arrival of Lieutenant General Lord Cathcart and transports loaded with approximately twenty-seven thousand British and German soldiers.

While the admiral was gathering his forces, the British consul at Copenhagen informed the Danish crown prince that if his fleet were not turned over, it would be taken by force. The prince could not allow himself to tamely submit to this demand, although there was little likelihood that the fleet could be saved. He refused and passed the order for the city to prepare to defend itself. Because the main body of the Danish army was then in Holstein, there were only about 5,500 soldiers and 4,000 seamen available to defend the city.

Delayed by weather, the fleet reached a point halfway between Helsingör and Copenhagen on 15 August. Gambier commanded the main force to anchor there while he sent a squadron under the command of Rear Adm. William Essington onward. Meanwhile, some troops were landed at Wedbeck before the rest of the fleet passed on toward Copenhagen. On 16 August the joint commanders in chief issued a proclamation restating the claim that they had come in peace and that if the Danes would surrender their fleet, it would be returned at the end of the war. If the Danes persisted in standing against the invasion force, the British commanders in chief were very sorry, but they would feel compelled to take action.

This was the situation when, on the seventeenth, a pack of Danish gunboats seized and burned a British merchantman just outside the harbor. Thus provoked, Gambier brought his fleet within four miles of the city and declared a blockade upon all Danish shipping.

While the navy blocked the enemy's passage by sea, the army landed and began to construct a battery to the north of the city. The Danes felt threatened by these works and attempted to bombard the soldiers from a squadron of small armed vessels. On 23 August a force of British bomb vessels and sloops-of-war entered the harbor and fought a sharp action before they were compelled to retreat. Eventually the gunners ashore drove the Danish vessels out of range.

The skirmish of the twenty-third was a preliminary to the main action of the twenty-fifth and twenty-sixth. More gunboats attempted to drive the British from their works—first from the west and then from the north. Neither of these attempts was successful, and the Danes were driven off after one of their vessels blew up and others suffered severe damage. For a few days relative quiet reigned. Then, on 31 August, the Danes again tried to assault the British batteries and the flotilla that guarded their seaward flank. This time they succeeded in blowing up one of the British vessels, but that did little to induce the invaders to leave. By the next day, the batteries were completely armed and ready to rain all manner of destruction down on Copenhagen.

Again the Danes were asked if they wished to surrender their fleet, and again they refused. On the evening of 2 September, the batteries opened fire on the city, and all through the night the citizens of Copenhagen fought fires that sprang up from the bombardment. They were allowed to rest the next day, but the following night brought more of the same. For three nights the Danes steadfastly refused to surrender, although their capital city was on the verge of total destruction. Finally, on the evening of 5 September, a cease-fire was called in order that terms could be negotiated, and on the seventh the Danish fleet and the city's defenses were surrendered to the British.

The fleet that fell to Gambier as part of the terms of surrender consisted of sixteen ships of the line, nine frigates, fourteen sloops-of-war, and a variety of smaller vessels. In return he suffered trifling losses. He announced that he had "added the navy of Denmark to that of the United Kingdom."[15] However, it later proved that only four of the ships of the line were fit for service.

On 21 October the admiral sailed for England, taking the prizes with him. Upon his return, he was created Baron Gambier of Iver and offered a pension of £2,000. He accepted the peerage, but he rejected the pension. In an era when admirals regularly took each other to court over prize money, Gambier's apparent lack of interest in material wealth is refreshingly rare.

In May 1808 Lord Gambier became commander in chief of the Channel fleet. He hoisted his flag aboard the *Caledonia* (120) and soon set sail for the coast of France. Although the British navy had constantly frustrated his plans, Napoleon commanded the construction of new ships in hopes that he would one day be able to employ them when the Royal Navy was otherwise occupied. Hearing that Martinique, then again a French possession, was soon to be attacked, the emperor commanded Rear Admiral Willaumez to sail at the soonest opportunity from Brest. He was to drive away whatever force the Royal Navy had in those waters, collect as many French vessels as he could, and sail for the West Indies.

At first it appeared that nature was on the side of the French. A storm drove the Channel fleet away from its station in February 1809. That allowed Willaumez to escape with eight ships of the line and a handful of smaller men-of-war. But as soon as they attempted to make contact with their countrymen at Lorient, the French were sighted by a British squadron of four ships of the line. Outnumbered, the English kept their distance while Willaumez hovered off Lorient, hoping to induce the squadron anchored there to come out and join him. But his compatriots would not emerge, and the British began to receive reinforcements. Leaving Lorient, the French rear admiral made for the Basque Roads, trailed by an enemy whose force had grown to seven ships of the line.

As soon as Willaumez had gone to ground in the Basque Roads, the senior British officer in the area, Rear Admiral Stopford, sent word to Admiral Gambier. Before the commander in chief arrived, the French made an attempt to escape but were foiled when one of their ships of the line ran aground and was wrecked. By the time his lordship appeared on the scene on 7 March, the French were bottled up in the Aix Road with little to protect them save a few shoals and a boom. They arranged themselves in a strong defensive position, as Gambier described to the Admiralty:

> The enemy's ships are anchored in two lines, very near to each other, in a direction due south from the fort, on the Isle D'Aix, and the ships in each line not further apart than their own length. . . . The most distant ships of their two lines are within point-blank shot of the works upon the Isle D'Aix: such ships, therefore, as might attack the enemy, would be exposed to be raked by the hot shot, &c. from the island, and should the ships be disabled in their masts, they must remain within range of the enemy's fire until destroyed, there not being sufficient depth of water to allow them to move to the southward out of distance.[16]

Lord Mulgrave, then First Lord of the Admiralty, thought that the situation offered a superlative opportunity to employ fireships. He wrote to Gambier to suggest this method of attack, to which the admiral replied that while it might be successful, he not only considered it a cruel form of warfare but feared that the risks might well outweigh the gains. Meanwhile, other officers in the fleet began to think that fireships would be the ideal weapon in the situation, and Rear Admiral Harvey circulated through the fleet, looking for volunteers. He found no shortage. By 19 March he had a long list to present to the commander in chief.

Unfortunately for the rear admiral, the Admiralty had its own ideas about who was the best candidate to lead the attack. Lord Mulgrave had selected a relatively junior captain, Lord Cochrane, to command the fireships. Doubtless the First Lord thought he had made a suitable selection. Cochrane had already made an enviable reputation for himself as a bold officer, quick-thinking and aggressive. He seemed a superior choice to lead this "hazardous, if not desperate" venture.

On the very day that Rear Admiral Harvey presented his list of volunteers to Gambier and was rejected, Cochrane was summoned from Plymouth to the Admiralty. According to his own account, he hesitated when the First Lord offered him command, because he feared exposure to the jealousy of his seniors in rank. But Mulgrave told him that no other officer had been considered for the undertaking and that he, the First Lord himself, would do everything in his power to draw off the slings and arrows of outraged superiors. Cochrane allowed himself to be persuaded and soon took ship aboard the *Impérieuse* (38) to join Gambier's fleet.

The young captain was not impressed with what he found upon his arrival. He relates in his autobiography: "[T]he fleet was in a state of great disorganization on account of the orders given to various officers for the distribution of tracts, and being naturally desirous of learning the kind of instruction thereby imparted, I found some of them a most silly and injudicious character, and therefore declined to distribute them."[17]

From Cochrane's account, the commander in chief was more interested in the souls of his men than in their ability to fight the enemy. Some of his officers supported him, but others were inclined to think that fighting the French was a far more important task. Given the animosity between Gambier and his second-in-command, there were bound to be factions, and Cochrane was soon in the middle of the fight.

At first both sides received the new arrival with courtesy. The commander in chief promised Cochrane every assistance, and Rear Admiral Harvey made it clear that in spite of being shouldered aside in favor of his junior, he was not inclined to hold it against him. However, this spirit of harmony was not to last.

When the fireships arrived off the Basque Roads on 10 April, Cochrane at once plunged happily into the task of improving some of them for their mission. He increased the cargo of explosives commonly carried by these vessels and added a few tons of shells and hand grenades for good measure. By the following afternoon he was ready to make his attack.

A force of sixteen fireships, bombs, and explosion vessels set sail on the afternoon of the eleventh. As night came on, they reached the entrance to the Basque Roads. The force was led by the *Mediator* (44), a larger and heavier vessel than the others, whose purpose was to break the boom the French had constructed to block the entrance to the harbor. The *Mediator* ran straight up onto the boom and, breaking it, sailed on with other vessels in her wake. Aboard one of these Cochrane remained to see the boom broken and the ships sailing in. Then he lit the fuses and escaped the ensuing explosion in a gig bound back for his own command.

At first the attack appeared to be proceeding according to plan. However, once the British vessels entered the harbor, they became lost because of the darkness of the night and the unfamiliarity of the road. Some were set on fire prematurely and exploded without effect, while others sailed off in the wrong direction. Ultimately the fireships had little direct impact upon the French. However, the fear of those floating bombs caused the enemy to cut their cables, and in confusion, they were driven aground.

By dawn on the twelfth, eleven French vessels could be seen ashore. Cochrane, who had returned aboard the *Impérieuse,* signaled the helplessness of the enemy to the admiral and suggested that by bringing in half the fleet, or even frigates alone, Gambier could utterly destroy the French. But it was not until 9:30 A.M., when the noble captain signaled that the enemy was preparing to heave off, that the commander in chief finally began to act. But Gambier appeared incapable of moving decisively. He wasted an hour by summoning the captains of the fleet aboard the flagship for a conference. It was 10:45 before he weighed anchor and drifted down to within six miles of the stranded French. There the majority of the fleet remained, no more effective against the enemy than it would have been in the middle of the English Channel. But Gambier would go no closer. The water was growing dangerously shallow for his larger vessels. He sent in a few of his smaller men-of-war to harass the French who were attempting to get off, but their shot had little effect.

On his own responsibility Cochrane brought the *Impérieuse* in as close as he could to the grounded Frenchmen and hoisted distress signals, hoping to lure more British vessels into the fray.[18] While the *Impérieuse* poured her shot into the sides of a French two-decker, Gambier debated whether to order some vessels to support his impetuous subordinate or to leave the rash young man to his fate. At last, more than half an hour after the request for assistance, he sent a few small men-of-war and two ships of the line to see what they could do. These vessels made a cautious approach, but eventually they came to Cochrane's assistance and opened fire on the nearest French who were still stranded. Between them they captured two of the enemy and set fire to two others.

While this had been going on, some of the French had succeeded in getting under way and took the opportunity to retreat into more sheltered water. But others remained exposed to any actions the British dared take against them. Eventually two more French ships were set on fire by landing parties before the British withdrew in the early morning hours of 13 April.

Although most of the fleet had left the Basque Roads, Cochrane and his squadron remained, determined to make another attempt. Soon after dawn they approached the remaining three Frenchmen who were still vulnerable and opened fire on them. They kept the cannonballs flying until late in the afternoon, when the ebbing tide compelled them to leave.

Meanwhile, Gambier sent Cochrane the following letter: "You have done your part so admirably that I will not suffer you to tarnish it by attempting impossibilities, which, I think, as well as those captains who have come from you, any further attempt to destroy those ships would be. You must, therefore, join me as soon as you can with the bombs, etc."[19] Cochrane had no desire to go farther than the tide compelled him as long as there were Frenchmen within reach. Eager to get back to his battle, he shot back the following reply: "I have just had the honor to receive your Lordship's letter. We can destroy the ships that are on the shore, which I hope your Lordship will approve of."[20] But Gambier was satisfied with what had already been accomplished and had no desire to risk damage to any of the vessels under his command in further fighting. He reiterated his command that Cochrane depart and made sure that he would listen by sending another captain to take his place.[21]

At last Cochrane left the scene of the action, but he was in a state of rage as he stormed aboard the *Caledonia*. Once again the officers of the flagship were treated to a row on the quarterdeck. The captain insisted that the enemy could still be destroyed if attacked with vigor, but the commanders who had been sent to help him had not done their utmost, because of personal jealousy. Gambier heard out this tirade and replied, "If you throw blame upon what has been done, it will appear like arrogantly claiming all the merit to yourself."[22] Then he wrote out unequivocal orders for Cochrane to proceed at once to England. The *Impérieuse* sailed for home on 15 April.

On 22 April the *Morning Advertiser* carried the commander in chief's account of events at the Basque Roads:

> The Almighty's favor to His Majesty and the nation has been strongly marked in the success He has been pleased to give to the operations of His Majesty's Fleet under my command. . . . I cannot speak in sufficient terms of admiration and applause of the vigorous and gallant attack made by Lord Cochrane upon the French line-of-battle ships which were on shore, as well as of his judicious manner of approaching them, and placing his ships in a position most advantageous to annoy the enemy and preserve his own ship,

which could not have be exceeded by any feat of valor hitherto achieved by the Royal Navy.[23]

The admiral's attempts to smooth over his difficulties with the captain were scornfully received by Cochrane, who wrote:

There is something very revolting in a truly religious mind in these derogatory phrases, which couple the beneficent Author of our being with the butcheries of war. Under no circumstances are they defensible. But when the name of the great and merciful Creator is made subservient to an attempt to palm off as a great victory that which, in reality, was a great disgrace . . . there is something shocking in the perversion of language which should only be uttered with the profoundest reverence, and on occasions in strict coincidence with the attributes of the sacred name invoked.[24]

Perhaps the main reason that Gambier appeared willing to forgive and forget his differences with Cochrane was because he had bigger fish to fry. His first objective was the court-martial of his second-in-command, whose words upon the quarterdeck of his flagship he was not so ready to forgive.

After Cochrane's departure the main fleet remained off the Basque Roads for another fortnight while the French brought off what ships they could salvage. The British made a few haphazard attempts to destroy those vessels that were still within their reach, but with little effect. Finally, when all the surviving Frenchmen had retreated beyond his reach, Gambier sailed for home, on 29 April.

Soon after the commander in chief's return to England, he had his second-in-command tried for insubordination. At his defense, Harvey apologized to Gambier and the court for his rash words. He stated that he had been under the influence of great irritation and that it was his excessive zeal for the good of the service that had caused him speak so injudiciously. The court heard him and, having maturely weighed the evidence, found the rear admiral guilty and cashiered him. However, because of Harvey's gallant conduct at Trafalgar and other deeds of note throughout his career, he was soon reinstated to his former rank.

Meanwhile, heavier weather was brewing for Admiral Gambier. Although he had been willing to forgive Cochrane for his words on 14 April, the frigate captain was not prepared to drop the matter of the perceived lack of support. As was common after a significant victory, Parliament was in the process of producing a vote of thanks to the commander in chief. But Cochrane, who was a member of the House of Commons, was against it, even though his own name would have been included in the vote of thanks.

The captain paid a visit to the First Lord to inform him of his intentions to block the vote of thanks, and what was more, he hoped that the matter of the Basque Roads would be looked into by a court of inquiry. Not wishing to preside over perhaps the worst intraservice quarrel since the Keppel-Palliser affair, Mulgrave tried to make a deal with Cochrane. He offered him the command of three frigates and carte blanche in the Mediterranean. But the young captain would have none of those bribes. He was determined to see his notion of justice done, whatever the cost to himself. The cost to himself was high, and whether justice was done is dubious.

On 26 July court was convened to try Lord Gambier on the charge that "Admiral Lord Gambier . . . the enemy's ships being then on shore, and the signal having been made that they could be destroyed, did for a considerable time neglect or delay taking effectual measures for destroying them."[25] The president of the court was a personal friend of the accused, and the next most senior officer detested Cochrane for exposing in Parliament his own venal performance of the duties of port admiral at Portsmouth. The witnesses called were supporters of Gambier nearly to a man, and those who were not were badgered by some of the judges, so the trial produced a predictable result and the admiral was honorably acquitted.

Following the verdict of the court-martial, Gambier received the delayed vote of thanks from Parliament and returned to his command in the Channel. Cochrane, on the other hand, was effectively ruined as an active naval officer for the remainder of the war. The only fighting he did until he left the country to enlist in the cause of Chilean independence was on the floor of the House of Commons.

Although Gambier remained commander in chief of the Channel fleet until 1811, little of moment took place after the action at the Basque Roads. The French had been so thoroughly shattered that there was scarcely a fleet worthy of the name to be watched, let alone fought. Admiral Sir Charles Cotton, former commander in chief of the Mediterranean fleet, succeeded Gambier at the end of his term.

Command of the Channel fleet was his lordship's last service as a naval officer, but in July 1814, he was called upon once more to serve his country. Since his departure from the Channel command, Britain had gone to war with the United States over issues of trade and the impressment of seamen. By 1814 both sides saw little profit in continuing the conflict. Bonaparte had been defeated, and most of the sources of contention had been removed, so the British government decided to appoint a peace delegation.

Lord Gambier was appointed to lead a delegation consisting of William

Adams, a lawyer, and Henry Goulburn, the under secretary for war. None of these men was considered especially distinguished, but most of Britain's primary diplomats were occupied with the negotiations to redraw the boundaries of Europe.

The admiral and his two assistants arrived at Ghent on 6 August. Soon afterward they met with the American delegates—John Quincy Adams, Henry Clay, Albert Gallatin, Jonathan Russell, and James Bayard—who had arrived a month earlier. At the opening of the negotiations, the British stated that impressment would be discussed, the border between the United States and Canada would be modified, and some accommodation should be made for their Indian allies. On their side, the Americans had been instructed to demand an end to impressment, prohibit British trade with the Indians, and insist on compensation for loss and damages to American property. After opening discussion, both sides realized they were too far apart to resolve anything without consulting their respective governments.

All through the autumn the two sides exchanged polite but unyielding notes. Then, as winter came on, each delegation grew more conciliatory. However, there were still some bitter disputes. On 10 December, the two sides became vociferous over the possession of the Passamaquoddy Islands off the coast of Maine. It was Gambier, "imposing and not a little pompous in his admiral's uniform but undeniably sincere," who defused the quarrel by suggesting that the commissioners move on to another topic.[26]

On 24 December 1814 the Treaty of Ghent was signed. Gambier brought the treaty home to his masters, who ratified it on 17 February 1815, and ended his service career. As a reward for leading the negotiations at Ghent, he was created a knight Grand Cross of the Bath on 7 June 1815. Then he settled down to a life of quiet retirement.

When the Duke of Clarence became King William IV on 22 July 1830, one of the titles he resigned was Admiral of the Fleet. At this time the most senior officer on the Navy List was Lord Gambier, who at the age of seventy-three became Admiral of the Fleet. Like most occupants of that office in the eighteenth and nineteenth centuries, he never hoisted his flag, and on 19 April 1833, he died. With his death, his title became extinct.

Chapter 8

JOHN DUCKWORTH

1748–1817

I N APRIL 1797 Capt. John Thomas Duckworth of the *Leviathan* (74) had just returned to England following an extended cruise in the West Indies. His ship lay in Plymouth Harbor while he went ashore to begin the business of replacing his dwindling supplies.

Although the captain had gone ashore on business, he took advantage of his freedom to order a meal at an inn, a welcome change from the salt provisions on which he had been subsisting since his departure from Jamaica. Meanwhile, the men in his ship, barred from coming ashore for fear that they would desert, were still consuming the same "rotten cheese, rotten beef and sour beer" that had sustained them throughout their passage of the Atlantic.[1] Captain Duckworth was eager to get fresh provisions to his men; he was a captain who took good care of the health and well-being of his crew. But the local victualers were dragging their feet about getting supplies out to the newly arrived third rate. Thus far the only visitors to come out to the *Leviathan* were mutinous sailors from the *Atlas* (98) who had thrown in their lot with the delegates at Spithead. Taking advantage of Duckworth's absence, the mutineers came aboard and soon had the Leviathans talked around to their point of view. They sent their officers ashore to take the news to the captain that none of them were wanted back aboard for a while.

When Duckworth learned that his ship's company had rejected him, he flew into a rage. He sent back his first lieutenant to tell the seamen that "Captain Duckworth [had] resolved never to command such a set of villains till he [had] proved to the world through a court-martial [their] baseness and his innocence."[2] It was characteristic of the man that he should feel unappreciated, but these words were not designed to make the captain any more welcome aboard the *Leviathan.* He was compelled to await developments ashore.

For more than a fortnight, Duckworth remained fuming on the beach while his ship's company stood out with the rest of the mutineers. As he fretted in his room ashore, the captain first dwelt upon the ingratitude of the men who had repudiated him after everything he had done for them. But later he began to feel more sympathetic. After all, not long before, he too had complained of the shortness of his pay and of the duties put upon him without much hope of thanks. By the time he was invited to return to his command, he was prepared to look upon the seamen under him in a new light. Already a humane commander, he resolved to become an example of a benevolent leader. He kept his resolve too. Although he was not always popular with his superiors, Duckworth was generally well liked by his subordinates.

Sir John Duckworth was one of the most controversial of Napoleonic era naval officers. Although his distinguished record includes notable feats at the Glorious First of June and the command of a squadron at the minor but highly successful action off San Domingo, there were enough questionable actions in his career to place weapons in the hands of his enemies. Unfortunately for him, two of his enemies were outspoken and influential. The first of these was the Earl of St. Vincent, a man with an opinion (generally bad) of everyone, and only too willing to share it. According to his lordship, Duckworth was an officer of limited ability, whose only redeeming feature was that he was a good trainer of midshipmen.[3]

An even more outspoken antagonist was William James, author of *The Naval History of Great Britain,* one of the two major works on the naval aspect of the French Wars written while many of those who had taken part were still alive. Throughout his work, James rarely misses an opportunity to give any action of Duckworth's the most uncomplimentary interpretation. But James was not an impartial observer. According to Laughton (1907): "James is so constant in his hostility to and disparagement of Duckworth that they awaken a presumption that when Duckworth was commander-in-chief at Jamaica (1801–3) he must, in some way, have annoyed James, then a lawyer practicing in the colonial court."[4]

However, Duckworth had his defenders. The *British Naval Biography* published in 1839 addresses some of the disparaging remarks made on the career of this officer: "The character of this gallant admiral, like that of most unsuccessful commanders, has been subjected to great and unjust disparagement. The expedition to Constantinople, which exposed him to this unpopularity, was one of the most arduous and doubtful ever undertaken, and its complete success was only prevented by the wholly inadequate force which was placed under his command."[5]

Some of Duckworth's actions during his career, especially in the case of the expedition to Constantinople, were dubious, but in general he appears to have been a competent commander. Occasionally it was his misfortune to find himself in a difficult situation from which even the most talented officer would be unlikely to obtain glory. At least Duckworth was fortunate in one respect. Although he did not receive the honors he thought his due, he was highly compensated with cold cash.

Judging by his letters, which are full of dramatic language, Duckworth appears to have been an individual who felt and expressed strong emotions. That being the case, it is not surprising that those around him had strong feelings about him. *The Dictionary of National Biography* sums him up as follows: "The contradictions are excessive; and though, at this distance of time, it is impossible to decide with any certainty, we may believe that he was a good, energetic, and skilful officer, and that, as a man, his character would have stood higher had he been much better or much worse; had he had the sweetness of temper which everybody loves, or the crabbedness of will which everybody fears."[6]

Duckworth was not above average height and was rather more plump than otherwise. His face was expressive, with a long nose, heavy eyebrows, and full-lipped mouth. As late as 1810 he was still wearing his hair in an old-fashioned style, with curls over the ears. Like his career, his person was more memorable for strong-marked traits than for any special virtues.

• • •

On 28 February 1748, another son was born to the Reverend Henry Duckworth, curate of Leatherhead in Surrey. As father of five promising lads who all had to make their own way in the world, the reverend had limited choices of where to place his sons to their best advantage. From the day he was born, John Thomas was destined for the navy.

Although Henry Duckworth was a mere curate, he apparently had some connections. He sent his sons to Eton, but in John's case, the formal education did not last long. A mere child of eleven, Master Duckworth was taken out of school and installed aboard the *Namur* (90) as a volunteer under the protection of Admiral Boscawen.

Duckworth's first year of naval service (1759) was an exciting one. Shortly after he joined the *Namur,* she sailed for the Mediterranean. She joined Vice Admiral Broderick off Cape Sicie in May and commenced the blockade of the French fleet at Toulon. The blockade continued for two months, but at the beginning of July the British ran short of supplies and had to return to Gibraltar. The French fleet took the opportunity to slip out in mid-August and head for the Straits of Gibraltar to join forces with Spanish allies at

Cadiz. Boscawen weighed anchor and went pelting after the enemy, catching them by surprise on 18 August. In spite of variable winds, the British caught the French rear and began to exchange broadsides. The *Namur* laid herself alongside the French flagship, and fought until the British vessel was disabled. Boscawen shifted his flag to continue the chase, which lasted into the next day and ended with two French ships of the line running aground and being burnt, and two others taken. Although the *Namur* was out of the action after the first hours of the battle, Duckworth had seen shots fired in anger for the first time—and was soon to see more.

With the coming of autumn, the *Namur,* minus her flag and commanded by Matthew Buckle as a private captain, returned to England. Soon she was placed under the command of Admiral Hawke and sent to blockade the French at Brest. On 20 November she took part in the Battle of Quiberon Bay, which is described in detail in chapter 1. Although the *Namur* did not take as prominent a role as the *Magnanime* or the *Torbay,* she charged in with the rest, risking both French shot and French rocks.

In the spring of 1760, Boscawen returned to the *Namur* and used her as his flagship for his final cruise of the Channel. He served as commander of the force off Brest until Hawke relieved him in August. Then, ill and worn out, he went home, and on 10 January 1761, he died.

Although Duckworth had lost his first patron very early, it does not appear to have adversely affected his career. He seems to have found others who took an interest in his progress. Captain Buckle as senior captain commanded a squadron off Brest in the spring of 1761 to keep the main French fleet from interfering with the British expedition to Belle Ile. After the British had successfully taken the island, the *Namur* returned to England, and the following year found her once more a flagship. Admiral Sir George Pocock hoisted his flag in her on 18 February and assumed command of the expedition soon to sail for Havana.

Joining forces with other vessels already in the West Indies, Pocock's fleet reached Havana in early June 1762. A fuller description of the Havana campaign is included in chapter 5. Like the *Valiant* (74), the *Namur* sent many of her men ashore to man the batteries of heavy guns bombarding the city and the fortress of El Morro. Duckworth served his turn at the batteries and saw many men fall ill from tropical diseases. But Duckworth appears to have been resistant to diseases of the climate. He survived several postings to the tropics during his career.

Havana surrendered on 12 August; however, several months were required to secure the territory and divide the plunder. The *Namur* did not sail for

England until 3 November. By the time she returned home, the Seven Years' War was drawing to a close. She was paid off, and Mr. Midshipman Duckworth came home to his family with a great store of tales for a lad of fifteen.

Like many other officers, Duckworth found it difficult to advance in peacetime. He successfully completed his requisite six years at sea, and then some, without receiving promotion. Finally, at the age of twenty-three, he was appointed an acting lieutenant. He obtained his commission in November 1771 and entered aboard the *Kent* (74), the guardship at Portsmouth.

The *Kent*'s commander was Capt. Charles Feilding, who had a reputation for being a difficult superior. However, Lieutenant Duckworth must have impressed him favorably, because not only did the two officers serve together in the Kent, but when Feilding was commissioned to the *Diamond* (32) in 1776, Duckworth followed him as first lieutenant.

During Duckworth's service in the Plymouth guardship, the only incident of note took place on 4 July 1774. Captain Feilding may have been strict in his enforcement of certain disciplinary matters, but safety does not appear to have been one of his major concerns. Aboard the *Kent* he allowed some gunpowder to be left about on the poop deck while a party of seamen scraped the rust off the iron guns. The powder took fire, and the ensuing explosion killed or wounded forty-five men.

Soon after Feilding and Duckworth transferred aboard the *Diamond,* the frigate sailed for the North American station with Lord Howe. They arrived off Sandy Hook in July and entered New York City in September. Once the rebels had been driven out of New York City and its immediate environs, the British turned their eyes northward. On 1 December a force of five fifty-gun vessels and eight smaller men-of-war sailed from New York Harbor, bound for Newport, Rhode Island. This squadron, commanded by Commo. Sir Peter Parker, landed troops on the eighth and took the town without opposition. For the following three years, Newport was the second major North American base of the Royal Navy, after New York.

While the *Diamond* was anchored in the harbor on 18 January 1777, she fired a salute in honor of the queen's birthday. Unfortunately, through carelessness, two of her guns had been left loaded, and the balls that emerged struck the *Grand Duke* transport, killing five men and wounding two. Less than a week later, the commodore convened a court-martial to try the frigate's first lieutenant, gunner, gunner's mate, and gunner's crew on the charge of neglect of duty. The court-martial was conducted with a minimum of ceremony, and all the accused were acquitted. However, when the minutes of the court-martial were submitted to Lord Howe, he disallowed the verdict. To him it appeared that the affair had been poorly handled. Not only were the deaths of five men not even mentioned in the charges against the defendants, but the names of the defendants never appeared in any part of the minutes. He declared that these men should be tried again, and this time on a charge of murder as well as neglect of duty.

At first the captains who had made up the original court refused to conduct a new trial, feeling that the matter had been pursued far enough and the accused found innocent. But, as Howe insisted that the matter be reopened—even threatened to remove these captains from their commands—they paid lip service to his demands. They gathered again, read the minutes of the original court-martial, and pronounced that the accused, "having been acquitted of neglect of duty, are in consequence thereof acquitted of murder or any other crime or crimes alleged to them."[7] Although this result was unlikely to have satisfied Lord Howe he decided not to pursue the matter further. Shortly afterward the *Diamond* was assigned to the West Indies.

For most of 1777 and 1778, the *Diamond* conducted the standard frigate duties of convoy and cruising. In early January 1779 Vice Adm. John Byron arrived at St. Lucia to take command of the station. Within two months of his arrival in the West Indies, he invited Lieutenant Duckworth to join him aboard his flagship, the *Princess Royal* (90).

In the spring of 1779, the British and the French forces in the Caribbean increased in size as the two nations jockeyed for control of the region. At the end of June, reinforcements from Brest joined Admiral d'Estaing at Fort Royal, giving the French numerical superiority. Meanwhile, the main British fleet had set out with a convoy, allowing the French, with twenty-five sail of the line, to take the British island of Grenada. Before Byron had any idea of what was happening, the French had captured the island and thirty richly laden merchantmen then lying in the harbor.

Then, on 6 July, the British fleet of twenty-one ships of the line arrived off the island. As soon as he learned of the enemy's approach, d'Estaing formed a line of battle, but when Byron first saw the French, they still appeared to be in a state of disorder. What was more, because many vessels masked others in the anchorage, he thought the enemy's fleet was inferior in numbers to his own. He decided that the best mode of attack would be to bring his own vessels in as quickly as possible. So, although his own fleet was not in formation, the British admiral commanded his captains to attack as they were, hoping to form their line as they entered the battle.

Under full sail, the British van swept down on the still clustered French rear. As they approached their targets, they had to pass down the full enemy line and receive considerable damage without having the option to reply. Then, by the time Byron's myrmidons finally reached the French rear, d'Estaing's fleet had formed into a line of battle compact enough that to attack it piecemeal would have been folly. So the lead British vessels came about and ran back up the French line, now on the starboard tack. The resulting action was a scrambling, disordered affair on both sides. There were large gaps in the British line, and many of d'Estaing's ships overlapped each other, so neither side could effectively bring the mass of its firepower to bear. The most notable occurrence during this action came when Rear Adm. Joshua Rowley, who had begun near the rear, cut out of line to support the van in an action very similar to Nelson's at the Battle of St. Vincent.

After the two fleets had been in action for about five hours, the French admiral dropped down to protect a portion of his force that had fallen behind. Byron, on the other hand, maintained his position to defend the convoy he had been escorting. The two fleets drew apart, and firing stopped. Although a few crippled British ships lay between the two forces, d'Estaing was not force- ful in his attempts to capture them; otherwise, the Battle of Grenada could have ranked as one of the worst defeats in British naval history. Instead, it is merely a debacle in which neither commander in chief shone.

That the *Princess Royal* took some part in the action is shown by the fact that she suffered three men killed and six wounded. But these casualties pale in comparison with those suffered by the *Grafton* (74), a much smaller ship, which lost thirty-five killed and sixty-three wounded.

A mere ten days after the battle, Lieutenant Duckworth was promoted to commander of the *Rover* (18), a sloop-of-war that had been the *Cumberland* before she had been taken from the Americans in 1777. When Byron sailed for England in August, the *Rover* remained in the West Indies, cruising for privateers. For nearly a year Duckworth remained in command of the sloop-of-war until he was made post into the *Terrible* (74) on 16 June 1780.

The new captain did not remain long in the *Terrible* before he returned to the *Princess Royal,* now as flag captain to Rear Admiral Rowley, the same officer who had shown initiative at the Battle of Grenada. At the command of Admiral Rodney, the *Princess Royal* sailed for Jamaica, but on her way she was caught by a hurricane off the coast of San Domingo. For nearly a fort- night in early October, violent storms lashed the ships of Rowley's squadron. One ship of the line foundered, and another was driven ashore with terrible loss of life. But the *Princess Royal* weathered the storm with relatively little damage.

In February 1781, Captain Duckworth read himself in aboard the *Bristol* (50), in which he took charge of a homeward-bound convoy. After an absence of five years, the captain finally set foot again on English soil. There the *Bristol* was paid off, and Duckworth was without employment for several months. But in 1782 he was appointed to command of the *Europe* (64), which he held until early 1783. Then he was transferred to the *Salisbury* (50), which he captained for a mere four months. When the *Salisbury* was paid off in April, the American War ended for Captain Duckworth.

Little of note took place for the captain during the ensuing ten years. In September 1792 he sat on the court-martial that tried ten of the *Bounty* mutineers. Of these, four were acquitted, two were found guilty but were pardoned, one escaped punishment on a technicality, and three were eventually hanged, in October 1792.

With the beginning of the French Wars in 1793, Duckworth was appointed to the command of the *Orion* (74) in the Channel fleet. Once again under the command of Admiral Howe, the captain cruised periodically off the coast of France. Prior to the meeting of the French and British fleets at the end of May 1794, the *Orion* was employed in protecting the frigates the commander in chief sent to watch the enemy. Being near the front of the British van on 29 May, the *Orion* took a prominent part in that day's action. She came close alongside the *Indomptable* (80) and exchanged broadsides for some time before the French admiral sent other vessels to the rescue. Even then, Villaret-Joyeuse was compelled to send the *Indomptable* home before the main action on 1 June.

On the day of Howe's great victory, Duckworth's command was positioned three ships behind the *Queen Charlotte* (100). In this location the captain was able to exchange broadsides with two French ships of the line until they bore up to avoid him. Then, seeing the *Queen Charlotte* mobbed by the enemy, Duckworth ordered his command forward to the assistance of the flagship, although the *Orion*'s rigging had been damaged by earlier exchanges. This timely aid was remembered later by the commander in chief, who when asked to name which captains had particularly distinguished themselves in the action, included Duckworth in his list.

Early in 1795 Duckworth left the *Orion* to take command of the *Leviathan* (74). Once again he traveled to the West Indies, this time as second-in-command of a squadron led by Rear Adm. William Parker. A short time after the arrival of the *Leviathan,* Rear Admiral Parker divided his fleet and sailed off, appointing Duckworth commodore in command of the station. Although pleased by his appointment, the newly made commodore appears to have suffered some irritations that arose from his new responsibilities. For one thing, Admiralty dispatches did not arrive swiftly enough to suit him, as he wrote: "I think it my duty to acquaint you for the information of their Lordships that the passage of the cutter with their dispatches was at least protracted a week from the circuitous voyage made by her arising from there not being a chart of any part of the West Indies on board, and the lieutenant commanding her being a total stranger to this country."[8]

At the time of Duckworth's arrival on the Jamaica station, the focus of the Royal Navy's efforts was on San Domingo. At the time the commodore was left in temporary command, the major city of Port au Prince had already fallen. The next goal was the city of Léogane.

In early 1796, troops were loaded into transports and escorted to Léogane, where they landed on 21 March. The *Leviathan* was among the vessels that bombarded the town while the troops attempted to land. However, the town was better defended than expected, and several of the men-of-war received extensive damage to their rigging. Eventually the British decided to cut their losses and abandon the attempt. Thoroughly disgusted with the proceedings, Duckworth wrote:

> The blundering and undigested expedition against *Léogane* has, I fear, totally done us up as to making any progress in St. Domingo, as by disabling the *Leviathan* and injuring the *Africa,* so as to make it requisite for them to go to Jamaica to repair their damages, we have not been able to keep a sufficient strength off Cape Francois to prevent the French from receiving reinforcements. . . . And indeed everything here bears the most unfavorable aspect, and I don't conceive our posts in this island will be much longer tenable. . . . Alas! Alas! How many millions have we thrown away from Government having, I conceive, been kept in ignorance, or at least badly informed about the state of the inhabitants of this island. But true it is (and I have observed it from my first arrival) that you have not a friendly Frenchman but those who are made so by local advantages.[9]

At the end of June, Rear Admiral Parker fell ill and was compelled to leave the station. As senior officer in the area, Duckworth became commander in chief. Apparently Parker's departure was so sudden that he was unable to provide his successor with instructions. Although he had had some experience in commanding a station, Duckworth appears to have been made anxious by bearing the full responsibility. His anxiety is reflected in this letter to the First Lord of the Admiralty: "To commence a command of such high consequence with only a choice of difficulties, your lordship will do me the honor to admit requires fortitude in any climate; but in this, where we are surrounded with scenes of horror and dissolution, nothing would support me in the undertaking but the reflection that under your lordship's auspices the most liberal construction will be put upon my conduct."[10]

Indeed, the captain had been stuck with the unpleasant task of cleaning up a mess of someone else's making. However, he wanted to make certain that the First Lord knew the facts of the situation so that if something went wrong, his career would not suffer for it. Lord Spencer proved sympathetic. He issued the order for Duckworth to hoist his broad pennant as a commodore and left him to run the station as best he could. Vice Adm. Sir Hyde Parker was sent out from the Mediterranean to take command of the station, and the *Leviathan* was ordered home. Within days of his return to England, Duckworth found himself in the midst of the fleet mutiny at Plymouth as described at the beginning of this chapter.

In early 1798 Duckworth served as commodore of a squadron patrolling off the coast of Ireland. The ships under his command cruised against a threatened attempt by the French to invade Ireland, but they never encountered the enemy. The *Leviathan* left for the Mediterranean before the main French landing was made in the autumn.

Toward the middle of the year Lord Spencer thought the time auspicious for the retaking of Minorca, which was then held by Spain. Flying a commodore's broad pennant in the *Leviathan,* Duckworth commanded a total of two ships of the line, two fifth rates, a frigate, and two sloops. Their mission was to protect the troopships, storeships, and other transports on their journey between Gibraltar and Minorca.

The British first landed in the vicinity of Fornello on 7 November and swiftly forced the Spaniards in the area to withdraw. While the army fought its way toward Port Mahon, Duckworth and his squadron chased off an inferior Spanish squadron. By the end of the week, the entire island was in British hands, without the loss of a single man. In gratitude, the nation made the army commander, General the Hon. Charles Stuart, a knight of the Bath, and Duckworth thought he should be granted a similar honor. Much to his disgust, he received no token for what he considered a valuable service.

Some authors are inclined to ascribe the fact that Duckworth was neither knighted nor made a baronet on this occasion to some cutting words from

Lord St. Vincent to the First Lord. But the commodore had his own ideas on the matter, as described in a letter to the commander in chief:

> Feeling that the success of every expedition depends much upon unanimity, and knowing your wishes, I have studied accommodation with uncommon assiduity . . . and before my colleague landed I thought I had succeeded to a miracle; but soon after, when he discovered the game was likely to be easily played . . . I saw he felt there would not be a sufficient portion of honour for us both, and became so proud and captious that it required great ingenuity and forbearance to follow up the ideas of a man who would sacrifice everything, the navy in particular, to military aggrandisement.[11]

Although Duckworth was disgusted at not receiving the rewards he plainly thought due him, he was not as outspoken about it as some other officers in a similar situation. He remained on the station as commander of the British naval forces in the vicinity of Minorca, and on 14 February 1799 he was promoted to the rank of rear admiral.

In May, after several months of independent command, Duckworth rejoined the main fleet, but soon he was sent to Naples to reinforce Nelson. Together the two admirals defended an area that included Sicily, Malta, and Egypt, but when Lord Keith succeeded to command of the Mediterranean fleet in the summer of 1799, he ordered Duckworth to return to Minorca. Then, when Keith's pursuit of the combined fleets left Cadiz uncovered, Duckworth was ordered to blockade the ships remaining there. Even after Keith returned to Cadiz late in the year, the more junior admiral remained in the western Mediterranean, which turned out to be a stroke of good fortune.

On 5 April 1800, while cruising off Cadiz in company with the *Swiftsure* (74) and the *Emerald* (36), Duckworth sighted a Spanish convoy and gave chase. Through the night the British closed the distance, and soon after daybreak on the sixth, they captured one Spanish ship and then another. Soon after capturing their second merchantman, they sighted six more sail in the offing, and leaving the *Swiftsure* to look after the prizes, the *Leviathan* and the *Emerald* bore down on the strangers. The Spanish watched the British approach but mistook them for members of the convoy. They did not discover their mistake until the *Emerald* was nearly upon them, summoning them to surrender. Two of the escorting frigates were shot up by the *Emerald*, which allowed the ship of the line to close and complete the capture. In two days, Duckworth had made four important prizes, especially as the merchantmen were richly laden. It is said that the rear admiral's share in the prize money amounted to £75,000.[12]

Two months after the capture of the convoy, Duckworth was sent to the Leeward Islands again, this time as commander in chief of the station. His arrival was well timed to take advantage of a situation arising in Europe. In the autumn of 1800, Czar Paul of Russia convinced Sweden and Denmark to support him in keeping British trade out of the Baltic. Although war was never officially declared, Britain decided that the acts of the Baltic nations were hostile enough to merit punishment. One penalty was the appropriation of the Danish and Swedish islands in the Caribbean.

Rear Admiral Duckworth and Lt. Gen. Thomas Trigg set out together in March 1801 and fell first upon the island of St. Bartholomew. Four days later they took St. Martin and then passed on to the double prize of St. Thomas and St. John, which fell the same day, 29 March. Two days later they added St. Croix to their cache, thereby exhausting the supply of Scandinavian islands in the West Indies. Although the islands were later returned by treaty, both the admiral and the general were made knights of the Bath. Not only did Duckworth gain honor by his conquests, but once again he received monetary compensation. Each of the islands contained property that the British felt should be forfeit to King George, and thence to His Majesty's army and navy.

Later in 1801 the rear admiral returned to Britain to enjoy the short period of peace at home, but in 1803, he was again sent to the West Indies, this time, by way of variety, as commander in chief of the Jamaica fleet. The *Leviathan* must have been Sir John's favorite, because he hoisted his flag in her again. Under his command he had a force of nine ships of the line, nine frigates, and seven smaller men-of-war.

During the peace San Domingo had been returned to the French, so with the reopening of hostilities, one of Duckworth's first actions was to blockade Port au Prince. Soon he made a major coup when two of his ships of the line captured the French second-in-command, who had taken passage in a frigate. By the beginning of autumn, the people of San Domingo were suffering exceedingly from the blockade, which allowed no food to pass. Rather than die of starvation in droves, they capitulated at last.

In 1804 the actions in the West Indies were small and not terribly successful. Duckworth, who was promoted to vice admiral on 23 April, remained at San Domingo and took little part in the skirmishes. The following spring Sir John was ordered home. Not wishing to remove a ship of the line from the Caribbean, the Admiralty directed him to come home in the frigate *Acasta* (40). Apparently the admiral did not care for the frigate's present commander, Capt. James Wood, so he ordered him to exchange with a captain more agreeable to him. Wood was furious. What was more, when Duckworth came aboard the *Acasta,* he brought with him a huge cargo of mixed goods. As transporting merchandise aboard a warship was against the Articles of War, Wood had an avenue through which to pursue his personal grievance against the vice admiral.

On 25 April 1805 Duckworth appeared before a court-martial, charged with oppression in the manner of replacing the captain of the *Acasta* and for transporting merchandise in one of His Majesty's ships. Sir John admitted that he had brought home a vast store of goods, but he explained that all of it had been intended for gifts and none of it was to be sold. Although there was some shaking of heads among members of the court, most accepted the explanation and acquitted the admiral of any wrongdoing.

Meanwhile, Duckworth enjoyed a rare period of leisure at home with his family. Then, in September, he hoisted his flag in the *Superb* (74), regarded as one of the fastest and finest third rates in the king's service. She was commanded by the distinguished Richard Goodwin Keats (whose exploits are detailed in chapters 9 and 10).

Sir John was commanded to make all speed for Cadiz to offer assistance to Lord Nelson, then blockading the combined fleet and expecting action shortly. But by the time Sir John reached Cadiz, the Battle of Trafalgar had already been fought. Vice Admiral Collingwood, who had succeeded Nelson as commander in chief, escorted his damaged vessels and prizes to Gibraltar, leaving Duckworth in command of the fleet blockading the enemy ships that had escaped the battle and reached the safety of Cadiz.

On 30 November Sir John learned that a French fleet had been sighted off Madeira. He bolted off a quick message to Collingwood to explain his intentions and then sailed in pursuit with six ships of the line.[13] However, by the time Duckworth reached Madeira, the enemy had left. He continued as far south as the Cape Verde Islands before he finally gave up the chase and turned back for Cadiz. But before he reached his station, he sighted another French squadron of six ships of the line. Immediately he altered course to give chase. Rather than face an equal number of ships of the line, the French admiral fled with all speed toward the southwest. Although the *Superb* was able to keep up, the rest of the squadron soon fell behind. Lest his flagship be compelled to face the united enemy alone, Duckworth finally pulled up and abandoned the chase a day after it began. By this time he was in the middle of the Atlantic and running short of water. As the prevailing winds were carrying him toward the West Indies, he decided to make for the islands. He sent the *Powerful* (74) back to the Cape Verde Islands on 2

January 1806, and reached Barbados on 12 January. He sailed two days later for St. Kitts, where he watered his squadron and joined forces with Rear Adm. Alexander Cochrane, who had the *Northumberland* (74) and the *Atlas* (74) under his command.

As he had lost touch with the enemy and had no notion of where they were bound, Duckworth elected to return to Cadiz. However, on 1 February a scouting sloop-of-war arrived with the report that a small squadron of French ships of the line had been seen making for San Domingo. Sir John sailed immediately and on 6 February sighted the enemy at anchor. The French had five strong ships of the line to face the smaller British seven.[14] Rear Admiral Leissègues feared to be trapped as Brueys had been at the Battle of the Nile (see chapter 10), and at once put to sea to meet the enemy. Delighted that the foe was coming out to fight him, Duckworth signaled his squadron, "This is Glorious."[15] His captains appear to have agreed with him, and made sail to come into action as swiftly as possible.

The French formed a line of battle close to shore, hoping to maintain a stout defense. But the British had the wind gauge and thus the ability to choose the mode of attack. Following the tactic then favored by the British in this situation, Duckworth divided his little fleet. With the leading four ships of the line (*Superb, Northumberland, Spencer,* and *Agamemnon*), he bore down on the enemy's van. His three remaining ships (*Canopus, Donegal,* and *Atlas*), under the command of Rear Admiral Louis, were sent to harass the enemy rear.

The first shots were exchanged at approximately 10:00 A.M., when the *Superb* and the leading French ship, the *Alexandre,* opened their broadsides. They did not remain engaged for long before the Frenchman dropped back and tried to rake the *Spencer* but was raked by her instead. Locked in combat, the two vessels drifted to leeward into the midst of the rest of Duckworth's squadron, which in the smoke and confusion, mistook the *Spencer* for an enemy. They fired a few shots into her but soon learned their mistake and ceased fire. The two combatants then fell among the smaller British division, which concentrated their fire on the *Alexandre* and soon dismasted her. She was eventually claimed as a prize.

Meanwhile, after the *Alexandre* had dropped behind, the *Superb* and the *Northumberland* attacked the huge French flagship. Duckworth described the action:

> The signal was now made for closer action, and we were enabled to attack the admiral in the *Impérial* (formerly the *Vengeur*) . . . [t]he action became general,

and continued with great severity till half past eleven, when the French admiral, much shattered, and completely beat, hauled directly to the land; and not being a mile off, at 20 minutes before noon, ran on shore. His foremast, then only standing, fell immediately; at which time the *Superb,* then only in 17 fathoms water, was forced to haul off the avoid the same evil.[16]

In the heat of the battle between the *Superb* and the *Impérial,* a chicken coop located on the British flagship's poop deck was smashed by a cannonball. One of the inmates, a gallant rooster, sprang from the wreckage and perched on the spanker boom, crowing with all his might. When the battle was over, the bird was decorated with ribbons and made into the flagship's mascot.

The *Diomède* too was forced ashore but she continued to annoy the British with her fire for some time afterward. Meanwhile, the *Donegal* and the *Brave* engaged in a close-fought ship-to-ship duel that ended with the Frenchman's surrender. The remaining French third rate, the *Jupiter,* was also engaged by the *Donegal* after she had first been pounded by the *Atlas.* Like her sister ship, she struck to Capt. Pulteney Malcolm. Then the only enemy ships still firing were the two that had run aground.

The *Atlas* exchanged broadsides with the *Impérial,* but her rudder jammed, and she ran into the *Canopus,* losing her bowsprit. The two vessels were swiftly cleared, and the problem with the *Atlas's* rudder repaired. She closed with the *Diomède* and fired into her until the *Spencer* came to her aid. Meanwhile, the *Canopus* fired into the *Impérial* until the French flagship ceased all resistance. The smaller men-of-war that had accompanied Leissègues successfully escaped.

By about noon, the British drew away from San Domingo, taking three French two-deckers with them, and leaving another two ships of the line fast aground. The winning side suffered 74 killed and 264 wounded, while the losing side lost more than 700 killed and wounded.[17]

Although the British left the scene of the battle the same afternoon, the two frigates, *Acasta* and *Magicienne,* returned two days later. By that time the *Impérial* had been completely evacuated, but the *Diomède's* crew was attempting to salvage what they could. The British frigates swooped in, captured the captain of the *Diomède* and about one hundred of his officers and men, and burnt the two grounded vessels.

Perhaps the British government felt that it had been too generous with honors in the past, or perhaps Lord Collingwood, who had been annoyed that Duckworth left Cadiz unguarded to go chasing after the French, sent a scathing letter to the Admiralty. Whatever the cause, the disgusted vice admiral received no advancement for his part in the Battle of San Domingo. His second-in-command, Rear Admiral Cochrane, was made a knight of the Bath; the third-in-command, Rear Admiral Louis, became a baronet. Gold medals were struck for all flag officers and captains, and several more junior officers received promotions. Duckworth himself received a £1,000 pension, but as he was already well endowed with funds, it is likely that he would have preferred to trade the money for a minor title.

In April, Duckworth returned to the Mediterranean, once again under the command of Vice Admiral Collingwood. But his lordship ordered him back to England, where he left the *Superb*. While Sir John was being lionized at home, actions that were soon to influence his career were taking place to the east.

All through the year of 1806, the French ambassador to the court of the Sublime Porte in Constantinople had been pressuring the sultan to act against Britain and her allies. The sultan closed the Dardanelles to Britain's ally Russia in September, but a month later reopened the passage. Although the sultan appeared to have changed his mind about hostilities against British allies, the Admiralty became alarmed at the trend and began thinking of sending a fleet through the Dardanelles to remind the Turks of what they would have to face if they went to war against England.

On 12 January 1807 Lord Collingwood received a dispatch directing him to detach a squadron to the Dardanelles and indicating that Duckworth was to command it. He swiftly relayed the information to his subordinate, who had rejoined him off Cadiz, but the instructions were unclear and left a great deal of latitude. However, Sir John set to with a will, and within three days he had his squadron assembled, with his flag in the *Royal George* (100), and set sail for the eastern end of the Mediterranean. To collect the squadron assigned to him, the vice admiral was required to make a couple of stops. He halted first at Gibraltar, where he remained for only one day before he sailed again for Malta, which he reached at the end of the month.

Now in command of a force of eight ships of the line, two frigates, two bomb vessels, and a storeship, Duckworth left Valetta on 4 February.[18] He arrived off the Dardanelles in less than a week, but as the wind was against him, he had to anchor to await improvement in the weather conditions. While he waited he learned more about the local situation and sent the following dispatch back to his commander in chief:

> I think it a duty I owe to his Majesty and my own honor, to observe to your Lordship that, our minister having left Constantinople sixteen days since, and the Turks [having] employed French engineers to erect batteries to flank every

turn in our passage through the Dardanelles, I conceive the service pointed out in my instructions as completely altered; and, viewed in whatever light it may be, [it] has become the most arduous and doubtful that ever has been undertaken. . . . I entreat your Lordship, however, to believe that, as I am aware of the difficulties we have to encounter, so I am resolved that nothing on my part [shall] be left undone that can ensure the means of surmounting them.[19]

While the squadron lingered outside the passage, calamity struck one of the ships in the squadron. The *Ajax* (74), one of the largest British-built two-deckers yet launched, caught fire on the evening of 14 February. The flames started somewhere in the after portion of the vessel but soon spread throughout the ship. The *Ajax*'s crew attempted to lower the boats, but the thick smoke that billowed over the deck so cut down the visibility that it was possible to lower only one small boat. So the captain gave the order to abandon ship and then jumped overboard. Altogether 381 individuals were saved, mainly by boats from other ships in the squadron, but approximately 250 perished in the disaster. The ship herself drifted ashore and blew up in spectacular fashion in the early morning hours of the fifteenth.

Finally, on 19 February, the wind shifted enough to allow the British to pass through the Dardanelles. There were castles on either side of the entrance, which opened fire as soon as the leading enemy vessel passed between them. At the recommendation of the British ambassador, the invaders did not fire back at the first set of castles, although they did engage the second set more closely. Neither side appears to have suffered heavy casualties from the engagement.

Duckworth's next encounter was with a small number of Turkish men-of-war that annoyed him after he passed the second set of castles. He sent his third-in-command, Rear Adm. Sir William Sidney Smith, to chastise them, and within half an hour, most of the Turkish ships had been taken or run aground and set on fire. In addition, the British overran a redoubt that had been covering the men-of-war, partially demolished it, and spiked the guns. Again the casualties were light.

After forcing the passage of the Dardanelles, Sir John appears to have become indecisive about what he should do. He led his fleet under easy sail to within a few miles of Constantinople and then sent one of his frigates ahead under a flag of truce. The frigate's captain sent ashore a message from the admiral demanding the surrender of the Turkish fleet and naval stores. The Turks made no response except to start to prepare for an attack, so on the twenty-second, the British again weighed anchor and drifted closer to

Constantinople. From this position, Duckworth sent the following bom-
bastic message to the sultan's court:

> I must tell you frankly I will not consent to lose any more time. I owe it to my
> Sovereign and to my own honor not to suffer myself to be duped; and those
> who are capable of thinking so meanly of others justly become themselves the
> object of suspicion. You are putting your ships of war in motion; you take
> every method of increasing the means of defense; but if the Sublime Porte
> wishes to save its capital from the dreadful calamities which are ready to burst
> upon it . . . you will be sent here very early tomorrow morning with full pow-
> ers to conclude with me the work of peace. . . . I now declare to you, for the
> last time, that no consideration whatever shall induce me to remain at a dis-
> tance from your capital a single moment beyond the period I have now
> assigned; and you are sufficiently acquainted with the English character not to
> be ignorant that, in a case of unavoidable necessity, we are less disposed to
> threaten than to execute.[20]

Apparently the sultan was not sufficiently acquainted with the English character to be aware of anything of the kind, and Duckworth did little to edu-
cate him further. Negotiations dragged on for another week before Sir John
decided it was time to move. Noticing that the Turks were constructing a
battery on an island within range of the some of the squadron, the admiral
sent a marine landing party with the support of a third rate and a bomb vessel. The Turks abandoned the batteries but took refuge in a monastery that
had been well designed for defense. A sharp fight developed before Duckworth decided that too many lives were being lost to no purpose and had
the marines evacuated. By dawn on the next day, the Turks had abandoned
the island.

On 1 March the British weighed anchor and sailed within sight of Constantinople to give the Turks a chance to come out and fight. But the sultan
was not foolish enough to face a force of seven ships of the line with only
five of his own, and wisely stayed at home. Duckworth decided he had wasted
enough time and saw little chance of improving his position. Clearly the
Turks were unwilling to treat with the British, and as he had insufficient
force to compel them, he started back the way he had come. He wrote the
following letter to the Admiralty to explain his reasons for departing without accomplishing his mission:

> I feel confident it will require no argument to convince your Lordship of the
> utter impracticability of our force having made any impression, as at this time
> the whole line of the coast presented a chain of batteries; that twelve Turkish

line of battle ships, two of them three deckers, with nine frigates, were with their sails bent, and apparently in readiness, filled with troops . . . besides, there were an innumerable quantity of small craft, with boats; and fire vessels had been prepared to act against us. With the batteries alone we might have coped, or with the ships, could we have got them out of their strong hold; but your Lordship will be aware, that after combating the opposition which the resources of our empire had been many weeks employed in preparing, we should have been in no state to have defended ourselves against them as described, and then repass the Dardanelles.[21]

It soon became clear that the journey back through the Dardanelles would be a great deal more hazardous than the initial passage. The enemy was better prepared and kept up a hot fire as the squadron passed within range. Some of the stone shot employed by the Turks were huge—more than six feet in circumference and weighing up to eight hundred pounds. However, they did less damage than was feared. With a few of these monstrous shot sticking out of their hulls, and losses amounting to 26 killed and 130 wounded, the British struggled through to safety. They were met outside by a Russian squadron, whose admiral urged Duckworth to turn back again. But the British commander had had enough of the Dardanelles. He led his fleet westward and arrived at Aboukir Bay on 22 March.

The Constantinople campaign is the most controversial portion of Duckworth's career. Throughout, he appears to have been hesitant and unsure of himself, when a firm hand seems to have been called for. In the admiral's defense it should be said that his instructions were unclear and poorly conceived. Brenton wrote: "Sir John Duckworth was a brave man, but was overruled, and finally condemned, I think unjustly."[22] The only fault he finds is that the admiral delayed for two days when he had his best opportunity for action.

Soon after his arrival in Egypt, Duckworth was summoned home aboard the *Royal George.* He had the opportunity to answer his accusers by demanding a court-martial upon himself but declined it, and as the government was in part to blame for the failure, the matter was dropped. The vice admiral was assigned to the Channel fleet under Admiral Gambier.

As described in chapter 7, a French squadron escaped from Brest on 21 February 1809. As soon as Gambier heard of the escape, he sent Vice Admiral Duckworth with eight ships of the line to find them. Unfortunately, the French evaded the squadron, and to make matters worse, Sir John received misleading intelligence about their destination. He ended up pursuing an imaginary squadron into the middle of the Atlantic, down to Lisbon, across to the West Indies, and finally into the Chesapeake before he learned that he had been chasing a phantom. Although that sort of thing could have happened to anyone, following his embarrassing performance at Constantinople it did little to improve his reputation.

After serving in the Channel into 1809, Duckworth was appointed governor of Newfoundland in 1810, and in the same year he was promoted to the rank of full admiral. Sir John's luck always seems to have been best on the western side of the Atlantic, and his term as governor was no exception. From being a flag officer of questionable merit in the Channel fleet, he became a popular administrator and station commander. The only dark cloud on his horizon during the period of his governorship (1810–13) was the death of his eldest son at the Battle of Albuera on 16 May 1811.

Duckworth married twice. His first wife, Anne Wallis of Cornwall, bore him a son and a daughter. The son entered the army and was slain as described above, while his daughter married Rear Adm. Sir Richard King. Sir John's second wife was Susannah Buller, daughter of the Bishop of Exeter, who bore him two sons.

Following Duckworth's return to England in 1813, he was created a baronet. At last he had the title that he had always wanted to pass on to his descendants. For a year the admiral remained at home. Then, in January 1815, he was appointed commander in chief at Devonport, a command he held for the next two years. As soon as his term at Devonport expired, he was appointed to command at Plymouth. Unfortunately, by that time his health was beginning to fail, and on 31 August he died.

Duckworth would have been disappointed at the outcome of all his efforts to finally win a hereditary title. Although he was survived by the two sons of his second wife, the Duckworth baronetcy was extinct by 1900.

Chapter 9

JOHN BORLASE WARREN

1753–1822

T HE EXPEDITION to the northwest tip of France was a closely
guarded secret. The area around Quiberon Bay was a noted hotbed of
royalist sympathies in June 1795, and the British government decided to
send aid to the supporters of Louis XVII. Approximately 3,500 émigré
troops had been loaded into transports with a large store of arms, ready to
join forces with the royalist sympathizers ashore. But lest the republicans
send reinforcements to the region, the destination was kept a profound
secret known only to the senior French officers, Lord Bridport, who commanded the Channel fleet at sea, and Commo. Sir John Borlase Warren,
officer in charge of the convoy.

The convoy's destination was such a secret that even flag officers such as
Vice Adm. William Cornwallis were kept in ignorance. Acting on his own
intelligence, the vice admiral had attacked a French convoy not far from the
landing site of the secret expedition. His attack drew the main fleet from
Brest under the command of Vice Admiral Villaret-Joyeuse westward. Finding himself in the presence of a force much larger than his own, Cornwallis
executed a skillful retreat and got his own squadron safely away. Unfortunately, this action placed the Brest fleet in dangerously close proximity to
the Quiberon expedition, which had been protected by the Channel fleet
part of the way but had since broken off.

To make matters worse, Villaret-Joyeuse encountered a storm, which
forced him to seek shelter at Belle Ile, the very point for which Warren's
squadron was making. Unaware of a large enemy force in the area, the invasion force sailed on through thick weather until the parting fog gave a scouting frigate a glimpse of the French just sailing out from Belle Ile. Immediately the captain hurried back to the commodore with his report. As the
Channel fleet was too far away to assist him, Warren decided that he would
have to hold off the Brest fleet with his available resources.

The commodore signaled his squadron of three ships of the line and assorted frigates and gunboats to form line of battle. Then they drew back to protect the transports. Villaret-Joyeuse sent one of his heavy frigates, the *Tribune* (36), to examine the enemy more closely. Hoping to entice this frigate close enough to take her as a prize, Warren commanded that a huge red cap of liberty, complete with tricolor cockade, be placed atop his flagship's figurehead.[1] This mockery of a symbol sacred to republican France was enough to draw the *Tribune* within range. However, after she had felt the effects of a few British broadsides, she put about and returned to her admiral. Hearing the frigate captain's report, Villaret-Joyeuse decided that the opposition appeared too formidable for him to risk an attack, so he continued on his way toward Brest, leaving Warren to continue in peace.

Thus the Quiberon expedition was able to land without loss. As for the French admiral, he had jumped nimbly out of the frying pan and into the fire. In avoiding the weak squadron he had thought a powerful fleet, he fell straight into the clutches of the Channel fleet, resulting in the Battle of Ile de Groix described in chapter 2.

• • •

Sir John Borlase Warren had an unusual background for an eighteenth-century naval officer. Originally intended for the Church, he received a bachelor's and a master's degree from Cambridge. But he never graced a pulpit. Instead, he inherited a title and a sizable fortune while in his early twenties and seemed prepared to live the life of a playboy. But then the threatened entry of the French into the American War of Independence induced him to reexamine the life he had been leading. He decided to face his perceived responsibilities and join the Royal Navy.

Judging by most contemporary sources, it was well for the Church of England that Sir John opted for the quarterdeck of a ship of war over the pulpit. He was noted for impetuosity in action and some unsteadiness of character that would have ill suited him to the role of parson but made him an ideal frigate captain or commander of small detached squadrons. Although he seems to have thought of his commands more as something he was doing for fun than as a deadly serious business, when the situation required it he could be as dedicated as any captain on the Navy List. Even that most severe of critics, the Earl of St. Vincent, thought highly of him for certain tasks. Of him he wrote: "He is a good fellow in the presence of the enemy, but runs a little wild in other matters when detached; he cannot bear being confined to a fleet . . . and will be miserable when he is obliged to serve en masse."[2]

A touch of the flightiness in Warren's character appears in his letters. Although his English was more literate than that of many sea officers of the day, and his education was reflected in his use of Latin, he swooped rapidly from one subject to the next and rarely said all he needed without adding a postscript. In writing of his battles, he had a tendency to exaggerate the force of the enemy, especially the vessels that escaped his clutches. Nonetheless, his career is remarkable for the number of actions and prizes taken.

As previously stated, Sir John was well suited to the role of frigate captain or commodore of a small squadron, but as a commander in chief he was out of his depth. He was not successful as admiral in command of the North American station during the War of 1812. This could have been because he was in ill health, but chances are that even if his constitution had been better he still would have lacked the steadiness of character that marks good commanders in chief. The Earl of St. Vincent said of him: "Sir John Warren . . . has honestly declared to me that he can neither stand long cruises nor being constantly attached to the fleet; which, looking back to the course of his services, and manner of life when ashore, is easily accounted for."[3]

Although not the ideal commander in chief, Warren was a highly talented and intelligent officer and deserves more attention than is commonly meted out to him. His career encompassed many notable actions, but while his colleague Pellew is widely known, Warren is virtually forgotten.

Generally, Sir John's history is one long tale of good fortune. He inherited a title and money as a young man and acquired more honor and wealth in the course of his naval career. He was tall and good-looking, and has generally been described as a man of rank and fashion.[4] Only in family matters did his habitual good luck fail to materialize. Of his five children, only a daughter survived him, but in her children his blood survives to this day.

• • •

Although John Borlase was the fourth son born to John and Anne Warren of Nottinghamshire, he was given his father's name. The Warrens were members of the local gentry, with aspirations of reviving a baronetcy that came from Sir John Borlase, whose only daughter had married the grandfather of the subject of this biography. Although the title had become extinct at the death of old Sir John, the Warren family struggled to have it revived, until it was settled on the eldest surviving son of Mr. Warren of Nottinghamshire upon the death of that gentleman.

When the eventual Sir John was born on 2 September 1753, he had older brothers who seemed likely to inherit the family wealth and honors. Therefore, young John Borlase was intended for the Church. He was apparently a bright lad, who did well enough at his studies to enter Cambridge at the age of sixteen. He was admitted to Emmanuel College in the autumn of 1769 and continued studies suitable for a future member of the clergy.

But in 1771 two things changed the course of John's life. In March his remaining elder brother died, suddenly making him the heir presumptive to title and fortune. This event appears to have caused young John to rethink his future. Although he did not abandon his course of study at Cambridge, he was entered on the books of the *Marlborough* (74), the guardship in the Medway, on 24 April. He had never been to sea before, but he was rated an able seaman. It is unlikely that Mr. Warren of Emmanuel College messed between the guns on the berth deck with Jack Tar. In fact it is unlikely that he spent much time aboard ship at this early stage of his career. Guardship duties were light and did not require constant attendance. Although on the *Marlborough*'s books, Warren continued his studies at Cambridge.

By the beginning of 1772, however, Warren's attendance aboard the *Marlborough* had become so irregular that he was actually listed on the ship's books as a deserter. But with a little friendly persuasion from family interest, the letter "R" for "Run" standing against the fledgling seaman's name was removed within a month. A few days later Warren was transferred to more active duty aboard the *Alderney* (12), a revenue cruiser.

Aboard the *Alderney* our hero's naval career might be said to have fairly begun. Within a couple of months, he was rated midshipman and saw a side of peacetime service that was much better suited to his character than the endless swaying at anchor of the guardship. He developed a love of sailing, especially in fast small vessels, and a devotion to the service.

Still, Warren's duties in the revenue cruiser were not arduous. He found time to complete his bachelor's degree at Cambridge in 1773 and to begin his studies for a master's degree. He continued sporadically in the *Alderney* until the spring of 1774 and then came ashore, apparently on a permanent basis. At the tender age of twenty-one, he became member of Parliament for Marlow. As was common in the era, it is probable that the seat in the House of Commons was gained by family interest and money. It appears that at this time in his life he intended to swallow the anchor and take up a political career. But once again, his situation changed.

John Warren senior died on 1 June 1775, leaving a sizable fortune to the newly made Sir John. A fortune and a title are heady possessions for a young man in his early twenties. At first Sir John appeared willing to act with a maturity unexpected in one so young and volatile. He continued his studies and finished his master's degree in 1776. However, once he had completed his degree, he seems to have felt that the time had come to sow his wild oats. Like some modern young men with a lot of money and few responsibilities, he bought an island and a yacht.

The island Warren bought was Lundy Island, in the Bristol Channel, and for the next year he amused himself by dashing about in his speedy little boat. Then the news from France took a turn for the worse in early 1777. Sir John had taken little interest in affairs in America while it had been apparently no more than a matter of subduing a few rebels. But when it appeared that the hereditary enemy was on the verge of entering the contest, the young baronet decided that he should bear a hand. He sold his yacht and "left Lundy to the rabbits."[5] Then he went aboard the *Venus* (36) as a gentleman volunteer and sailed for North America.

When Warren joined the fleet under Lord Howe in the autumn of 1777, the Royal Navy was at work in the Delaware River. The baronet was present at the capture of Philadelphia and in December transferred aboard the *Apollo* (32), under the command of Philemon Pownall, a bold captain (of whom more will be told in chapter 11). While Warren was in the *Apollo,* France entered the American War, and the British evacuated Philadelphia for fear of being trapped in the Delaware by an enemy fleet.

As described in chapter 1, the British fleet returned to New York just in time to discourage Admiral d'Estaing from entering the harbor, in July 1778. During the frantic few days while the enemy hovered off the coast, Sir John was promoted to lieutenant of the *Nonsuch* (64) under Capt. Walter Griffith. Although he had officially been in the navy six years before he received his commission, very little of that time had actually been spent aboard ship. By most accounts Warren was never much of a seaman, but he seemed to have made up for his lack of practical experience with intelligence and dash.

When Howe sailed for Newport to meet the French in August, the *Nonsuch* was one of his fleet. The little third rate took part in the maneuvers between the rival fleets in August and September before returning to New York.

Most of the ships of the North American squadron, the *Nonsuch* included, prepared to spend the winter in the Caribbean. However, Lieutenant Warren decided against sailing with his ship to the south. Either he had heard the fearsome reputation the West Indies had for disease or he had found the war in North America less exciting than he had anticipated. For whatever reason, he resigned his commission to the *Nonsuch* in October and sailed for home. Once again Sir John might have taken up his playboy existence, but the navy still had a hold on him. By March 1779 he had succeeded in obtaining a commission aboard the *Victory* (100) in the Channel fleet.

The spring of 1779 was a time of turmoil for the Channel fleet. At around the time that Warren joined the ship, the *Victory* ceased to be the flagship of Admiral Keppel. Because of the bad blood between the First Lord of the Admiralty, Lord Sandwich, and Keppel's supporters, finding a replacement for the commander in chief proved difficult. At last the position was given to the elderly Sir Charles Hardy, who hoisted his flag aboard the *Victory* and led the fleet to sea on various brief occasions through the summer.

Although Channel fleet service under the circumstances could not have been inspiring for an eager young man like Warren, Sir John remained for the few months required to transform him from a mere lieutenant to a master and commander. His lucky break came toward the end of June, when one of the Channel fleet cruisers captured the French corvette *Helena* (14). Within a fortnight, the little man-of-war was purchased for the navy's use, and Warren appointed to command her. Service in the *Helena* was truer to Sir John's character than being fastened to a flagship. He was free to cruise, dash about with dispatches or, at worst, defend a convoy. For nearly two years he commanded the corvette and carried on various missions in home waters.

Although small ships generally spent more time at sea than did ships of the line, Warren still found time enough for courtship ashore. In December 1780 he married Caroline Clavering, the daughter of Lt. Gen. Sir John Clavering, and carried her off to his ancestral home in Nottinghamshire. They eventually had five children. Sadly, three died young, and their eldest son was killed in Egypt as an officer in a Guards regiment.

Not only did Warren find time for courtship, but also he was able to perform some of his parliamentary duties. He became a follower of Lord Sandwich, an alliance he hoped would speed him toward his true goal—command of a frigate. As he wrote to the First Lord in February 1780:

> I was very happy in being able to comply with your Lordship's wishes in being in town time enough to attend the debate on Monday. I am sure your Lordship cannot doubt of my personal attachment to yourself or desire of concurring in any measure where you think your own interest concerned.
>
> On the other hand I hope your Lordship will not think me unreasonable in requesting an immediate and public proof of your Lordship's approbation, by giving me a frigate and a station in the spring, either in the South Sea or off Lisbon.[6]

The desired promotion was longer in coming than Sir John wished, but it came eventually. In February 1781 Sir John was transferred into the *Merlin* (18), which he commanded for only a few months. Then, on 25 April, he achieved his heart's desire by being made post into the *Ariadne* (20), which he commanded for the rest of the year. For the summer the *Ariadne* cruised off Britain's east coast, and enjoyed a few minor adventures. She gave chase to a stranger who proved too large for the *Ariadne* to handle alone but whom, fortunately, she could outrun. Later she pursued an American privateer, only to lose her in heavy weather. Once the summer cruising season was over, Warren wrote to the Admiralty explaining that his private affairs demanded too much of his time and could they please appoint a temporary captain for the *Ariadne* until he chose to return. As it turned out, Sir John's departure from his first frigate was permanent. However, in March of the following year he became captain of the *Winchelsea* (32).

When he received his commission to the *Winchelsea*, Warren placed more demands on the First Lord of the Admiralty. He could not be bothered with the mundanities of fitting out his new command, so he asked for a relief captain to take care of that tedious business for him. Then he would be only too happy to arrive on board, take up the reins of command, and set sail in search of rich prizes. After that, his only demand was that he not have to sail so far that he could not come home every once in a while to visit his wife. Sandwich thought his demands absurd and refused to grant him a relief captain. With the change of administration, Sir John kissed hands to the new First Lord and remained in command of the *Winchelsea*, with the exception of a winter sabbatical, until the end of the war.

Although the Treaty of Paris ended Captain Warren's term in command of a king's ship for a time, he continued to maintain contact with the navy. He offered his services in 1786, and when the Admiralty failed to find a ship for him, he decided to travel to the Continent. With his family he spent most of 1787 jaunting between France and Switzerland. When he returned, he felt again the need for a deck under his feet, and served as a volunteer under the command of Commo. John Leveson-Gower, one of the peacetime commanders of the Channel fleet. At each new armament and reincarnation of the fleet, Warren saw a little more sea time. In the summer of 1790, he joined the *Valiant* (74) as a volunteer under the command of the Duke of Clarence but grew bored when it did not appear that the fleet would sail, and went ashore. He applied again for employment the following year, but did not stride his own quarterdeck again until early 1793.

Just before the French wars broke out, Sir John was appointed to command of the *Flora* (36), flagship of a frigate squadron under Rear Adm. John MacBride. As was typical at the beginning of a war, the Royal Navy was seriously undermanned, and Warren's main challenge was to find a crew for his frigate. One of the best places for a bold captain to pick up prime seamen was off Gravesend, where the homeward-bound merchantmen tended to concentrate. On 10 March he acquired forty men in the following manner:

> I dropped [anchor] near the *Lord Harlow* Indiaman, which ship had acted in the most outrageous manner, in recruiting the boats sent from H.M. ships. From the accounts I received and the appearance of the soldiers in the ships who were all armed and acting in conjunction with their crews, I accepted the offer of a part of 30 men . . . to embarque and act as marines in the river. . . . Afterwards veered alongside the Indiaman, when they received me armed, I told them the consequences of their resistance and to avoid the shedding of blood, I promised that if they would enter voluntarily, they would have liberty to do so; upon which they threw down their arms.[7]

The seamen of the *Lord Harlow* may not have wanted to join the navy, but if they volunteered, they would at least receive a bounty and better treatment. If they had held out against Warren and his press gang, they would have received nothing except hard knocks, and if they had killed a member of the gang, they would have become hunted men.

While patrolling off Brest in January 1794, the *Flora* captured her first prize—the sixteen-gun *Vipère*. This was merely the first of many enemy men-of-war that Warren was to capture or destroy during the next several years.

Soon after the capture of the *Vipère*, Rear Admiral MacBride was sent on to other duties, and Sir John received orders to hoist the broad pennant of a commodore. On 23 April, Warren was cruising off Le Havre with a squadron of five frigates.[8] There he encountered a French squadron consisting of three frigates and a corvette.[9] When the two squadrons first encountered one another on the evening of the twenty-second, the wind was in the south-southwest, with the British on the starboard tack and the French to windward on the larboard tack. Having the advantage of the wind gauge, and hoping to avoid what was likely to be an unprofitable action, the French, under the command of the Commodore Desgareaux in the *Engageante* (36), formed line of battle. Making all sail, they crossed in front of the British line, but no sooner had the French crossed than Warren commanded his squadron to tack. This maneuver, aided by a slight shift in the wind direction, placed his frigates on the same tack as the enemy and gave them the wind gauge.

Shortly after dawn on the twenty-third, the *Flora,* at the head of the British line, closed with the enemy and exchanged broadsides with the *Babet* (20), *Pomone* (44), and *Résolue* (36) in succession. Then, with her spars and rigging severely damaged, the flagship fell back, and the *Arethusa* (38) took her place. The actions of the *Flora* and the *Arethusa* held the enemy long enough for the *Melampus* (36) and the *Concorde* (36) to come up. Although the *Flora* could scarcely make steerage way, she was able to close with the *Babet* and compel her to surrender. Meanwhile, the *Résolue* and the *Engageante* tried to break away, leaving the *Pomone* to face the *Arethusa* and the *Melampus* alone. The huge frigate fought for an hour before she hauled down her flag.

Seeing that the *Résolue* and the *Engageante* were attempting to escape, Warren signaled the *Melampus* and the *Concorde* to pursue them. The *Concorde* was the swiftest of the British frigates and soon caught up with the Frenchmen. But her captain could do little but engage in a delaying action against two opponents of her own size. He had hoped that the *Melampus* would be able to come to his assistance, but she was too badly damaged to catch up. At last he selected the *Engageante* and threw his own vessel close alongside her. For close to two hours, the frigates pounded at each other until the Frenchman was completely dismasted and forced to surrender. While this battle raged, the remaining enemy frigate escaped.

To engage an enemy force only slightly weaker than one's own and capture three out of four was a respectable if not exceptional showing. The losses suffered by both sides were surprisingly lopsided. The complete tally of casualties in Sir John's squadron amounted to 10 killed and 25 wounded, whereas the French lost between 110 and 140 killed and wounded from two of the prize ships alone.[10]

Some reports of the battle exaggerated the power of the French squadron, giving the impression that Warren had won a great victory, for which he was made a knight of the Bath. However, Warren's feats are now forgotten to the extent that it is a commonly stated myth that no naval officers under the rank of rear admiral were made knights of the Bath between Jervis in 1781 and Cochrane in 1809.[11]

All through the summer of 1794, Warren and his wolf pack of frigates prowled the waters of the Channel. On the morning of 23 August, his squadron, which consisted of six frigates—*Flora* (36), *Arethusa, Diamond* (38), *Artois* (38), *Diana* (38), and *Santa Margarita* (36)—whose commanders were a virtual constellation of rising stars, sighted the *Volontaire* (36) and two eighteen-gun corvettes off Brest.[12] The *Diamond, Artois, Santa Margarita,* and *Diana* attacked the frigate immediately and forced her upon the rocks, where she was "disabled and irrecoverably lost."[13] As for the corvettes, Warren went after them himself, taking the *Arethusa* with him. The Frenchmen tried to flee into the shelter of Audierne Bay, but the British continued to come in after them. At last the corvettes too ran themselves aground under a battery. Still the *Flora* and *Arethusa* would not abandon their prey. They remained in the bay, exchanging shots with the battery and the grounded corvettes until the French vessels had been completely dismasted. Then Pellew took two boats full of seamen and marines ashore to finish the destruction of the corvettes.

That was the last major action Warren saw in 1794. At the beginning of the following year, he was sent with his squadron to Brest to confirm a rumor that the French fleet had sailed. Upon his arrival, he sent Sir William Sidney Smith and the *Diamond* into the harbor to gain better intelligence. Sir Sidney hoisted French colors and sailed well into enemy waters until he came within speaking distance of a ship of the line. This two-decker appeared to be making repairs, and the audacious Smith, who spoke excellent French, asked if she needed any assistance. He received a refusal and then the information that the ship had been damaged while sailing with the rest of the fleet. With this intelligence, the *Diamond* returned unmolested to her compatriots.

Soon after this scouting expedition, the commodore shifted his broad pennant into the *Pomone,* the same vessel his squadron had captured the previous year. Now, with her battle wounds repaired, she was a fit flagship for a frigate squadron.

Through the spring of 1795, Sir John and his pack cruised the Channel, snapping up any enemy vessel that crossed their path. On 26 February the *Pomone* captured the *Curieuse* (12), on 15 April the *Jean-Bart* (16) fell to her guns, and the next day she took the *Expedition* (16).

When the Channel weather became more moderate, the Admiralty decided that the time was ripe to foster a descent on Quiberon. As noted at the beginning of this chapter, royalist sympathies were reported to be strong in Normandy, so it was thought that if émigré troops were landed, partisans would rise up to join them. To Commodore Warren fell the task of escorting the transports across the Channel and then guarding them from interference once they had landed. He had at his command three ships of the line, six frigates, and a number of cutters, gunboats, and armed transports.[14]

These vessels carried approximately 3,500 French soldiers and volunteers under the command of the Comte de Puisaye, who was seconded by the Comtes d'Hervilly and de Sombreuil.

Although all the soldiers had been embarked by 12 June, the expedition did not set sail until nearly a week later. But finally, under the protection of the main Channel fleet, they put to sea. For two days the expedition kept company with Admiral Bridport before parting near Belle Ile. This precaution should have been sufficient to keep the French fleet away from the squadron, except that Vice Admiral Villaret-Joyeuse turned up where he was not expected. As described at the beginning of this biography, Warren found himself face to face with the French fleet but managed to make his force look formidable enough that Villaret-Joyeuse had second thoughts about attacking. The French turned away, leaving Sir John's squadron free to enter Quiberon Bay on 25 June.

Two days later the first troops were landed. Although a small force of about two hundred republicans were waiting to oppose them, they were soon driven off, and the Anglo-French force was able to complete its landing without loss. Soon after the landing, royalist partisans, called Chouans, began to arrive to join forces with the expeditionary party. Warren had been supplied with a large stock of arms and ammunition, which he distributed to the Chouans as they arrived. The initial response was enthusiastic, as the commodore reported to Lord Bridport: "I have already armed between three and four thousand Royalists, and the numbers that come down to join us are inconceivable. I never saw so affecting a scene as the reception of the troops by our friends. Old men and young cried; and men, women and children, brought butter, eggs, milk, bread, wine, and whatever they had, both to our people and the troops, and would not receive a farthing in payment."[15]

At first the expedition yielded promising results. The troops swiftly captured Fort Penthièvre, and more and more partisans rallied to the royal standard. The British and Royalist officers arranged to have the Chouans trained as soldiers, but Warren considered them unreliable and hoped to be reinforced from England. As the republican forces continued to increase in the area in response to the royalist threat, the commodore grew ever more anxious to have additional regulars join him, but none were forthcoming.

The commander of the republican forces in the vicinity of Quiberon Bay was General Lazare Hoche. Although only twenty-eight, he was one of the most respected republican military commanders. When he arrived on the scene, he stationed his troops in a strong position on the heights of St. Barbe.

On 16 July the Comte d'Hervilly with five thousand troops, including two hundred marines, assaulted the republican works, but was driven back with severe losses.[16] The comte himself was wounded, which deprived the émigrés of one of their most active leaders. Although this action demoralized some of the Chouans, who began to desert, the regulars remained undaunted.

But on 20 July the situation was drastically altered. A howling storm blew up that night, and under cover of the weather, a party of émigrés who had been on guard duty deserted to the enemy. Soon afterward they returned with a large body of republican troops, who stormed the fort and drove the royalist forces and their allies to the beach, where they were once again embarked aboard the ships of the squadron.

While covering the retreat, the Comte de Sombreuil was overwhelmed; he surrendered upon terms. However, once he and his men had been disarmed, the republicans ignored the terms, marched the prisoners to Nantes, and tried them by drumhead court-martial. De Sombreuil and most of his officers were shot, and the ranks enlisted in the republican army.

Warren had tried to negotiate with the republicans for de Sombreuil's release, but there was no one with the authority or the courage to treat with the British. The Frenchmen nearest him had dissolved into a state of utter chaos after they gained possession of a large supply of rum that had been stored in six poorly defended transports. The republicans became drunk nearly to a man, and afterward as many as fifty died as a result of their overindulgence.

Although he was short of supplies, the commodore had no wish to completely abandon the enterprise. He led the squadron and transports to two nearby islands, thinking they could be used as a temporary base while the government in London decided what to do next. Once he had secured the islands, he sent ashore some of the refugees he had taken aboard at Quiberon. In this way he was able to conserve the supplies they had been eating, but still his stock of provisions was running low. The islands supplied some water, and he had flour enough to have bread made, but he knew that on such a limited diet, his men would soon be falling sick. His letters to the Admiralty during the latter part of July and the beginning of August are full of appeals for beer and cattle to be sent to him directly.

Hearing that the island of Noirmoutier in the Loire River was in royalist hands, Warren hoped to salvage something from the wreck of his expedition and provide more supplies for his men by placing a garrison on the island. Unfortunately, by the time he arrived off the island, the republicans had retaken it and set up some stout defenses. The British were unable to land any troops, and were soon forced to put about for the nearby Ile d'Yeu, which they captured to use as a base. It was there that a supply convoy finally reached Warren in mid-September, enabling the British to hold on for some months longer.

Still hoping to gain something from their possession of a few small islands and from the prevalence of royalist sympathies in certain districts, the government sent Sir John an additional four thousand British troops in early October. With these reinforcements came the Comte d'Artois, brother of the executed Louis XVI.

The original intent of sending the troops was to capture Noirmoutier via a narrow sandbar, which connected the larger island with the Ile d'Yeu. However, after the troops arrived, it was discovered that the sandbar was impassible and Noirmoutier was too heavily defended. Finding the military situation tenuous at best, the Comte d'Artois hesitated to risk his life by landing, and returned to England in November, which destroyed the morale of the royalists ashore. From that point, any attempts to capture more territory from the republicans were doomed. Lord Spencer soon realized that there was no point in prolonging an expedition that was unlikely to yield lasting results. He sent Warren the orders for his recall on 22 October.

The commodore had been anxious to depart for some time. Immediately upon receiving his orders from the First Lord, he set about reembarking the troops. However, he was stopped by Rear Adm. Henry Harvey, commander of a squadron of the Channel fleet. Apparently the admiral feared that the weather conditions would interfere with the embarkation or that the ships would be wrecked in leaving the road. As a result of Harvey's delays, the evacuation of the Ile d'Yeu was not completed until 10 December.

Warren successfully escorted his transports home and soon returned to his accustomed role as commander of a frigate squadron. On 20 March 1796 the *Pomone* was in company with the *Anson* (44), *Artois,* and *Galatea* (32) when Warren sighted a large French convoy guarded by four frigates and a corvette.[17] Immediately the British gave chase. After about two hours of pursuit, the *Pomone* and the *Artois* captured two merchant brigs and, soon afterward, another brig and a three-masted ship.

By this time the French frigates were prepared to defend the rest of the convoy. On opposite courses, the two squadrons passed each other at a good fighting distance and exchanged broadsides that did little damage to any vessel, except to the rigging of the *Galatea.* As soon as they completed the first pass, Warren tacked his squadron and started back after the enemy. By evening he had gained the wind gauge and prepared to cut the French line. Unfortunately, by this time the enemy had nearly reached the safety of their own coast. Taking advantage of the gathering darkness and the treacherousness of the coast, most of the French managed to slip away. However, Sir John's squadron managed to take two more prizes before they were forced to abandon the pursuit.

Less than a month later, Warren's squadron captured the *Robuste* (22), also off the coast of France. But their next major exploit occurred on 22 August. While cruising off the mouth of the Gironde River, the squadron encountered the French frigate *Andromaque* (36), which was attempting to enter the river. The *Galatea* was nearest and put on all sail to cut the enemy off from her place of refuge. By hoisting French signals, Captain Keats of the *Galatea* induced the commander of the *Andromaque* to drop anchor, but soon the Frenchman discovered his error and cut his cable. This, however, gave the British more time to close. The *Andromaque* attempted to escape to the south, hotly pursued by the *Galatea* while the *Pomone* and *Anson* remained to the north to prevent her from cutting back. Through night and storm the British frigate hung in the wake of her quarry, and at dawn she was joined by the *Artois* and the *Sylph* (18). Finding the situation hopeless, the French captain ran his ship on shore. Captain Keats sent a number of boats ashore to take off prisoners, and once the *Andromaque* had been completely evacuated, he sent the *Sylph* to complete the frigate's destruction. For this and other deeds, the commodore was presented with a 100-guinea sword by the newly formed Patriotic Fund.

Shortly after the encounter with the *Andromaque,* the squadron put back to Falmouth. But in early October, Warren planned to go cruising after rich prizes that were due to be coming from South America to Spain. Indeed, he sailed with that in mind, but when he was compelled by foul weather to return, he received orders to remain closer to home in case the French should attempt an invasion, which seemed likely, considering the force that was gathering at Brest. Characteristically, Sir John was not enthusiastic about the change of plans, and Lord Spencer felt compelled to reassure him:

The present situation of things at Brest and the tenor of the orders which we have in consequence of it been under the necessity of giving to Admiral Thompson . . . making it absolutely necessary for him to have the assistance of a considerable number of frigates, we send you out to join him for a time and assist the operations . . . intending by and by to release you from the fleet and send you cruising again on your old ground. I write this that you may not be alarmed and fancy we are going to attach you as a fixture to the great lumbering three-deckers in the Western squadron.[18]

Although Warren himself doubted that the French would be ready to invade for some time, he was compelled to comply with his orders. He remained attached to the lumbering three-deckers for the balance of the year.

Eventually, near the end of 1796, the French invasion force sailed for Ireland. Although Warren's squadron was cruising in search of the enemy, he failed to spy them on this occasion. (The fate of this expedition has been discussed in chapter 2 and is described in greater detail in chapter 11.)

The spring of 1797 brought the fleet mutinies, which have already been described in several of the previous chapters. Warren had the good fortune to be at sea with his squadron for most of the period of the Spithead mutiny, so he missed the worst of that episode. However, when his men heard of the deal Lord Howe had made with other members of the Channel fleet, they felt they had been cheated out of their share in the rewards. After all, they had kept their stations when the rest of the fleet had been in a state of mutiny, and they agreed that they were at least as entitled to dispose of unwanted officers as those who had refused to sail. The frigates' people formed a delegation and compelled the commodore to leave his station for Plymouth. There they presented him with a list of officers they wished to have removed, with his friend Captain Keats of the *Galatea* at the top.

Sir John cooperated with his men as best he could. He forwarded their requests to the Admiralty and sat in negotiation with them. His reward was that his men never became mutinous, but discipline suffered severely for a time, as he related to Lord Spencer:

> My Lord,—I did not write to your lordship sooner, because it was necessary to see what course the present fever in the ships here might take. . . . I have been obliged to undergo many trials of patience and condescension, and have experienced all the mummery of being chaired. My men, being the first to return to their duty, have incurred the guilt of not being violent enough; they have likewise been alarmed at the idea of my leaving them. The ship gets forward, and perhaps matters may go on tolerably well, but the example of the *Galatea* is dreadful. . . . The seamen are now drunk and disorderly, and some have been committed; but perhaps in a day or two they may be tired and return to their duty on board their respective ships.[19]

Eventually the trouble passed, and Warren returned to his accustomed station off Brest. On the evening of 16 July, the *Pomone*, sailing in company with the *Anson, Artois,* and *Sylph,* sighted a French convoy composed of fourteen vessels escorted by the *Calliope* (28) and two corvettes. When the British gave chase, the corvettes were able to escape, but the frigate was forced ashore. It was followed by the *Anson* and the *Sylph,* which anchored in shallow water and bombarded the French as they attempted to carry stores out of the *Calliope.* By the next day the French frigate had been pounded to pieces by the surf. Of the rest of the convoy, eight ships were captured and three run aground and destroyed.[20]

Less than a month later, Sir John, this time in company with the *Jason* (38), *Triton* (32), and *Sylph,* sighted another small convoy under the protection of a corvette and a few gun vessels. This convoy sought refuge in the mouth of a nearby river with the corvette and one of the gun vessels under the guns of a fortress. Even this failed to daunt the captain of the *Sylph,* who requested and received permission to attack the two French men-of-war. The sloop-of-war opened fire, which was returned by both enemy ships and the fort. The valiant little *Sylph* held on alone for half an hour until the *Pomone* and the *Jason* were able to come to her assistance. The pounding from the three British vessels induced the captain of the French gun vessel to attempt to escape upriver, but no sooner had he gotten under way than his ship sank. The corvette too was severely damaged, but the presence of the fort prevented Warren's squadron from finishing the work they had begun.

The commodore's last major exploit in the *Pomone* was the destruction of the cutter *Petit Diable* (18) on 28 August. While the rest of the squadron was chasing a convoy, the *Pomone* closed with the escorting cutter, and thinking her lightly armed and manned, Sir John sent a boat to take possession. But the cutter defied the boat, causing the *Pomone* to open fire. Within a few minutes, the *Petit Diable*'s mast had gone overboard. The ship, out of control, ran aground and was lost upon the rocks.

For some time Warren had been requesting the use of a ship of the line. He wrote to Lord Spencer: "[M]y Lord, it were possible to have such a ship of the line as the *Leviathan* upon the Falmouth station, it would be a very pleasant circumstance. . . . I could then act with the frigates as usual; and if it should meet with the approbation of the Board, to cruise off Cape Ortegal should be of more use than off Brest; except when the fleet were in Torbay."[21] In the autumn of 1797, Sir John's broad pennant was transferred aboard the *Canada* (74). In the following spring Warren and his wolf pack were back to their old tricks off the French coast. Unfortunately, the commodore appears to have had a little trouble adjusting to one of the differences between a ship of the line and a frigate.

On the morning of 22 March 1798, the *Canada* was cruising with the *Anson* and the *Phaeton* (38) when she sighted the French frigate *Charente* (36). The three British vessels gave chase, but as the frigate was fleet, they gained slowly. It was not until after midnight that the *Phaeton* approached within gunshot and opened fire. To escape the guns of the frigate, the *Charente* turned toward the land, which put her in range of the guns of the *Canada*. Warren opened fire and continued in pursuit until his flagship ran aground on a sandbank. Sir John made a distress signal, which caused the frigates to abandon their own pursuit. The Frenchman also ran aground shortly thereafter. After two and half hours on the sandbar, the *Canada* floated off, carried by the rising tide and lightened by emptying a portion of her water supply over the side. Meanwhile, the French frigate was compelled to throw most of her guns overboard before she was able to sail again and seek refuge in the Bordeaux River.

The remainder of the spring and summer was spent cruising without any results worthy of note. But with the coming of autumn, the French at Brest were again preparing to make a descent upon Ireland. Approximately three thousand troops were embarked with artillery and a vast supply of stores aboard the ships of the squadron commanded by Commo. J. B. F. Bompart. This squadron consisted of one ship of the line and nine heavy frigates.[22]

Blessed with good sailing weather on the night of 16 September, Bompart weighed anchor, hoping to slip unobserved past the British scouts. But the following morning the squadron was sighted by Captain Keats, now commanding the *Boadicea* (38), who was cruising in company with the *Ethalion* (38) and the *Sylph*. Ordering his companions to shadow the enemy, Keats sped northward to alert the Channel fleet. The next day the *Amelia* (44) joined the two British vessels in trailing the French, who tried without success to drive them off. Two days later the *Anson* joined the gathering pack.

Hoping to fool the British, Bompart steered toward the south as if he were bound for the West Indies. But the British were not deceived. Concluding that the destination of this squadron was Ireland, the senior captain sent the *Sylph* to warn Warren, who was cruising off the coast of Donegal. The three frigates remained within sight of the enemy until the weather turned dirty on 4 October. Then, being forced off, they turned northward in search of Warren.

Meanwhile, Sir John had sailed on 23 September as soon as he learned that the French were out, and guessing that the enemy meant to make for Ireland, he placed his squadron across their most likely course. When the

Anson, Amelia, and *Ethalion* joined him on 10 October, the commodore's total force consisted of three ships of the line and five frigates.[23]

The following afternoon the two squadrons sighted each other. Thinking that the enemy might escape, Warren instantly signaled his ships to give chase, hoping they would be able to form line of battle as they came up. While the British continued in pursuit of the French that night, a sharp gale sprang up, which damaged a few of the vessels on either side, including Bompart's flagship. Fearing that the British would catch him in his crippled state, the French commodore sought to decoy the enemy away from his squadron by ordering the most damaged of his vessels, the *Biche* (36), to make for the shore and to fire distress signals. However, these orders never reached the intended recipient, and the *Biche* went her own way into the night. When the sun rose, Bompart found the British nearly upon him. Indeed, the leading vessels were almost within random shot. However, Warren allowed the chase to continue until his squadron had further closed the distance and most of his vessels were in a position to support those first engaged.

At approximately 7:00 in the morning, the two squadrons formed a rough line of battle on the starboard tack bearing southwest. The British were to windward and slightly astern of the French. The battle began when Sir John commanded the *Robust* (74), his leading vessel, to close with the enemy rear. The *Embuscade* (36) and the *Coquille* (36) fired their stern chasers at the two-decker, but did little damage. The ship of the line returned their fire for a short time, but then passed on to leeward to attack the French flagship.

No sooner had the *Robust* dashed forward than her place in battle with the *Embuscade* and *Coquille* was taken by the *Magnanime* (44), which passed to leeward and opened up with her starboard guns. She did considerable damage, but to avoid colliding with the *Robust*—by that time locked in close combat with the *Hoche*—she was forced to break off. She was annoyed by the shot of the *Loire* (40), *Immortalité* (40), and *Bellone* (36) until she was able to bring her own broadside to bear. Aided by the *Foudroyant* (80), she soon sent the French frigates packing. Then the *Magnanime* joined the *Robust* in attacking the enemy flagship. If the *Hoche* had not difficulties enough, she was also engaged astern by the *Amelia* (44) and more distantly by the *Canada*. Finally, with her masts tottering and nearly sinking from shot holes between wind and water, the *Hoche* hauled down her flag shortly before 11:00. Meanwhile, the *Foudroyant* shifted her fire to the *Embuscade,* which forced her to surrender. The frigate became the prize of the *Magnanime*.

Leaving the damaged *Robust* and *Magnanime* to look after the prizes, Warren and the rest of his squadron pelted after the remaining Frenchmen. The frigates realized that their best hope of escape was to gain the wind gauge by crossing the bows of the British. Five of the seven managed to pass to windward, where they fought a brief action with the *Anson* before making their escape. But the *Bellone* and the *Coquille* were trapped. The *Bellone* was engaged first by the *Foudroyant,* then the *Melampus,* and finally the *Ethalion* before she surrendered. Meanwhile, the rest of Sir John's squadron mobbed the *Coquille* and forced her to haul down her flag. Then the *Melampus, Foudroyant, Amelia,* and *Canada* sailed on to assist the *Anson,* which appeared to be in difficulties. At the approach of these vessels, the Frenchmen made off. Not long afterward elements of the British squadron took three of the survivors of the action of 12 October. Of Bompart's squadron, only three eventually returned to France. The losses reported were 13 British killed and 75 wounded. The French lost no fewer than 395 killed and wounded.[24]

Warren's victory was no great tactical triumph. His squadron so greatly exceeded the force of his foe that he would have been justified in continuing the general chase rather than forming line of battle. It is probable that if he had not delayed at that critical moment he could have captured more of the enemy than he did.

Although Warren's action might have achieved more, it successfully removed the last threat of an invasion of Ireland. The English public, already celebrating the recently arrived news of Nelson's victory at the Nile, greeted this new victory with enthusiasm. Both houses of Parliament passed a vote of thanks in honor of Sir John's squadron, and each commander was entitled to the coveted gold battle medal.

On 14 February 1799 Warren was promoted to the dignities of a rear admiral. At first his life was uneventful, but in July he hoisted his flag aboard the *Téméraire* (98) and joined the Channel fleet. In September the idea of making a landing on the French coast was again bandied about, and Sir John was decidedly in favor of it. But perhaps the fiasco at the Helder (see chapter 5) caused Lord Spencer to think better of that notion. Instead, he preferred to encourage the more active flag officers in the Channel fleet to conduct cutting-out expeditions rather than full-scale invasions.

Warren's squadron undertook one such cutting-out expedition on 10 June 1800. In a daring nighttime raid, the crews of several boats cut out three small men-of-war and eight merchantmen from the harbor of St. Croix, at the cost of four men. A fortnight later the same company stormed and destroyed three small forts and batteries at the mouth of the Quimper River.[25] In this way the British continually harassed the French coast but never remained in one place long enough for the enemy to strike back.

Shortly after the events above, Sir John was detached from the Channel fleet for an expedition to Ferrol. At that time a squadron of six Spanish ships of the line was at anchor, protected by the guns of the forts overlooking the harbor.[26] The British government thought the situation providential for sending in soldiers to capture the forts, thereby enabling a squadron to sail in and capture the Spanish ships. Rear Admiral Warren was chosen to command the naval portion of the expedition with his flag in the *Renown* (74), while command of the army's forces went to Lt. Gen. Sir James Pulteney. In the British squadron were five ships of the line, five frigates, a sloop-of-war, and a large number of transports.[27]

Although Warren might have left something to be desired as a commander in a fleet action, he was accounted one of the best in raiding the enemy's coast. Admiral St. Vincent applauded his appointment in a letter to Lord Spencer: "Sir J. Warren is arrived on the very nick of time to become colleague to Sir James Pulteney: for indeed, my Lord, there is not other of the rank prescribed shaped for such an enterprise."[28]

The British arrived off Ferrol on 25 August. Immediately they set to work. The *Impétueux* (74), with a frigate, a sloop-of-war, and a gunboat, sailed into the harbor and began to fire on one of the forts. They made things so hot for the Spanish gun crews that the fort was abandoned, and the troops were able to land unopposed.

The British soldiers and a naval landing party climbed the heights in time to repel Spanish forces that arrived to try to drive them off. By the next morning the invaders had secured the heights. However, once he had the opportunity to collect some intelligence of dubious value, Sir James Pulteney decided that the enemy force in the area was too strong for him to hope to hold the heights long. He sent word to Warren to prepare to take the soldiers back aboard the transports again, and by midnight of the twenty-sixth, every Englishman had returned aboard the ships. The naval officers thought the expedition would have been a success if it had been pressed home, but they could not induce the general to agree with them. They proceeded to Gibraltar to join forces with Lord Keith. (The tale of how Admiral Keith sailed with the full power and majesty of his fleet to Cadiz, intending to compel its surrender, and of how he was turned away by news of the plague is told in chapter 6.) Once again Sir John and his squadron returned to Gibraltar.

Although the notion of attacking Cadiz was abandoned, a British squadron was still required to watch over the Spanish ships of the line anchored in the harbor. Early in 1801 Warren's squadron took that post and began the sort of blockading service that was anathema to a man of Sir John's volatile disposition. Undoubtedly, the rear admiral was relieved to hear that a French squadron under the command of Rear Admiral Ganteaume had escaped from Brest, apparently bound for the Mediterranean. Learning on 8 February that the enemy was not far away, Warren left his station to go in pursuit. He reached Gibraltar two days later, only to learn that the French were a day ahead. Thinking that they might be bound for Toulon or Cartagena, he pressed on, sending scouting frigates to search for the French, but found no sign of them.

In early March the admiral learned that the king of Naples had concluded a treaty with the French, and fearing for British interests in Sicily, he set sail in that direction. But on his way he was joined by a couple of ships of the line, whose captains informed him that Ganteaume was at Toulon after all. Immediately Sir John put about and made all sail. At daybreak on 25 March, his squadron sighted the enemy off the coast of Sardinia. Although the two forces were of roughly equal strength, the French did not wait to offer battle. They put on a turn of speed and before long were out of sight. Suspecting that Ganteaume was bound for Egypt, Warren continued in that direction, arriving off Alexandria on 19 April. It was there that he learned that Ganteaume had never been anywhere near Egypt. The disappointed admiral sailed back to the west.

Although Sir John was cheated of his chance to do battle with Ganteaume, who had returned to Toulon, he later learned that a small French squadron was besieging allied British and Tuscan troops on Elba. Once again he changed course and arrived in time to chase off the French and raise the siege. He then sent a force of seamen and marines ashore to assist the army in driving off enemy troops that had been landed on the island. Then Warren reembarked his men, leaving the army to hold Elba until the Peace of Amiens was signed.

When the preliminary peace was signed in October, Sir John came home, but he was not to remain idle for long. In 1802 he was appointed a member of the Privy Council and was later sent to St. Petersburg as ambassador extraordinary to congratulate the new czar, Alexander I, on his accession. On 9 November 1805 Warren was promoted to vice admiral and not long afterward appointed to command of a squadron of seven ships of the line.[29] He hoisted his flag in the *Foudroyant* and prepared to sail for Madeira in search of a French squadron that had escaped from Brest. This was the same squadron that eventually made its way to the West Indies, where it was defeated by Vice Admiral Duckworth. Upon reaching Madeira, Warren learned that the French were too far ahead of him to be worth pursuing, so he turned for home. In the early morning of 13 March 1806, his squadron encountered the *Marengo* (74) and *Belle Poule* (40), which had been sent to prey on East Indiamen in the South Atlantic. Like the British, they were on their way home.

The two French vessels, which had been accustomed to hunting large merchantmen, did not expect to find a squadron of warships in such isolated waters. The lack of light and their preconceived notions caused them to mistake Warren's vessels for a convoy of homeward-bound Indiamen. Hoping to pick up a few rich prizes, the *Marengo* and *Belle Poule* closed. The *London* was the first to detect the enemy and turned from the rest of the squadron to confront them, followed by the *Amazon* (38). When dawn broke, the *London* was separated from her compatriots by some distance and within easy shot of the French. As soon as it was light enough, she opened up with her broadside upon the *Marengo*. Finding that the intended victim had sharp teeth, the *Belle Poule* fled. Meanwhile, the *Marengo* traded fire with the British until she had damaged the *London*'s rigging enough that her captain thought she had a chance of escape. However, her own rigging was badly damaged, and the rest of the squadron was closing in. The French ship of the line was caught late in the morning and was forced to haul down her colors. Meanwhile, the *Amazon* made all sail after the *Belle Poule* and soon brought her to action. For two hours the two frigates enjoyed a running fight until the *Belle Poule* lowered her colors.

Warren's squadron brought their prizes into Spithead. Then, when news arrived of another French squadron loose in the West Indies, they were sent southward. All through the summer they hunted their quarry but never caught sight of them. Eventually they turned for home, and the squadron was disbanded.

For the next three years, Sir John commanded the North American station, which at that time was peaceful. He returned home in 1810. Then, shortly after Britain went to war against the United States in 1812, Warren, a full admiral as of 1810, was again appointed commander in chief of the North American station, to which the West Indies station had been added. He arrived in Halifax in September 1812, with a small squadron and his flag in the *St. Domingo* (74).[30]

At the age of fifty-nine, Warren was not exceptionally elderly for commanding a foreign station. However, he appears to have been in ill health and lacking the vigor that characterized his earlier career. For conducting the active part of his campaigns, he relied upon his second-in-command, the forty-year-old Rear Adm. George Cockburn.

In 1813 Warren centered his operations on the Chesapeake, which, with New England, was the most active area for shipping off the American coast. The British government decreed that the entire southeastern coast of the United States was to be blockaded, and to that end the admiral anchored his larger vessels near Baltimore. He sent smaller men-of-war of every description cruising over his vast command, which extended from Canada to the West Indies.

But Cockburn was not content with the blockade. He was eager to take more aggressive action, and so, in April, Warren gave him command of a squadron of light ships and unleashed him to ravage various towns up the creeks and waterways that emptied into the bay. For the space of a month, the rear admiral wreaked havoc throughout the region. After Cockburn had marauded for a few weeks, he reembarked his men and sailed for Bermuda to take on troops for some larger-scale attacks Warren had in mind. So when Sir John had all his forces gathered in June, he determined to make Norfolk his target.

The Norfolk expedition was divided into two parties—a land party and a naval party that set out in fifteen boats. Neither met its objective. The land party became lost in the swamps and eventually reembarked without meeting the enemy. As for the naval division, they set out to attack Craney Island, which was defended by a small battery. But they found the water too shallow for their boats to approach close enough to land the men without a long walk through the water, and the battery kept up a destructive fire. Three of the attacking boats were sunk, and the rest put about and returned to the fleet, having accomplishing nothing except the loss of ninety-one men.

Annoyed by the failure at Norfolk, Warren dispatched Cockburn against the village of Hampton. After a sharp fight the British took the town, and, against orders, they looted it and put it to the torch. After that experience Sir John decided to control his forces more closely. He continued to make raids, but these accomplished little. The main focus of his final period in command was the tightening of the blockade.

In the spring of 1814, the British government decided it needed a healthier commander in chief for the North American station. Warren was relieved by Vice Adm. Sir Alexander Cochrane and went home to enjoy the remainder of his life in peace. Although ill health prevented Sir John for taking any more commands after he left the North American station, he maintained his old friendships. While on a visit to Sir Richard Keats at Greenwich on 22 February 1822, he suddenly took ill and died. He was buried in the family vault in Oxfordshire.

Although Warren was unfortunate in that most of his children died young, his daughter Frances married well. In 1802 she wed the man who eventually became the fourth Lord Vernon.

Chapter 10

JAMES SAUMAREZ

1757–1836

THE SITUATION had gone from a promising opportunity to a complete disaster in such a short time that it was difficult at first for the crew of the *Caesar* (80) to comprehend the extent of their reversal. Only the day before, the squadron under the command of Rear Adm. Sir James Saumarez had heard that a French squadron of four ships of the line had slipped out of Toulon, headed for Gibraltar. As commanding officer of the nearest force of sufficient size to face the French, Saumarez had immediately left his post before Cadiz and made sail for the south with six ships of the line.

The French admiral, Linois, had been attempting to pass through the Straits of Gibraltar against a head wind when he learned that the British had been alerted to his presence. Not wishing to be caught between the guns of the fleet and those crowning the Rock, Linois immediately put into Algeciras, a port a short distance to the east. It was there that Saumarez found him the morning after he sailed from Cadiz.

Sir James had been second-in-command at the Battle of the Nile nearly three years earlier. He remembered well how Nelson had swooped in on the anchored French in spite of approaching darkness and the close proximity of the shore. The reward for Nelson's audacity had been a splendid victory, and there seemed no reason to believe that the result on this occasion would be any different. Not only did the British have their enemy trapped, but they also had numerical superiority.

With the *Venerable* (74), commanded by Capt. Samuel Hood, in the lead, Sir James's squadron sailed in on a light breeze. Unfortunately, the breeze did not prove reliable. As soon as the British came within the bay, they found themselves subjected to scattered calms that swiftly broke up their tight formation. Still they came on, approaching as close to the enemy as the winds would allow and then dropping anchor to hold them in place while the gun crews worked their pieces. Some of the British vessels were able to get within a good fighting distance, but others were essentially useless because they were unable to turn their broadsides on the enemy.

In this piecemeal fashion a bloody action developed. The British vessels in a convenient situation for fighting exchanged broadsides with the French. Meanwhile, the Spanish batteries that overlooked the bay opened up on them and on those ships that had not been able to enter the fight.

It had fallen to the lot of the *Pompée* (74) to fight the French flagship *Formidable* (80). To her great misfortune, the British ship was in a position where only her forward guns would bear, while her opponent could employ her full broadside. Observing the *Pompée*'s plight, Admiral Saumarez ordered the *Hannibal* (74), which was anchored near his flagship, to cut her cable and sail to the assistance of the *Pompée*. Obedient to this command, Captain Ferris of the *Hannibal* made sail toward the French flagship, but before he could reach his destination, his ship ran aground almost at point-blank range from some of the Spanish batteries.

Valiantly the *Hannibal* opened up with her guns on the batteries and the *Formidable* while those of her crew who were not manning the guns struggled to free her of the bottom. In spite of the best efforts of her ship's company and seamen sent to her by the *Caesar* and the *Venerable*, she could not get free.

Meanwhile, fearing that the British would get between him and the shore, Linois ordered his captains to cut their own cables and run their ships deliberately ashore. Saumarez too commanded his squadron to cut, hoping to gain a more favorable position for attacking the enemy. But again the wind failed him, and some of his vessels were badly damaged aloft. Rather than risk losing another ship, Sir James was compelled to take the five vessels that remained afloat and retreat, abandoning the *Hannibal* to her fate. For the British, who had grown accustomed to capturing enemy vessels in every fleet and squadron encounter, the loss of even one vessel was a heavy blow. But Admiral Saumarez was undaunted. He retreated to Gibraltar to refit his squadron and plot his revenge.

Sir James Saumarez's career is remarkable for the number of fleet actions in which he took part, which included Dogger Bank, Kempenfelt's action against de Guichen, the Saintes, St. Vincent, and the Nile. Unlike some of the admirals whose biographies are included in this book, he had served as a subordinate in many fleet actions before he was called upon to command one of his own. Although his first attempt to command a battle in his own right was unfortunate, the sequel reflected a reversal of his fortunes.

Saumarez is rightfully considered one of the most distinguished admirals of the generation that reached flag rank between 1800 and the end of the Napoleonic Wars. Whenever called upon to face the enemy, he did so without hesitation or confusion. Within a service in which courage was expected, he appears to have been exceptionally brave. Although there is little evidence of real genius, there can be no doubt he was a better seaman and fleet commander than many of his contemporaries.

Because Sir James rarely mixed personal observations and opinions with Admiralty correspondence, his is a difficult personality to define. In situations that would have induced many of his contemporaries to thoroughly curse the bureaucrats at the Admiralty, he remained remarkably calm. Although of Whiggish sentiments, he stayed out of the worst partisan wrangles. He took no part in the periodic quarrels between senior officers and generally appears to have been liked by his subordinates. Accounts of his actions in battle indicate that he was a "team player"—in other words, an officer who was willing to risk his life, ship, and reputation for the good of the fleet. Unlike some of his contemporaries, he did not actively seek titles and glory, but he did expect to receive credit for his actions, and could grow resentful when he received less than what he considered his due. However, if he felt resentment, he rarely published it before the world.

As a captain Saumarez was patient and rather methodical. Unlike most other commanding officers of the time, he did not punish offenders within a day or two of their offenses. Instead, he waited from a fortnight to as much as a month, until he had a number of malefactors collected. Then he would punish them all at once.

Portraits of Saumarez show a handsome man with a supercilious expression that might have hinted at arrogance. However, a contemporary stated that he was "rather formal and ceremonious in his manner, but without the least tincture of affectation or pride."[1] It is likely that, like Lord Howe, he was well disposed toward others but so reserved that the light of personality was difficult to discern.

* * *

On 11 March 1757 a third son, James, was born to Matthew and Carteret Saumarez on the Island of Guernsey. Although for a long time politically allied to the British Isles, Guernsey and the other Channel Islands are physically closer to France than to England, and closer in other ways as well. Many of the names of families that have resided a long time in the islands are French in origin, and the family of Saumarez was one of the oldest and most distinguished in Guernsey.

When James was born, the name of Saumarez was already familiar in naval circles. His uncle Philip had served under Anson in his voyage around the world. As one of a brotherhood that included Admirals Saunders and Keppel, it appeared that Philip's future was assured. However, in 1747 he was killed in action as captain of the *Nottingham* (60).

Although James's uncle was no longer alive by the time James was born, Philip's friends in the navy were willing to look after a young relative of his. It is likely that with the potential for some powerful patrons, Saumarez had been intended for sea service from an early age. When he was little more than ten years old, his name was entered in the books of the *Solebay* (28), but he remained in school for another three years.

In August 1770 James Saumarez joined the *Montreal* (32) under the command of Captain Alms and soon sailed to the Mediterranean for a lengthy stay abroad. He cruised aboard the *Montreal* until November, when he was transferred aboard the *Winchelsea* (32). While Saumarez sailed aboard the *Winchelsea,* the frigate's primary mission was to protect British interests in Smyrna from the Turks.

Still in the Mediterranean, the midshipman joined the *Levant* (28) in February 1772, in which he remained until he finally returned to England in April 1775. At the age of eighteen, Saumarez sat for and passed his exam for lieutenant, but he was not immediately commissioned. Instead, hoping that proximity to a senior officer would soon win him lieutenant's rank, he went aboard the *Bristol* (50), which was soon to bear the broad pennant of Commo. Sir Peter Parker across the Atlantic.

On 26 December 1775 Parker's squadron weighed anchor from Portsmouth, but they did not yet go far. The ships put into Cork to collect the troops commanded by Lord Cornwallis and the transports they would be escorting to the southern portion of the rebelling colonies. They sailed from Ireland in January, and after a "boisterous passage" they arrived off Cape Fear in May.[2] There they were joined by more troops, under the command of Sir Henry Clinton, who assumed overall command of the expedition that was to be directed against Charleston.

The total force weighed anchor on 1 June and reached its destination on the fourth. For the first three days, the squadron sent out boats to reconnoiter the area, examining the city's defenses and charting the safest passage for the larger vessels to cross the bar into the harbor. The frigates were able to cross immediately, but the *Bristol* drew too much water to make the passage without removing her guns. She did not join her smaller sisters until the tenth.

Meanwhile, Clinton began landing his troops on Long Island and setting up camp. The next island south, Sullivan's Island, was occupied by the rebels, and only a narrow channel separated the two pieces of land. The general hoped to march his men across the channel and take the fortress on the south end of Sullivan's Island, facing the harbor, by its less defended rear. Unfortunately, Clinton's intelligence failed to discover that the depth of the channel was seven feet, and the current was dangerously swift. The first soldiers to attempt the crossing were nearly drowned, so the general abandoned his attempt to assault Sullivan's Island by that route.

Foiled in their attempt to attack the Americans by land, the British opted for an all-out assault by sea. On the twenty-seventh the ships took advantage of a favorable breeze to carry them closer to the island, but it was not until the next day that the wind was steady enough for the attack to take place. In the last hour before noon, the squadron, consisting of two fifty-gun ships, four small frigates, a sloop-of-war, and a bomb vessel, ranged itself into position to attack the fort. Most of the squadron formed a line ahead and anchored with springs in their cables to keep their broadsides presented to the fortress. Immediately they began to pour a veritable hail of iron upon the rebel construction, which appeared a flimsy thing built of mud and palmetto logs. But in spite of heavy bombardment, the fortress remained intact and in condition to fire back. The spongy palmetto logs absorbed most of the force of the cannonballs, and the shells fell into the mud, where they failed to explode.

In response, the Americans kept up a slow but punishing fire. Their cannonballs shattered the hulls of the men-of-war and slew men in alarming numbers. During the hottest part of the fighting, a cannonball severed the spring in the *Bristol*'s anchor, and the current began to shift the flagship's head around so that her bow was exposed to the fire of the fortress. When a volunteer was called upon for the hazardous duty of replacing the spring, Saumarez stepped forward. With admirable coolness, he made three attempts under heavy fire to restore the spring before he succeeded at last, and the *Bristol* was able to present her broadside to the Americans again.

The flagship's casualties amounted to more than 30 percent of her total force (40 killed and 71 wounded of a complement of approximately 350 men), truly horrible losses in an era when 10 percent was considered worthy of comment. According to Clowes: "Among the injured was the Commodore himself, whose cool heroism must have been singularly conspicuous, from the notice it attracted in a service where such bearing is not rare. At one time when the quarterdeck was cleared and he stood alone upon the poop ladder, Saumarez suggested to him to come down; but he replied, smiling, 'You want to get rid of me, do you?' and refused to move."[3]

Parker's refusal to move may have owed as much to embarrassment as to courage under fire, which is also far from unique in the annals of military history. The location of the commodore's wound was not much in keeping with the dignity of his rank. The seat of his breeches had been shot away, exposing a tender portion of his anatomy to the elements. Most British accounts pass over this undignified detail, but rebels reveled in the commodore's embarrassment, and a ballad was written in commemoration.

After receiving terrible punishment, the British could hold out no longer. One of the frigates ran aground and eventually blew up, and the rest withdrew. There were no further attacks on Charleston during that campaign, and the squadron sailed northward as soon as the ships had made the repairs necessary for the passage.

Although the assault on the fortress on Sullivan's Island had been a black eye for the Royal Navy, it had not been a complete misfortune for everyone involved. Because of the number of officers who were killed in battle, promotions could be made from among those who had shown themselves to be worthy. Saumarez became an acting lieutenant aboard the *Bristol* on 11 July. His commission was confirmed two months later.

At the beginning of August, Parker's squadron joined the main fleet off New York. The reinforcements were welcome to Admiral Howe, who was attempting to capture the city. Toward the end of the month, he sent a small force, including the *Bristol,* to assist the army. But unfavorable wind and tidal conditions prevented them from advancing any closer than three miles.

Soon after the British army captured New York in September, Parker transferred his broad pennant aboard the *Chatham* (50), and took Saumarez with him. The fleet spent the autumn securing the city, and once Howe felt he could spare some of his force, he sent Sir Peter with five fifty-gun ships and eight smaller men-of-war to Rhode Island. On 8 December the squadron arrived at Newport, to the complete surprise of the American forces. The rebels fled, leaving the British to take the town unopposed.

While Howe conducted his campaigns in 1777, the *Chatham* remained at Newport to maintain that harbor for the navy's use. That corner of North America remained quiet for the rest of 1777, but in the following year Newport came once again into the world's eye. When the French entered the war early in 1778, they needed a good port in close proximity to a major British base, and Newport appeared to be the best choice.

In February 1778 Saumarez was appointed to command of the *Spitfire* (8) schooner, in which he patrolled the waters off Newport. However, as the French closed in at the beginning of August, the *Spitfire* and other British men-of-war were trapped at Newport. Rather than allow the ships to fall into enemy hands, Commodore Brisbane, the senior officer on station, ordered that they should be destroyed. The little *Spitfire* was burned to the waterline, thereby depriving Lieutenant Saumarez of his first command. On coming ashore, he became the commodore's aide-de-camp as the British ships' companies joined the soldiers in the fortifications. Through the remainder of the month, they hung on in the face of the French fleet and American forces until the withdrawal of the French to Boston compelled the rebels to abandon their siege.

The Americans' departure left the way clear for the British seamen to disperse to locations where they would be needed. Saumarez took a passage for England aboard the *Leviathan* (74) and was soon appointed to the *Victory* (100) upon his return. As flagship of the Channel fleet, the *Victory* served under several different masters in the period 1778 through 1781. When Saumarez first came aboard, it is likely that she still carried Admiral Keppel's flag, although Adm. Sir Charles Hardy soon assumed command. The sixty-three-year-old flag officer led his fleet to sea in the summer of 1779, but could do little except retreat in the face of a substantially larger combined French and Spanish fleet. When Hardy died in the spring of 1780, the command passed first to Adm. Francis Geary, who retired due to ill health in August, and then to Vice Adm. George Darby.

Throughout this time Saumarez remained a lieutenant aboard the *Victory*. But when Vice Admiral Sir Hyde (aka "Old Vinegar") Parker, an old shipmate of Philip Saumarez's, was appointed commander in chief of the North Sea fleet in early 1781, he requested that James join him in his flagship, the *Fortitude* (74), as second lieutenant. During the summer months, the fleet escorted convoys through the North Sea and the Baltic. Early in the morning of 5 August, Parker's squadron of seven assorted two-deckers, seven frigates, and a number of smaller men-of-war was returning from the Baltic with a convoy when they encountered a Dutch squadron of seven small two-deckers, seven frigates, and a few smaller vessels that were attempting to bring out a convoy. The Dutch were commanded by Rear Adm. Johan Zoutman.

Parker immediately signaled his convoy to head westward for England while he turned toward the enemy, who stood to leeward of him. Meanwhile, the Dutch admiral gathered his own merchantmen into a compact formation and placed his squadron between them and the British. He formed line of battle on the larboard tack, waiting with typical Dutch fortitude for his enemy to close with him. Parker was eager for the fight and commanded his men-of-war to spread every stitch of canvas. Some of his vessels were old and in poor condition, but they managed to remain in good order as they charged down upon the Dutch in line abreast.

Against the French the British would have lost a good many spars, and the squadron would have been in a state of disorder long before they came to within what their admiral considered a good fighting range. But the Dutch waited patiently until their enemies were ready. Then the signal for battle was hoisted by both flagships, and the squadrons opened up on each other from the murderous distance of about fifty yards.

The Battle of Dogger Bank was a highly ritualized combat. Not only did the leeward opponent wait patiently for the attackers to be ready before firing a shot, but Parker purposely sought out the enemy flagship, the *Admiraal de Ruijter* (68), as the only foe worthy of his metal. The Dutch flagship was farther back in line than her British counterpart, causing the two lines of battle to be slightly overlapped. The rearmost English vessel was left without an opponent, while the foremost two British ships of the line were left to face three of the enemy.

For close to four hours, the two fleets stood toe to toe and traded broadsides in an impressive, if inconclusive, slugging match. After the second hour, the Dutch convoy retreated back toward the Texel, but the squadron continued fighting until the British drew away. Both sides were too badly damaged to renew the action. They remained within sight of each other until the Dutch took the opportunity to follow their convoy back into port. The British turned for home themselves shortly afterward.

As was typical in fights between the British and the Dutch, who both tended to aim at the hulls of the enemy rather than at the rigging, the casualties were quite high considering the forces involved. The British losses were 104 killed and 339 wounded, while their enemies suffered 142 killed and 403 wounded.

· · ·

Although there were no official rewards distributed for the inconclusive action at Dogger Bank, Saumarez was promoted to commander less than a month later. He assumed command of the *Tisiphone* (8) fireship and went to join the Channel fleet.

At the time the *Tisiphone* joined the fleet, the French were preparing to sail from Brest. Part of their force was intended for the West Indies and the rest for India. In November the British detached a squadron under the command of Rear Adm. Richard Kempenfelt to keep a closer watch on the enemy, but unfortunately it was not at hand when the French commander Rear Admiral de Guichen sailed on 10 December. The French fleet consisted of nineteen ships of the line, several frigates, and a large convoy carrying troops and provisions for de Grasse in the West Indies.

Kempenfelt's fleet of thirteen ships of the line, four frigates, and the *Tisiphone* sailed from Britain on 2 December, hoping to catch the French when they weighed anchor. They failed to catch them fresh out of Brest, but as they were beating about in the fog on the twelfth, the weather suddenly cleared, revealing the enemy to leeward. It was most unfortunate for de Guichen that his convoy had fallen behind him in the fog and now lay between him and the British. Stripped of the protection of the fleet, which was too far to leeward to turn back quickly, the transports and other vessels scattered. But the enemy was too quick for some of them to escape. Bearing down with every sail set, Kempenfelt's fleet soon forced the surrender of many of de Guichen's convoy. Some managed to escape later during the night, but in the morning fifteen remained under the British flag.

Kempenfelt brought his prizes back in triumph to England, but learning that a small French force was still on its way to the West Indies, he commanded the *Tisiphone* to warn Rear Admiral Hood of their approach. Saumarez made a quick passage, arriving at Barbados late in January 1782. There he learned that Hood's fleet was off St. Kitts. Making sail again, he joined the fleet at anchor on the thirty-first.

Once again the misfortune of others turned to the benefit of Saumarez. The captain of the *Russell* (74) was ill, and Hood needed active commanders to assist in his escape from the waiting French fleet. He posted Saumarez into the *Russell* on 7 February, and a week later escaped the French by employing the masterful ruse described chapter 3.

Leaving the baffled French behind him, the rear admiral rejoined Admiral Rodney on 25 February. The campaign that followed, in which the French sailed to attempt to join the Spanish fleet in April and were caught by Rodney off the Saintes, is described in detail in chapter 3. Here, only the actions of the *Russell* will be described.

Although new to the command of a ship of the line, Captain Saumarez distinguished himself in battle. His position was eighth in the line, well ahead of where the French line was broken, so the *Russell* did not take part in that history-making maneuver. But when the enemy turned to flee, Saumarez was one of the first in pursuit. Because of her captain's quick thinking, the *Russell* was on hand to exchange broadsides with the French flagship, *Ville de Paris* (110), along with several other British ships.

The price the *Russell* paid for facing a first rate was a heavy one. Out of an official complement of six hundred men, she lost ten killed and twenty-nine wounded, one of the largest percentages of casualties suffered by any British vessel involved in the Battle of the Saintes.[4]

Soon after the battle, a ship of the line was needed to help protect a homeward-bound convoy. Rodney delegated the *Russell* for this task. The convoy reached England safely, and because the war appeared to be approaching its end, the third rate was paid off and Saumarez put on half pay.

Although Saumarez had commanded a post ship for only a few months, he had been marked as an officer of merit. In 1787 and again in 1790, when matters abroad caused the British government to temporarily mobilize extra naval forces, he was among the captains called into service. As each of these mobilizations were limited and of short duration, only the best officers were chosen, so it is significant that Saumarez was among them. He commanded the *Ambuscade* (32) in the autumn of 1787, and the *Raisonnable* (64) in 1790.

Most of the period between 1782 and 1793 may have been peaceful for Captain Saumarez, but it was not without event. On 27 October 1788 he married Martha de Marchant, the nineteen-year-old daughter of a Guernsey gentleman. The couple wasted no time, and within a year Mrs. Saumarez bore a son, who was named for his father. He proved to be the first of seven children born to the couple. They seem to have been an exceptionally healthy brood compared with many of the other families mentioned in this work, because most of them lived into old age.

Another way in which Captain Saumarez occupied himself between the wars was in recruiting Channel Islanders for service in the Royal Navy. In 1790 he made an extensive tour of Guernsey and managed to persuade eighty-five men to join the service. Then he wrote to the Admiralty requesting reimbursement for his expenses. Apparently, the government was reluctant to part with its funds for obtaining recruits at that time, because Saumarez was still looking for his money in 1796, when the Admiralty informed him that he could not be paid until they had received all his receipts. Throughout what must have been a highly frustrating correspondence, the captain never once resorted to telling his parsimonious masters what he probably actually thought of them. One has to admire his patience and diplomacy.

When war broke out with France early in 1793, the captain was appointed to the *Crescent* (36) and ordered to cruise the western approaches for enemy merchantmen and privateers. All through the summer the frigate cruised and then, with the approach of autumn, returned to Portsmouth for a brief refit. Then, on 19 October, the *Crescent* sailed with dispatches for the commander of the force cruising off the Channel Islands. But learning that there was a French frigate at Cherbourg that cruised at night and returned to port during the day, Saumarez made a detour. At dawn on the twentieth he sighted the *Réunion* (36) making for her home port.

The wind was blowing offshore, compelling the Frenchman to tack toward his goal. The *Crescent* had the wind more abeam, and she was fresh from her refit. Taking advantage of her edge in speed, she charged between the *Réunion* and the shore and drew alongside. The two frigates pounded at each other at close range and soon suffered damage to their spars and rigging. The *Crescent* lost her foretopsail yard and foretopmast, while her opponent was deprived of her foreyard and mizzentopmast. Temporarily out of control, the *Réunion* drifted until her stern was exposed to the British frigate's fire. The raking broadsides wreaked havoc before the *Réunion*'s captain was able to regain a modicum of control. But even then, the French frigate was too badly mauled to hold out much longer, and after a gallant defense lasting more than two hours, the *Réunion* finally lowered her flag.

The discrepancy between the casualties suffered by the two sides in this close-fought action is remarkable. On the British side, not a man was hurt, except one who had his leg broken by the recoil of a cannon. As for the French, they are believed to have suffered thirty-three killed and forty-eight wounded.[5]

Saumarez's victory was one of the first over a ship of equal force since the beginning of the war, and was therefore made much of. Soon after he returned to Portsmouth, with his prize to leeward, he was knighted, and his first lieutenant was promoted to the rank of commander.

The following year the *Crescent* cruised out of Plymouth as part of the frigate squadron commanded by Rear Adm. John MacBride. Periodically, Saumarez was detached with a few other vessels to cruise independently. On one of these occasions, on 8 June, while in company with the *Druid* (36) and the *Eurydice* (24), he encountered a powerful French squadron composed of two cut-down ships of the line, two large frigates, and a brig. Hoping to take advantage of their superiority in numbers and weight of shot, the French bore down on Saumarez's small force. Of the three, the *Eurydice* was the worst sailor, so Sir James ordered her captain to seek shelter at Guernsey nearby while he and the *Druid* held off the enemy.

Falling back slowly, Saumarez allowed the French to within distant gunshot and engaged them at long range, giving the *Eurydice* enough time to gain a considerable lead on her sisters. Then, when he felt certain that his smallest frigate would reach safety, he clapped more sail on his own yards and started off toward Guernsey with the *Druid*. Of the two, the *Crescent* was the better sailer, and began to pull away from her companion. The enemy sought to take advantage by cutting off the *Druid*. But discerning their intentions, Saumarez hauled his wind and turned to present his broadside to the French, firing as he proceeded along their line. As he had hoped, his action distracted their attention from the other two frigates. The enemy commodore felt certain that he could claim this audacious frigate as his prize. However, Saumarez knew those waters well, and in addition, he had an expert pilot aboard. They knew of a dangerous channel nearby that had never been used before by men-of-war but was sometimes employed by local traffic and fishermen. When she reached the passage, the *Crescent* threaded her way between the shoals where the French dared not follow and made her escape.

That was Saumarez's last adventure as captain of a frigate. In February 1795 he was appointed to command of the *Marlborough* (74) but was soon transferred to the *Orion* (74). He accompanied the Channel fleet on Howe's last cruise, and when the fleet sailed again under Lord Bridport to protect the Quiberon Bay expedition in June, the *Orion* went along.

After parting with Warren's expedition bound for Quiberon, the Channel fleet encountered the French under the command of Vice Admiral Villaret-Joyeuse on 22 June. The Battle of Ile de Groix is described in chapter 2, but the details of the *Orion*'s share in the action are included here. As one of Bridport's fastest-sailing ships of the line the *Orion* was among those ordered to chase after the retreating French. The chase continued through the night, and in the morning Saumarez found himself just behind the *Queen Charlotte* (100) at the front of the pack. At 6:00 in the morning, the *Orion* opened fire on the *Alexandre* (74). The French ship tried to fight her off, but with the assistance of the *Irresistible* (74) and the *Queen Charlotte,* the *Orion* compelled the *Alexandre* to strike her flag in little more than an hour.

With the surrender of the *Alexandre,* the battle ended for the *Orion*. By the time she could have caught up with the rest of the action, the French ships that had been caught had surrendered, and Bridport had called off his fleet from pursuing the enemy any farther. For her part of the action, the *Orion* lost six killed and eighteen wounded. Her number of killed was the highest in the fleet, except for that of the larger *Sans Pareil* (80).

The remainder of 1795 and most of the year following was peaceful for the Channel fleet. At the beginning of 1797, the *Orion* was included in a squadron under the command of Rear Adm. William Parker, with orders to reinforce Admiral Jervis off the coast of Spain. As described in chapter 4, Admiral Parker and his reinforcements arrived in the nick of time. On 6 February, the squadron from the Channel joined the Mediterranean fleet off Cape St. Vincent, bringing the total British force in those waters to fourteen ships of the line. Meanwhile, a Spanish fleet of twenty-seven ships of the line had departed Cartagena, bound for Cadiz. On 14 February, Admiral Jervis learned that the Spanish fleet was only a short distance away and immediately set forth to meet them.

As soon as the Spanish fleet came into sight, the British commander in chief sent six of his fastest ships of the line, the *Orion* among them, to scout ahead. Their compatriots soon followed, and once battle was joined, Saumarez found himself again in the heart of the action. The *Orion* was fourth in the British line of battle when the action off Cape St. Vincent began. After an initial exchange of broadsides with the leading Spanish vessels, Jervis's fleet tacked in succession. The *Orion* was successful in this maneuver, but her next astern, the *Colossus,* was too badly damaged aloft to tack and was compelled to wear. According to James, this change in course placed the *Colossus* in great danger from the guns of a Spanish three-decker.

This manifestation of an attack upon her disabled companion induced the *Orion,* in a very gallant manner, to back her main topsail and lay by to cover her. The Spanish ship, however, made no such attack, and the *Orion* pressed on to the assistance of the van.[6]

For a time the *Orion* left the main action as she hurried to catch up with the main body of the Spanish fleet. But eventually she joined her compatriots, the *Blenheim* (90) and the *Irresistible,* around the vast *Santissima Trinidad* (130). These three vessels so harassed the largest ship afloat that she is said to have hauled down her flag. Saumarez was convinced to the end of his days that she had surrendered. He would have sent a prize crew aboard, except that he was intent upon pursuing more of the enemy, thinking he could return to claim his prize later.[7] However, soon afterward a large fraction of the Spanish fleet closed around the stricken *Santissima Trinidad* and drove the British away. Although the *Orion* attempted to break in and regain her prize, the Spanish succeeded in towing the huge four-decker to safety. The battle ended with the retreat of the vessels towing the *Santissima Trinidad.* Although the *Orion* had taken an important part in the Battle of St. Vincent, her only casualties were seven men wounded.

The remainder of 1797 was comparatively peaceful for one involved in as many battles as Saumarez. The Mediterranean fleet, including the *Orion,* divided its time between protecting the trade and keeping an eye on the Spanish fleet at Cadiz. In the spring of 1798, the *Orion* was lying off Gibraltar when Rear Adm. Sir Horatio Nelson arrived from England. With Nelson's return, Admiral St. Vincent decided that the time was ripe for reclaiming that sea from the enemy who had enjoyed undisturbed occupation for nearly two years.

With his flag in the *Vanguard* (74), Nelson assumed command of a squadron consisting of the *Orion,* the *Alexander* (74), and three smaller men-of-war. This force sailed on 9 May to seek intelligence on French activities at Toulon. Learning that a fleet was on the point of sailing from that port, Nelson attempted to intercept it, but his flagship was severely damaged in a storm on the twenty-first. In addition, the three smaller vessels in his squadron became separated, and were never able to rejoin. When the storm subsided the *Alexander* and the *Orion* escorted the *Vanguard* to Sardinia for repairs.

Thanks in part to Saumarez's assistance, the repairs took less than a week, but valuable time had been lost. The French sailed from Toulon on 19 May and reached the coast of Corsica by the end of the month. Meanwhile, Nelson weighed anchor again for Toulon. By the time he reached his destination, he learned that not only was he was too late to stop the enemy from sailing, but he could gain no intelligence about their intended destination. The only good news was that reinforcements were on their way.

On 7 June Nelson was joined by eleven two-deckers, which brought his total force to fifteen vessels, of which only one was smaller than a fifty-gun ship, and that a mere brig. Without scouts to hunt for the enemy, the admiral was forced to rely on whatever intelligence he could gather ashore. Making a guess from the direction the French had sailed when they first departed Toulon, Nelson made for Corsica. There one of his vessels gathered the false information that the French were at Syracuse, which sent the British fleet to Naples. Although the enemy was nowhere to be seen, Nelson did learn that Malta was a likely destination; but when he arrived he found that the island had already been taken. When the French fleet departed Malta, it appeared to be headed toward Egypt, so Nelson hastened his squadron farther to the southeast. The British arrived at Alexandria on 28 June but, finding no sign of the French, put back for Syracuse, where they remained for reprovisioning.

Meanwhile, the French had already made themselves masters of Alexandria. Only days after the British left that city astern, Bonaparte's fleet put in, landed troops, and took possession within twenty-four hours. The troops had all been landed, and the French fleet, under the command of Vice Admiral Brueys, was resting peacefully at anchor in Aboukir Bay when the British finally returned on 1 August.

Nelson's fleet had remained at Syracuse until 24 July. Then, on a hunch, the admiral led his fleet back toward Alexandria. He arrived in the morning of the first day of August, but he did not discover the enemy's anchorage until afternoon. He set off immediately to attack them, but it was not until a few hours later that he was close enough to start the fight.

Brueys had placed his fleet in what he thought to be an impregnable position. His vessels were anchored bow to stern, with their starboard sides facing the open ocean and their larboard sides toward the nearby shoreline. In addition, the fleet was protected by a battery constructed on an island at the head of the line. He doubted that the enemy could pass between his ships and the land, so, caught between two fires, they would have to do battle on his terms. Even then, combat was only a last resort. Bonaparte had commanded Brueys not to fight if he could avoid action. According to James, he was only waiting for darkness to fall before he weighed anchor and escaped.[8]

By the time the British appeared, the hour was growing late, and the French admiral was confident that Nelson would wait until daylight rather than risk his fleet in the shallow waters with darkness coming on. However, having chased for so long after this fleet, the British commander would not allow a second more than necessary to pass before he engaged. At 3:00 in the afternoon he made the signal to prepare for battle, and his ships swept down on the head of the French line.

Finding that the enemy appeared to be mad enough to assail him so late in the day, Brueys ordered his flagship, the *Orient* (120), to clear for action by bundling surplus items to the larboard side, which he did not expect to be engaged in the coming fight. However, the British had another plan.

Captains Foley of the *Goliath* (74) and Hood of the *Zealous* (74) suspected that there was enough water between the head of the French line and the shore for them to cut through and engage the enemy on the landward side. Followed by the *Orion* and the *Theseus* (74), they bore for this narrow passage, while the remainder of the fleet made for the seaward side of the French fleet.

The first shots of what was to prove one of the most decisive naval victories ever fought were fired shortly before 6:30. Soon afterward the *Goliath* and the *Zealous* rounded the head of the French line and anchored to larboard. As always, Saumarez was not far from the front. His command was the next ship after the *Zealous* to get around the enemy's van and pass between the French and the shore. The frigate *Sérieuse* (36) happened to get in the *Orion*'s way. The two-decker opened up with such a broadside that the smaller man-of-war was soon reduced to a shattered hulk. Then Saumarez passed onward to anchor abreast of the *Peuple Souverain* (74). Although she was compelled to anchor at a farther-than-optimum distance to avoid colliding with the *Theseus,* the *Orion* poured devastating broadsides into the Frenchman.

After facing the *Peuple Souverain* alone for a time, the *Orion* was joined by the *Defence* (74), which anchored on the Frenchman's starboard side. As the darkness grew, the flames of a drifting fire raft were sighted from the *Orion.* After a few tense moments, the blazing raft was fended off and the two-decker returned her full attention to her principal foe. In her duel with the *Peuple Souverain,* the *Orion* suffered considerable damage to her masts and yards but lost no spars. Her opponent lost both fore- and mainmasts and, eventually parting her cable, drifted out of the action.

When her original foe left the line, the *Orion* turned her attention on the *Franklin* (80), the next astern. But eventually the *Leander* (50) came between the *Orion* and the *Franklin,* and not wishing to risk hitting a friend, Saumarez ordered a cease-fire.

At 10:00 the *Orient* exploded. She had caught fire earlier in the action, and when the flames reached her magazine, she blew up with a deafening roar. Only some seventy of her original crew numbering around nine hundred were saved from the conflagration, and for a short time, all firing ceased.

After ten minutes of silence, the guns began to speak again, but for the *Orion,* the action was drawing to a close. She remained at anchor while around her the enemy surrendered in droves. In all, out of a fleet of thirteen ships of the line, nine were taken, two burned, and two escaped. For her part of the action, the *Orion* suffered thirteen killed and twenty-nine wounded, including the captain, who was injured by a splinter in the side.

Although Nelson did little to single out any particular officer in his report except his own flag captain, who took command when the admiral was wounded, Saumarez felt slighted. As second-in-command he apparently felt that he should have been given credit beyond that of the other captains, but no particular mention was ever made of his role in the action. Although Sir James was not the sort of officer to feud with his superior, he nonetheless felt a certain amount of resentment toward Nelson afterward.[9]

Following the Battle of the Nile, the British vessels and the French prizes thought worth salvaging required repairs. They remained at Aboukir until

14 August, when Saumarez was sent to escort the prizes to Gibraltar. Soon after Sir James successfully escorted the crippled prizes to Gibraltar, he was ordered to return home. He reached Portsmouth in November, and shortly thereafter the *Orion* was paid off.

On 14 February 1799 Saumarez received the honor of being appointed a colonel of marines, which may have helped ease the sting of not being accorded what he considered his due for the Battle of the Nile. The duties of a colonel of marines were not demanding, but only the most distinguished captains were chosen for the rank. Later in the same year, he was given command of one of the largest third rates in the British service, the *Caesar*. He was to remain in this vessel, despite promotion to flag rank, until the signing of the Peace of Amiens.

In 1800 Saumarez once again found himself serving under Admiral St. Vincent, this time in the Channel fleet. As a senior captain noted for ability and courage, he was given command of a squadron of ships patrolling the dangerous inshore waters off the coast of France. Because of the unpredictable weather and the presence of numerous rocks and shoals, command of the inshore squadron required an officer of exceptional intelligence and fortitude. St. Vincent could think of few other captains or flag officers who would be capable of taking on such a challenge, and he had faith in Saumarez.

Unfortunately, the commander in chief was slightly disappointed by Sir James's performance once he was installed with his squadron off the infamous Black Rocks, on which many ships had met their doom. St. Vincent wrote to the First Lord of the Admiralty: "Sir James Saumarez does not stand the work at the advanced posts with the firmness I expected, whence it is evident that the man who faces a Frenchman or Spaniard with intrepidity, does not always encounter rocks and shoals with the same feeling."[10]

However, there were virtually no other officers who met the commander in chief's demanding standards better than did Saumarez, so he continued in command of his squadron. Later, even St. Vincent showed some sympathy for the stresses of the station, as he wrote to Lord Spencer: "Sir James Saumarez will never complain, but I am told by those who have lately seen him, that he is as thin as a shotten herring."[11] For most of the autumn, Sir James's squadron remained close off the coast of France; then, with the coming of winter, it returned home.

On the first day of 1801, Saumarez became a rear admiral. Although he was then entitled to hoist a blue flag to the top of his mizzenmast, there was little material change in his condition. He remained aboard the *Caesar* and continued in command of the inshore squadron, which took up station again in the spring.

Following the conclusion of his first cruise as a rear admiral, Sir James was ordered home and commanded to prepare to leave for a foreign station. Shortly before he was ready to depart, he was gratified with the news that he had been made a baronet. On the day that Sir James was gazetted (13 June), Rear Admiral Linois sailed with a squadron of three ships of the line from Toulon, intending to unite his small force with a Spanish squadron.[12] The following day Saumarez departed for Cadiz, where he was to keep watch over the main Spanish fleet. The squadron under his command consisted of seven ships of the line, a frigate, and a gun brig.[13]

When Saumarez reached his new station, he sent the *Superb* (74) and the gun brig, *Pasley,* northward on a separate blockade while he patrolled with the rest off Cadiz. But scarcely had the admiral settled down to the blockade when he learned that Linois's squadron had put into Algeciras. The admiral paused only long enough to send his frigate, the *Thames* (32), northward to fetch the *Superb* to Gibraltar. Then he departed for the south. As the *Superb* had the reputation of being one of the fastest line-of-battle ships in the fleet, Sir James hoped that if the frigate did not take long to find her, she would be able to join him before he encountered the enemy. The *Superb* and the two smaller men-of-war did in fact sight Saumarez's squadron for a while off Gibraltar, but then lost sight again in the calms.

As described in the opening scene of this chapter, Saumarez discovered Linois still anchored at Algeciras on 6 July. The French appeared vulnerable, so the British determined to attack immediately. But the fickle winds betrayed them, and soon some of Sir James's squadron were receiving a severe pounding from Linois's ships and from a number of fortresses ashore. The *Caesar* and the *Pompée* were badly damaged, and the *Hannibal* had the misfortune to drift ashore where she could not get off. The British admiral was compelled to return to Gibraltar with nothing to show for his engagement against an inferior force, save two crippled craft and one lost ship of the line.

The French were jubilant at the news and doctored the account of the battle to make the victory seem even more impressive. According to *Le Moniteur:*

> If the French had any advantage in point of situation, the English had double their force, and several of their vessels carried ninety guns each. . . . For two hours, the *Formidable,* the French Admiral's ship, successfully opposed three

English ships. One of the British squadron, which was singly engaged with a French vessel, struck her colors. . . . Immediately after, the *Hannibal,* exposed to the fire of three French ships, which fired from two decks, also struck her colors. . . . The first English ship that struck her colors was retaken by a great number of gunboats and other vessels sent out from Gibraltar. This action covers the French arms with glory, and shews what they are capable of accomplishing.[14]

Although he had been defeated, Saumarez was not ready to concede. At Gibraltar he was joined by the *Superb* and the two smaller men-of-war. Hoping to restore his squadron to fighting condition in time to catch Linois when he put to sea again, the admiral instituted a program of intensive labor. After a brief assessment of the damage, Saumarez decided that the *Pompée* would require too many repairs for her to be ready to sail in the time required. He was also inclined to give up hope on his own flagship, and for a time transferred to the *Audacious* (74). But his flag captain promised that his ship's company would work eagerly night and day to make certain the *Caesar* would be ready to face the enemy in time.

Following a frenzy of activity, all the damaged vessels except the *Pompée* were more or less ready for sea by 12 July. It was not a moment too soon. At dawn on that day, Linois's squadron and a Spanish force that had joined him from Cadiz loosened their sails. With the addition of the Spaniards, the enemy's fleet had been increased to nine ships of the line, including two huge three-deckers of 112 guns apiece.[15] With his own squadron reduced to five ships of the line, Saumarez would be severely outnumbered, but that did not trouble him. As soon as he heard that the enemy was preparing to come out, he gave the orders for his own ships to be warped out of the Gibraltar mole, where they had been undergoing their repairs.

In spite of the British eagerness to be at the enemy, there were delays. The *Caesar* cleared the mole by 3:00 P.M., but some of the rest of the squadron took longer. When Saumarez signaled his ships to inquire into their state of readiness for battle, a few were compelled to reply that they were not yet ready. It was not until after 6:30 that the entire squadron finally signaled that they were prepared for action, and by that time, the enemy had a comfortable lead. However, Sir James did not allow that to concern him. He hoisted a blue light aboard his flagship so that the other vessels could keep track of him in the failing light. Then he clapped on all sail after the foe.

Each ship made the best speed she could. As one of the fastest ships of the line in the British service, the *Superb* was soon well ahead of the rest. Not long after 11:00, she opened fire on one of the Spanish three-deckers. Apparently the Spanish had not been expecting an attack to come out of the dark, so the broadside threw them into a state of confusion. The Spanish ship drifted into the path of the other three-decker, and soon the two vessels were fouled. The *Superb* remained on the scene long enough to pour in three broadsides, and then charged forward again. Meanwhile, the two Spaniards were doing very well—against each other. Each taking the other for an enemy, they continued firing with enthusiasm. Eventually a sail fell over the guns of one of the vessels and caught fire. The flames quickly spread, until both three-deckers were alight from stem to stern. The *Caesar,* coming up just as the flames began, gave the Spaniards a broadside, but seeing their state, continued on her way, seeking out a more formidable foe. It was well for the *Caesar* that she did not linger. Shortly after midnight first one three-decker and then the other exploded, killing most of the 1,700 men who were aboard the two vessels.

Meanwhile, the *Superb* had shot on ahead and soon came alongside the *San Antonio* (74), which she fought single-handedly until she was on the point of surrendering. The *Caesar* came up just as the Spaniard (sailing under French colors) was hauling down her flag. Leaving the *Superb* with her prize, the flagship drove on after the fleeing enemy, accompanied by the *Venerable,* commanded by the ubiquitous Capt. Samuel Hood. Sighting an enemy to leeward, Hood gave chase, and soon left the *Caesar* astern. At 5:00 A.M., the *Venerable* brought her foe to bay and exchanged broadsides for about an hour. During this action the winds died, making it impossible for the rest of the squadron to come to Hood's aid, although Saumarez ordered his flagship towed toward the two combatants.

Finally, at about 6:00, an offshore breeze riffled the still waters and cleared away the obscuring smoke of the battle. When the curtain lifted, it exposed the *Venerable* with her mainmast gone and the enemy ship making off as fast as she could. Still separated from the rest of the squadron and severely damaged in her rigging, the two-decker drifted and eventually collided with a submerged sandbar. The concussion caused her foremast and mizzen to quiver and then topple overboard, leaving her dismasted.

Noticing the cripple that appeared to be within their grasp, the retreating enemy put about and started cautiously to return. Still at the mercy of unreliable winds, Saumarez feared that he would have to take the crew off the *Venerable* and destroy her before she could be taken. He sent his flag captain in a boat to offer Hood that option, but the *Venerable*'s commander thought he could save the ship.

By this time the rest of the squadron had finally caught up with the *Caesar.* They closed ranks near the dismasted third rate, discouraging the enemy from making any further attempt to take her. The allies thought better of attacking, and made good their escape into Cadiz. Shortly afterward, the *Venerable* was brought off the sandbar, and by sunset was cruising along with the rest under a jury rig.

When the news of the battle reached Britain, Sir James and his squadron received a vote of thanks from Parliament. Even so tough a judge as the Earl of St. Vincent was impressed. He said, "This gallant achievement surpasses everything I have met with in reading or service."[16] Although no gold medals were struck in honor of the Battle of Algeciras, the gallant admiral was made a knight of the Bath and granted a pension of £1,200 per annum. The first lieutenants of the three ships of the line that had been most active in the battle were promoted to commander.

The battle was Sir James's last service before the Peace of Amiens. When the war resumed in the spring of 1803, he returned to sea as commander of the Guernsey station. This command was especially convenient for him, because he was able to live in his own house ashore for much of that time.

In January 1807 Saumarez was promoted to vice admiral and made second-in-command of the Channel fleet. When Sir James assumed this role, the commander in chief of the fleet was the Earl of St. Vincent. Later in the year, the senior admiral finally retired, but Saumarez was too junior to succeed him. It eventually transpired that Admiral Gambier assumed command of the station, but apparently Sir James disliked him so much that he refused to serve with him and asked to be relieved of his command.

The vice admiral was not ashore long. In the spring of 1808, he hoisted his flag aboard the *Victory* as commander in chief of a squadron in the Baltic. This squadron consisted of twelve ships of the line, five frigates, and a number of smaller men-of-war.[17] For his immediate subordinates, Saumarez enjoyed the services of two old friends—Sir Samuel Hood and Richard Keats, now both rear admirals.

The need for a large British fleet in the Baltic was created by the signing of the Treaty of Tilsit, between Russia and France, in June 1807. Russia was the greatest power in the Baltic area, and where she placed her alliances, she generally compelled the Scandinavian countries to follow suit. This had happened before in 1801, when Russia had sponsored the Armed Neutrality in alliance with Denmark and Sweden. The alliance had ended with the defeat of the Danes by the British at the first battle of Copenhagen and by the assassination of Czar Paul. But in 1807 it again appeared likely that the Baltic sea powers would be allied against Britain.

Denmark joined the coalition against England, only to have her capital captured (as described in chapter 7). Although pressured by Russia, Sweden was more resistant to an alliance with Napoleon, especially as King Gustavus IV Adolphus believed that the French emperor was the Beast of the Apocalypse.[18] Both Russia and Denmark proceeded to invade the holdout, hoping to force Sweden's hand. War was already being waged in Sweden and Finland when Saumarez arrived on the scene in April 1808. His instructions were to collaborate with the Swedish navy against the common enemy.

British government sent ten thousand troops in addition to the fleet under Sir James; but as the Swedes and the English could not agree on the best use for these troops, they were sent back to Britain in July. Meanwhile, Saumarez and his ships lay off Göteborg waiting for a decision to be made about the optimal deployment of the force under his command. It was not until August that the Royal Navy had its opportunity to act.

On 25 August a fleet action was fought by eleven Swedish ships of the line assisted by two British 74s under the command of Rear Admiral Hood. Against them were nine Russian ships of the line. The Russians fled in the face of the superior force, and the allies gave chase, but soon the Swedes were left behind. The British continued on and eventually captured one of the Russians. The rest retreated into Roggersvik, where they were blockaded until the beginning of October. Saumarez assumed command of the blockading fleet at the end of August.

Rather than spend the winter iced in, the British fleet elected to leave the Baltic every October, returning each spring. This move preserved the ships in good condition and their men in better health than if they had been forced to winter in subarctic regions. However, events moved on while they were absent. As soon as the blockade was removed, the Russian fleet returned to its main base at Kronstadt. Then, in March 1809, King Gustavus IV Adolphus was deposed, and his place taken by a junta sympathetic to the French.

In spite of the change in government, the British fleet was sent back into its station in May. Saumarez arrived off Göteborg on the fifth, but soon decided that events required his presence, and that of his fleet, in other parts of the Baltic. He spent the season of 1809 cruising the Gulf of Finland to prevent the Russians from completely overwhelming Sweden. His actions were in part successful, but the Swedes were still compelled to sign a humiliating treaty with Russia in September. Although forced to accede to the czar, Sweden maintained friendly relations with Britain, and English shipping was allowed to continue unmolested in the Baltic.

In 1810 Saumarez's main service was keeping the Swedes from abandoning their friendly relations with his government. In spite of a politically volatile situation at Stockholm, brought about by the death of the crown prince and the election of a French field martial to the throne, the admiral's talent for diplomacy kept up cordial relations. He declined to attempt to influence the local situation, and when some of his subordinates occasionally exceeded their orders, he smoothed the matter over, preventing those actions from becoming international incidents.

Sir James's efforts kept the Swedes neutral for most of the year, but once his fleet departed in November, the threat of Russia became too great for Sweden to hold out against alone. With regret, Sweden declared war on England. In spite of the change of situation, Saumarez and his fleet returned to the Baltic in the spring of 1811. They cruised for the season without major incident, and by the time they returned again in 1812, the situation had changed for the better. Thanks to Napoleon's designs against Russia, Sweden was no longer threatened from that quarter, and in January she resumed trade with Britain.

Saumarez's command in the Baltic ended in 1813. By that time the Baltic nations had become British allies, and the area seemed secure enough that the size of the fleet could be reduced. Before he hauled down his flag, Sir James was invested with the Swedish Order of the Sword, in honor of his efforts at maintaining peaceful relations between the two nations.

In June 1814 Saumarez was promoted to the rank of admiral, but his days of wartime fleet command were over. He remained at home in Guernsey during the closing years of the Napoleonic Wars and through the early years of the peace that followed. In 1819, he was appointed Rear Admiral of England, and two years later he was made Vice Admiral of England.

From March 1824 to May 1827, Saumarez served as commander in chief of the Plymouth station. When he lowered his flag for the last time, at the age of seventy, the admiral retired from a career that had officially spanned sixty years. But he did not retire from public life. During the 1820s the great issue in British politics was parliamentary reform. Although the House of Commons had a majority in favor of weeding out the rotten boroughs, the conservative House of Lords prevented any progress on the issue. Although Saumarez had never been a member of Parliament, his sympathies were known to be with the reformers. The Duke of Clarence, too, sided with the reformers, and when he became King William IV in 1830, he pledged himself to making reform a reality. One of his actions was to make a few new peers who might help swing the balance in the House of Lords more toward reform. As a former naval officer and a friend to many of the great admirals of the era, the new king was delighted to have the opportunity to advance one of his former colleagues to the peerage. Sir James's services to his country were sufficient that few could complain when he was created Baron de Saumarez on 15 September 1831. With his assistance, the Reform Bill was passed into law in 1832.

In February 1832 Lord de Saumarez was made general of marines, the last naval officer to hold that distinction. Then, on 9 October 1836, he died peacefully at home in Guernsey, at the advanced age of eighty-nine. His title passed to his eldest son and later to a younger son, John St. Vincent Saumarez, from whom the title descends to the present day.

Chapter 11

EDWARD PELLEW

1757–1833

THE INDIAMAN *Dutton* was in grave danger. Outward-bound from England in January 1796, she encountered a fierce gale off Plymouth, and her captain thought it safest to put into Catwater until the storm abated. But the buoy on the reef off Mount Batten had broken adrift. The *Dutton* blundered on in blissful ignorance, until her stern struck the reef and her rudder tore loose from its pintles. The passengers and crew watched in horror as their ship, now unmanageable in a raging sea, was driven ever closer to the shore. Although some of the crew labored to save the ship, others despaired and sought to drown their fears by breaking into the spirit room.

Inevitably the *Dutton* rammed sideways against the shore, and as the waves broke over her, the masts came crashing down. With the fractured hull listing to one side and the waves boiling around her, word was passed for every man to save himself. The captain, his officers, and many of the more nimble men reached the shore and managed to secure a line to keep the wreck from being swept back out to sea. But there were many left aboard the battered hulk, especially soldiers and their families who had been embarked on a voyage to the West Indies. They feared the perilous passage from the ship to shore, but there was no safety for them where they lay. The gale was still rising in its fury, and the incoming tide was viciously pounding the hull against the rocks. Soon the *Dutton* would be nothing more than driftwood, and her passengers would be at the dubious mercy of the elements.

Not far away, the heavy frigate *Indefatigable* (38) was refitting. Her captain's character was well suited to the name of his ship. Already noted for saving the lives of drowning men, Sir Edward Pellew was always ready to leap to the assistance of any human in distress. Seeing the plight of the *Dutton,* he called out to the crowd of citizens who had gathered on the beach to watch the unfolding disaster, asking if anyone would join him in attempting to rescue those still trapped aboard the wreck. Although others were reluctant, a Mr. Edsell, the port admiral's signals midshipman, stepped forward.

Realizing that there was no time to be lost, the two officers approached the wreck, and using the line that fastened the *Dutton* to the shore, they hauled themselves aboard. Once they reached the stranded vessel, they attached a strong hawser to the shore and fitted it with hauling lines and travelers by which the *Dutton*'s passengers and remaining crew could be transported ashore. It was difficult and dangerous work. As they clung to the hawser, the two naval officers were alternately lifted high or plunged into the sea. But their labors achieved the desired result. Everyone aboard the Indiaman was brought safely ashore, Pellew and Edsell last of all.

Edward Pellew's life was defined by service—service to God, service to king, and service to humanity. Like most officers of his era, he was intensely religious and tended to publicly give credit to God for his victories and achievements. Unlike some of his contemporaries, he seems to have been driven more by a sense of duty to his king and country than by a quest for personal glory. An even more significant aspect of Pellew's personality was his willingness to risk his life for the sake of others. As described in chapter 10, Saumarez was ready to come to the aid of fellow commanders in difficulties during a battle. Pellew's form of assistance came in a more personal fashion. If he saw a man fall into the water, he would immediately plunge in himself and swim to the man's rescue. This willingness to risk his life for the sake of others was noted early by his superiors and was one of the reasons that someone of his relatively lowly origins was promoted quickly.

Pellew's deeds speak for themselves, but his correspondence gives little indication of his personality. He did not embellish his writing with dramatic figures of speech, nor did he indulge in sarcasm. His correspondence occasionally includes criticisms of colleagues, but generally he kept to the unadorned facts of a situation and rarely exercised the opportunity for self-glorification. His only observable flaw as a civic leader was his tendency toward nepotism. His son Fleetwood, serving under his command in the East Indies, was promoted to the rank of commander at the exceptionally immature age of seventeen. Many officers of the era used their rank and position to advance their kinsmen and favorites at an accelerated rate, but Pellew's nepotism was more pronounced than most. If his father's letters are to be believed, Fleetwood, young as he was, proved an exemplary captain.

The *Dictionary of National Biography* describes Pellew as "tall and handsome and of remarkable strength and activity."[1] While the record of his deeds certainly merits the latter half of the assessment, existing portraits do not show a man of exceptionally good looks. He had regular features, blond hair, and blue eyes, but a jowly face paired with large ears and a small chin spoiled his appearance.

• • •

Samuel Pellew was the captain of a passenger vessel sailing out of Dover when his second son, Edward, was born on 19 April 1757. He and his wife, Constance, were natives of Cornwall, but they had moved to Dover to allow Captain Pellew to visit his family between voyages. When Edward was seven years old, his father died, and his widowed mother moved the family back to her former haunts at Penzance. Edward was to identify with his Cornish roots throughout his life, even to the point of manning one of his ships partly with Cornish miners.

Pellew attended school at Truro for a few years, but in 1770 he was entered aboard the *Juno* (32), the first of many frigates on which he was to serve. His first captain was John Stott, who had commanded the *Scarborough* (24) at the capture of Quebec. Initially, Pellew appears to have won Stott's favor, but later they had a falling-out that nearly ruined the junior officer's career.

The main event of naval significance in 1771 was the dispute between Britain and Spain over ownership of the Falkland Islands. Both nations laid claim to this archipelago and appeared ready to go to war over it. Soon after Pellew joined her ship's company, the *Juno* sailed for the Falklands to protect British interests there and to be on hand should Spain threaten the islands by sea. However, when France refused to side with her usual ally over the issue, Spain was forced to back down.

In 1772 the *Juno* returned to England, and her captain was transferred into the *Alarm* (32). He selected Pellew as one of the followers he took with him into his new command, and soon set sail to the south. For the next three years Pellew served aboard the *Alarm* in the Mediterranean. But in 1775 he and a few other junior officers quarreled with their captain, who decided that he could no longer tolerate their presence. He unceremoniously set them ashore in Marseilles, leaving them to find their own way home as best they could. They might have been in difficulties obtaining a passage, except that Pellew soon encountered an old friend of his father's who commanded a merchantman bound for Lisbon. The skipper offered the stranded officers places aboard his ship as far as Portugal, an offer they gladly accepted. At Lisbon it was easy for them to find a ship that would take them back to England.

Not long after his return, Pellew went aboard the *Blonde* (32) under the command of Philemon Pownoll. Pellew was lucky to have gained the notice of one of the most promising young captains in the king's service. Not only did Pownoll possess influence, but also he was noted for his abilities as a sailor and a leader of men.

In the spring of 1776, the *Blonde* set sail with a distinguished passenger aboard. Major-General "Gentleman Johnny" Burgoyne was on his way to North America to assume command of an expedition he expected would cut the rebelling colonies in two. From Montreal, Burgoyne, with approximately eight thousand men, was to push south to the Hudson River, while Major-General William Howe was to travel up the river to meet him. Unfortunately, no one saw fit to inform Howe of his portion of the project.

Because the best route through the wilderness of North America was by water, the army was accompanied by a naval detachment, including Midshipman Pellew of the *Blonde*. From the end of June to the beginning of July, Burgoyne's force drove the American army southward, until they came to Lake Champlain. There the rebel commander, Benedict Arnold, ordered a number of gunboats to be built to try to hold back the enemy.

Halted at the northern end of the lake by the news that the Americans had naval superiority in that location, the British too began to construct a number of ships to challenge the rebels' squadron. All through the summer and into the autumn, the two sides feverishly built one vessel after another, until the American force consisted of two schooners, one sloop, four row galleys, and eight or nine smaller gunboats. To face them, the British had an eighteen-gun sloop-of-war, three schooners, an armed barge, and about twenty gunboats. Commanding this miniature fleet was Capt. Thomas Pringle. Pellew was appointed master's mate of the schooner *Carleton* (12), commanded by Lieutenant Dacres.

On 4 October the British finally set sail to seek out the enemy. Arnold knew that his opponent was more powerful and that in an open fight, he was likely to emerge the loser. So he made a plan to ambush the foe as they passed Valcour Island. He hid his ships behind the tall trees that covered the island and waited for the enemy to sail past, which they did on 11 October. Sailing before a strong northeasterly wind, Pringle's men did not spot the Americans until they had already passed Valcour Island. Thus, Arnold gained the wind gauge before the first shot was fired.

As soon as the British noticed the Americans astern, they dropped anchor and began firing. However, they were at too great a distance for their shot to do much damage, and they could not proceed to windward without exposing themselves to the enemy's fire. Of all the British squadron, the *Carleton* was closest to the enemy and bore the brunt of the action in the early stages. The fire concentrated on the *Carleton* took a terrible toll upon her officers. Lieutenant Dacres was knocked unconscious, and his second-in-command was severely wounded. Of the officers, only Pellew remained fit for duty.

Seeing the schooner's plight, Pringle signaled her to retreat and join the rest of the squadron, but the ship's head was not in the right direction to allow her to slip away. Rather than ask one of the seamen to take such a risk, Pellew himself scrambled out onto the bowsprit, ignoring the heavy musket fire directed at him, and hauled the jibsail around to catch the wind to direct the ship's head toward the south.

Eventually the British flagship managed to close with the Americans, and being larger than anything Arnold had, she did severe damage before she broke off the action because of darkness. While their enemies slept, the rebels slipped away, but they were unable to get far. At dawn Pringle discovered them trying to make off to leeward, and setting all sail, soon overtook a number of them. He captured three ships, and ran six more aground, where they were burned by the Americans. Only three successfully made their escape, essentially putting an end to Arnold's squadron as an effective fighting force. However, it had served its purpose of delaying the British advance for another year.

With Lake Champlain firmly in their possession, the British settled down to wait for spring before continuing their advance to the south. Pellew, who had been given command of the *Carleton* as a reward for his courage, remained with Burgoyne's troops in Canada through the winter. In December he received word from Lord Howe that he would be promoted to lieutenant if he could reach the admiral in New York. A month later he received a promise of a commission from Lord Sandwich, provided Pellew could make his way back to England. However, the young officer decided to remain where there was likely to be action.

In June 1777 Burgoyne once again set forth from Montreal and sailed unmolested down Lake Champlain. With help from the navy, the British smashed through a boom the rebels had set up at Ticonderoga and defeated them at Hubbardton on 7 July. But following this promising beginning, the campaign began to bog down. Instead of taking the less direct but more reliable water route, Burgoyne opted for the land road, which the Americans obstructed with fallen trees and pitfalls. Harassed all the way by the rebel army, the British finally crossed the Hudson River near Saratoga on 13 September. At Bemis Heights, Burgoyne dug in, hoping that troops would arrive from New York to rescue him. But Major General Clinton had no desire to travel far from his base of operations. He contented himself with creating a diversionary attack that accomplished nothing. After two costly attempts to break out from the encircling American troops, the British were forced to surrender on 17 October.

Among those taken prisoner was Pellew; however, he was soon released and transported back to England. As promised, Sandwich promoted him to lieutenant on 9 January 1778, and placed him aboard the *Princess Amelia* (80), the Portsmouth guardship. Although Lieutenant Pellew was eager to get back into action, the First Lord could not commission him to a fighting vessel because of the terms of the officer's parole. He was forbidden to fight until he had been formally exchanged. It was not until late in the year that Sandwich was free to transfer him aboard the *Licorne* (32), a frigate recently captured from the French.

In the spring of 1779, Pellew sailed for Newfoundland. He spent the summer cruising off the coast of North America, but the *Licorne* encountered no serious opposition. She returned to England late in the year, and in 1780 Pellew rejoined Philemon Pownoll aboard the *Apollo* (32). Assigned to the Channel fleet, the *Apollo* cruised along the coast of France and the Low Countries. On 15 June she encountered the powerful privateer *Stanislaus* (26) off Ostend. The British frigate immediately came in to attack, her broadsides blazing. But she soon found herself in a more desperate battle than she had expected. The privateer fought back fiercely, flinging clouds of cannon shot and musket balls. Captain Pownoll was mortally wounded, but as he lay dying, he called out to his first lieutenant, "Pellew, don't give His Majesty's ship away."[2]

Even without his commander's last words, Pellew was determined to fight on. He blasted the *Stanislaus* so severely that she was dismasted, and she drifted ashore. Unfortunately, the coast she grounded upon was neutral, so the crew of the *Apollo* could not go ashore and burn her. Later, however, she was taken off and sold to the British government.

Following her battle with the *Stanislaus,* the *Apollo* returned again to England. Lord Sandwich was so impressed with the accounts he heard of the action that he promoted Pellew to commander of the *Hazard* (8) sloop on 1 July. The young commander remained in service in the Channel until the *Hazard* was paid off early in 1781. Shortly after leaving the *Hazard,* Pellew was appointed to the *Pelican* (16), in which he was again sent to patrol the Channel. He had been in command for little more than a month when he encountered three privateers. Although outnumbered, Pellew did not hesitate to plunge after them, and rather than face the wrath of the *Pelican,* all three vessels ran aground.

For this service and because of the promise he had shown in the past, Pellew was promoted by Lord Sandwich to the rank of post captain into the *Suffolk* (74), on 25 May. But command of the third rate was only temporary. Little more than a week later, the captain found himself on the deck of his own first frigate command—the *Artois* (40). Once again he ventured out into the Channel, and on 1 July he captured an unusually large privateer. That was the last action Captain Pellew saw during the American War of Independence. With the end of the conflict, the *Artois* was paid off, and the captain placed on half pay.

Before long Pellew had someone with whom to share his 110 pounds a year half pay. On 28 May 1783, he married Susannah Froude, a lady nearly a year his senior. The couple would have six children. Within a few months of the wedding, the Pellews journeyed to the south of France. In his correspondence to the Admiralty, the captain explained that his health required a warmer climate, but it is likely that life ashore had palled for an individual accustomed to constant activity. Travel may have been seen as a remedy for stagnation.

The couple did not remain abroad long, and in the spring of 1786, Captain Pellew was appointed to the command of the *Winchelsea* (32). This frigate patrolled the banks off Newfoundland in the summer and wintered in Cadiz or Lisbon. While the captain was off the coast of North America in 1 July 1786, his wife gave birth to their eldest son, who was blessed with the unlikely name of Pownoll Bastard Pellew. (His middle name came from his godfather, a Mr. Bastard.)

During the first half of 1787, the *Winchelsea* cruised the Channel in search of smugglers. Smuggling was rife in the English Channel and the North Sea, and the Royal Navy did what it could to curb the traffic. However, the smugglers' small craft usually were able to keep out of sight or could outmaneuver most of the heavier men-of-war. In spite of all her cruising in the first half of 1787, the *Winchelsea* succeeded in capturing only a single smuggler.

In early 1789 Pellew ended the *Winchelsea*'s commission and soon assumed command of the *Salisbury* (50), flagship of Vice Admiral Milbanke, who was commander in chief of the North American station. He remained in active service until December 1791, when the *Salisbury* was paid off, and Captain Pellew was stranded without a ship again.

With only his half pay to live on and a growing family to feed, Pellew tried his hand at farming. Unfortunately, he was less successful as a farmer than he had been as a naval officer, and he became discouraged. He even considered accepting a command in the Russian navy, but declined it, and before long his life took a turn for the better.

On 11 January 1793, even before war had been officially declared on the French republic, Pellew received his commission to the *Nymphe* (36). As described in chapter 9, the principal difficulty for a captain trying to fit out a vessel was gathering enough men. Writing from Torbay in February, Pellew complained that his frigate was badly undermanned and that many of the men he had were ill. As a Cornishman, he decided to do his recruiting in familiar territory, so he sailed to Falmouth, where he enlisted the assistance of the local press gang. On the night of 21 March, Pellew "ransacked the whole town in company with the officers of the gang" and gathered up a sizable contingent of likely seamen.[3] Unfortunately, in spite of the captain's protests, the Admiralty demanded that he surrender his prisoners to a tender for the benefit of captains who had been less active in trying to man their own vessels. Nevertheless, by the beginning of April, the *Nymphe* was ready for her first cruise of the new war.

On 18 June the *Nymphe* sailed out from Falmouth and only a day later captured her first prize. Her lookouts sighted the *Cléopâtre* (36) early in the morning of the nineteenth, and Pellew gave the order to make all sail after her. He had been chasing the other frigate for only an hour before the French captain, finding that he would not be able to escape, hove to and gallantly awaited his approach. Without firing a shot, the *Nymphe* drew to within speaking distance, at which point the two ship's companies exchanged patriotic cheers. Only then did Pellew give the signal for his gun crews to open fire.

The two frigates pounded each other savagely, but the *Cléopâtre* received the worst of it. Within forty-five minutes she had lost her wheel and her mizzenmast. Out of control, the Frenchman swung into the wind and collided with her opponent, her jibboom passing between the *Nymphe*'s fore- and mainmasts. For a moment the British vessel's damaged mainmast tottered, but then the intruding jibboom snapped, allowing the two frigates to lie alongside each other, bow to stern. Meanwhile, as soon as the two vessels collided, a boarding party from the *Nymphe* charged onto the deck of the *Cléopâtre* and, within ten minutes, hauled down the tricolor. About an hour had passed between the first shot and the last, and Pellew had a prize to escort back to England. The cost to both sides was high—fifty British killed and wounded and sixty-three French, including her captain, who was killed. With typical generosity, Pellew later sent monetary assistance to his dead enemy's widow.

Within less than a fortnight of the action against the *Cléopâtre,* the king summoned Pellew before him and dubbed him a knight. Sir Edward and the *Nymphe* enjoyed some less notable cruising in the Channel, and in January 1794 Pellew left her for the *Arethusa* (38). In April the *Arethusa* joined the squadron under the command of Commo. Sir John Warren. She took part in the action against the three French frigates on 23 April that is detailed in chapter 9.

Later in the year a second frigate squadron was formed and placed under Sir Edward's command. While on his first cruise in company with the *Artois,* the *Diamond* (38), and the *Galatea* (32), Pellew encountered the *Révolutionnaire* (40) off Ushant. The entire squadron gave chase, but the *Artois* was the first to get into action. The two frigates exchanged broadsides at close range for about forty minutes before the *Diamond* joined in. Finding himself outnumbered and unable to escape, the French captain finally hauled down his flag.

Once again the new year brought a new ship for Captain Pellew. In January 1795 he took command of the *Indefatigable* (38), a cut-down ship of the line, or razee. His squadron joined that of Commodore Warren off Brest, and on 18 February they attacked a convoy of twenty merchantmen under the escort of a frigate. So effective was the attack that virtually the entire convoy was captured or destroyed. Then, a month later, the wolf pack flushed out another convoy and captured most of it.

With the coming of spring, Warren's squadron was broken up. Warren himself went to command the naval force assisting the landing of troops at Quiberon Bay. Meanwhile, Pellew and a few others remained off the coast, protecting the expedition from interference by sea. After a year spent largely under sail, the *Indefatigable* was due for a refit. She put into Plymouth, and it was there that her captain helped save the lives of the passengers and crew of the *Dutton.* For his bravery and self-sacrifice, Pellew was created a baronet on 5 March 1796.

Not long after his new civilian rank was gazetted, Sir Edward sailed again to the coast of France. Warren, who had been gone from England for nearly a year, needed to return home, so Pellew was sent to replace him. At that point, the main duty was getting off the surviving troops and transporting them back to England. This Sir Edward managed with his usual efficiency and, incidentally, captured another French convoy.

On 12 April, Pellew was again in command of a frigate squadron off Brest, when Captain Cole of the *Révolutionnaire* sighted the French frigate *Unité* (36). He gave chase and approached within hail shortly before midnight. The rest of the squadron was not far behind, and Cole urged his French counterpart to surrender. But Captain Linois refused and gave the order for his men to fire. However, his mutinous crew forced him to strike within twenty minutes. The action with the *Unité* was short, but the next action between a British and a French frigate in the Channel was five times as long.

The *Indefatigable* was in company with the *Amazon* (36) and the *Concorde* (36) off Cornwall on 20 April when she sighted a suspicious sail to seaward. Immediately all three vessels made sail after the stranger, which proved to be the *Virginie* (40). For fifteen hours the four frigates continued southward toward Brest, the British slowly closing the distance. Finally, the *Indefatigable* was in a position to fire on the foe. Pellew described the action:

> A little past midnight I commenced action with the enemy, which was closely continued under a crowded sail, for one hour and forty-five minutes. The enemy, who fought gallantly, was by this time much crippled, her mizzenmast and main topmast being shot away. The *Indefatigable* was not much less disabled, having lost her gaff and mizzen topmast . . . . In this situation we passed the enemy without the power of avoiding it . . . and I had long discovered that we had not only to combat a ship of large force, but that her commander was completely master of his profession, in whose presence I could not commit myself with impunity by throwing my ship in the wind, without submitting to be raked by him.
>
> At this period *La Concorde* appeared close under her stern, and upon the enemy's seeing her she fired a gun to leeward and struck her light as a signal of surrender.
>
> Altho' a very few minutes would have placed the *Indefatigable* again alongside of her, I am confident she would not have surrendered without further resistance had not the *Concorde* so timely come up.[4]

In the preceding narrative some of Pellew's personality can be discerned. The enemy was so heavily outgunned that once he caught her, it was virtually a certainty that he would take her. But, to add glory to the action, he describes the foe as both powerful and well commanded. However, he is generous enough to give plenty of credit to the captain of the *Concorde*.

In June the frigate squadron captured two gun brigs off Ushant with contemptuous ease. Sir Edward reported to the First Lord, "[I]t is a great pleasure to me to prevent the abundant mischief such little spiteful rascals are calculated to commit upon our trade."[5]

Later in the summer the *Indefatigable* was given a special task to perform. The enemy was assembling an invasion fleet at Brest, but its intended destination was unknown. Sir Edward was sent to scout along the enemy's coast and try to discover what they were about. Although the frigate snooped about the coast for most of the autumn, Pellew was unable to discover anything more specific than that a major invasion was being prepared for some part of the world. He was inclined to believe they were bound for Portugal, although in fact the expedition was intended for Ireland.

When the French fleet sailed on 16 December, the *Indefatigable* was waiting to shadow them. She dogged them all day, but in the night, she lost contact. Desperately Pellew cast about, searching for any sign he could find of the fleet, but not a trace could he see. He decided that if he could not find the French within twenty-four hours, he would head for Lisbon to warn the Portuguese of the potential invasion. With an uncharacteristic note of self-doubt, he wrote to Lord Spencer, "God knows, my lord, if I shall be doing right, but left in a wilderness of conjecture I can only say that the sacrifice of my life would be easy if it served my gracious King and my country."[6] In the end, he changed his mind and returned to England instead of proceeding to Lisbon.

The *Indefatigable* arrived at Falmouth on 20 December and returned to renew her search for the French two days later. By that time most of the expedition had put into Bantry Bay, where rough weather compelled the soldiers to stay in the ships. By the time the weather cleared, the invaders were short of supplies, and their commanding officer decided to return home, which he reached on 1 January 1797. The intended invasion of Ireland had been a complete failure, but only the weather had stood in the way of the French. The main fleet saw scarcely a sign of the Royal Navy from the time they left Brest to the time they returned.

Others were not so lucky. During the first stormy crossing of the Channel, several vessels were unable to follow the main fleet into Bantry Bay. These proceeded farther north to find shelter in the mouth of the Shannon. Then, having spent a short time making repairs, they too decided to return to France. One of these vessels was the *Droits de l'Homme* (74). As she neared the coast of France in foggy weather on 13 January, her captain sighted a pair of vessels that appeared to be pursuing him. The two vessels were the *Indefatigable* and the *Amazon* (36), which had been cruising the area, waiting for such an opportunity. Although a ship of the line under normal circumstances is more than a match for two frigates, the two British captains continued in pursuit, and the Frenchman fled.

As the chase continued through the afternoon, the wind strengthened from the west. A sudden squall carried away the *Droits de l'Homme*'s fore-

and maintopmasts, which slowed the larger man-of-war, allowing the *Inde-fatigable* to close to within gunshot by 5:30. Coming upon the Frenchman from astern, Pellew had his command haul up to rake her with a broadside, but before he could reload, the enemy had also hauled up and returned the favor. Because of the high seas, the two-decker was unable to open her lower gunports and use her larger guns. However, even her upper battery was formidable. In addition to her broadside, she peppered the decks of the *Inde-fatigable* with musketry. Pellew described the scene as he attempted to surge ahead of the *Droits de l'Homme* to rake her across the bow and the Frenchman blocked his way: "When he endeavour'd to run me on board his lion-head was at least 6 feet above our taffrail, and a heavy fire of musketry assailed us through his head doors."[7] In other words, the French ship was so much taller than her foe that her figurehead loomed more than six feet over the stern, giving her soldiers armed with muskets a clear shot at the *Inde-fatigable*'s quarterdeck.

The battle continued between the ship of the line and the razee for more than an hour before the *Amazon* was able to come to Pellew's assistance. She hauled up and directed a broadside into the *Droits de l'Homme*'s quarter. Then the Frenchman maneuvered so that the smaller vessels were both on the same side. The action continued until 7:30, at which point the two British men-of-war shot ahead and did not return to the attack until an hour later. This time they chose a more orderly approach. Each took a side of the two-decker's bow and positioned themselves to rake her. The *Droits de l'Homme* fought back like a bear in a pit, occasionally clawing her smaller and more nimble opponents but never getting close enough for her greater weight to work to her advantage. After three hours of action, her mizzen fell overboard, but she fought on.

For most of a long winter night, the two frigates continued to batter their foe, only once withdrawing for a few quick repairs. Then, at 4:20 A.M., the sudden appearance of land to leeward gave the ships' companies something more urgent to concern them. Immediately all three vessels fought to clear the shore, but after so sharp an engagement, the *Droits de l'Homme* was too damaged to reach safety. She struck upon a sandbank at 7:00 in the morning of 14 January and became a total wreck. The *Amazon* soon afterward also took the ground, but virtually her entire crew was saved. The men of the *Droits de l'Homme* were not so fortunate.

The two-decker was stranded on a sand spit at some distance from land, and the state of the weather prevented well-meaning citizens from coming to the rescue of the distressed soldiers and mariners. Several attempts were made over the course of three days for boats and rafts to leave the ship, but the only persons who made shore successfully were some British prisoners. It was not until four days after the wreck that the weather moderated enough for the survivors to be rescued. By that time, many who had survived the action had perished by drowning or from hunger and exposure. More than three hundred of the *Droits de l'Homme*'s passengers and crew died during the battle and its aftermath.[8]

The *Indefatigable* was also in great distress from the weather. Pellew described the state of his command during the latter part of the battle: "The ship was full of water, the cockpit half-leg deep, and the surgeon absolutely obliged to tie himself and patient to the stanchions to perform an amputation."[9] But thanks to the superb seamanship of her captain, the heroic efforts of the already exhausted crew, and a modicum of luck, the *Indefatigable* weathered the rocks with about a mile to spare.

In the autumn the *Indefatigable* had another cruise and enjoyed continued success. She captured the *Ranger* (12) near the Canary Islands. Then, eleven days later, while she was returning to Britain, the privateer *Hyène* (24) approached her. The French captain, looking upon the stout hull of the *Indefatigable*, wishfully decided that he had happened upon a rich Indiaman. He managed to approach within gunshot before he was undeceived. As soon as he discovered his mistake, the *Hyène*'s captain came about and fled with all speed, but the frigate's shots were faster, and well aimed. They struck down the privateer's foremast, allowing the *Indefatigable* to come up and take her for a prize.

The *Indefatigable*'s next memorable fight came on 7 August 1798. Pellew sighted the *Vaillante* (20) at dawn and immediately gave chase. The enemy was fresh from the dock with clean copper and hoped that she could outsail the bigger vessel. But Sir Edward handled his command so well that the Frenchman was never able to get out of his sight. After twenty-four hours, the *Indefatigable* was finally within range to fire on the *Vaillante*. Once a few shots had whistled through her rigging, the Frenchman's crew decided to haul down their flag. Pellew sent a prize crew aboard to take possession. When they boarded the prize, the British learned that the *Vaillante* had been bound for the penal colony at Cayenne and that she had twenty-five Catholic priests housed in execrable conditions in the bilges.

Sir Edward was shocked at the dreadful treatment of the priests. He ordered them to be brought up on deck, treated by his surgeon, and given the run of the ship for their voyage back to England. For the prize crew he selected mainly Irishmen who would give the reverend fathers due respect.

The priests were landed safely and founded a monastery in Dorsetshire where they prayed every day for the Protestant captain who had saved them from the deadly miseries of Cayenne.

The normally humane Pellew occasionally showed that he had a harsh streak. One example was when he was called upon to sit in judgment upon one of the mutineers from the *Hermione* (32). On 21 September 1797 some of the crew of the *Hermione* rose up and murdered the sadistic Capt. Hugh Pigot and most of his officers. After surrendering their ship to the Spanish at La Guaira, the mutineers had scattered, but some were discovered and brought to trial. Pellew had been friendly with the Pigot family, so when one of the mutineers was brought before him and found guilty, he urged his fellow judges to have the man strung up immediately: "The circumstance of the case demanded, in his opinion, unusual severity, which might be expected to have good effect upon the Fleet; while there was every reason to conclude, from the prisoner's demeanour before them, that if delay were allowed, he would meet his fate with hardihood which would destroy the value of the example."[10]

Accordingly, the mutineer was hanged within an hour of his conviction. The man lost much of the demeanor he might have had if he had been allowed a few days' time, but the value of the example was questionable. The fleet was shocked by the suddenness of the event, and the consensus among Pellew's peers was that to hang a man before he had had the opportunity to make his peace with God was extraordinarily cruel.

By the beginning of 1799, Sir Edward had been a post captain for eighteen years. In an era when frigate commands were generally held by more junior captains, he had remained in small ships for an exceptionally long period. But at last he became too senior to command a frigate any longer. In March he was appointed to the *Impétueux* (74) in the Channel fleet.

In the first months of his new command, Pellew must have often regretted leaving the *Indefatigable*. Not only had he lost the harmonious ship's company he had assembled over four years, his independence, and a good chance of prize money, but also the *Impétueux* was a vessel full of troubles. There was little wrong with the ship herself. It was her ship's company that was the main source of trouble. They had been an unruly lot ever since the Spithead mutiny two years before, and Sir Edward had been placed in command with the hope that he would be able to bring them to heel.

Lord Bridport denied Pellew's request to transfer a large number of trusty officers and men from the *Indefatigable*. So, not wishing to be completely at the mercy of the *Impétueux*'s mutinous crew, the captain recruited a small company of tough Cornish miners to stand as a buffer between him and his ship's company. As soon as Sir Edward arrived on board, he tightened the noose of discipline. He had not often had to employ the cat-o'-nine-tails upon the crews of his frigates, but aboard the two-decker, punishments were awarded virtually every day. The situation developed into a test of wills between captain and crew.

The tension aboard the *Impétueux* grew with each passing day as the vessel stood outside of Brest. Finally, on 30 May, matters came to a head. Certain members of the ship's company clamored for a boat to take them to Bridport's flagship so that they could present a written complaint against their captain. Pellew refused to let them have the boat but promised them he would carry the letter himself. This pledge was not good enough for the men, whose demands grew ever louder and more threatening.

Deciding he could do no more by persuasion, Sir Edward dashed down into his cabin and seized his sword. Meanwhile, he passed the order for his officers to be armed and for the marines to come to order. Then Pellew dived among the mutineers and picked out nine men he considered the ringleaders. His bold action temporarily restored order aboard the *Impétueux*.

However, this incident did not end the captain's difficulties. When Sir Edward requested that the commander in chief convene a court-martial to try his mutineers, Bridport refused. Finding that they had little to fear, the rebellious element again became unruly. It was not until Lord St. Vincent took command of the Channel fleet in 1800 that Pellew was finally able to gain the backing he sought. Following a court-martial, three of the ringleaders were hanged.

At the beginning of June, the British again tried to sponsor a counterrevolution in the north of France. Pellew was placed in command of a squadron consisting of seven ships of the line and five frigates and was directed to land troops in Quiberon Bay and cooperate with the royalists ashore. A few raids did some damage, but in general, the republicans were found to be too strong, so the expedition soon returned to England.

For a short time Sir Edward served again under the command of Rear Admiral Warren, and in August took part in the expedition against Ferrol. As reported in chapter 9, this foray was unsuccessful, because of the lack of harmony between the army and the navy, as well as an epidemic ashore.

With two abortive expeditions behind him, Pellew returned to the Channel, where he remained until the Peace of Amiens. The *Impétueux* was paid off late in 1801, sending her captain ashore to seek occupation in other fields. This time, instead of farming, Sir Edward entered politics, at which he was only slightly more successful. He was elected a Tory member of Parliament for Barnstaple in July 1802.

In March 1803, with war breaking out anew between Britain and France, Pellew read his commission aboard the *Tonnant* (80). Once again he sailed the waters of the Channel and the Bay of Biscay he knew so well. Later he was placed in command of a squadron and sent down to Ferrol to keep watch over the Spanish fleet there.

After Pellew had been in command of the *Tonnant* for a year, Parliament began a debate over St. Vincent's practices as First Lord of the Admiralty. Knowing that Sir Edward was bound to support his old patron in the face of his Tory colleagues, some of the old admiral's friends had him recalled from his command. He returned reluctantly, but soon observed that St. Vincent would need the support of all his friends. He gave his assistance and thereby made enemies of several Tories who thought he should have toed the party line rather than obey his conscience and personal loyalties.

On 23 April 1804 Pellew was promoted to rear admiral and was soon appointed commander in chief of the East Indies station. He hoisted his flag in the *Culloden* (74) on 4 July and sailed a week later. For more than five months, the *Culloden* sailed south and eastward, protecting a valuable convoy. She finally parted with her charges at the end of November and proceeded to Penang, where the admiral hoped to encounter his predecessor, Vice Admiral Rainier. But the former commander in chief was not there, having gone chasing after an enemy squadron that had eluded him. Although Sir Edward continued to follow after his predecessor in hopes of transferring the command formally, they never were able to meet.

Sir Edward's period of sole command did not last long. Shortly after Pellew had been appointed to his command, St. Vincent left the Admiralty. Still smarting from Sir Edward's apparent treachery, the new First Lord wanted to have him removed from his post, but after some bargaining, Pellew was allowed to proceed. Nonetheless, after his departure, the incoming government wanted to see the rear admiral punished, so they decided to divide his command. Sir Thomas Troubridge was junior to Pellew on the captain's list but had been made a rear admiral on the same date. He was appointed to command half of the East Indies station in February 1805, and he set sail with his flag in the *Blenheim* (74) in April. Meanwhile, unaware of the trouble brewed for him at home, Pellew shuttled between Bombay and Madras. Because of the climate and the seasonal patterns of trade in those waters, the commander of the station generally spent the winter months at Bombay and the summer at Madras.

When Sir Edward first arrived at the station he found the fleet too weak for his liking, so he purchased a few local ships to be fitted out as frigates. The two largest were the *Carron* and the *Shah Kaikuseroo,* which he renamed the *Duncan* (38) and the *Howe* (20), respectively. Other than these few new ships, the fleet at the time Pellew took over consisted of seven two-deckers, ten frigates, four sloops, a cutter, and a hulk. These were more than enough when accumulated to deal with the main opponent, Rear Admiral Linois. However, the British had numerous valuable ships that were vulnerable to raids by enemy frigates and privateers. Pellew's main responsibility was to supply escorts for the convoys.

Troubridge arrived at Madras at the end of August. Although his orders made it clear that the Admiralty had elected to divide the station between the two flag officers, Pellew was determined to use his few months' seniority to advantage and take the new arrival under his command. Sir Thomas would have none of it. He immediately wrote a letter of protest to the Admiralty.

> I must request that you will be pleased to move the Lords Commissioners of the Admiralty speedily to afford such further explanation of their Lordships' orders to Sir Edward Pellew as he seems to require . . .
>
> I most cheerfully proceed under the command of Sir Edward Pellew, because it is my duty to yield obedience to a senior officer, and because I hope the result may prove beneficial to His Majesty's Service; but I am persuaded that their Lordships will agree with me in opinion, that as effectual Co-operation might have been given by me as Commander in Chief agreeably to their Lordships' appointment, as under the present circumstances, by which, in defiance of their Commission I am placed as second in Command of the Squadron only.[11]

Having sanctimoniously relieved himself of his grievance, Troubridge proceeded to relieve Pellew of half his fleet. They sailed in company on 6 September to escort the China convoy, but both the convoy and the escorts were divided in two. In early October the two admirals parted, the junior to continue with the convoy to its destination, and Pellew to return with his half of the fleet to Madras. Although Sir Edward's correspondence to the Admiralty was diplomatic and uncritical, his private correspondence betrayed his frustration and contempt for Troubridge: "Sir Thomas is more outrageous than ever, and from a public correspondence full of invective and low insinuation, has now commenced a private one of no less scurrility and abuse. Language which degrades the Gentleman is ever flowing from his lips. . . . I wish to God I was out of it."[12]

For more than a year, the situation remained the same. Relations between the co–commanders in chief went from bad to worse, until Troubridge was at the point of challenging Pellew to a duel. The duel never took place, because in October 1806 the junior admiral was assigned to command of the Cape of Good Hope station. In early January 1807 he departed aboard his decrepit flagship, still seething with resentment. On his passage to his new command, the admiral encountered a tremendous storm. On 1 February the *Blenheim* went down with her entire ship's company, taking with her the officer whom the Earl of St. Vincent considered the best in the service. It is typical of Pellew that when he learned that the *Blenheim* had been reported missing, he sent Troubridge's son, who commanded the *Greyhound* (32), to Mauritius in search of news. Although the French governor of the island was as helpful as he could be, no trace of the admiral or his flagship was ever found.

Relieved of the tensions of a divided command, Pellew began to look about for employment for his ships. The Dutch had colonies at Batavia and Java, which were vulnerable to attack by the much more numerous British. Around the same time that Troubridge was appointed to the Good Hope station, Pellew was planning an attack on Batavia. He sailed from Madras on 22 October and arrived at the Dutch colony on 27 November. At the first sight of the British, the ships in the harbor ran themselves aground. Pellew ordered some boats from his squadron to row out to the stranded vessels and set them alight. Approximately twenty-five ships of various kinds were destroyed in this manner.

At the forefront of the action was Sir Edward's seventeen-year-old son, already a commander and acting captain of the *Terpsichore* (32). His proud father could not restrain his enthusiasm as he described to a friend how his son battled a Dutch frigate: "He fought her until the water overflowed her magazine, as they had scuttled her. I assure you, a prettier exploit I never saw. You will say, Aye, Aye, here is the Father. I have therefore done —but I assure you I say not half what others say of him. And so let it rest; it is a great comfort to see that one has not reared a bevy of Pigeons."[13]

Having completed the destruction of the Dutch naval forces at Batavia, the admiral returned to Madras, taking a few turns in his course to hunt for any Dutchmen who had escaped his net. He did not remain at Madras long, but soon proceeded to Bombay to spend the late winter and early spring of 1807. It was while he was there that he received some good news. One of his cruisers, the *Caroline* (36), had captured a Spanish vessel with a valuable cargo and $500,000 aboard. As commander in chief of the station, Pellew received an eighth of the value of the prize, amounting to £26,000, a most welcome addition.

The admiral returned to Madras in June, with a plan. The Dutch colony on the island of Java was nearly as vulnerable as that on Batavia had been, and this time he hoped to accomplish more than mere destruction. He needed soldiers to take permanent possession of the island, so he pressed the British governor of India, Lord Minto, to provide him with troops. Grudgingly the governor allowed Pellew about five hundred men. Although the admiral would have liked more, he decided to carry on with his plan with what he could get. His squadron sailed from Madras in mid-October. They stopped first at Penang, where more vessels were added to the fleet, and then weighed anchor for Java.

Pellew arrived off the Javanese coast on 5 December, only to discover that his flagship could not reach the main settlement of Grisee because of her deep draft. He sent a message to the Dutch governor, inviting him to surrender, which was received with derision. While the enemy sneered at his presumption, he lightened his flagship enough that she was able to pass up the river to Grisee. Faced with the gun power of two ships of the line and numerous smaller men-of-war, the Dutch asked for terms. Because Pellew lacked sufficient force to hold Java, the terms did not include ceding the island to Britain. Although he had not made a permanent conquest, Pellew congratulated himself that he had destroyed the entire naval force of Holland in the East Indies.

The British departed Java less than a month after their arrival and returned again to Madras in early 1808. From there the admiral thought of another rich prize that had thus far eluded him. It was the Dutch convoy from Japan, laden with the few exports the Japanese allowed to leave their country. To capture it would be a coup nearly beyond the most extravagant dreams of any commander in chief. Pellew had learned some information about the movements of the convoy, but wishing to learn more, he sent one of his sons to Nagasaki for intelligence. The visit did little to improve the admiral's chances of catching the Dutch convoy, but it so alarmed the Japanese that they formed a navy to keep more such visitors away.

Pellew spent most of the year 1808 in the standard round of Madras to Bombay and back. His cruisers captured many enemy vessels, but the richest prizes eluded them. Meanwhile, Lord Minto's eyes had turned toward China. Because the French were thought to be intending to establish themselves at Macao, the British decided that they would have to act quickly to thwart the enemy's plan. Pellew did not sail for China himself, but delegated command of the squadron to Rear Admiral Drury.

Toward the end of 1808 Pellew, now a vice admiral, felt that he had accomplished all his goals in the East Indies station. His health was beginning to deteriorate, and he grew homesick for the shores of England. In October he wrote to the Admiralty to ask to be relieved of his command. His wish was granted, and after nearly five years abroad, he returned to Britain in the middle of 1809.

Within less than a year of his return, Sir Edward was appointed commander in chief of the North Sea fleet. He had been offered the position of second-in-command under Lord Collingwood in the Mediterranean, but preferring to play the lead in a lesser theater, he elected to take the North Sea command. He remained in that position for a year, until matters changed in the Mediterranean. Lord Collingwood died in March 1810, and was replaced by Sir Charles Cotton. But in 1811 Cotton was appointed commander in chief of the Channel fleet, leaving the way open for Pellew to assume command in the Mediterranean, flying his flag in the *Caledonia* (120).

In the spring Sir Edward took up the station off Toulon, where the French fleet remained at anchor. Once or twice they made signs of coming out, but to Pellew's frustration, they never gave him a chance to get at them. It was not until the blockading squadron had been reduced to two frigates that Vice Admiral Emeriau thought to give his crews some exercise. They made an attempt to capture the two blockading frigates but were unsuccessful, and when the main British fleet was known to be within a few hundred miles, they scampered back into their hole.

Although Emeriau made a few feeble demonstrations in 1812, the fleets never came within range. The following year, however, was a trifle more eventful. On 5 November 1813 the main British fleet was blown off station by a stiff gale. This, the French admiral decided, was the perfect opportunity to give his crews some much needed sea time. At first the conditions favored his being able to exercise his fleet in peace, but suddenly the wind shifted, allowing the enemy to approach too close for comfort. Emeriau gave the signal to gather his flock and guide it back to safety. They were still attempting to escape when the British van came up. The *Scipion* (74) and three other third rates attempted to cut off five larger ships of the line. They exchanged a few broadsides, but the French managed to elude their pursuers, and by the time Sir Edward was able to come up, the enemy was out of range.

The French fleet made one more demonstration early in 1814, but the long war was drawing to a close. Britain and her allies entered Paris on 31 March, effectively putting an end to the conflict.

Amid the celebrations that followed the conclusion of the war, Sir Edward Pellew became Baron Exmouth of Canonteign on 14 May, and less than a month later was promoted to full admiral. Following Napoleon's exile to Elba, Exmouth returned to England to enjoy the fruits of his wartime labors. In 1815 he was made a knight Grand Cross of the Bath and presented with other honors. But when the emperor returned to the Continent, the admiral became once more commander in chief of the Mediterranean, with this flag in the *Boyne* (98). Although Napoleon's final run was soon terminated, Exmouth remained on station. The main enemy had been defeated, but there was a need for a peacekeeping force in the Mediterranean.

With the great naval powers preoccupied by their globe-spanning conflict, the Barbary pirates had enjoyed a free run. They had captured a large number of merchant ships and taken many slaves. But with the French Wars over, attention now turned toward what had been a minor irritant.

In March 1816 Exmouth toured the nations of Tunis, Tripoli, and Algiers to negotiate the release of Christian slaves taken during the conflict. He also stipulated that no more Christians should be enslaved henceforth. The rulers of Tunis and Tripoli decided not to risk the displeasure of the nation that could wield such a powerful fleet, but the dey of Algiers refused to outlaw the slavery of Christians in his country. After heated words between the British and Algerian delegations and an attack on some England officers by a mob, the admiral returned to his native land to gather a fleet that could teach the dey and his people a lesson.

With his flag in the *Queen Charlotte* (100), Exmouth sailed from Plymouth on 28 July. He was accompanied by a fleet of six two-deckers, four frigates, five sloops-of-war, and four bomb vessels.[14] They reached Gibraltar on 9 August and found that they had been preceded by a Dutch squadron with similar intentions. Vice Admiral van Capellen had five frigates and a sloop under his command. He asked permission to join Exmouth's fleet, and was received with pleasure.

The combined fleet sailed on 14 August and arrived off Algiers nearly a fortnight later. With such an impressive force to back him, Exmouth thought that the dey would now be willing to negotiate. He sent in demands for the release of all Christian slaves, for Algiers to sign a treaty with the Dutch, and for reparations to be paid. But the dey was not to be cowed. His defenses were formidable, and he relied on them to keep the enemy at bay.

Algiers was defended by batteries armed with one thousand 32-, 24-, and 18-pounders. These remained silent while negotiations were still under way. But shortly after 2:30 in the afternoon of 27 August, a single gun opened up on the *Queen Charlotte.* Exmouth took this as a declaration of war, but before he returned fire, he urged the gathering crowd on shore to seek shelter. Then he gave the command for his flagship to open up with her broadside.

The other vessels of the combined fleet came as swiftly as they could to the *Queen Charlotte's* assistance. They formed a long line abreast of the batteries, the British in the van and the Dutch toward the rear. Broadside after broadside was directed at the batteries, which returned a fierce fire. The *Impregnable* (98) and the *Glasgow* (40) were severely damaged by enemy shot, but no vessel was compelled to leave the line. Meanwhile, the town and warehouses along the shore were set on fire by shot and shell from the combined fleet. Later in the evening, an explosion vessel was run ashore near one of the batteries and set off where it would do the most damage.

By 10:00 in the evening, after more than seven hours of constant action, the allied fleet had fired nearly fifty thousand rounds. Although that nearly exhausted the allies' supply of ammunition, it had brought the Algerians to the brink of defeat. Seeing that there was little more he could do, Exmouth signaled for his fleet to withdraw, and by 2:00 A.M. the action was over. In the battle the British lost 128 killed and 690 wounded. Dutch losses were 13 killed and 62 wounded. The minimum casualties estimated for the enemy were 4,000.[15]

As soon as it was light again, the admiral renewed his demands and indicated that he would renew the bombardment at need. But the dey and his people had had enough. They agreed to all his terms and ended the era of taking Christian slaves. On 4 September the fleet departed for Gibraltar.

Upon his return to England in late September, Exmouth was bombarded with honors. He was made a viscount of the United Kingdom and awarded orders of merit by Spain, Naples, the Netherlands, and Sardinia. Within a year after his return from Algiers, Lord Exmouth was made commander in chief at Plymouth, following the sudden death of Admiral Duckworth. He flew his flag in the *Impregnable* for the next three and a half years before retiring from active service on 1 February 1821.

Although the admiral had retired from service at the age of 63, his distinguished career was not forgotten. When the position of Vice Admiral of

England fell vacant in February 1832, he was appointed to it. But by that time, Exmouth was already in ill health. Upon his appointment, he wrote to his brother, "I shall have it only for one year."[16] Indeed he held the rank for slightly less than that. He died peacefully at home on 23 January 1833.

The title of Viscount Exmouth passed to his eldest son, Pownoll Bastard Pellew, while two of his younger sons enjoyed highly successful naval careers. The second son, Fleetwood, rose to the rank of admiral, and like his father before him, commanded the East Indies station.

Glossary

aback With the wind blowing against the front of a sail, pressing the sail against the mast.

abaft Behind.

able seaman An experienced sailor who can work the sails and steer the ship.

admiral of the red, white, or blue Each of the three squadrons—red, white, or blue—denoted seniority in the Royal Navy. The blue squadron was most junior, the white squadron next, and the red squadron most senior. As an admiral increased in rank, he became first rear admiral of the blue, then rear admiral of the white, rear admiral of the red, vice admiral of the blue, and so on.

afterhold A storage area near the stern of a ship.

back To turn a sail so that the wind catches the front of the sail.

ball mizzen The driver reduced to its minimum area.

barge A ship's boat reserved for a captain or admiral's personal use.

berth deck The highest enclosed deck in the forward part of a ship where the seamen sling their hammocks.

bilges The lowest portion of a ship's interior, where liquid generally collects.

boatswain A warrant officer in charge of maintaining a ship's sails and rigging, among other duties.

bomb ketch A warship with two masts and one or two mortars mounted where the foremast is usually stepped.

bomb vessel A warship designed to carry mortars for siege work.

boom (1) A barrier typically constructed of logs fastened with a chain; (2) the spar that supports the foot of some fore-and-aft sails.

bowsprit A spar thrusting out from a ship's bow, used to attach the forestays.

brace A line attached to a yard that is used to shift the position of the yard in a horizontal direction.

brig A sailing vessel with two masts, both of which bear square sails.

bring to To stop a ship by backing a sail, or to cause another ship to do the same.

broad pennant A swallow-tailed red flag flown by a commodore's flagship.

broadside The firing of all of a warship's guns on one side together.

bulwarks The upper sides of a ship's hull.

cable (1) A thick rope to which the anchor is attached; (2) an eighth of a mile.

cap-a-bar Misappropriation of government stores.

capstan A wooden cylinder mounted vertically on deck used to reel in the anchor cable.

carte blanche Open orders.

cathead A beam that juts out from a ship's bow and is used to weigh the anchor.

chains Metal fittings that fasten the ends of the shrouds to the ship's sides.

chainshot A cannon projectile consisting of two half cannonballs joined by a short chain, mostly used to destroy sails and rigging.

chock A wooden or iron fitting used to keep a running line on track.

close hauled Sailing as close as possible to the wind.

cockade A piece of material worn in a hat as a token of national or party loyalty.

corvette A small French warship, smaller than a frigate.

cruiser A frigate or sloop-of-war with orders to cruise after prizes.

cutter A small sailing vessel with a single mast and fore-and-aft sails.

driver The large fore-and-aft sail on the mizzenmast.

farthing A quarter of a penny.

fifth rate A warship with a single full gundeck mounting thirty to forty-four guns.

fireship A small ship designed to be filled with flammable materials and set on fire to drift into enemy vessels and catch them on fire.

first rate A warship with three full gundecks and mounting one hundred cannon or more.

flag captain Captain of a commodore's or admiral's flagship.

flat boat A boat with an extremely shallow draft.

forecastle An open deck in the foremost portion of a ship.

foremast The foremost of a ship's three masts.

foresail The largest and lowest sail attached to the foremast.

foreyard   The horizontal spar that supports the foresail.

fourth rate   A small two-decked warship with between forty-four and sixty guns.

frigate   A fast warship with twenty to forty-four guns and only one complete gundeck.

gaff   The upper spar that supports some types of fore-and-aft sails.

galleon   A large merchant vessel.

galley   A ship designed to be propelled by oars.

gangway   A narrow raised platform that connects the forecastle to the quarter-deck on either side.

gig   A small ship's boat, generally used by officers.

guardship   A warship that spends most of its time at anchor in a major port, whose crew serves as a harbor police force.

gunboat   A boat carrying a small number of cannon aboard to be used in landings or inshore battles.

gun brig   A two-masted man-of-war.

gunport   A square hole cut into a warship's hull to allow the cannons to protrude.

halyard   A line that is used to hoist a yard or a flag up the mast.

hawser   A heavy line five or more inches in diameter.

heave to   To halt a ship in the water by backing a sail.

Indiaman   A large merchant ship built for trade to the East or West Indies

jack   A flag.

Jack Tar   A nickname for a common seaman.

jibboom   A spar that extends out from the end of the bowsprit.

jibsail   A fore-and-aft sail suspended from a line running from the foremast to the bowsprit.

keel   The beam that runs the length of the bottom of a ship's hull to which the ribs are attached.

larboard   The left side of a sailing vessel (pre-mid-nineteenth-century).

launch   A large ship's boat.

leeward   Downwind.

letter of marque   (1) Papers carried by a privateer enabling that vessel to capture enemy vessels; (2) a ship carrying such papers.

line abreast   A fleet formation in which the ships are sailing side by side.

lugger   A sailing vessel with "lug" sails—a quadrilateral sail bent to a yard that is slung obliquely in a fore-and-aft position.

mainmast   The middle of a ship's three masts—usually the tallest and thickest.

maintop   A platform located at the conjunction of the mainmast and maintopmast.

merchantman   A merchant sailing ship.

mess   A group of seamen or officers who eat together.

midshipman   An officer in training, usually between the ages of twelve and thirty, ranking as a warrant officer.

miss stays   To fail in the attempt to tack.

mizzen   The aftermost of a ship's three masts.

mole   A loading and discharging place for vessels, usually protected by a breakwater.

moor   To anchor a ship using two anchors—one on either side of the bow.

mortar   A short, thick piece of artillery designed to throw shells at a high trajectory.

offing   In sight of land, but well to seaward.

paid off   Taken out of commission.

pintle   The hinge upon which the rudder turns.

poop deck   On a large warship, an open deck abaft and above the quarterdeck.

post captain   Captain of a ship of "rate," i.e., possessing twenty guns or more; only a post captain could eventually be promoted to the rank of admiral.

prison hulk   An old ship of the line converted into a floating prison.

privateer   A privately owned vessel granted a commission by the government to attack ships belonging to a hostile power.

purser   A warrant officer whose duty is to look after and measure out the provisions for a ship's company.

purser's steward   A petty officer who assists the purser.

quarter   The aft part of a ship, e.g., the lee quarter, the downwind rear portion of a ship.

quarterdeck   An open deck located abaft the mainmast and forward of the mizzen, where typically the captain and officers stand to command the ship.

quarter gallery   A small room that projects from the side near a ship's stern.

rake   To present one's broadside to an enemy's bow or stern, thereby enabling one to fire without being fired upon.

razee   A frigate produced by removing the upper deck from a ship of the line; a cut-down ship.

read in   The act of a captain reading his commission aloud to the ship's company upon first taking command of a ship.

reeve   To pass a rope through a block or hole.

rigging   The lines that support the masts and yards and that are used to control the orientation of a ship's sails.

road   An anchorage.

rocket vessel   A small warship especially designed to fire Congreve rockets.

running rigging   The lines that run through blocks and control the position and shape of the sails.

Sally Port   At Portsmouth, where ship's boats are loaded and unloaded.

schooner   A sailing vessel with two or more masts set with fore-and-aft sails.

scuttle   To sink a ship deliberately by knocking holes in the hull under the waterline.

seam   The joint between two pieces of wood in a ship's hull.

second rate   A three-decked warship with between ninety and ninety-eight guns.

ship of the line   A warship with two or more full decks of guns designed to fight in the line of battle.

shot locker   Storage place for cannonballs.

shroud   A line that supports the mast on the sides.

sixth rate   A warship bearing between twenty and thirty guns on one deck.

sloop-of-war   A three-masted fighting vessel with twelve to eighteen guns, usually commanded by a commander.

slow match   Cord soaked in potassium nitrate—it burns slowly and is used to set off cannon or light fuses.

soundings   Measurements of water depth.

spanker   The lowermost sail on the mizzen, set fore-and-aft.

spar   Any wooden part of a ship's rigging, such as a mast or yard.

spring   A line attached to the anchor cable and run through a windlass to be used in maneuvering an anchored vessel.

spritsail   A small square sail suspended under the bowsprit.

starboard   The right side of a vessel.

stay   A line that runs forward of a mast and holds it in place.

staysail   A fore-and-aft sail suspended from a stay.

stern chaser   A cannon mounted over the stern of a warship.

stern gallery   A walkway along the stern of a ship of the line, usually adjoining a captain's or admiral's cabin.

stocks   Framework in which a hull is mounted when under construction.

tack (n)   The direction from which the wind is blowing relative to the position of a ship, i.e., if a ship is on the starboard tack, the wind is blowing from the starboard side of the ship.

tack (v)   To change directions by turning the ship's bow into the wind.

taffrail   A rail that runs along the upper part of a ship's stern.

tender   Small support vessel.

third rate   A warship with two full gundecks and between sixty and eighty cannon; usually the most common ship of the line.

three-decker   A warship with three full gundecks.

topmast   A second, thinner mast, attached to the top of the foremast, mainmast, or mizzenmast.

topsail   A sail above the foresail, mainsail, or spanker.

traveler   A moving ring to which a block is attached.

two-decker   A warship with two full gundecks.

veer   A change in wind direction to the right.

wardroom   The common room for officers in a ship of the line.

warp   To move a ship by means of ropes fastened to fixed posts.

wear   To change directions by turning the ship's stern into the wind.

weather quarter   The after end of the ship nearest the wind.

wind gauge   Having the wind gauge is to be positioned upwind of an opposing ship or fleet, allowing the captain or admiral to choose whether to attack or hold back.

xebec   A shallow-drafted ship with a foremast that slopes toward the bow, commonly used by Barbary pirates.

yard   A horizontal spar used to support the top of a square sail.

yardarm   The outer end of a yard.

yardrope   A rope attached to the end of a yard as preparation for suspending a noose for a hanging.

Notes

Chapter 1. Richard Howe

1. *Dictionary of National Biography,* s.v. Howe.
2. PRO ADM1/1887.
3. Warner, *Glorious First of June,* 15.
4. Ibid., 16.
5. Cokayne, *Complete Peerage,* s.v. Howe.
6. Numbers in parentheses following ships' names are rated for number of guns.
7. Mackay, *Admiral Hawke,* 173–74.
8. Lavery, *Shipboard Life and Organization,* 70.
9. *Soleil Royal* (80), *Tonnant* (80), *Formidable* (80), *Orient* (80), *Intrepide* (74), *Glorieux* (74), *Thésée* (74), *Héros* (74), *Robuste* (74), *Magnifique* (74), *Juste* (70), *Superbe* (70), *Dauphin Royal* (70), *Dragon* (64), *Northumberland* (64), *Sphinx* (64), *Solitaire* (64), *Brilliant* (64), *Eveille* (64), *Bizarre* (64), and *Inflexible* (64).
10. *Royal George* (100), *Union* (90), *Duke* (90), *Namur* (90), *Mars* (74), *Warspite* (74), *Hercules* (74), *Torbay* (74), *Magnanime* (74), *Resolution* (74), *Hero* (74), *Swiftsure* (70), *Dorsetshire* (70), *Burford* (70), *Chichester* (70), *Temple* (70), *Revenge* (64), *Essex* (64), *Kingston* (60), *Intrepid* (60), *Montagu* (60), *Dunkirk* (60), and *Defiance* (60).
11. Lyon, *Sea Battles in Close-up,* 38.
12. Coggins, *Ships and Seamen of the American Revolution,* 20.
13. Partridge, *Sir Billy Howe,* 48.
14. Ibid., 242.
15. Miller, *Sea of Glory,* 348.
16. *Dictionary of National Biography,* s.v. Howe.
17. *Annual Register,* 1783.
18. Dugan, *The Great Mutiny,* 153.
19. *Dictionary of National Biography,* s.v. Howe.
20. Lewis, *Correspondence of Miss Berry,* 1:392.
21. Ibid., 1:425.
22. Blunt, *Mrs. Montagu,* 2:296.
23. The larger number is to be found in James, *The Naval History of Great Britain,* 1:138; the smaller number is in Clowes, *The Royal Navy,* 4:216.

24. *Queen Charlotte* (100), *Royal George* (100), *Royal Sovereign* (100), *Barfleur* (98), *Impregnable* (98), *Queen* (98), *Glory* (98), *Gibraltar* (80), *Caesar* (80), *Bellerophon* (74), *Montagu* (74), *Tremendous* (74), *Valiant* (74), *Ramillies* (74), *Audacious* (74), *Brunswick* (74), *Alfred* (74), *Defence* (74), *Leviathan* (74), *Majestic* (74), *Invincible* (74), *Orion* (74), *Russell* (74), *Marlborough* (74), *Thunderer* (74), and *Culloden* (74).

25. *Montagne* (120), *Terrible* (110), *Révolutionnaire* (110), *Républicain* (110), *Indomptable* (80), *Jacobin* (80), *Juste* (80), *Scipion* (80), *Achille* (74), *America* (74), *Convention* (74), *Entreprenant* (74), *Eole* (74), *Gasparin* (74), *Jemmapes* (74), *Impétueux* (74), *Montagnard* (74), *Mont-Blanc* (74), *Mucius* (74), *Neptune* (74), *Northumberland* (74), *Pelletier* (74), *Tourville* (74), *Tyrannicide* (74), and *Vengeur* (74).

26. *Bellerophon, Russell, Marlborough,* and *Thunderer.*

27. Tracy, *Naval Chronicle,* 1:92.

28. Dugan, *Great Mutiny,* 148.

Chapter 2. Alexander Hood

1. Clowes, *Royal Navy,* 3:83.

2. PRO ADM1/1891.

3. Ibid.

4. Barrow, *Mutiny of the Bounty,* 198.

5. Cokayne, *Complete Peerage,* s.v. Hood, Alexander.

6. *Couronne* (80), *Duc de Bourgogne* (80), *Glorieux* (74), *Palmier* (74), *Bien-Aimé* (74), *Dauphin Royal* (70), *Vengeur* (64), *Alexandre* (64), *Indien* (64), *Saint Michel* (60), *Amphion* (50), *Bretagne* (110), *Ville de Paris* (100), *l'Orient* (74), *Fendant* (74), *Magnifique* (74), *Actif* (74), *Réfléchi* (64), *Eveille* (64), *Artesien* (64), *Actionnaire* (64), *Saint Esprit* (80), *Robuste* (74), *Conquerant* (74), *Intrepide* (74), *Zodiaque* (74), *Diadème* (74), *Solitaire* (64), *Roland* (64), *Sphinx* (64), *Triton* (64), and *Fier* (50).

7. *Monarch* (74), *Hector* (74), *Centaur* (74), *Exeter* (64), *Duke* (90), *Queen* (90), *Shrewsbury* (74), *Cumberland* (74), *Berwick* (74), *Stirling Castle* (64), *Courageux* (74), *Thunderer* (74), *Sandwich* (90), *Valiant* (74), *Bienfaisant* (64), *Victory* (100), *Foudroyant* (80), *Prince George* (90), *Vigilant* (64), *Terrible* (74), *Vengeance* (74), *Worcester* (64), *Elizabeth* (74), *Robust* (74), *Formidable* (90), *Ocean* (90), *America* (64), *Defiance* (64), *Egmont* (74), and *Ramillies* (74).

8. Clowes, *Royal Navy,* 3:413.

9. Keppel, *Life of Augustus Viscount Keppel,* 2:39.

10. Ibid., 49.

11. Clowes, *Royal Navy,* 3:422.

12. Keppel, *Life of Augustus Viscount Keppel,* 2:75–76.

13. Ibid., 77.

14. Ibid., 78.

15. *Dictionary of National Biography,* s.v. Hood, Alexander.

16. PRO ADM1/5312.

17. Ibid.

18. Brenton, *Naval History of Great Britain,* 1:128.

19. James, *Naval History of Great Britain,* 1:154.

20. Ibid., 186.

21. *Royal George* (100), *Queen Charlotte* (100), *Queen* (98), *London* (98), *Prince of Wales* (98), *Prince* (98), *Barfleur* (98), *Prince George* (98), *Sans Pareil* (80), *Valiant* (74), *Orion* (74), *Irresistible* (74), *Russell* (74), and *Colossus* (74).

22. *Peuple* (120), *Alexandre* (74), *Droits de l'Homme* (74), *Formidable* (74), *Fougueux* (74), *Jean-Bart* (74), *Mucius* (74), *Nestor* (74), *Redoutable* (74), *Tigre* (74), *Wattigny* (74), and *Zélé* (74).

23. James, *Naval History of Great Britain,* 1:275.

24. Brenton, *Naval History of Great Britain,* 1:233.

25. Manwaring and Dobrée, *Floating Republic,* 29.

26. Dugan, *Great Mutiny,* 133.

27. Ibid., 139.

28. Ibid., 170.

Chapter 3. Samuel Hood

1. *Dictionary of National Biography,* s.v. Hood, Alexander.

2. Hurst, *Golden Rock,* 138.

3. Rodger, *Wooden World,* 75.

4. PRO ADM1/1892.

5. Clowes, *Royal Navy,* 3:301.

6. Blanco and Sanborn, *American Revolution,* 1:768.

7. Macintyre, *Admiral Rodney,* 158.

8. Blanco and Sanborn, *American Revolution,* 1:769.

9. Clowes, *Royal Navy,* 3:480.

10. *Alfred* (74), *Belliqueux* (64), *Alcide* (74), *Invincible* (74), *Monarch* (74), *Barfleur* (90), *Terrible* (74), *Princesa* (70), *Ajax* (74), *Resolution* (74), *Montagu* (74), *Gibraltar* (80), *Centaur* (74), *Russell* (74), *Prince William* (64), *Torbay* (74), *Intrepid* (64), and *Shrewsbury* (74).

11. Hurst, *Golden Rock,* 155–56.

12. Ibid., 158.

13. *St. Albans* (64), *Alcide* (74), *Intrepid* (64), *Torbay* (74), *Princesa* (70), *Prince George* (98), *Ajax* (74), *Prince William* (64), *Shrewsbury* (74), *Invincible* (74), *Barfleur* (98), *Monarch* (74), *Belliqueux* (64), *Centaur* (74), *Alfred* (74), *Russell* (74), *Resolution* (74), *Bedford* (74), *Canada* (74), *Prudent* (64), *Montagu* (74), and *America* (64).

14. Macintyre, *Admiral Rodney,* 232.

15. Clowes, *Royal Navy,* 3:534.

16. Ibid., 537.

17. *Victory* (100), *Britannia* (100), *Windsor Castle* (98), *Princess Royal* (98), *St.*

George (98), *Alcide* (74), *Terrible* (74), *Egmont* (74), *Robust* (74), *Courageux* (74), *Bedford* (74), *Berwick* (74), *Captain* (74), *Fortitude* (74), *Leviathan* (74), *Colossus* (74), *Illustrious* (74), *Ardent* (64), *Diadem* (64), *Intrepid* (64), and *Agamemnon* (64).

18. Clowes, *Royal Navy,* 4:211.

19. James, *Naval History of Great Britain,* 1:208.

20. *Dictionary of National Biography,* s.v. Hood, Samuel.

Chapter 4. John Jervis

1. Dugan, *Great Mutiny,* 122.

2. Berckman, *Nelson's Dear Lord,* 240.

3. Corbett, *Private Papers of Earl Spencer,* vols. 4, 5.

4. Ibid.

5. James, *Old Oak,* 2.

6. Berckman, *Nelson's Dear Lord,* 38.

7. Ibid., 258.

8. Creswell, *British Admirals of the Eighteenth Century,* 39.

9. Keppel, *Life of Augustus Viscount Keppel,* 2:79.

10. Ibid., 170.

11. James, *Old Oak,* 39.

12. Clowes, *Royal Navy,* 3:448.

13. Corbett, *Private Papers of Earl Spencer,* 2:211.

14. *Culloden* (74), *Blenheim* (98), *Prince George* (98), *Orion* (74), *Colossus* (74), *Irresistible* (74), *Victory* (100), *Egmont* (74), *Goliath* (74), *Barfleur* (98), *Britannia* (100), *Namur* (90), *Captain* (74), *Diadem* (64), and *Excellent* (74).

15. *Santissima Trinidad* (130), *Concepción* (112), *Conde de Regla* (112), *Mexicano* (112), *Principe de Asturias* (112), *Salvador del Mundo* (112), *San Josef* (112), *Neptuno* (80), *San Nicolas* (80), *Atalante* (74), *Bahama* (74), *Conquistador* (74), *Firme* (74), *Glorioso* (74), *Oriente* (74), *Pelayo* (74), *San Antonio* (74), *San Domingo* (74), *San Firmin* (74), *San Francisco* (74), *San Genaro* (74), *San Ildefonso* (74), *San Juan* (74), *San Pablo* (74), *San Ysidro* (74), *Soberano* (74), and *Terrible* (74).

16. Uden and Cooper, *Dictionary of British Ships and Seamen,* 195.

17. Berckman, *Nelson's Dear Lord,* 113.

18. Dugan, *Great Mutiny,* 377.

19. Ibid.

20. Corbett, *Private Papers of Earl Spencer,* 2:473.

21. Berckman, *Nelson's Dear Lord,* 169.

22. Pratt, *Empire and the Sea,* 297.

23. Corbett, *Private Papers of Earl Spencer,* 3:314.

24. *Dictionary of National Biography,* s.v. Jervis.

25. Thursfield, *Five Naval Journals,* 104–5.

26. *Dictionary of National Biography,* s.v. Jervis.

27. Creswell, *British Admirals of the Eighteenth Century,* 194–95.

Chapter 5. Adam Duncan

1. Camperdown, *Admiral Duncan,* 111.
2. Thursfield, *Five Naval Journals,* 105.
3. Blunt, *Mrs. Montagu,* 2:337.
4. Keppel, *Life of Augustus Viscount Keppel,* 1:272–73.
5. *Dictionary of National Biography,* s.v. Duncan.
6. PRO ADM51/3998.
7. Ibid.
8. Keppel, *Life of Augustus Viscount Keppel,* 1:344–45.
9. Syrett, *Siege and Capture of Havana,* 271.
10. PRO ADM51/3998.
11. Keppel, *Life of Augustus Viscount Keppel,* 1:365.
12. Clowes, *Royal Navy,* 3:249.
13. Camperdown, *Admiral Duncan,* 21.
14. PRO ADM1/1705.
15. PRO ADM1/1706.
16. Camperdown, *Admiral Duncan,* 23.
17. Barnes and Owen, *Private Papers of Earl of Sandwich* 2:247.
18. PRO ADM2/106.
19. Ibid.
20. Camperdown, *Admiral Duncan,* 26.
21. PRO ADM51/609.
22. PRO ADM1/1707.
23. Camperdown, *Admiral Duncan,* 367.
24. Hamilton and Laughton, *Recollections of James Anthony Gardner,* 70–71.
25. Camperdown, *Admiral Duncan,* 56.
26. Ibid., 66.
27. Ibid., 307–8.
28. Ibid., 98–99.
29. Ibid., 101.
30. Corbett, *Private Papers of Earl Spencer,* 2:122.
31. Ibid., 132.
32. Camperdown, *Admiral Duncan,* 141.
33. Corbett, *Private Papers of Earl Spencer,* 2:147.
34. Ibid., 150.
35. Ibid., 184–85.
36. Ibid., 188.
37. The sixteen two-deckers were *Russell* (74), *Director* (74), *Montagu* (74), *Veteran* (64), *Monarch* (74), *Powerful* (74), *Monmouth* (64), *Agincourt* (64), *Triumph* (74), *Venerable* (74), *Ardent* (64), *Bedford* (74), *Lancaster* (64), *Belliqueux* (64), *Adamant* (50), and *Isis* (50).

38. *Gelijkheid* (68), *Beschermer* (56), *Hercules* (64), *Admiraal de Vries* (68), *Vrijheid* (74), *Staten-Generaal* (74), *Wassenaar* (64), *Batavier* (56), *Brutus* (74), *Leijden* (68), *Mars* (44), *Cerberus* (68), *Jupiter* (72), *Haarlem* (68), *Alkmaar* (56), and *Delft* (54).

39. *Gelijkheid, Hercules, Admiraal de Vries, Vrijheid, Wassenaar, Jupiter, Haarlem, Alkmaar,* and *Delft.*

40. Camperdown, *Admiral Duncan,* 269–70.

41. Corbett, *Private Papers of Earl Spencer,* 2:197.

42. Camperdown, *Admiral Duncan,* 261.

43. Windham, *Windham Papers,* 2:68–69.

44. Corbett, *Private Papers of Earl Spencer,* 3:179.

Chapter 6. George Keith Elphinstone

1. James, *Naval History of Great Britain,* 1:76.

2. Ibid., 77.

3. Clowes, *Royal Navy,* 1:190.

4. Miller, *Sea of Glory,* 418.

5. Dupuy and Dupuy, *Outline History of the American Revolution,* 153.

6. Colledge, *Ships of the Royal Navy,* 25.

7. PRO ADM1/1763.

8. James, *Naval History of Great Britain,* 1:79.

9. The ships of the line were *Victorious* (74), *Arrogant* (74), *America* (64), and *Stately* (64).

10. The two-deckers were *Monarch* (74), *Tremendous* (74), *America* (64), *Ruby* (64), *Stately* (64), *Sceptre* (64), *Trident* (64), and *Jupiter* (50).

11. The two-deckers were *Dordrecht* (66), *Revolutie* (66), *Van Tromp* (54), *Castor* (40), and *Braave* (40).

12. *Ville de Paris* (112), *Barfleur* (98), *Prince George* (98), *London* (98), *Princess Royal* (98), *Namur* (90), *Foudroyant* (80), *Gibraltar* (80), *Montagu* (74), *Northumberland* (74), *Marlborough* (74), *Warrior* (74), *Hector* (74), *Defence* (74), and *Majestic* (74).

13. Shankland, *Beware of Heroes,* 120.

14. The two-deckers were *Foudroyant* (80), *Swiftsure* (74), *Ajax* (80), *Tigre* (80), *Kent* (74), *Minotaur* (74), and *Northumberland* (74).

15. Clowes, *Royal Navy,* 4:456.

16. Shankland, *Beware of Heroes,* 140.

17. Brenton, *Naval History of Great Britain,* 2:635.

18. Ibid., 637.

19. *Dictionary of National Biography,* s.v. Elphinstone.

Chapter 7. James Gambier

1. Clowes, *Royal Navy,* 5:257.

2. Ibid., 256.

3. Dundonald, *Autobiography of a Seaman,* 1:357.

4. Ibid., 358.

5. Lavery, *Shipboard Life and Organization 1731–1815,* 69–70.

6. Tracy, *Naval Chronicle,* 1:109.

7. Barnes and Owen, *Private Papers of Earl Sandwich,* 2:39.

8. Rodger, *Insatiable Earl,* 189.

9. PRO ADM1/1839.

10. Padfield, *Nelson's War,* 23.

11. Gardiner, *Fleet Battle and Blockade,* 33.

12. *Dictionary of National Biography,* s.v Gambier.

13. *Prince of Wales* (98), *Pompée* (74), *Minotaur* (74), *Centaur* (74), *Ganges* (74), *Superb* (74), *Spencer* (74), *Vanguard* (74), *Valiant* (74), *Mars* (74), *Defence* (74), *Maida* (74), *Brunswick* (74), *Resolution* (74), *Hercule* (74), *Orion* (74), *Alfred* (74), *Goliath* (74), *Captain* (74), *Ruby* (64), *Dictator* (64), *Nassau* (64), *Inflexible* (64), *Leyden* (64), and *Agamemnon* (64).

14. Clowes, *Royal Navy,* 5:209.

15. Ibid., 216.

16. Tracy, *Naval Chronicle,* 4:236.

17. Dundonald, *Autobiography of a Seaman,* 1:361.

18. Ibid., 264.

19. Ibid., 394.

20. Ibid., 395.

21. Ibid., 396.

22. Ibid., 397.

23. Tute, *Cochrane,* 110–11.

24. Dundonald, *Autobiography of a Seaman,* 1:426–27.

25. Brenton, *Naval History of Great Britain,* 2:284–85.

26. Reilly, *British at the Gates,* 245.

Chapter 8. John Duckworth

1. Dugan, *Great Mutiny,* 118.

2. Ibid.

3. Horsfield, *Art of Leadership in War,* 61.

4. Laughton, *Letters and Papers of Charles, Lord Barham,* 3:xxxi.

5. *British Naval Biography,* 597.

6. *Dictionary of National Biography,* s.v. Duckworth.

7. Ibid.

8. PRO ADM1/1717.

9. Corbett, *Private Papers of Earl Spencer,* 1:283–84.

10. Ibid., 285.

11. Ibid., 2:488–89.

12. *Dictionary of National Biography,* s.v. Duckworth.

13. *Superb* (74), *Canopus* (80), *Spencer* (74), *Donegal* (74), *Powerful* (74), and *Agamemnon* (64).

14. The French ships were *Alexandre* (84), *Impérial* (120), *Diomède* (84), *Jupiter* (74), and *Brave* (74).

15. Tracy, *Naval Chronicle,* 3:261.

16. Brenton, *Naval History of Great Britain,* 2:107.

17. British losses according to Clowes, *Royal Navy,* 5:192; French losses according to Brenton, *Naval History of Great Britain,* 2:109.

18. The ships of the line were *Royal George* (100), *Windsor Castle* (98), *Canopus* (80), *Pompée* (74), *Ajax* (74), *Repulse* (74), *Thunderer* (74), and *Standard* (64).

19. Clowes, *Royal Navy,* 5:220–21.

20. Ibid., 225–26.

21. Tracy, *Naval Chronicle,* 4:31.

22. Brenton, *Naval History of Great Britain,* 2:190.

Chapter 9. John Borlase Warren

1. Corbett, *Private Papers of Earl Spencer,* 1:75.

2. Ibid., 4:14.

3. Ibid., 13–14.

4. *Dictionary of National Biography,* s.v. Warren.

5. Ibid.

6. Rodger, *Insatiable Earl,* 187.

7. PRO ADM1/2678.

8. *Arethusa* (38), *Flora* (36), *Melampus* (36), *Concorde* (36), and *Nymphe* (36).

9. *Engageante* (36), *Pomone* (44), *Résolue* (36), and *Babet* (20).

10. Clowes, *Royal Navy,* 4:484.

11. Ibid., 5:270.

12. Sir Edward Pellew (*Arethusa*), Sir William Sidney Smith (*Diamond*), and Eliab Harvey (*Santa Margarita*), to name a few.

13. James, *Naval History of Great Britain,* 1:233.

14. *Robust* (74), *Thunderer* (74), *Standard* (64), *Pomone* (44), *Anson* (44), *Artois* (38), *Arethusa* (38), *Concorde* (36), and *Galatea* (32).

15. Corbett, *Private Papers of Earl Spencer,* 1:76.

16. James, *Naval History of Great Britain,* 1:278.

17. *Proserpine* (40), *Unité* (36), *Coquille* (36), and *Tamise* (36).

18. Corbett, *Private Papers of Earl Spencer,* 1:364–65.

19. Ibid., 2:139.

20. James, *Naval History of Great Britain,* 2:96.

21. Corbett, *Private Papers of Earl Spencer,* 2:139–40.

22. *Hoche* (74), *Romaine* (40), *Loire* (40), *Immortalité* (40), *Coquille* (36), *Bellone* (36), *Résolue* (36), *Embuscade* (36), *Semillante* (36), and *Biche* (36).

23. *Canada* (74), *Foudroyant* (80), *Robust* (74), *Magnanime* (44), *Anson* (44), *Amelia* (44), *Ethalion* (38), and *Melampus* (36).

24. Clowes, *Royal Navy,* 4:348.

25. Ibid., 531.

26. *Real Carlos* (112), *San Hermenegildo* (112), *San Fernando* (96), *Argonauta* (80), *San Antonio* (74), and *San Augustin* (74).

27. The ships of the line were *London* (98), *Renown* (74), *Impétueux* (74), *Courageux* (74), and *Captain* (74).

28. Corbett, *Private Papers of Earl Spencer,* 4:10.

29. *Foudroyant* (80), *London* (98), *Ramillies* (74), *Hero* (74), *Namur* (74), *Repulse* (74), and *Courageux* (74).

30. *Poitiers* (74), *Sophie* (18), *Magnet* (16), and *Mackerel* (4).

Chapter 10. James Saumarez

1. *Dictionary of National Biography,* s.v. Saumarez.

2. Clowes, *Royal Navy,* 3:372.

3. Ibid., 376.

4. Gardiner, *Navies and the American Revolution,* 127.

5. James, *Naval History of Great Britain,* 1:116.

6. Ibid., 40.

7. Brenton, *Naval History of Great Britain,* 1:341.

8. James, *Naval History of Great Britain,* 2:181.

9. Ibid., 341.

10. Corbett, *Private Papers of Earl Spencer,* 4:18.

11. Ibid., 19.

12. *Formidable* (80), *Indomptable* (80), and *Desaix* (74).

13. *Caesar* (80), *Pompée* (74), *Spencer* (74), *Venerable* (74), *Hannibal* (74), *Audacious* (74), and *Superb* (74).

14. Tracy, *Naval Chronicle,* 2:219.

15. *Real Carlos* (112), *San Hermenegildo* (112), *San Fernando* (94), *Formidable* (80), *Indomptable* (80), *Argonauta* (80), *San Augustin* (74), *St. Antoine* (74), and *Desaix* (74).

16. Brenton, *Naval History of Great Britain,* 1:553.

17. The ships of the line were the *Victory* (100), *Centaur* (74), *Superb* (74), *Implacable* (74), *Edgar* (74), *Brunswick* (74), *Mars* (74), *Orion* (74), *Goliath* (74), *Vanguard* (74), *Africa* (64), and *Dictator* (64).

18. Ryan, "Ambassador Afloat," 239.

Chapter 11. Edward Pellew

1. *Dictionary of National Biography,* s.v. Pellew.

2. *British Naval Biography,* 625.

3. PRO ADM1/2310.

4. Tracy, *Naval Chronicle,* 1:262.

5. PRO ADM1/2493.

6. Corbett, *Private Papers of Earl Spencer,* 1:371.

7. Ibid., 380.

8. *Dictionary of National Biography,* s.v. Pellew.

9. Corbett, *Private Papers of Earl Spencer,* 1:381.

10. Pope, *Black Ship,* 269.

11. Parkinson, *War in the Eastern Seas,* 279.

12. Ibid., 284.

13. Ibid., 297.

14. The two-deckers were the *Queen Charlotte* (100), *Impregnable* (98), *Superb* (74), *Minden* (74), *Albion* (74), and *Leander* (50).

15. Clowes, *Royal Navy,* 6:230.

16. *Dictionary of National Biography,* s.v. Pellew.

Bibliography

Books

Annual Register or General Repository of History, Politics, and Literature for the Year 1783. London: G. Robinson, 1784.

Anson, Walter Vernon. *The Life of Admiral Lord Anson.* London: John Murray, 1912.

Barnes, G. R., and J. H. Owen. *The Private Papers of John, Earl of Sandwich.* Vols. 69, 71, 75, 78. London: Navy Records Society, 1932.

Barrow, Sir John. *The Life of Richard Earl Howe.* London: Murray, 1838.

———. *The Mutiny of the Bounty.* Ed. Gavin Kennedy. Boston: D. R. Godine, 1980.

Berckman, Evelyn. *Nelson's Dear Lord.* London: Macmillan, 1962.

Blanco, Richard L., and Paul J. Sanborn, eds. *The American Revolution 1775–1783: An Encyclopedia.* New York: Garland, 1993.

Blunt, Reginald, ed. *Mrs. Montagu, "Queen of the Blues."* New York: Houghton Mifflin, n.d.

Bradford, Gershom. *The Mariner's Dictionary.* New York: Weathervane Books, 1952.

Brenton, Edward Pelham. *The Naval History of Great Britain.* London: Henry Colburn, 1837.

British Naval Biography. London: Scott, Webster and Geary, 1839.

Bryant, Arthur. *The Years of Endurance (1793–1802).* London: Collins, 1947.

Camperdown, Third Earl of. *Admiral Duncan.* London: Longmans, Green, 1898.

Chandler, David, ed. *The Oxford Illustrated History of the British Army.* Oxford: Oxford University Press, 1994.

Clowes, William Laird, et al. *The Royal Navy, A History from the Earliest Times to the Present.* London: Chatham Publishing, 1901.

Coggins, Jack. *Ships and Seamen of the American Revolution.* Harrisburg, Penn.: Stackpole Books, 1969.

Cokayne, George E. *The Complete Peerage of England, Scotland, Ireland, Great Britain and the United Kingdom.* Rev. and enl. ed., ed. Vicary Gibbs. London: St. Catherine Press, 1916.

Colledge, J. J. *Ships of the Royal Navy.* London: Greenhill Books, 1987.

Corbett, Julian S. *Private Papers of George, Second Earl Spencer.* Vols. 46, 48, 58, 59. London: Navy Records Society, 1913.

Creswell, John. *British Admirals of the Eighteenth Century.* London: Allen & Unwin, 1972.

Dugan, James. *The Great Mutiny.* New York: G. P. Putnam's Sons, 1965.

Dundonald, Thomas Cochrane, Tenth Earl of. *The Autobiography of a Seaman.* 2 vols. London: Richard Bentley, 1860.

Dupuy, R. Ernest, and Trevor N. Dupuy. *The Encyclopedia of Military History.* New York: Harper & Row, Publishers, 1977.

———. *An Outline History of the American Revolution.* New York: Harper & Row, 1975.

Dupuy, R. Ernest, Gay Hammerman, and Grace P. Hayes. *The American Revolution—A Global War.* New York: David McKay, 1977.

Fleming, Thomas. *1776, Year of Illusions.* Edison, N.J.: Castle Books, Edison, 1996.

Fry, Plantagenet Somerset. *Rulers of Britain.* London: Paul Hamlyn, 1967.

Gardiner, Robert, ed. *The Campaign of Trafalgar 1803–1805.* London: Chatham, 1997.

———. *The First Frigates.* London: Conway Maritime Press, 1992.

———. *Fleet Battle and Blockade.* Annapolis: Naval Institute Press, 1996.

———. *Navies and the American Revolution.* Annapolis: Naval Institute Press, 1996.

Glover, Michael. *The Napoleonic Wars.* London: B. T. Batsford, Ltd., 1979.

Guttridge, Leonard F. *Mutiny.* Annapolis: Naval Institute Press, 1992.

Hamilton, Sir R. Vesey, and John Knox Laughton, eds. *Recollections of James Anthony Gardner.* Vol. 31. London: Publications of the Navy Records Society, 1905.

Hannay, David, ed. *Letters Written by Sir Samuel Hood.* Vol. 3. London: Publications of the Navy Records Society, 1895.

Harbron, John D. *Trafalgar and the Spanish Navy.* Annapolis: Naval Institute Press, 1988.

Hodges, H. W., and E. A. Hughes. *Select Naval Documents.* Cambridge: Cambridge University Press, 1922.

Horsfield, John. *The Art of Leadership in War.* Westport, Conn.: Greenwood Press, 1980.

Hurst, Ronald. *The Golden Rock.* Annapolis: Naval Institute Press, 1996.

James, Hartwell. *Sea Kings and Naval Heroes.* Philadelphia: Henry Altemus Company, 1901.

James, William. *The Naval History of Great Britain.* London: Richard Bentley, 1860.

James, William M. *Old Oak; The Life of John Jervis, Earl of St. Vincent.* London: Longmans, Green, 1950.

Jerdan, William. *National Portrait Gallery of Illustrious and Eminent Personages of the Nineteenth Century.* London: Fisher, Son, & Jackson, 1830.

Keppel, Thomas. *The Life of Augustus Viscount Keppel.* London: Henry Colburn, 1842.

Laughton, Sir John Knox, ed. *Letters and Papers of Charles, Lord Barham.* Vols. 32, 38, 39. London: Publications of the Navy Records Society, 1907.

Lavery, Brian. *Nelson's Navy.* London: Conway Maritime Press, 1989.

———. *Shipboard Life and Organization 1731–1815.* Vol. 138. London: Navy Records Society, 1998.

Lewis, Lady Theresa. *Extracts of the Journals and Correspondence of Miss Berry.* London: Longmans, Green, 1865.

Lewis, Michael. *The Navy of Britain.* London: Allen & Unwin, Ltd., 1949.

Lloyd, Christopher. *St. Vincent and Camperdown.* London: B. T. Batsford Ltd., 1963.

Lyon, David. *Sea Battles in Close-up: The Age of Nelson.* Annapolis: Naval Institute Press, 1996.

Macintyre, Donald. *Admiral Rodney.* London: Peter Davies, 1962.

Mackay, Ruddock F. *Admiral Hawke.* Oxford: Clarendon Press, 1965.

Mahan, A. T. *The Influence of Sea Power upon History, 1660–1783.* Boston: Little, Brown, 1918.

———. *The Influence of Sea Power upon the French Revolution and Empire, 1793–1812.* Boston: Little, Brown, 1894.

Manwaring, G. E., and Bonamy Dobrée. *The Floating Republic, an Account of the Mutinies at Spithead and the Nore in 1797.* New York: Harcourt, Brace, 1935.

Masefield, John. *Sea Life in Nelson's Time.* London: Book Club Associates, 1984.

Michael, Wolfgang. *England under George I: The Beginning of the Hanoverian Dynasty.* London: Macmillan, 1936.

Miller, Nathan. *Sea of Glory.* Annapolis: Naval Institute Press, 1974.

Padfield, Peter. *Nelson's War.* London: Book Club Associates, 1976.

Parkinson, C. Northcote. *War in the Eastern Seas, 1793–1815.* London: Allen & Unwin, 1954.

Partridge, Bellamy. *Sir Billy Howe.* London: Longmans, Green, 1932.

Partridge, Eric. *A Dictionary of Slang and Unconventional English.* New York: Macmillan, 1937.

Pivka, Otto von. *Navies of the Napoleonic Era.* London: David & Charles, 1980.

Pope, Dudley. *At Twelve Mr. Byng Was Shot.* London: Weidenfeld and Nicolson, 1962.

———. *The Black Ship.* London: Weidenfeld and Nicolson, 1963.

———. *Life in Nelson's Navy.* London: Unwin Hyman, 1989.

Pratt, Fletcher. *Empire and the Sea.* New York: Henry Holt, 1946.

Preston, Anthony. *History of the Royal Navy.* New York: Greenwich House, 1983.

Price, Anthony. *The Eyes of the Fleet.* New York: W. W. Norton, 1990.

Reilly, Robin. *The British at the Gates.* New York: G. P. Putnam's Sons, 1974.

Rodger, N.A.M. *The Insatiable Earl.* London: W. W. Norton, 1993.

———. *The Wooden World.* London: Collins, 1986.

Rutter, Owen, ed. *The Court-Martial of the* Bounty *Mutineers.* Birmingham, Ala.: The Notable Trials Library, 1989.

Ryan, Anthony. "Ambassador Afloat: Vice-Admiral Sir James Saumarez and the Swedish Court, 1808–1812." In *The British Navy and the Use of Naval Power in the Eighteenth Century,* edited by Jeremy Black and Philip Woodfine. Atlantic Heights, N.J.: Humanities Press International, Inc., 1988.

Shankland, Peter. *Beware of Heroes.* London: William Kimber, 1975.

———. *Byron of the* Wager. New York: Coward, McCann & Geoghegan, 1975.

Smith, George, and Sir Sidney Lee, eds. *The Dictionary of National Biography.* London: Oxford University Press, 1938.

Syrett, David, ed. *The Siege and Capture of Havana.* Publications of the Navy Records Society, vol. 114. London: Navy Records Society, 1970.

Terraine, John. *Trafalgar.* New York: Mason/Charter, 1976.

Thursfield, Rear-Admiral H.G., ed. *Five Naval Journals 1789–1817.* Vol. 91. London: Navy Records Society, 1951.

Tracy, Nicholas, ed. *The Naval Chronicle.* London: Chatham Publishing, 1998.

Tuchman, Barbara W. *The First Salute.* New York: Alfred A. Knopf, 1988.

Tunstall, Brian. *Naval Warfare in the Age of Sail.* London: Conway Maritime Press Ltd., 1990.

Tute, Warren. *Cochrane.* London: Cassell, 1965.

Uden, Grant, and Richard Cooper. *A Dictionary of British Ships and Seamen.* Middlesex: Kestrel Books, 1980.

Walder, David. *Nelson, a Biography.* New York: Dial Press/J. Wade, 1978.

Warner, Oliver. *Command at Sea.* New York: St. Martin's Press, 1976.

———. *The Glorious First of June.* London: B. T. Batsford Ltd., 1961.

———. *Great Sea Battles.* New York: Macmillan, 1963.

———. *The Life and Letters of Vice-Admiral Lord Collingwood.* London: Oxford University Press, 1968.

Wertenbaker, Thomas Jefferson. *Father Knickerbocker Rebels.* New York: Charles Scribner's Sons, 1948.

Wilcox, L. A. *Anson's Voyage.* New York: St. Martin's Press, 1970.

Windham, William. *The Windham Papers.* London: Herbert Jenkins, Ltd., 1913.

Woodman, Richard. *The Victory of Seapower.* London: Chatham, 1998.

Primary Documents

Letters

PRO ADM1/1705—Captains' Letters D, 1778.

PRO ADM1/1706—Captains' Letters D, 1779.

PRO ADM1/1707—Captains' Letters D, 1780.

PRO ADM1/1709—Captains' Letters D, 1781.
PRO ADM1/1710—Captains' Letters D, 1782–83.
PRO ADM1/1711—Captains' Letters D, 1784–87.
PRO ADM1/1717—Captains' Letters D, 1795.
PRO ADM1/1761—Captains' Letters E, 1772–76.
PRO ADM1/1762—Captains' Letters E, 1777–83.
PRO ADM1/1763—Captains' Letters E, 1784–90.
PRO ADM1/1838—Captains' Letters G, 1779–80.
PRO ADM1/1839—Captains' Letters G, 1781–82.
PRO ADM1/1840—Captains' Letters G, 1783–90.
PRO ADM1/1886—Captains' Letters H, 1746–48.
PRO ADM1/1887—Captains' Letters H, 1749–50.
PRO ADM1/1888—Captains' Letters H, 1751–52.
PRO ADM1/1889—Captains' Letters H, 1753–54.
PRO ADM1/1890—Captains' Letters H, 1755.
PRO ADM1/1891—Captains' Letters H, 1756.
PRO ADM1/1892—Captains' Letters H, 1757.
PRO ADM1/1893—Captains' Letters H, 1758.
PRO ADM1/1894—Captains' Letters H, 1759.
PRO ADM1/1895—Captains' Letters H, 1760.
PRO ADM1/1896—Captains' Letters H, 1761.
PRO ADM1/1897—Captains' Letters H, 1762.
PRO ADM1/2307—Captains' Letters P, 1782–83.
PRO ADM1/2308—Captains' Letters P, 1784–90.
PRO ADM1/2310—Captains' Letters P, 1793.
PRO ADM1/2486—Captains' Letters S, 1784–90.
PRO ADM1/2488—Captains' Letters S, 1790–92.
PRO ADM1/2490—Captains' Letters S, 1794.
PRO ADM1/2493—Captains' Letters S, 1796.
PRO ADM1/2676—Captains' Letters W, 1781–3.
PRO ADM1/2677—Captains' Letters W, 1784–92.
PRO ADM1/2678—Captains' Letters W, 1793.
PRO ADM1/2680—Captains' Letters W, 1795.
PRO ADM1/2682—Captains' Letters W, 1796.
PRO ADM1/2686—Captains' Letters W, 1798.
PRO ADM2/106—Admiralty Out-letters, 1779.

Logs

PRO ADM51/50—Captain's Log of the *Antelope* 1756.
PRO ADM51/117—Captain's Log of the *Blenheim* 1781–82.
PRO ADM51/175—Captain's Log of the *Centurion* 1754.
PRO ADM51/301, 302—Captain's Log of the *Edgar* 1783–86.

PRO ADM51/609—Captain's Log of the *Monarch* 1778–80.

PRO ADM51/1001—Captain's Log of the *Torbay* 1756–1759.

PRO ADM51/1049—Captain's Log of the *Warwick* 1777–81.

PRO ADM51/1190—Captain's Log of the *Circe* 1796–98.

PRO ADM51/1195—Captain's Log of the *Director* 1797–98.

PRO ADM51/1213—Captain's Log of the *Adamant* 1797.

PRO ADM51/1331—Captain's Log of the *Caesar* 1800–1801.

PRO ADM51/3998—Captain's Log of the *Valiant* 1760–64.

PRO ADM52/1699—Master's Log of the *Diamond* 1777.

Court-Martial Records

PRO ADM1/5312—Proceedings of the Court-Martial of Admiral Keppel, 1779.

Index

Abercromby, Sir Ralph, 128, 147–48
Aboukir Bay, 147, 188, 228–29
Acasta, 181–82, 184
Achille, 24
Adamant, 104–5, 122–25
Addington, Henry, 100
Admiraal de Ruijter, 221
Africa, 33, 178
Agamemnon, 183
Aigle, 137
Ajax, 186
Alarm, 84, 240
Albany, 83
Albemarle, Earl of. *See* Keppel, George
　(Earl of Albemarle)
Albuera: battle of, 189
Alcide, 6
Alderney, 193
Alexander, 227
Alexander I, 210
Alexandre, 43–44, 67, 183, 225
Alexandria, 145, 147–48, 227–28
Alfred, 65
Algeciras, 16, 91, 214, 231, 234
Algiers, 258–59
Amazon (36), 248–49
Amazon (38), 211
Ambuscade, 223
Amelia, 206–8
America, 24
Andromaque, 203
Anson, 202–3, 205–7

Anson, Lord George, 2–3, 81, 107,
　217
Antelope, 31–32, 56
Antigua, 4, 62, 67, 157
Apollo, 14–15, 194, 243
Arbuthnot, Merriot, 115, 134–35,
　157
Ardent, 126, 156
Arethusa, 198–99, 246
Ariadne, 196
Arnold, Benedict, 241–42
Arrogant, 157
Artois, Comte d', 200
Artois (38), 198–99, 202–3, 205, 246
Artois (40), 244
Atlas (74), 183–84
Atlas (90), 46
Atlas (98), 170
Audacious, 22, 36, 146, 232

Babet, 198
Baltimore, 4–5, 106
Bantry Bay, 45–46, 70, 248
Barbados, 2–3, 8, 62, 65, 89, 91, 111,
　183, 222
Barfleur (90), 60, 70, 72
Barfleur (98), 139, 143
Barham, Lord. *See* Middleton, Charles
　(Lord Barham)
Barrington, Samuel, 85, 87
Basque Roads, 9, 152, 163–64,
　166–68

Bastia, 76

Batavia, 255–56

Bath, 26, 42

Bay of Biscay, 20, 33, 253

Beaulieu, 124

Bedford, 70

Belle Ile, 8, 31, 42–43, 109–10, 155, 173, 190, 200

Belle Poule, 211

Bellerophon, 22, 150

Bellone (32), 57

Bellone (36), 207–8

Biche, 207

Bickerton, Sir Richard, 149

Bideford, 56

Blenheim (74), 253, 255

Blenheim (90), 117, 226

Blonde, 241

Boadicea, 206

Bombay, 253, 255–56

Bompart, J. B. F., 206–8

Bonaparte, Napoleon, 97, 102, 145, 150, 160, 162, 168, 227–28, 235–36, 258

Bone, Johnny, 118

Bonetta, 137

Boscawen, Edward, 5–6, 81, 107, 172–73

Boston, 10, 15, 58–59, 220

Bounty, 177

Boyne, 89, 258

Braddock, Edward, 107

Brave, 184

Brest, 19, 21, 32, 34, 40, 42, 45–46, 50, 57, 83, 86, 91, 98–99, 101, 103, 110, 143, 159, 162, 173, 188, 190–91, 197, 199, 203–6, 210–11, 221–22, 246–47, 247–48, 252

Bridgewater, 30

Bridport, Lord. *See* Hood, Alexander (Lord Bridport)

Bristol, 177, 217–19

Britannia, 38

Broderick, Thomas, 172

Brueys, F. P., 183, 228

Bruix, Eustache, 143–44

Brunswick, 24, 159

Buckle, Matthew, 173

Buckner, Charles, 141

Burford, 3–4

Burgoyne, John, 23, 241–42

Bushnell, David, 11

Byng, John, 31–32, 37, 56, 108

Byron, John, 15, 34, 57, 156, 175–76

Cadiz, 17, 78, 87, 90–92, 95–98, 143–44, 147, 173, 180, 182–85, 209–10, 214, 226–27, 231–32, 234, 244

Caesar, 214–15, 230–33

Caldwell, Benjamin, 90, 158

Caledonia, 152, 162, 166, 257

Calliope, 205

Calvi, 76

Camperdown: battle of, 125–28

Canada, 169, 212, 242

Canada, 70, 205–8

Canopus, 183–84

Cape Finisterre, 108, 144

Cape François, 67, 72, 178

Cape Gata, 82

Cape of Good Hope, 139–40, 255

Cape St. Vincent, 127, 133–34, 215

Cape Town, 139–41

Captain, 93–95

Carleton, 241–42

Carnatic, 89

Caroline, 256

Carron, 254

Carysfort, 137

Cartagena, 90–91, 98, 144, 210, 226

Cayenne, 250–51

Centurion (50), 15

Centurion (60), 3, 107–8

Charente, 206

Chariot Royale, 108

Charleston, 55, 131, 134–36, 157, 217, 219

Chatham, 117, 154–55

Chatham, 219

Chatham, Earl of. *See* Pitt, John (Earl of Chatham)

Cherbourg, 7, 224

Chesapeake Bay, 12, 63, 65, 68, 189, 212

China, 254, 256–57

Chouans, 200–201

Clarence, Duke of. *See* William IV

Cléopâtre, 245–46

Clerk of Elden, 102

Clinton, Sir Henry, 13, 134–35, 217–18, 243

Cochrane, Lord Thomas, 152, 163–68, 198

Cochrane, Sir Alexander, 183, 185, 212

Cockburn, Sir George, 212

Collingwood, Lord Cuthbert, 94, 96, 103, 182, 184–85, 257

Colossus, 43–44, 95

Colpoys, Sir John, 49

Colville, Lord Alexander, 80, 84, 133

Comet, 4

Concorde, 198, 247

Conflans, Hubert de, 7–8

Constantinople, 171, 185–89

Cook, James, 28

Copenhagen, 160–62, 234

copper, 84

Coquille, 207–8

Cordova, Don Jose de, 91–95

Cordova, Don Luis de, 17

Cork, 50, 108, 136, 217

Cornwall, 134, 189, 240, 247

Cornwall, 5

Cornwallis, Lord Charles, 16, 63–65, 71, 134, 136, 217

Cornwallis, Sir William, 42, 65, 101, 129, 190

Corsica, 75–76, 90–91, 138, 227

Cotton, Sir Charles, 168, 257

Courageux, 59

Crescent, 223–25

Culloden, 32, 41–42, 48, 81–82, 92–93, 95, 253

Culloden: battle of, 4, 106

Cumberland, 176

Cumby, 78–79

Curaçao, 9, 61

Curieuse, 199

Curtis, Sir Roger, 97

Dacres, James, 241–42

Danae, 83

Darby, George, 220

Dartmouth, 6, 31

Defence, 158–59, 229

de Guichen, Rear Admiral, 215, 222

Delaware River, 12–13, 137, 194

Denmark, 160, 162, 181, 234–35

Dennis, Sir Peter, 133

de Ternay, Commodore, 83–84, 133

Devonshire, 81

Diamond (32), 174–75

Diamond (38), 198–99, 246

Diana, 198–99

Dickson, Sir Archibald, 128–29

Digby, Robert, 65

Diomède, 184

Director, 126

Dogger Bank: battle of, 215, 221

Dolphin, 5

Dominica, 67–70

Donegal, 183–84

Douglas, Sir Charles, 69–70

Droits de l'Homme, 46, 248–50

Druid, 224–25

Drury, William, 257

Duckworth, Sir John, 98, 144, 211, 259; as admiral, 180–89; as captain, 176–80; character of, 170–72; early years of, 172–76

Duncan, 254

Duncan, Alexander, 106

Duncan, Lady Mary, 113, 127

Duncan, Lord Adam, 102, 104–5, 136; as admiral, 118–29; at battle of Camperdown, 125–27; as captain, 109–18; character of, 105; early years of, 106–9

Dundas, David, 75–76, 89

Dundas, Henrietta, 113

Dundas, Henry (Lord Melville) 127, 129

Dundas, Robert, 118

Dunkirk, 6, 13, 114

Dutton, 238–39, 246

Eagle, 10, 12, 15

Ecureuil, 33

Edgar, 118

Egypt, 145, 147–48, 180, 195, 210, 227

Elba, 75, 150, 210, 258

El Moro, 111, 173

Elphinstone, George Keith, 73, 98, 180, 157, 209; as admiral, 138–51; as captain, 134–38; character of, 131–32; early years of, 132–34

Elphinstone, Lord Charles, 132

Elphinstone, William, 132–33

Embuscade, 207

Emerald (32), 133

Emerald (36), 180

Endymion, 157

Engageante, 197–98

Essex, 7

Essington, William, 161

Estang, Comte Henri d', 13–15, 156, 175–76, 194

Ethalion, 206–7

Europe, 64, 177

Eurydice, 224

Excellent, 94, 96

Exeter, 30, 53

Exmouth, Lord. *See* Pellew, Edward (Lord Exmouth)

Expedition, 199

Experiment, 82

Falkland Islands, 9, 240

Falmouth, 203, 205, 245, 248

Fancourt, Devereux, 100

Feilding, Charles, 174

Ferrol, 205, 209, 252–53

Firebrand, 30–31

Flora, 197–99

Foley, Sir Thomas, 228

Formidable (80), 8, 215, 231

Formidable (90), 35, 43–44, 46, 70

Fort La Malgue, 131, 138

Fort Moultrie, 135, 157

Fort Royal, 61–62, 67, 89, 175

Fortitude, 220

Foudroyant, 38, 82, 85–88, 117, 143, 147–48, 207–8, 210

Fox, Charles James, 72

France, 5–6, 8, 13, 19–20, 39–40, 50, 56, 60, 84–85, 89–90, 100–102, 106, 109, 116, 118, 124, 136, 143, 145, 147, 150, 157–60, 162, 177, 190, 194, 196, 203, 208, 230, 234, 240, 243–44, 246, 248, 252–53

Franklin, 229

Fraternité, 45

Galatea, 202–4, 246

Galles, Morard de, 45

Gambier, James, 155–56

Gambier, John, 154

Gambier, Lord James, 152–53, 188, 234; as admiral, 159–69; as captain,

156–59; character of, 153–54; early
years of, 154–56
Ganteaume, Admiral, 148, 210
Gardner, Sir Alan, 99
Garland, 53
Geary, Francis, 87, 220
General Mifflin, 157
Genoa, 84, 90, 146–47
George III, 25, 33, 58–59, 181
George IV, 103
Gibraltar, 2, 16–17, 31, 39, 45, 73,
75, 82, 86–88, 90–91, 97–98,
116–17, 138, 144–45, 147, 172,
179, 181, 185, 209–10, 214–15,
227, 230–32, 258–59
Glasgow, 259
Gloire, 137
Glory (44), 5
Glory (98), 41
Gloucester, 80–81
Goliath, 228
Goodall, Samuel Cranston, 74
Goree, 108–9
Gosport, 83–84, 133
Grafton (70), 55
Grafton (74), 176
Grand Duke, 174
Grasse, Comte Francois de, 16,
61–70, 104–5, 222
Graves, Lord Thomas, 41, 63–65
Greenwich, 80, 154, 213
Greenwich, 54
Greenwich Hospital, 34, 77, 80
Grenada, 175–76
Grenville, Thomas, 29, 53
Greyhound, 255
Guadeloupe, 67, 69–71, 89
Guernsey, 216, 223, 225, 234,
236–37
Guillouet, Louis (Comte d'Orvilliers),
34–36
Gustavus IV Adolphus, 235

Haldane, Robert, 106
Halifax, 10, 58, 137, 211
Hallowell, Sir Benjamin, 92
Hannibal, 215, 231–32
Hardy, Sir Charles, 86, 116, 195, 220
Harvey, Eliab, 152–53, 163–64, 167
Harvey, Sir Henry, 202
Havana, 105, 110–12, 173
Hawk, 30
Hawke, Lord Edward, 6–9, 15–17,
31–32, 56–57, 81–84, 109, 173
Hazard, 243
Helder, 120, 128–29, 208
Helena, 195
Hercule, 28, 50
Hercules, 126
Hermione, 251
Héros, 8–9, 17
Hervey, Augustus, 17
Hervilly, Comte d', 200–201
Hibernia, 101
Hoche, 50, 207
Hoche, Lazare, 45, 200
Holland, 16, 89, 118, 120, 128, 256
Holmes, Charles, 55, 57
Hood, Alexander, 28, 50
Hood, Alexander (Lord Bridport), 26,
81, 85, 98–99, 143, 190, 200, 225,
251–52; as admiral, 39–51; as cap-
tain, 31–39; character of, 52–53;
early years of, 28–31
Hood, Lord Samuel, 28, 108, 131,
136–38, 155, 159, 222; as admiral,
60–69, 72, 99; and battle of the
Saintes, 69–71; as captain, 55–60;
character of, 52–53; commands
Mediterranean fleet, 73–77; early
years of, 53–55
Hood, Sir Samuel, 28, 214, 228,
233–35
Hotham, Lord William, 63, 76–77
Howe, 254

Howe, Lord Richard, 39–42, 46–47, 49, 56, 87–88, 99, 102, 106, 117, 127, 132, 139, 150, 156, 158–59, 174–75, 177, 194, 204, 216, 219, 225, 242; in America, 10–15; and battle of the First of June, 22–25; as captain, 5–9; character of, 1–2; commands Channel fleet, 16–21; early years of, 2–4; as First Lord of the Admiralty, 17–18; later years of, 25–27

Howe, Lord William, 2, 10–13, 27, 241

Hudson River, 11, 241–42

Hyène, 250

Ile d'Aix, 6, 56–57, 163

Ile de Groix, 44, 191, 225

Ile d'Yeu, 200, 203

Imbert, Baron d', 73

Immortalité, 207

Impérial, 183–84

Imperieuse, 164–66

Impétueux, 24, 209, 251–52

Impregnable, 259

Indefatigable, 238, 246–51

India, 33, 256

Indomptable, 23, 40, 177

Invincible (74), 40, 42, 54, 159

Invincible (battleship), 77

Ireland, 45–46, 50, 76, 179, 206, 208, 217, 248

Irresistible, 43, 66, 226

Italy, 84, 90, 113, 127, 144

Jacobin, 23–24, 39

Jacobites, 106

Jamaica, 4, 63, 67–68, 71–72, 81, 91, 112, 170–71, 176, 181

Jamaica, 55

James, William, 131, 171

Janus, 17–18, 30

Japan, 256

Jason, 205

Java, 255–56

Jean-Barte, 199

Jervis, John (Earl of St. Vincent), 38, 50, 105, 116–17, 128–29, 132–33, 143–44, 146, 150, 170, 180, 191–92, 198, 209, 226–27, 230, 234, 252–53, 255; as admiral, 88–103; and battle of St. Vincent, 92–95; as captain, 83–88; character of, 78–80; early years of, 80–83; as First Lord, 100–101

Jervis, Swynfen, 80–81

Juno, 133, 240

Jupiter, 184

Juste, 24

Karel Doorman (aircraft carrier), 130

Katherine, 34, 38

Keats, Sir Richard, 160, 182, 203–4, 206, 213, 234

Keith, Lord. *See* Elphinstone, George Keith

Kempenfelt, Richard, 39, 215, 222

Kent, 85, 128, 174

Keppel, Lord Augustus, 15, 17, 34–37, 56, 71, 85–86, 105, 107–16, 195, 217, 220; court martial of, 26, 38–39, 47, 52, 59–60, 99, 114–15, 168

Keppel, George (Earl of Albemarle), 111–12

King, Sir Richard, 189

Kleber, Jean-Baptiste, 145–47

Knowles, Sir Charles, 4–6, 13

Laforey, Sir John, 157

Lagos Bay, 95–96

Langara, Don Juan de, 74, 91

Languedoc, 15

Leander, 229

Leghorn, 146–47
Le Havre, 7, 57, 83, 197
Leisségues, Rear Admiral, 183–84
Le Moniteur, 231
Lestock, Richard, 29–30, 53
Levant, 217
Leveson-Gower, John, 196
Leviathan, 170, 177–81, 205, 220
Lichfield, 108
Licorne, 243
Lincoln, 134–36
Linois, 214–15, 231–32, 247, 254
Linzee, Robert, 75
Lion (60), 54
Lion (64), 137
Lisbon, 91, 96, 102–3, 188, 195, 240, 244, 248
Lively (20), 55, 133
Lively (32), 90
Loire, 207
London, 39, 43–44, 49, 211
Long Island, 11, 218
Lord Harlow, 197
Louis, Sir Thomas, 183, 185
Louisbourg, 55, 81, 83
Lovely Sukey, 31
Ludlow Castle, 53
Lushington, Franklin, 3–4

MacBride, John, 119–20, 122, 197, 224
Madeira, 182, 210–11
Madras, 140, 253–56
Magicienne, 184
Magnanime (44), 207–8
Magnanime (74), 6–9, 173
Malcolm, Sir Pulteney, 184
Malta, 146, 180, 185, 227
Man, Robert, 90–91
Marengo, 211
Marlborough, 22, 59, 70, 159, 193, 225

Mars, 50
Marseilles, 73–74, 240
Martinique, 4, 61, 65, 67, 89, 111, 162
Mary, 81
Mathews, Thomas, 29–30, 32
Mediator, 164
Melampus, 198, 208
Melville, Lord. *See* Dundas, Henry (Lord Melville)
Merlin (10), 31
Merlin (18), 196
Middleton, Charles (Lord Barham), 154–55, 160
Minerva, 32–33
Minorca, 31–32, 56, 98, 134, 144, 147, 179–80
Minotaur (74), 146
Minto, Lord, 256
Mitchell, Andrew, 128–29
Monarch, 32, 70, 114–17, 125, 139, 149
Monmouth, 82
Montagnard, 23, 40
Montagne, 23
Montagu, John, 54
Montague, John (Earl of Sandwich), 15–16, 35, 39, 59, 71, 86, 87, 115, 136, 155, 195–96, 242–44
Mont-Blanc, 23
Montreal, 241–42
Montreal, 217
Moonlight Battle, 87, 116
Morning Advertiser, 166
Morning Intelligencer, 37
Morning Post, 37, 85
Mucius, 43, 158
Mulgrave, Lord, 138
Mulgrave, Lord Henry, 163–64, 168

Namur, 172–73
Naples, 118, 180, 210, 227, 259

Napoleon I. *See* Bonaparte, Napoleon
Naval Academy, 59
Nelson, Lord Horatio, 2, 28, 51, 76, 79, 93–97, 103, 105, 136, 176, 180, 182, 208, 214, 227–29
Neptune (90), 83
Neptune (98), 159
Nestor, 43
Netherlands, 139, 259
New York, 10–14, 22–24, 26, 63–65, 72, 83, 134, 136–37, 155–57, 174, 194, 219, 242–43
Newfoundland, 6, 21, 83–84, 96, 133–34, 159, 189, 243–44
Newport, 14–15, 26, 174, 194, 219–20
Nile, battle of: 2, 145, 183, 208, 214–15, 229–30
Nile River, 6, 148
Nonsuch, 194
Nootka Sound, 18–19, 39, 89
Nore, 119, 127; mutiny, 96, 121–23, 141–43
Norfolk, 212
Normandy, 57, 199
North, Lord, 117, 155
Northumberland, 24, 150, 183
Norwich, 107
Nottingham, 81, 217
Nymphe, 65, 245–46

Onslow, Sir Richard, 120, 126, 128
Orde, Sir John, 97–98
Orient, 228–29
Orion, 43, 66, 177, 225–27
Orvilliers, Comte d'. *See* Guillouet, Louis (Comte d'Orvilliers)
Osborn, Henry, 82
Owen, Thomas, 108–9

Pakenham, Sir Thomas, 42, 159
Palliser, Sir Hugh, 15, 35–39, 60, 85, 99, 114–16, 168
Paris, 60, 84, 196, 258
Parker, Sir Hyde Jr., 179
Parker, Sir Hyde Sr., 15, 220–21
Parker, Sir Peter, 135, 174, 217–19
Parker, Sir William, 96–97, 177–78, 226
Pasley, 231
Pasley, Sir Thomas, 21–22
Patriote, 23
Patriotic Fund, 203
Paul I, 123, 181, 234
Peace of Amiens, 148, 159, 210, 230, 234, 252
Pearl, 3
Pégase, 87–88
Pelican, 243–44
Pellew, Edward (Lord Exmouth), 192, 199, 238–39; as admiral, 253–60; as captain, 244–53; character of, 239–40; early years of, 240–44
Pellew, Fleetwood, 239, 260
Pellew, Pownoll Bastard, 244, 260
Penang, 253, 256
Perseus, 134, 136
Petit Diable, 205
Peuple, 43–44
Peuple Souverain, 229
Phaeton, 159, 206
Philadelphia, 12–13, 55, 194
Phoenix, 15
Pigot, Hugh Jr., 251
Pigot, Hugh Sr., 71–72
Pitt, John (Earl of Chatham), 18, 25–26, 76–77
Pitt, William, 18, 100–101, 120, 128–29, 154
Pitt, William Morton, 154
Plymouth, 27, 37, 42, 49, 56, 85, 106, 149, 157, 164, 170, 174, 179, 189, 204, 224, 236, 238, 246, 258–59

Pocock, Sir George, 111–12, 173
Pomone, 198–99, 202–5
Pompée, 215, 231–32
Porcupine, 83
Port au Prince, 178, 181
Port Royal, 112
Portland, 54
Portsmouth, 3, 16, 17, 25, 27, 38–39,
    42, 45, 47, 49, 54, 58–59, 82,
    87–89, 99, 108–9, 117–18,
    137–38, 143, 155–56, 159, 168,
    174, 217, 224, 230, 243
Portugal, 45, 91, 102, 160, 240, 248
Powerful, 182
Pownall, Philemon, 194, 241, 243
Prince (90), 81
Prince (98), 46
Prince George (90), 30, 32, 50, 132
Prince George (98), 94, 159
Prince of Wales, 160
Princess Amelia, 9, 114, 243
Princess Mary, 29
Princess Royal, 175–77
Pringle, Sir Thomas, 119, 141,
    241–42
Protecteur, 87
Puisaye, Comte de, 200
Pulteney, Sir James, 209

Quebec, 82–83, 240
Queen, 24, 39, 43–44
Queen Charlotte, 18–19, 23–25, 43,
    48, 143–44, 146, 177, 225, 258–59
Quiberon Bay, 8–9, 42, 44, 190–91,
    199–201, 225, 252; battle of, 2, 9,
    32, 35, 68, 71, 83, 109, 155, 173

Raccoon, 137
Rainier, Peter, 140, 253
Raisonnable, 17, 223
Raleigh, 156–57
Ramillies, 24

Ranger, 250
Redoubtable, 43
Renown (50), 15
Renown (74), 209
Républicain, 24, 41, 158
Repulse, 57
Résolue, 198
Réunion, 224
Révolutionnaire (40), 246
Révolutionnaire (110), 22–23
Rhode Island, 14, 156, 174, 219
Rippon, 5
Robust, 34–36, 38, 56, 58–59, 131,
    138, 207–8
Robuste, 203
Rodney, Lord George Brydges, 53,
    57–58, 60–63, 67, 69–72, 83,
    86–87, 102, 116–17, 176, 222–23
Romney (50), 58, 134
Romney (54), 29, 46, 53
Rotterdam, 136
Rover, 176
Rowley, Joshua, 176
Royal Exchange, 109
Royal George, 4, 32, 39–41, 44–45, 50,
    81, 185, 188
Royal Sovereign, 30
Royal William, 27, 59
Russell, 22, 43, 66, 70, 124–25,
    222–23
Russia, 73, 179, 160, 181, 185,
    234–36

Saint-Andre, Jean Bon, 20
Saintes: battle of the, 69, 71–72, 215,
    222–23
Salisbury, 88, 155, 177, 244
Salvador del Mundo, 94
San Antonio, 233
San Augustin, 117
San Domingo, 176, 178, 181,
    183–84; battle of, 171, 183–85

Sandwich, Lord. *See* Montague, John (Earl of Sandwich)
Sandy Hook, 10, 13–15, 174
San Josef, 94
San Nicholas, 94
Sans Pareil, 23, 41, 43–44, 46, 69, 225
Santa Margarita, 198–99
Santissima Trinidad, 93–95, 226
San Ysidro, 94
Saratoga, 13, 241
Sardinia, 210, 259
Saumarez, Lord James, 214–15, 239; as admiral, 230–37; as captain, 222–30; character of, 215–16; early years of, 216–22
Saumarez, Philip, 217, 220
Saunders, Sir Charles, 30–32, 34, 52, 81–82, 84, 217
Savannah, 134
Scarborough (24), 240
Scipion, 257
Scorpion, 83, 133–34
Scotland, 4, 11, 118, 128–29
Seaford, 81
Séduisant, 45
Sérieuse, 229
Severn, 3, 81
Shah Kaikuseroo, 254
Sheerness, 53
Shoreham, 106
Sicily, 180, 210
Simon's Bay, 139–41
Smith, Sir William Sidney, 75, 145, 147–48, 186, 199
Smith, Thomas, 28–30, 47, 53
Solebay, 217
Sombreuil, Comte de, 200–201
Spain, 3, 9–10, 16, 18, 31, 39, 74, 86, 89–90, 168, 179, 203, 226, 240, 259
Speculator, 124

Spencer, Lord George, 26, 47–48, 73, 77, 98, 105, 118, 120–21, 123–24, 128, 140–41, 179, 202–5, 208–9, 230, 248
Spencer, 183–84
Sphinx, 81
Spitfire, 220
Spithead, 5, 13, 14, 25, 32, 39–41, 44–46, 57, 72, 86–87, 90, 98, 110, 114, 116, 159, 211; mutiny, 26–27, 47–49, 96–97, 120–21, 141–43, 170, 204
Stag, 133
Stanislaus, 243
Staten General, 126
Staten Island, 10–11
St. Bartholomew, 181
St. Croix, 181, 208
St. Domingo, 211
St. Eustatius, 60–61, 63, 65
St. George, 32, 82
St. Helens, 17, 48, 87, 115, 143
St. John, 181
St. Kitts, 65–67, 89, 183, 222
St. Lawrence River, 83
St. Lucia, 60, 67, 89, 175
St. Malo, 7, 14, 53
St. Martin, 181
Stopford, Sir Robert, 163
St. Thomas, 181
Stuart, Sir Charles, 179
St. Vincent: battle of, 79, 92–95, 176, 215, 226; Cape, 86, 91
St. Vincent, Earl of. *See* Jervis, John (Earl of St. Vincent)
Subtile, 54
Suffolk (70), 4
Suffolk (74), 113–14, 165, 244
Sullivan's Island, 218–19
Superb, 83, 182–85, 231–33
Sweden, 160, 181, 234–36
Swiftsure (70), 82

Swiftsure (74), 180
Sylph, 203, 205–6

Tartar, 56
Téméraire, 208
Terpsichore, 96, 255
Terrible, 55, 65, 176
Texel, 119–20, 122–28
Thalia, 78
Thames, 231
Thames River, 113, 141
Thésée, 8, 35
Theseus, 228–29
Thompson, Sir Charles, 96, 203
Thrale, Hester, 132, 149–51
Thunder, 156
Thunderer, 22, 34, 58
Ticonderoga, 2, 241
Tigre, 44
Tisiphone, 221–22
Tonnant, 253
Torbay, 19–20, 110, 145, 205, 245
Torbay, 8, 35, 56, 70, 108–9, 173
Toulon, 29, 73–76, 82, 90–91,
    97–98, 131, 138, 172, 210, 214,
    227, 231, 257
Tourville, 158
Trafalgar: battle of, 23, 79, 102, 149,
    152, 160, 167, 182
Trajan, 23
Tremeraire (74), 23
Tremeraire (98), 208
Trent, 57
Trente-et-un Mai, 23
Tribune, 191
Trident, 133
Trigg, Thomas, 181
Triton, 133
Triton (32), 205
Troubridge, Sir Thomas, 41, 93, 96,
    253–55
Tryal, 106

Tryton, 5
Turtle, 11–12
Tyrannicide, 40

Unité, 246–47
United States, 13, 168–69, 211
Ushant, 21, 56, 58, 100, 102, 109–10,
    246–47; battle of, 35–36, 38, 85,
    114

Vaillante, 250
Valcour Island, 241
Valiant, 43, 109–12, 173, 196
Van Capellen, 258
Vanguard, 227
Vanstabel, Pierre, 20
Venerable (aircraft carrier), 130
Venerable (74), 119–26, 182, 187,
    214–15, 233–34
Vengeur, 24, 39, 183
Venus, 194
Vestal (28), 137
Vestal (32), 56–58
Victory, 16, 35, 73, 75, 85, 86, 90,
    92–94, 195, 220, 234
Villaret-Joyeuse, Louis Thomas,
    20–23, 38, 40, 42–44, 158, 177,
    190–91, 200, 225
Ville de Paris, 46, 68–71, 98, 100, 223
Villeneuve, Pierre, 91
Vipère, 197
Virginia Capes: battle of, 64, 136
Virginie, 247
Volontaire, 199
Vrijheid, 126

Waldegrave, William, 96
Warren, John, 192–93
Warren, Sir John, 147, 190–91, 246,
    252; as admiral, 208–13; as captain,
    196–208; character of, 191–92; ear-
    ly years of, 192–95

Warwick (50), 136–37
Warwick (60), 33
Washington, George, 10, 14
Waterloo: battle of, 150
Watson, Charles, 54
Wattigny, 43
Willaumez, Rear Admiral, 162–63
William IV, 103, 129, 136, 169, 196, 236
Winchelsea (20), 53–54
Winchelsea (32), 196, 217, 244
Windham, Sir William, 127

Winter, Jan de, 124–26
Wolfe, James, 83

xebec, 82

Yarmouth, 119–22, 124, 128, 160
Yarmouth, 154

Zealous, 228
Zélé, 68–69
Zoutman, Johan, 220

About the Author

Lee Bienkowski has a Ph.D. from the University of Kentucky and has studied naval history for twenty years. She has written articles for *American History* and *Military History* magazines. A native of Boston, she currently resides in St. Augustine, Florida.